The Swastika and the Stage

Based on extensive archival research, this is the first full-length study in English of theatre in the Third Reich. It explores the contending pressures and ambitions within the regime and the Nazi party, within the German theatre profession itself and the theatregoing public. Together, these shaped theatrical practice in the Nazi years. By tracing the origins of the Nazi stage back to the right-wing theatre reform movement of the late nineteenth century, Strobl suggests that theatre was widely regarded as a central pillar of German national identity. The role played by the stage in the evolving collective German identity after 1933 is examined through chapters on theatre and Nazi ethnic and racial policy, anti-religious campaigns, on the *Thingspiel* and the uses of history. The picture is completed by chapters on the role of theatre in Nazi repression, propaganda and the regime's self-representation at home and abroad. The book thus traces the evolving fortunes of theatre in the Third Reich, from the financial constraints of the Great Depression, via the ostentatious lavishness of the late 1930s, to the years of 'total war', and the resulting physical destruction of most German playhouses.

GERWIN STROBL is Lecturer in Modern History at Cardiff University. He is the author of *The Germanic Isle: Nazi Perceptions of Britain* (Cambridge, 2000), and has published articles in journals including *New Theatre Quarterly*, *German Life and Letters* and the *Journal of Contemporary History*.

CAMBRIDGE STUDIES IN MODERN THEATRE

Series editor
David Bradby, *Royal Holloway, University of London*

Advisory board
Martin Banham, *University of Leeds*
Jacky Bratton, *Royal Holloway, University of London*
Tracy Davis, *Northwestern University*
Sir Richard Eyre
Michael Robinson, *University of East Anglia*
Sheila Stowell, *University of Birmingham*

Volumes for Cambridge Studies in Modern Theatre explore the political, social and cultural functions of theatre while also paying careful attention to detailed performance analysis. The focus of the series is on political approaches to the modern theatre with attention also being paid to theatres of earlier periods and their influence on contemporary drama. Topics in the series are chosen to investigate this relationship and include both playwrights (their aims and intentions set against the effects of their work) and process (with emphasis on rehearsal and production methods, the political structure within theatre companies and their choice of audiences or performance venues). Further topics will include devised theatre, agitprop, community theatre, para-theatre and performance art. In all cases the series will be alive to the special cultural and political factors operating in the theatres examined.

Books published
Brain Crow with Chris Banfield, *An Introduction to Post-Colonial Theatre*
Maria DiCenzo, *The Politics of Alternative Theatre in Britain, 1968–1990: the Case of 7:84 (Scotland)*
Jo Riley, *Chinese Theatre and the Actor in Performance*
Jonathan Kalb, *The Theatre of Heiner Müller*
Richard Boon and Jane Plastow, eds., *Theatre Matters: Performance and Culture on the World Stage*
Claude Schumacher, ed., *Staging the Holocaust: the Shoah in Drama and Performance*

The Swastika and the Stage

German Theatre and Society, 1933–1945

Gerwin Strobl

CAMBRIDGE
UNIVERSITY PRESS

CAMBRIDGE UNIVERSITY PRESS

Cambridge, New York, Melbourne, Madrid, Cape Town, Singapore, São Paulo, Delhi

Cambridge University Press
The Edinburgh Building, Cambridge CB2 8RU, UK

Published in the United States of America by Cambridge University Press,
New York

www.cambridge.org
Information on this title: www.cambridge.org/9780521880763

First published 2007
Reprinted 2009

Printed in the United Kingdom at the University Press, Cambridge

A catalogue record for this publication is available from the British Library

ISBN 978-0-521-88076-3 hardback

This book is dedicated to the memory of my grandparents Franz and Marie, Herbert and Emmi, who loved the theatre and supported it actively in good times and bad; and to my parents Werner and Dity, who passed on to me their own great enthusiasm for the stage; to Borgi, who shares it and has been communicating it to her students; and to Guido and Filip who, we hope, will also grow to relish *Theaterluft*.

Contents

List of illustrations

Acknowledgements

I am grateful to the British Academy for a Small Grant, to Cardiff University for a Research Grant, and to Professor Jonathan Osmond for his support and encouragement. I am indebted to the Archiv der Stadt Linz, the Bundesarchiv Berlin, the Oberösterreichisches Landesarchiv, the Stadtarchiv Düsseldorf, the Stadtarchiv Heidelberg, the Süddeutscher Verlag, and especially to Herrn Riepe, for their helpfulness and kindness. Without their support this book could never have taken shape. The Deutsches Theatermuseum in Munich, the Österreichisches Theatermuseum in Vienna and the Theaterwissenschaftliche Sammlung der Universität Köln threw open their collections. Ullstein-Bilderdienst agreed to provide some illustrations (albeit in exchange for a very large cheque). Thanks are also due to friends in Austria, Britain and in Germany, and above all to my family, who were indulgent enough to put up with my enthusiasm for 'my topic' and were kind enough to forgive the prolonged *Funkpausen* during the writing-up. Special thanks, finally, are due to Dipl.-Ing. Bodo Weih, who rescued the manuscript from a dying computer and, as always, to my father, Prof. Werner Strobl, for giving so generously of his time in helping to track down elusive sources.

Introduction: why write a book about the theatre in the Third Reich?

Theatre played a significant role in German national life before and during the Second World War. It was a genuine mass phenomenon involving millions of Germans and Austrians. The German repertoire system, and the lavish funding that sustained it, enabled the stage to hold its own even in competition with the cinema. An extensive network of state and municipal theatres gave the theatre a greater geographical and social range than in other countries. The role it had played in defining German national identity from the eighteenth century onwards lent it additional prestige. In the Weimar years, moreover, theatre had become one of the principal battle grounds in the 'cultural wars' between left and right. There were heated exchanges in council chambers, furious polemics in the press, and in the playhouses themselves, 'incidents', boycotts and barely disguised threats.

These threats and the violent expulsion of the Weimar cultural elite after 1933 have inevitably shaped perceptions of theatre in the Third Reich ever since. Outside Germany, and to an extent inside Germany too, the Nazi years are perceived as a yawning gap in the history of the German stage, a black hole of destruction from which no light can escape. It is telling that six decades on from the fall of the Reich, not a single full-length study exists in English of the German stage in the Nazi era, and in German, too, the ongoing neglect is striking. That neglect is all the more remarkable given the attention lavished by the regime on the stage and the vast political and financial investment in the theatre made by the Nazis.

This book, then, seeks to fill a gap and to explore some of the things that happened to, in and around the theatre between 1933 and

1945. The aim is to provide a clearer picture overall of the development of the German stage in the twentieth century, and a more rounded view of life in the Third Reich. The book does not intend to provide a revisionist perspective on the course of German and Austrian culture, but it has been guided by the thought that if theatre under the swastika had been as uniformly bad as some of the returning émigrés claimed after 1945, then the playhouses in the Reich would surely have collapsed; for even in a dictatorship people cannot be *made* to go to the theatre, if they have no desire to do so. The book will thus both highlight areas where Nazi theatre incontrovertibly failed and areas where something more successful emerged, either by design or accident.

The first six chapters of the book probe the ideological intentions that shaped the theatre in the Third Reich. Chapters 1 and 2 explore both the immediate and the wider background. The third considers the reasons for the striking proliferation of history plays and some of the inherent problems playwrights encountered after 1933. The fourth chapter then explores the way theatre became a factor in the relationship of the German people with their neighbours, while the fifth sets out the grim detail of Nazi racism on and behind the stage. A chapter on religion and theatre completes the picture. The remaining three chapters then examine the political reality under which theatre had to operate in the Third Reich: censorship in all its forms, the combination of patronage and intimidation, the clash between propagandistic intent and traditional German concepts of *Kultur*, and finally the trajectory of German theatre from the near-bankruptcy of the 1932–3 season via conspicuous Nazi opulence to the physical destruction of the war years.

1   Weimar: politics in the playhouse

Theatres were among the first Nazi targets during the Seizure of Power: several of Germany's municipal or state playhouses were symbolically stormed by SA detachments; others were taken over by Nazi activists who had been operating for some time inside individual theatre companies.[1] Within a few weeks of Hitler becoming chancellor, the swastika flag was flying on most German theatres. In the wake of the flags came various supervision committees, which began to translate the symbolic takeover into a real one.[2] Theatre had possessed high political significance in the Weimar republic. It had probably been the most consistently controversial branch of the arts.[3] Inevitably, it was also the first part of German culture to undergo thorough nazification. The threats, betrayals and general brutality involved have been chronicled in the testimonies and memoirs of those silenced inside Germany after 1933.[4] Their tale is one of a culture snuffed out: of its exponents driven into exile or premature retirement, and its plays and practices banished for more than a decade. As the Third Reich expanded, the devastation spread. Yet more people were forced out of their positions in the theatre, and some had to flee a second or even a third time. Unsurprisingly, the tone of these accounts is sombre. They echo Sir Edward Grey's famous words, voiced some thirty years earlier: of the lamps going out over Europe, never to be lit again in the writers' lifetime.

Historians, theatre specialists and literary critics have largely followed that perspective. It is a view based on sound critical judgement. At its heart lies the contrast between the excellence of the ousted culture and the frequently mediocre offerings that sought to take its place. Yet it is not just a question of weighing Nazi culture and finding it wanting. The traditional ideal of scholarly detachment is difficult to sustain in the light of Nazism's record. Not a few theatre practitioners were driven to suicide; many more vanished in the Third Reich's killing apparatus.[5] In the case of Nazi Germany, even cultural historians or literary critics will find themselves confronted with evidence of murder.

Such knowledge has informed the research. It has tended to influence the perspective of accounts as much as their tone. Focusing on the culture of the victims (rather than the preferences of the persecutors) has been, at least in part, a posthumous attempt to right the wrongs of the 1930s and 1940s. It is an honourable stance but it comes at a price. It obscures from our view a large part of the historical reality of 1933, and of the cultural scene in the preceding years.[6] It runs the risk of portraying Nazi thugs in isolation, as though they had suddenly erupted out of nowhere. It implies, moreover, that the Nazi party and its constituency were uniformly strangers to culture. Yet this is not the case; the various artistic interests of the Nazi hierarchy are well documented, and the party also included a substantial number of dedicated theatregoers.[7] These particular theatre audiences, and a great many more outside the Nazi party, did not regard 1933 as darkness descending. They hailed it – often very vocally – as a bright new dawn.

A study of the Third Reich's theatre needs to take account of that. It must seek to explain why some cultured Germans should actually have rejoiced at the purge of the theatres in 1933. To do this we must leave behind the familiar metropolitan atmosphere of Berlin and turn to the provinces. For that is where Nazi theatre had its artistic, intellectual and political roots.

The word 'provincial' is not a neutral term in most languages. It tends to suggest, at the very least, a certain lack of sophistication. Yet, this is misleading in a German context. For unlike French or English culture, German cultural life had traditionally been highly decentralised.[8] Lack of political unity had enriched the nation culturally. The parallel with Ancient Greece so dear to German nationalist hearts contained perhaps a grain of truth: the institutions of high culture were indeed more broadly diffused in Germany than in most other European countries.[9]

Theatre had reflected this. Munich, Frankfurt, Dresden, Hamburg, Düsseldorf, Leipzig or Stuttgart were artistically far from provincial. Their theatres shone and often eclipsed many genuine capital cities elsewhere, including – repeatedly – Berlin itself. Yet that is not all: the survival up to 1918 of the old German kingdoms and principalities had added a further dimension. Princely ambition came into play. Take, for instance, the quixotic Prince of Reuß, who ran his own theatre company even after 1918: directing it, supporting dramatists and occasionally writing plays for it himself.[10] His private funds kept the venture afloat even in the dark days of the depression. Only the Red Army would finally snuff out the Reuß theatre tradition.

Most German ruling houses favoured less immediate forms of cultural ambition. Yet this still translated into substantial support for the stage. It allowed even very small *Residenzstädte* – the quintessentially German 'court towns' – to compete with the larger urban centres. In the latter half of the nineteenth century German acting and directing styles had in fact been revolutionised by one such court theatre: that of the diminutive duchy of Saxe-Meiningen and its exiguous capital. The 'Meiningen style' proved as influential on the German stage as the Meiningen orchestra did in the Western symphonic tradition.[11] It was only the Weimar republic that finally swept aside Meiningen's theatrical legacy, along with the institution of the court theatre itself.

The end of the monarchies in 1918 altered the theatrical scene: the court theatres became state institutions. Their funding now depended on box office takings and subsidies from regional bodies.[12] While theatres in large states like Prussia adapted successfully, those in the smaller *Residenzstädte* struggled to survive. The financial instability of the Weimar republic, together with changed leisure habits and the rise of the cinema, also posed serious challenges to Germany's many municipal theatres. Conditions improved temporarily in the mid-1920s, but it was only a reprieve. By the end of the republic, numerous theatres were threatened with closure or were being forcibly merged with companies from neighbouring cities.[13] The mood was correspondingly sombre. Talk of the imminent disappearance of theatre as an art form was widespread.[14]

Berlin did not escape the general crisis, yet, as the largest conurbation by far, there were economies of scale working in its favour. It also received generous press coverage, which allowed Berlin theatre to radiate out into the provinces. The presence in Berlin of what was then the world's largest film industry also benefited the city's theatre culture: actors began to work both for the studios and the stage. Theatres in the rest of Germany found it hard to compete. Outside Germany, the cultural dominance of one city might seem natural; to many Germans it was a new and unwelcome phenomenon.

Berlin's pre-eminence was enhanced by events abroad. The collapse of the Habsburg Empire had weakened the competition across the border. After 1918, the desperate penury of the new Austrian republic progressively dimmed the glow of the Viennese stage. Many of its younger talents began to gravitate to Berlin. By 1929 the satirist Erich Kästner was moved to observe, 'Berlin actors, as everyone knows, are without exception Viennese.' Eventually, this would itself become a factor in the political equation. It would cripple the Austrian government's attempts, after January 1933, to use culture as a weapon against the Third Reich.[15]

Prague was almost entirely eclipsed. The marginalisation of Austro-German culture by the new Czech authorities robbed that traditionally bilingual city of one of its great historical assets. The old German Landestheater had been at the forefront of artistic innovation even during the war. With a large pool of literary and artistic talent, and an economy unburdened by reparations, the new Czechoslovak state could have been a major player in Austro-German culture after 1918. Projecting itself abroad in theatre, film or print might ultimately have been in its own political interests. Yet it threw away that chance.[16] What Prussia had failed to achieve on the battlefield was thus thrust upon her in defeat: her capital, for better or worse, was now the undisputed centre of *Mitteleuropa*.

The equation in the popular mind of the inter-war years with the bustle of Berlin is therefore not entirely unjustified. The problem arises with how one interprets that bustle. We now tend to focus, retrospectively, on the cultural foment of a great metropolis come into its own. Many contemporaries noticed only the impoverished scene in the rest of the German lands.[17] To them, post-war culture seemed in its metropolitan bias alone a catastrophic departure from German tradition.

The Nazi party sided with those who had lost out, and drew strength from their grievances. It is no accident that National Socialism began in Munich, or that the first town it conquered through the ballot box was Coburg. Munich had 'glowed' culturally, as Thomas Mann put it, in the days of the monarchy. It was grey and exhausted in the republic. Coburg had disappeared altogether from wider view: 1918 saw it demoted from *Residenzstadt*, complete with palace, court theatre and royal relations on half the thrones of Europe, to lifeless provincial backwater.

Nazi theatre, like National Socialism in general, sprang from the wish to reverse that decline. The party and the culture it favoured both wore their regional badges with defiance. Embracing 'small town' Germany promised electoral gains. It also allowed the Nazi party to portray itself as the true heir and defender of German tradition. After all, the spiritual home of German *Kulturpatriotismus* – the town of Weimar – was itself a small provincial town.

Weimar tends these days to be equated in Britain and America with the republic to which it had lent its name. That association is one of history's most sublime jests: as improbable in its way as an English republic proclaimed in Stratford-upon-Avon. To Germans the primary association of the name 'Weimar' continues to be cultural: not *Republik* but *Klassik*; Goethe and Schiller, Herder and Wieland, and the Golden Age of German Literature. That association has given the town a unique status. To many, it has represented the very soul of Germany.[18] Coincidentally or not, Weimar also became an early stronghold of the Nazi party. Long before 1933, Weimar's hallowed literary institutions were, in the words of a perceptive observer, 'Nazi-infested, without being able to account for it to themselves'.[19]

That connection between high culture and National Socialism in the town of Goethe was not without consequences. It conferred a degree

1 The Reichsdramaturg Rainer Schlösser, the head of the Nazi theatre administration and the Reich's chief theatre censor.

of respectability on the Nazi movement, it provided a pattern for other parts of Germany, and it created a network of cultural activists who shaped the Reich's *Kultur* after 1933.[20] That was perhaps especially true of the theatre. Weimar had been home, for instance, to Rainer Schlösser. As Reichsdramaturg, an office and a title invented for him, he would become head of the Nazis' theatre administration and the chief censor of the Third Reich's stage. Schlösser could claim the Weimar classics as his birthright. His father had been a professor of literature and director of the prestigious Goethe-and-Schiller Archive. His younger brother went on to become a noted Shakespeare scholar. (Weimar had been, since Goethe's day, the official headquarters of Germany's Shakespeareans.)[21] The town,

8

in other words, possessed a recognisable cultural aristocracy, into which Schlösser had been born.[22] It provided an ideal launchpad for his own career as a literary critic. This, in turn, was to bring him to the attention of the emerging Nazi hierarchy. Weimar was also home to Hans Severus Ziegler. Ziegler, like Schlösser, possessed a doctorate in German Literature and contributed to the same right-wing literary journals.[23] He, too, caught the eye of the party hierarchy. When the Nazis first tasted regional power in 1930, Ziegler was invited into government. He was given control of the theatres in the state of Thuringia, which contained the town of Weimar (and the old principalities of Reuß and Saxe-Meiningen, which we encountered earlier).[24] Weimar, moreover, offered a publishing platform to the young dramatist Hanns Johst, who was to provide Nazi theatre with several canonical plays, and who would go on to become president of Goebbels' Reich Chamber of Literature.[25] Weimar, finally, was home also to Baldur von Schirach: another central figure in the Nazi cultural establishment. Schirach, too, had contributed to the literary journals that published Schlösser and Ziegler. In the Third Reich, Schirach became leader of the Hitler Youth: a position he used, amongst other things, to develop a Nazi Youth Theatre and to sponsor aspirant Nazi dramatists.[26] Later still, as the Führer's vice-regal representative in Vienna, Schirach was an influential patron of the arts, powerful enough to take on Goebbels even. Schirach, like Schlösser, wrote competent verse and had the classics coursing through his veins: his father, Carl von Schirach, had been *Intendant* – artistic and managing director – of Weimar's court theatre: the very institution Goethe had led a century earlier.

The point about all this is simple enough: the usual epithets for Nazi activists – 'barbarian', 'semi-literate' or 'philistine' – clearly do not describe these men. The Weimar group were men of some ability, and even of literary flair. Schlösser and Schirach also possessed undoubted elegance and style. In Goethe's day, they might have been praised for their 'refined manners and sensibilities'.[27] Nazi theatre, therefore, cannot simply be explained away as the triumph of barbarism and the second-rate.[28]

The biographies of the Weimar group reveals a further important aspect: the role of the year 1918 in disrupting individual lives, and the lasting bitterness this often produced. It is a commonplace in the historical literature that entire sections of German society rejected the republic. The imperial officer corps, in particular, never forgave the 'November State' for depriving them of their privileged position. This was exactly the case of the Reichsdramaturg Rainer Schlösser, whose own youthful hopes of a military career had ended abruptly in 1918.[29] For Schlösser there followed years of financial hardship. The sudden experience of poverty, after a comfortable boyhood, achieved what even the war had failed to do: it put iron in his soul.

Others despaired: Baldur von Schirach's elder brother took his own life. The collapse of everything he had believed in, combined with the prospect of unemployment, made death seem preferable. A few weeks later, it was the turn of Schirach-*père* to find himself unemployed. Carl von Schirach was summarily dismissed from his post as *Intendant* by the new Social Democrat minister of culture.[30] The minister felt that princely appointments should not survive into the republican era.[31] For Schirach, therefore, the new beginning began with the death of a son and an irreparable blow to his own career. Middle-aged and diligent, rather than inspired, he found himself competing against an army of younger men returning from the trenches. Unsurprisingly, he failed to secure another post anywhere. It was only fifteen years later – in 1933 – that he would come to lead a theatre again: then it would be the turn of the republic's supporters to be purged from office.[32]

Schirach's dismissal had been no isolated case. As the old court theatres were converted into republican institutions, there was an almost complete change in artistic management. Some *Intendanten* followed the example of their princes and abdicated, so to speak; others were simply sacked.[33] The revolution may have left intact the traditional bastions of conservatism in the Army (or what was left of it), in the civil service and education but it was rather more thorough in the theatre.[34] Histories of Weimar culture tend not to dwell upon this fact. We are told, for instance, in one classic account, that the great Leopold Jeßner was 'imposed' on Berlin's Prussian State Theatre in 1919.[35] But the incident is presented as an example of modernist light piercing conservative darkness. The fact that someone's life had been destroyed in the process is rather lost sight of. The shattered careers of men like Carl von Schirach were, we are to understand, merely the collateral damage of history. As the young Carlo Mierendorff put it in his campaign to remove the *Intendant* at Darmstadt, 'Partiality is the prerogative of a revolution. Revolution is about creating justice by depriving some of their rights.'[36]

Those deprived of their rights took a less sanguine view. Resentment of the new state was acute. 'A government which does not ally itself, from the outset, with the main exponents in the arts and sciences will always bear the stigma of the usurper', as the conservative poet Börries von Münchhausen, would later observe.[37] The point about all this is not to elicit sympathy for the fallen courtiers of the theatre world. By the standards of most revolutions, they had been treated tolerably well in 1918. Their dismissal, moreover, often led to higher artistic standards.[38] Some of the former *Intendanten* had been appointed with few perceptible qualifications other than the confidence of their prince. The most egregious example had been Joseph Lauff. He had been moved by Wilhelm II from commanding an artillery battery to running the court theatre at Wiesbaden: 'ordered to report to the Muses', as the satirist Ludwig Thoma put it. Such decisions had even led some conservatives to advocate reform.[39] Yet the old *Intendanten* had loved the theatre, and had earnestly sought to serve it. Their brusque dismissal may have been no great loss artistically but it was ungracious, and perhaps unwise. The republic had created a group of prominent and articulate victims. Not all of them were content simply to fade from the scene.[40] The *ancien régime* in the theatre, moreover, had not been without its supporters among the audiences, as the republic would discover to its cost.

Initially, the shock of revolution had paralysed German conservatives: many feared for their lives. In the early months of the republic looting, abductions and arson were not uncommon. In Saxony, marauding bands roamed the land; neighbouring Thuringia was effectively under martial law; Bavaria the scene of bloody civil strife. Even where things seemed to have quietened down, street battles could suddenly erupt again. In Berlin, the first-night audience of Wedekind's *Marquis von*

Keith emerged from the theatre to find itself in the line of fire. Reality seemed like a tableau from the play they had just seen.

It was in this atmosphere that Weimar theatre was born, and it was with this atmosphere also that German conservatives associated it ever after. In conservative eyes, the stage reflected to an alarming degree the pandemonium outside. It was not just a case of sacked *Intendanten* and a new left-wing repertoire: there were even *Räte* – soviets – who attempted, for a while, to run theatres as collectives.

The dismay was widespread: in June 1919, a glittering list of cultural luminaries, headed by Max Reinhardt and Richard Strauss, made their concern known in print. They warned against the folly of attempting to 'make artistic decisions by majority vote'.[41] Politics, they feared, was in danger of snuffing out *Kultur*. Left-wing culture, in turn, appeared to have taken over politics. This seemed exemplified by events in Munich: the short-lived Bavarian Soviet Republic of 1919 played a crucial role in defining the mindset of the German right after the war. Munich seemed a warning that Germany might easily follow Russia into the Bolshevik abyss.

That apparent danger was personified by Kurt Eisner, who had moved from writing theatre reviews to leading a revolution, and by two prominent playwrights: Erich Mühsam and Ernst Toller. Both men had been instrumental in establishing the Munich *Räterepublik*; both wielded power in the self-appointed government and delivered fiery orations; both, moreover, had a history of revolutionary activity. In January 1918, as Germany was preparing for one final push to win the war, they had incited munitions workers to go on strike. That was exactly what right-wing Germany meant when it spoke of the 'stab-in-the-back'; and far from being a myth, the activities of Mühsam and Toller had been all too real. Mühsam, moreover, had already been arrested before the war for trying to foment rebellion. The details were lurid: he had sought to recruit his revolutionaries among Munich's pimps, prostitutes and petty thieves.[42]

In the biographies of people like Mühsam or Toller, right-wing Germany thought it identified the themes of their writing: treason and mutiny, an apparent affinity with the criminal underworld, and a predilection for the aesthetics of the brothel. At the end of the

Weimar era, Rainer Schlösser was to summarise all these points for the main Nazi paper, the *Völkische Beobachter*. He entitled his articles 'A Cultural Chamber of Horrors', and invited his readers to put a stop to such outrages by voting for Hitler.[43]

The antisemitism that pervaded most right-wing pronouncements about Weimar theatre – for Mühsam and Toller were both Jewish – must not blind us to the wider concerns involved. Antisemitism was the grand narrative: but it depended for its effectiveness on selected verifiable facts, which then lent credibility to Nazi fabrications. Activists like Mühsam provided the antisemites with supposed proof of their conspiracy theories.

Before the war, Mühsam's antics had seemed harmless. The judges in 1909 had found his revolutionist band of rent boys and pickpockets sufficiently ludicrous to dismiss the case against him. Ten years on, his activities appeared in another light. And so now did the fact that he was Jewish. Likewise, the intention of the modernists to shock or provoke audiences with their plays and ecstatic exhortations – 'Onanists! Pederasts! Fetishists! ... Pimps! Whores! ... Syphilitics! Brothers!' etc. – had seemed the trademark of a minority before the war.[44] After 1919, their erotic obsessions were presented on all the major stages of Germany. Here too, it now mattered if the playwrights and directors championing that kind of theatre happened to be Jewish. Cultural and political factors reinforced each other. The term 'cultural Bolshevism' may have been polemical and often slanderous: but it was not meaningless rhetoric. There were very definite images associated with those words in right-wing minds. Those images now added new potency to ancient prejudice.

In the town of Weimar, the chief proponent of cultural antisemitism was Adolf Bartels: the mentor of Schlösser, Ziegler and young Schirach. Bartels had initially been a lonely figure. His antisemitism had been too loud and vulgar for the tastes of polite society.[45] Yet as the pressures of modernity – social, cultural and political – increased, polite society, or parts of it, became radicalised. That process began before the Great War, and effectively transformed German conservatism after the guns fell silent.

Carl von Schirach is a case in point. Before 1914, there had been nothing radical about him. Yet after the revolution (and his own dismissal), this changed. Surveying the theatrical scene in 1925, he concluded, 'The first principle ... now should be: removal with a broom of iron of all alien [fremdrassigen] elements. Between one half and two-thirds of all people working in the theatre [should be removed]. And if New York's Yiddish Theatre won't take them, pack 'em off to Jerusalem.'[46]

By 1925, when Schirach was writing this venomous letter, a cultural fronde was perceptible everywhere. Much of it was organised and coordinated through letters like Schirach's.[47] The public face of these cabals was a little more decorous. Manifestos were published, appeals appeared in the press, and plans and projects abounded. The people involved were a motley crew recruited among the déclassé servants of the sunken Empire: former Intendanten and court poets, dramatists who had lost their audiences, admirals without a fleet and generals deprived of their command. The atmosphere of those circles is captured in a satirical sketch of the period. It has various worthies congregating in Weimar to celebrate Shakespeare's birthday: the bibulous eulogies of the Bard promptly culminate in the call to build new dreadnoughts.[48]

Such satires worked because they contained a large element of truth; but they also revealed the inadequacy of early conservative plotting. The traditionalists lacked a vision for the future. The rhetoric of past greatness was not enough to bring down the republic – not even in the theatre. The more perceptive conservatives began to seek out new allies. Carl von Schirach, one of the men satirised in the 'Bard and the dreadnoughts' sketch, joined the Nazi party. He did so long before it began to flourish at the polls.[49] His political migration towards the furthest fringes of the right may have been unusually rapid; its general direction was common enough. The process is aptly summed up in the title of a post-war theatre memoir: Von S.M. zu N.S. – 'From His Majesty to Nazism'.[50] Whatever the exact mixture of the fuel that propelled individuals along similar trajectories, professional resentment and personal grudges were always important ingredients.[51]

At one level, therefore, the events of 1933 were about settling scores: a case of paying the republic's supporters back, *with interest*, for the slights and injustices of 1918. Yet there was perhaps also another factor, which was important psychologically. It may have allowed conservatives, in their own minds, to equate their own welfare with that of Germany as a whole. The mental link was simple enough. Events in the theatre after the revolution had been politically motivated. This probably gave individual fates wider relevance. To protest against a personal blow thus became a patriotic duty.[52] That duty seemed all the more pressing since the new authorities' actions had infringed a central tenet of traditional German beliefs. The *Bildungsbürgertum* – the educated middle classes – had long adhered to a strict separation between the political and artistic realms. *Kultur* was, in every sense of the phrase, above politics. Even today the famous line in *Faust*, 'Fi, 'tis an ugly song, 'tis a political song', will draw appreciative reactions from some German audiences.

Such an attitude is not quite as neutral ideologically as its supporters liked to imagine. It is evidence, as has often been pointed out, of a fundamentally conservative outlook. Yet this conservatism of temperament had allowed considerable stylistic latitude. Before the Great War, traditionalists in the Reichstag – and outside it – had famously ended up championing modern art: not because they liked it but because the Kaiser had attempted to ban it.[53] The attempts of Wilhelm II to influence the theatre repertoire had similarly backfired. The cancellation of the Imperial box in Berlin's Deutsche Theater in 1895 had failed to dissuade that theatre from championing naturalist plays. A decade later, Max Reinhardt was likewise undismayed by the Kaiser's boycott. German *Bürger* were prepared to render unto Caesar what they considered to be Caesar's but they were implacable in the defence of Art and its Sacred Freedom. *Kultur* has rightly been called the secular religion of the German middle classes.

The sacking of Carl von Schirach in Weimar, or the change of *Intendanten* elsewhere, needs to be seen against that background. To conservatives, it amounted to a declaration of war on German proprieties. If trees were to be judged by their fruit, the new republic was no German timber. The stigma of being *undeutsch* would hang over it throughout its brief existence. It was no use for (the Social Democrat) president Ebert to evoke German cultural traditions during his stay in Weimar. Actions, thought part of his audience, spoke louder than words. Was Ebert not delivering his speech in a theatre whose *Intendant* had been removed by political fiat a few weeks earlier?

In February 1919, two months after the abrupt end of Schirach's career, the German Constituent Assembly had taken up residence in Weimar's erstwhile court theatre. Fear of revolutionary crowds in Berlin had prompted the government to seek refuge in the heart of conservative Germany. The new constitution was debated in a building guarded, at its entrance, by a twin statue of Goethe and Schiller.

Theatre as the seat of German law-making was a transitory phenomenon; the more general blurring of culture and politics was not. Some of the newly appointed *Intendanten* exceeded the conservatives' worst fears in that regard. The most egregious example, in the eyes of his many critics, was the man installed by the new government in the Kaiser's own court theatre in Berlin.

Leopold Jeßner has become emblematic of the republic's stage. His appointment in 1919 marked the nadir of German conservatism; his resignation in 1930, after relentless hounding in speech and print, the first triumph of the resurgent right. He seems the perfect embodiment of the traditional thesis of Weimar: a culture cut short. That thesis, however, largely fails to notice the relish with which republican cultural activists had rubbed salt into conservative wounds.[54]

Take Jeßner's famous inaugural production in Berlin. It defined the way much of Germany viewed him and, by extension, the republic's new theatre style.[55] At first sight, Jeßner's choice of play might seem a conciliatory gesture: Schiller's *Wilhelm Tell* was especially dear to German nationalists.[56] But there was nothing conciliatory about the production. Jeßner made it an unambiguously republican affair. He dressed the villain in something reminiscent of a Prussian uniform, and he included a number of other allusions to the *ancien régime*. He also cut the play's most famous patriotic lines. The ensuing riot in the auditorium, which threatened to stop the first performance, has entered the mythology of Weimar culture.[57]

The *Tell* of 1919 might pass for initial revolutionary exuber-
ance. Yet in its gleeful assault on conservative sensibilities, it was
hardly alone. Jeßner himself was to achieve even greater offence with
his 1926 production of *Hamlet*. That play, too, had held a special place
in middle-class hearts. 'Germany *is* Hamlet', as the nineteenth-
century poet Freiligrath had famously declared.[58] Jeßner used that
association for his own ends. For the 'play within the play', audiences
glimpsed on stage a scaled-down version of the type of auditorium in
which they were sitting, complete with a mirror image of the former
royal box. In it was seated Claudius, dressed in the Kaiser's familiar
uniform: the actor even affected the exiled monarch's withered arm.[59]

The production caused deep offence among traditionalists.
Many felt personally insulted by the implied verdict about the older
Germany, and thus about their own generation. The matter was even
taken up by the Prussian diet.[60] The affair rumbled on for months, and
the production became notorious throughout Germany. Years later,
after the Nazis had come to power, and republican theatre had become
but a memory, Jeßner's *Hamlet* was still routinely held up as the
epitome of all that had been rotten in the state of Weimar.[61]

These productions, and others like them, are more than just
sources of theatrical anecdotes. They are instances of a history of the
theatre widening out into one nation's social history, and reaching
ultimately into its political history, too. They need to be seen in
context, in other words. That context should not be the familiar one
of the Glory That Was Weimar, but of the other Weimar: the Weimar
of Rainer Schlösser, or of Schirach-*père et fils*; the Weimar that had
become 'Nazi-infested' without quite knowing how that had
happened.

Viewed in that context, both the productions themselves and
the recorded reactions to them begin to look rather different. Let us
begin with Jeßner's *Wilhelm Tell* and the ensuing riot. The disturban-
ces during the first night have traditionally been regarded as a pre-
meditated protest. The actor Albert Bassermann had voiced those
suspicions during the performance itself, when he decided to step
out of character, had walked up to the footlights and called on the
audience 'to throw out the paid louts'. Yet the critic Alfred Kerr, a

vocal champion of Weimar theatre, questioned that explanation. Perhaps, he suggested, the protesters were simply disgruntled *habitués* of the old court theatre: 'loyal regular audiences . . . accustomed to *Kitsch*': in a word, 'monarchists of the arts'.[62]

That is a persuasive image of what happened repeatedly after 1918. Doubtless, such protests were often linked with a distaste for the republic. The problem for us, decades on, is to establish the precise motivation. Such an endeavour is not an exercise in splitting hairs. Politically, there was little the Weimar republic might have done to win over its enemies. The question is, might it have been able to neutralise at least parts of the cultural opposition? Or, to put it another way: did its cultural experiment needlessly exacerbate its political travails? An important clue comes, retrospectively, from the files of the Nazi Propaganda Ministry. It is a letter of complaint, written in 1936. The writer introduces himself as a veteran of the recent cultural wars. He had lived through the days when a visit to the theatre had entailed arming oneself with pungent projectiles. What makes the letter interesting is that its author was protesting about productions *in the Third Reich*; that he did so on unambiguously cultural grounds, and that he likened what he had just seen to the republican theatre of yore. To cap it all, he half-threatened the Propaganda Ministry with a resumption of the old audience protests.[63]

This attitude accords with Alfred Kerr's assessment of 1919 and indeed with earlier audience protest in Imperial Germany.[64] It also fits with wider middle-class behaviour. German *Bürger* were initially prepared after 1918 to tolerate the republic for fear of something worse (i.e. Bolshevism).[65] This was reminiscent of their earlier readiness to let the Kaiser govern, in spite of considerable unease about his style of government. (Fear of social democracy had kept them quiescent then.) But just as the Kaiser's attempts to interfere in the arts had provoked from them sudden defiance, so now it was meddling with *Kultur* that goaded them to insurrection.

It is another review of Jeßner's *Tell*, this time in a conservative newspaper, that may explain the point. The reviewer did not approve of the scenes at the first night. He urged his readers rather loftily to 'try and behave like Europeans'. Yet, significantly, he also questioned the wisdom of the production. *Tell*, he thought, was the stuff the nation's dreams were made of. There were definite 'mental images' attached to the play. 'If one now sets out to take all that away from people,' he added, 'one had better be certain that one has something of value to offer [them] ... in exchange.'[66]

That was the dilemma of the republic's theatre, and the cause of its ultimate failure. We now accept that Weimar did have something to offer: it refreshed a tradition that had become stale. The problem was, it was too uncompromising to carry a substantial proportion of the old audiences with it. Republican theatre made little effort to win those audiences over, especially while the political situation still favoured it. It never wooed, it rarely even met halfway; all too often, it simply ranted or harangued.[67] Years later, when the spirit of the republic's early years was revived in the German theatre of the 1960s, the dramatist Peter Handke wrote a play entitled *Publikumsbeschimpfung* – 'Insulting the Audience'. That is exactly how the republic's theatre appears to have felt to conservative audiences four decades earlier.[68]

The boyhood memory of the critic Friedrich Luft is apposite here. In 1919, his theatre-loving father had taken him to see Jeßner's *Wilhelm Tell*. The boy liked the performance. The father did not. He was too much of a European to jeer or walk out. Yet, as the younger Luft relates, his father never again set foot in the State Theatre thereafter: he had been deeply offended.[69] We should resist the temptation to feel superior when describing such responses. It is very easy to dismiss them as ignorant and philistine, and then bask in the glow of one's own sophistication. It is no less easy to tar the people involved with the brush of crypto-Nazism and speak of *les bourgeois enragés* who had paved the road to the Third Reich. That may constitute part of the truth, indeed a substantial part of the truth, but it is not quite the whole truth.

No less a figure than Max Reinhardt, the greatest exponent of German theatre before the war, might act as witness for the defence. Reinhardt was made extremely uneasy by the new style in Berlin. He disliked it so much that he withdrew to his native Austria (which conspicuously refused to adopt the Weimar model of modernity).[70] In his decision to leave, Reinhardt was encouraged by Hugo von Hofmannsthal: again, no marginal figure in the Austro-German culture of the day. Hofmannsthal's mood was apocalyptic. He saw the republic's stage as 'the end of all sophisticated German theatre', and a practice which 'put into question everything achieved since 1770 [i.e. the eighteenth-century theatre reforms]'.[71] This may sound melodramatic: but, in one sense at least, events seemed to bear Hofmannsthal out.

Theatre depends on audiences, and these began to thin out noticeably. Many Berlin theatres in the early 1920s found they were being deserted en masse by the people who had supported them loyally over the years. As insolvency threatened, desperate measures were adopted: a tide of trivia was channelled into the city to help refloat the beached vessels of modernism.[72] Reinhardt's own former flagship, the Deutsche Theater, staged the notoriously vapid *Alt-Heidelberg*. It is the equivalent perhaps of the Royal Shakespeare Theatre at Stratford-upon-Avon deciding to put on Agatha Christie's *The Mousetrap*. The hagiographies of Weimar culture are noticeably reticent on this subject.

The Nazis were not: empty theatres and *Alt-Heidelberg* became central arguments in their campaign against the republic's cultural policies.[73] The Nazis effectively hijacked wider cultural anxieties. Neither Reinhardt nor Hofmannsthal, after all, can be accused of Nazi leanings: both were cosmopolitan in outlook, both of Jewish extraction, indeed both were anathema to the Third Reich in every regard. Their Austrian retort to the new Berlin theatre style – the Salzburg festival – would be eviscerated artistically after the *Anschluß*.[74] Yet both men had foreshadowed some of the Nazis' arguments about Weimar theatre; and both also shared in effect the dismay of Friedrich Luft's father, who had been stunned into bitter withdrawal from theatregoing by Jeßner's *Wilhelm Tell*.

It is perhaps worth taking another look, then, at the underlying issues of that production, and of others like it. In its review of *Tell*, the conservative *Deutsche Allgemeine Zeitung* had noted that something was being taking away from the audiences. A German historian in our own day has coined the evocative term 'cultural dispossession' for the same process.[75] What was being taken away was the reassurance of the classics: the plays German *Bürger* had encountered in the school room, had performed in amateur productions and had leafed through again, in an idle hour, in their libraries or drawing rooms. These plays had formed part of the middle classes' mental landscape. Reminders of them recurred constantly: in the puns and allusions of the newspapers, or in the quotations with which the *Bildungsbürger* liked to sprinkle their conversation. And now, in the theatre, that familiar line, knowingly anticipated with a smile, was cut or traduced.[76]

It bears repeating that the animus provoked by the theatre of the Weimar republic was not simply a reaction against 'the modern': against the likes of Brecht, Bronnen, Toller, etc., conservative audiences tended to steer clear of their offerings in any case. If a drama contained in its title the words 'anarchy' or 'machine wreckers', one knew what to expect.[77] It was the modernist assault on the classics – and thus on the middle classes' home ground – that caused the deepest offence. It was this also that set the theatre apart from all the other branches of the arts. George Grosz or Otto Dix and their ilk may have produced objectionable daubs but at least they did not go and deface a Dürer canvas. Schönberg may have been writing ear-splitting music but even he would not have dreamt of tearing up a Beethoven score. The republic's theatre directors, it seemed, had no such scruples.[78]

It was for that reason, more than any other, that the word *Theaterskandal* became part of the discourse of the period. It has been well said that 'a history of the [Weimar] republic's theatre could very easily be presented as a history of the republic's theatre scandals'.[79] Making sense of the period, then, is a question of perspective: of deciding where the gaze should fall. If we focus, as most histories of the Weimar era do, exclusively on the events *on stage* until the brownshirts suddenly burst into the auditorium, we do not get the full picture. We miss the effect Weimar theatre had on a substantial part of the German public. That is not to say that the studies about the Weimar republic have been wrong: it is just that they have often been incomplete. Take the *cause célèbre* of Jeßner's *Tell*. That iconic production did offer fine acting; it was a brilliantly imaginative reinterpretation of a German classic, and an exuberant celebration of republican freedom. Seen from that perspective, the ensuing *Theaterskandal* is no more than the contemptible work of philistines and reactionaries.

Yet if the focus widens to take in the enraged sections of the audience, the picture alters: and so, it should be noted, does the message of Jeßner's production. *Wilhelm Tell* is about rebellion and its roots. In one of the play's most famous scenes, the villain of the piece, Geßler, places his hat on a pole in a market square and forces the Swiss peasants to abase themselves not simply before his person but before a mere item of his clothing. It is that deliberate humiliation that sparks the revolt. The word *Geßlerhut* – Geßler's hat – has become proverbial in the German language. Perhaps it never occurred to the republic's cultural activists that their artistic radicalism would have on conservative audiences the same effect that Geßler's hat, on stage, had on the Swiss peasants. In the play, and in real life, the response was to withdraw initially in the face of overwhelming power – the republic was securely entrenched at first – and then, conspiratorially, to plot revenge.

There was no repeat in the Prussian State Theatre of the first night's protests. Conservative audiences behaved like Europeans: many simply stayed away; but their resentment festered, and out of it grew a sense of being exiles in their own country. As Rainer Schlösser, the future head of Nazi theatre, would put it a few years later, people found after 1918 'that their Germany had vanished'.[80] Alienation, in other words, was not simply a theatrical device in the Weimar republic: it was a recognisable social phenomenon emanating from the stage. And social phenomena are the raw materials of politics. It has long been acknowledged that the Nazi party skilfully exploited cultural discontent. But that discontent had not been *created* by the Nazi party. Rejection of republican culture, likewise, was not automatically evidence of Nazi leanings; but it did often make people susceptible to wider Nazi arguments. That is precisely what Count Kessler had observed during his visit to the literary shrines in Goethe's Weimar: nazification had occurred almost below the level of consciousness. Moreover, it linked cultural activists with professional axes to grind – people like Schlösser, Ziegler,

Schirach-*père et fils* – with a vast army of potential foot soldiers: the 'monarchists of the arts'.

The origins of Nazi theatre can be found in the alliance of those two groups. The deposed professionals sought to recover their former positions; the audiences their sense of reassurance and the former pleasure of theatregoing.[81] Both were determined to wrest 'their' theatre from hostile hands; and both were in vengeful mood. Retribution should fall upon the heads of those who had set out to humiliate them, and had made fun of all they held dear.[82] At the root of the conflict, then, was the issue of identity: of how individuals defined themselves as members of a group, of an estate – to use the terminology of the German right – or of a class, to use the preferred term of the left. Above all, it was about how people conceived the wider German nation and their own place in it. And it was about how all these definitions were, in turn, affected by the social, economic and political crises of the inter-war years. Time was out of joint, and so was the nation. The stage reflected this all too accurately. That explains the extraordinary passion with which Weimar theatre was discussed by supporters and opponents alike. Outside observers were struck very forcefully by the fervour involved. Take the Austrian writer Robert Musil: a modernist himself, sympathetic to Weimar culture, Musil saw in the republic's theatre a *Psychopathologie* of the age: a telling allusion to a work by Freud.[83] The Nazis would not have approved of the reference to Freud, and indeed they did not approve of Musil, but the suggestion of Weimar theatre revealing precarious mental balances was very close to their own thinking.[84]

Musil's fellow modernist (and fellow Austrian), the later Nobel laureate Elias Canetti, also noticed an obsessive quality about Weimar theatre. Canetti lived through part of the 1920s in Frankfurt. At that time, the city was Berlin's principal rival in the new theatre style. In his memoirs, Canetti looks back on those years from the vantage of a life divided between Vienna, Zürich, Frankfurt and London. All these cities possessed lively theatre cultures. Yet nowhere, Canetti recalls, had the stage recurred so obsessively in conversation as in Frankfurt. Heated discussions about the latest productions in the municipal

playhouse became his dominant memory of that city, and by extension of Germany in the 1920s.[85]

Much was at stake emotionally for both sides. For the supporters of the republic, the new theatre style was about distancing themselves from an older world, a world that had not quite perished in the
carnage it had unleashed in Flanders and on the Russian plain.[86] The
court theatre style, and much of the traditional repertoire, were judged
guilty by association. The emotions of the republicans coloured their
theatre: it was a curious mixture of retrospective anger, joy at their
political liberation and a belief in the future that seems touchingly
naive in retrospect.

Yet emotions also shaped the reactions of conservative audiences. To them, the new style was a gratuitous reminder of the changes
war, defeat and revolution had brought to middle-class lives.[87] We
must imagine Germany's conservatives in the early 1920s not as the
formidable political class they had been in Wilhelmine days nor – yet –
as Hitler's vengeful auxiliaries. At the beginning of the republic, they
were a deeply traumatised section of society. The decline in their
fortunes had been precipitous. Money, status, possessions and self-
confidence had all utterly melted away in a few short years. At such
times one craves reassurance: yet there was none. There was little
hope of a genuine economic recovery, no prospect of political stabili-
sation at home or of restored national prestige abroad. That left only
the consolations of the mind: chief among them that personal treasury
of lyric or dramatic verse which no revolutionary could ransack, no
mercenary Allied government extort, and which inflation itself could
never debase.[88] That is why experimentation with the classics provoked such irrational anger among German conservatives. It threatened to complete their dispossession. After the Second World War, one
of the central figures of the emerging East German cultural bureaucracy, the poet Johannes R. Becher, looked back on the Weimar years
and diagnosed a comprehensive failure of the left. They – and Becher
includes himself in this – had completely misjudged the situation.
They had misread the political developments; and they had been
blind to the emotional needs of their fellow Germans. The avant-
garde, Becher suggests, had lived in self-imposed exile among their

own countrymen. Their artistic approach had 'isolated [them] from national problems', and had opened the field to the far right. Becher went on to say that it had only been later, during his actual emigration, that he himself 'discovered' Germany, 'the German people, and the German poetry that I had earlier dismissed out of hand'.[89]

Becher was speaking of literature: yet much the same went for the theatre. The failure of its star directors to appreciate the need for comfort amid the disintegration of national life is glaringly obvious in retrospect. Their unwillingness to explore the national disasters with at least a minimum of tact or compassion for the defeated sections of German society is no less striking; and their contemptuous attitude towards the past completes the picture. Let us turn, once more, to Jeßner and Piscator, as the epitome of the republic's theatre style; let us examine, in the light of Becher's comments, what had struck reviewers at the time.

It was the directors' 'tin ear for verse' which had dismayed the critics.[90] Even Alfred Kerr was troubled. He showed his unease through a parody of Goethe's 'Erlkönig'. Piscator, Kerr suggested, would turn Goethe's haunting verse into something like this: 'Rides, late, night, wind, father, child; ... child dead.'[91] Kerr was moved to ask, 'Where, Piscator, is the poetry?' It is a question remarkably similar to Becher's observation about the avant-garde. Kerr's related claim, moreover, that Schiller was being robbed of 'the poetic', and his drama 'of soul and spirit itself' effectively anticipates later Nazi claims.

Even Kerr's terminology does not seem hugely different from the later argot of the Nazis. Consider his spontaneous (and untranslatable) phrase *entdichtert* – 'with the poetry removed'. The phrase contains that very term *Dichter* – 'poet' – which the Nazis bestowed on the writers of whom they approved, to distinguish these from the mere *Literaten* – the soulless *littérateurs* of the republic.[92] Here, in other words, were expressed some of the principal charges the Nazis would later enter against the republic's theatre: and they came from a source with impeccable republican credentials.

Consider also the opinion of Kerr's principal rival, the critic Herbert Ihering. Ihering's early championing of Jeßner (and Brecht) had marked him out as another pillar of republican theatre. Yet, as the 1920s wore on, he could not disguise a growing disenchantment with Jeßner's artistic style. By 1930, his condemnation was categorical. Ihering was probably partly responsible for bringing about Jeßner's resignation.

Consider further the voice of a Prussian conservative, Paul Fechter, the critic of the influential *Deutsche Allgemeine Zeitung*. Fechter had been uneasy about the new style from the start; but he genuinely tried to be fair to it. He always sought to find at least some aspect to praise in his reviews. Yet faced with Jeßner's *Hamlet*, his dismay was bottomless.[93] Add to this the earlier voices of Reinhardt and Hoffmannsthal, representing pre-war theatre, and the pan-European perspective of Austrian Catholicism, and it becomes clear that the objections were not limited to any one ideological grouping. Weimar theatre had managed to unite a very large segment of Austro-German opinion against it. Becher was right: the left-wing avant-garde had chosen to live in self-imposed exile among their own countrymen; what is more, they had smoothed the path for the takeover by the far right.

That takeover, then, needs to be rethought. Much more was involved in the collapse of the republican cultural experiment than a simple triumph of the Nazis. The stormtroopers who burst into the theatres were merely the most radical part of a broad front of opponents. The motivations ranged from love of tradition or nostalgia for the sunken Empire to a dislike of the republic's *Sachlichkeit*, its much-vaunted sobriety. 'We are sick of that barren and cold tone,' wrote Hans Severus Ziegler in 1932.[94] Ten years earlier, Paul Fechter had already wondered after seeing Jeßner's stripped-down *Don Carlos*, 'whether that sobriety was not the result of a poverty within', suggesting a 'heart that feels nothing'.[95]

Let us recall the context in which such sentiments were expressed. Weimar audiences were not 'normal' theatre audiences. They had survived a war of unprecedented savagery; they had seen the mass death of civilians in the winter of 1918 through famine, rampant infant mortality and the Spanish influenza pandemic; they had experienced defeat, the collapse of their state, national humiliation abroad, occupation of parts of Germany by foreign armies bent on vengeance; civil strife in the streets, entire regions under martial law;

the collapse of values, traditions and symbols; and then – not once but twice within a decade – mass destitution: first through hyperinflation and then the Great Depression.

Such, then, was the context of complaints about 'a poverty within' and 'a heart that feels nothing', or of Kerr's plaintive question, 'Where . . . is the poetry?' We might see in such responses evidence of a fatal German preference for emotion over reason.[96] But when misery grows beyond measure, reason tends to give way not just in Germany. After the depression of the 1930s, the citizens of a great democracy were ready to believe in large numbers that extraterrestrials had invaded their country. The story of Orson Welles' radio broadcast may say as much about America as the *Theaterskandale* say about Germany. What both prove above all, however, is that people between the wars were deeply traumatised.

In the United States, the emotional needs of a shaken electorate were catered for in the movies, the art form that America made its own. Politically, the nervous masses were reassured by the leadership of President Roosevelt, who saved democracy by breaking all its previous rules. It was Germany's misfortune that it lacked a charismatic figure willing to save the republic; but it was perhaps its misfortune also that its brilliant cerebral theatre resolutely refused to dispense comfort. The emotional warmth and the feast for the eyes which, in their different ways, Reinhardt and the Meininger had both provided were now lacking. There was no more 'enchantment'.[97]

An important section of German society which continued to look to the stage rather than the screen sought enchantment elsewhere. They found it in a new style of politics: in Hitler's highly theatrical *Gesamtkunstwerk* of uniforms, music, lighting and carefully chosen settings.[98] That Nazism offered strong aesthetic stimuli and a powerful emotional release may not be a new insight; it helps explain, however, why a surprisingly high percentage of *cultured* Germans were ready to throw in their lot with Hitler. 'The festivals of the new German Reich', explained one contemporary observer, were true 'works of art' with 'carefully thought-out structures'. 'The greatest of these', 'the party rally', he added, was an 'exemplary theatricalisation of reality'.[99] The Nazis were thus able to exploit desires which republican culture had wilfully refused to satisfy.[100]

The Weimar era is often presented as a simple choice between republican culture and Nazi barbarism: between innovation on the one hand and sterile traditionalism on the other. There was, supposedly, no respectable alternative to Weimar.[101] Yet, in the theatre at least, the facts suggest otherwise. Take one of the most prominent directors outside Berlin: Saladin Schmitt in Bochum. His productions were the polar opposite to those of Jeßner, Piscator or Karl Heinz Martin. Yet they were hardly sterile: Schmitt created a lively theatre culture in an industrial town, something that might otherwise be thought to constitute part of a progressive agenda.[102] His repertoire, although thoroughly conservative, was not unadventurous either. He regularly confronted his audiences with unfamiliar, difficult works (albeit by canonical authors). Above all, Schmitt nurtured over the years an acting ensemble noted for the harmony of its playing.[103]

Consider also people like Jürgen Fehling in Berlin and Otto Falckenberg in Munich. Both men were clearly innovative, yet remained in many ways closer to Reinhardt than to Jeßner.[104] Schmitt, Fehling and Falckenberg continued to work in Germany after 1933, and all three remained true to their artistic visions, which were not those of the Nazi cultural apparatus.[105]

Finally, there was Max Reinhardt himself. His work after 1918 – in Austria, and in Berlin – must be considered a conscious refutation of republican theatre. Reinhardt was living proof that there existed a cultured, humanist alternative to Weimar. He continued to champion new plays and new playwrights, and his directing style never became repetitive.[106] The difference was that Reinhardt sought to appeal to the senses and emotions of his audience; much of Weimar theatre to their intellect. Where republican theatre had deployed emotional effects, as in its initial expressionist phase, it had aimed to shock. Reinhardt saw the stage as a source of pleasure, a sublime *jeu d'ésprit* and an end in itself. Jeßner, Piscator, Brecht or Karl Heinz Martin, and the critics who supported them, regarded it as a tool for social change.[107]

Consider the reception by the Berlin critics to Soviet theatre on tour, and the underlying agenda will become obvious. The crude agitprop of 'the Blue Aprons' troupe induced ecstasy in Alfred Kerr:

'ultramodern, alluring ... healthy, confident; marvellous, marvellous'.[108] Tairov's Chamber Theatre, per contra, was pronounced 'bourgeois snobbery from Soviet Russia'.[109] Alfred Döblin concurred. Tairov's colourful costumes were 'one hundred percent bourgeois'.[110] Meyerhold fared no better. His production of Ostrovsky's *Forest* was 'pretty but quite reactionary'.[111] Ihering identified Meyerhold's central deficiency: he produced 'depoliticised theatre'.[112] Piscator delivered the *coup de grâce*, 'Meyerhold is an artist in the true sense of the word but we live in an age where the arts have become irrelevant'.[113] What mattered in the theatre, he added, was 'enlightenment and education'. A significant part of middle-class Germany begged to differ. Republican theatre offered them no home. The Nazis did.

It bears repeating: not all of those who had grown tired of the republic's politicised theatre were Nazis. During one of Jeßner's final performances in the Prussian State Theatre in 1930, a critic counted all of seven paying spectators in the audience.[114] Piscator, meanwhile, had been responsible for the serial collapse of box office ventures. Indeed, it has been said – perhaps with a touch of hyperbole – that the only man still interested in Piscator at the end of the republic was Goebbels.[115] Before the Great War, radical theatre reformers had dreamt of a theatre 'emancipated' from its audiences.[116] By the end of the Weimar era, republican theatre had achieved that utopia.

Clearly, the depression was a contributing factor in the decline of modernist theatre. Yet contrast Jeßner's deserted auditorium with a suggestively large attendance a year later, and thus a year deeper into the depression. The occasion was Zuckmayer's new drama, *The Captain of Köpenick*. The play was subtle, smiling and suffused with warmth. It reflected the character of a man who managed to maintain friendships across the political spectrum: from the left to the (non-Nazi) right.[117] In retelling the celebrated case of a Berlin down-and-out who had impersonated an army officer, Zuckmayer's play provided a satirical comment on Imperial Germany. In 1906, an unemployed cobbler had managed to acquire a captain's uniform. The newly resplendent captain had promptly taken command of a company of soldiers he had chanced upon in the street. He marched them to Köpenick town hall on the outskirts of Berlin, and ordered them to secure the building. He then made off with the contents of the town's treasury: no one had dared to challenge a man in uniform.

Here was political education about the recent past (and possible future); here, moreover, was a play that portrayed a criminal as the victim of a conservative political system: driven to crime if he was to survive. Yet Zuckmayer lectured no one. What is more, his play betrayed a deep love of Germany – for all its manifest faults, so to speak. The audiences thanked him for it. They came in record numbers, at a time when money was scarce. Significantly, it did not seem to matter that Zuckmayer was, in Nazi terms, half-Jewish.

Patriotism was the Achilles' heel of the Weimar republic. The emphasis placed by its supporters on the word 'republic' allowed the right to appropriate the name of 'Germany'. It was a fatal tactical error of the left not to contest this. Theatre played its part in this fateful mistake. Let us return, one more time, to the beginning of republican theatre: Jeßner's *Wilhelm Tell* of 1919.

Schiller had written the play during a period of German impotence exploited by France. At that time, under Napoleon, France had annexed the Low Countries, much of Western Germany, and had snuffed out Swiss independence. *Tell*, in other words, had very specific historical connotations familiar to German audiences. Those connotations Jeßner had sought to destroy. He turned a play of *national* liberation into one of *political* liberation. He did so, however, at a time when the German *nation's* very existence seemed threatened, as its enemies were gathering at Versailles. Hence the outrage of conservative theatregoers. Jeßner's reading of the play seemed to them equally blind to past or present: dictated only by an apparent lack of patriotism. Inevitably, that stance came to be associated with Jeßner's Jewish background.

In 1923, Jeßner returned to *Tell*. The date is crucial: France was now attempting to sever the occupied Rhineland from Germany, as she had done in Schiller's day. There was no obvious way in which the disarmed and economically crippled German nation might have resisted. (In the end, it was Britain that stopped the French.) At that moment of national impotence, Jeßner staged his second *Tell*. This time, he gave it a traditional reading. He did not have to add anything to make the play patriotic. All he had to do was to provide a realist 'Swiss' setting, thus restoring the historical context. He also reinstated the lines he had cut four years earlier ('Ans Vaterland, ans teure'). The effect was electrifying. During the play's central patriotic scene the audience actually chanted the familiar words of the 'Rütli Oath', pledging themselves to defend their country as the actors on stage were doing in the play. Theatrical make-believe fused with reality. It did so again at the end of the performance: the audience rose spontaneously and began to sing the national anthem.

Before we dismiss this as archetypal German behaviour, as part of what was *wrong* with the Germans, let us not forget Olivier's *Henry V* during the war. Let us bear in mind also Hollywood's familiar patriotic paroxysms. Each nation fashions its own crutches with which to limp through reality. To outsiders, those crutches may sometimes look embarrassingly crude but they seem to work for the people they were designed for. No one should expect thanks for seeking to dash those crutches from people's hands. Yet that is precisely what Weimar theatre sought to do. The 'patriotic' *Tell* had been an exception, and Jeßner was severely criticised for it: not by the antisemites this time, but by his friends.[118]

Patriotism is more than just flag-waving: it is about identity. In Germany, national identity has centred, historically, on culture. It was no accident that Wagner's *Meistersinger* became a national icon: its solemn injunction to 'honour our German masters' struck a chord. Music, literature and indeed the theatre were central to German national identity. The project of a 'national theatre' had preceded political unification. It was conceived in the eighteenth century as a stepping stone towards political unity. The tradition of equating the theatre with the nation persisted into the twentieth century. On the eve of the Great War, Thomas Mann felt moved to declare, 'We Germans are born with an awe of theatre known to no other nation.'[119] It was no nationalist boast. Mann, the novelist, was in fact resentful of the stage's importance. Arnold Zweig – like Mann, a novelist – saw in the theatre the only institution where 'the nation could sit in judgement upon itself'.[120]

Given such sentiments, it was perhaps only fitting that the revolution should have gone further in German theatre than in most other national institutions. In Russia, the Bolsheviks destroyed the monuments of the tsars, sold off their art treasures and desecrated many of the churches. The German revolution did none of these things. Yet it did something that shocked traditionalists almost as much: it invaded the stage and melted down the classics to turn them into political brass. Piscator's production of Schiller's *Robbers* put a man wearing the mask of Trotsky on stage. Erich Ziegel in Hamburg had turned the villain in *Robbers* into a cigar-puffing capitalist. Karl Heinz Martin added new scenes to Büchner's *Danton* to fit a left-wing reading. In Nuremberg, they had added to *Tell* a new prologue 'by a rhymster of the class struggle'.[121] Jeßner's *Hamlet* placed the Kaiser at Elsinore. A whole range of core pieces of the classical repertoire were similarly pressed into political service: *Macbeth* and *Richard III*, *Don Carlos*, *Fiesco*, *Wallenstein*, etc. In each case, the play was reduced to one central idea: political power as the driving force in human lives. To sustain that interpretation, everything else was cut.[122]

The price paid was correspondingly high. Vast swathes of the classical repertoire, which resisted a political reading, went unperformed. 'The death of the classics' became a recurring term in the cultural and political discourses of the period. The plays that were put on appeared in severely truncated form. Brecht himself recorded, with a *tricoteuse's* relish, Jeßner's 'deliberate amputations'.[123]

Some in the audiences enjoyed the novelty of it. Others may have applauded, as Alfred Polgar suspected, for fear of being thought philistines.[124] Many reacted with open dismay. Consider, paradigmatically, Fechter's exasperation with the *Don Carlos* he had just seen. It was not just that the showpiece monologues had all been cut; nearly all the scenes with Princess Eboli were likewise gone. There was practically no 'female moment' left in the play.[125] Yet life was not exclusively male and did not simply consist of politics.

Apart from its obsession with the political, republican theatre possessed another controversial characteristic. It was supremely visual. Few theatrical epochs in the history of any nation can rival the Weimar stage's use of space, and its mastery of movement. Yet the same cannot be said about language.[126] That showed in various ways:

Piscator used a conveyor belt in his adaptation of *Schweijk*. He achieved striking visual effects with it. The noise of the machine also rendered the actors practically inaudible.[127] Berthold Viertel advocated an end of 'melodic sophistication' on stage.[128] Jeßner's players saw to that. They became famous for their 'staccato' delivery or *Telegrammstil* ('telegraphese'): they reproduced 'the punctuation rather than the melody', as Ihering later put it.[129] Jeßner himself readily sacrificed classical cadences to achieve the surging scenes and headlong tumbles on his trademark stairs.[130] Karl Kraus, the great humanist Jewish writer, summed it up succinctly. The new Berlin theatre was the 'death of the word': amid the 'shoving' and 'pounding', the 'syntax was being trampled underfoot' and the word drowned out by a 'regimented rhythm'.[131]

Yet language is central to identification. Weimar theatre all too often denied its audiences the possibility of identifying with the characters on stage. One consequence of this was the proliferation of the so-called *Zeitstück*. These dramatised versions of contemporary affairs were hugely popular.[132] Their topics openly appealed to the audiences' emotions: e.g. the rights or wrongs of abortion (§ 218), the fate of children in care (*Revolte im Erziehungshaus*), judicial murder (*Sacco und Vanzetti*), etc. These plays have usually been regarded as a kind of theatrical judgement on a dysfunctional society. Yet might their popularity with audiences not also be seen as a judgement on a dysfunctional theatre?[133]

For the relationship between auditorium and stage had changed. Republican theatre, by and large, sought to highlight ideas. These could only emerge through the director's reworking of the chosen play. The corollary of this was to disenfranchise audiences. Realist theatre had proceeded from the assumption that directors and audiences saw the world the same way. It gave the viewers the feeling of participating as equals. Jeßner or Piscator reduced the audience to an ignorant crowd requiring enlightenment by the director's anointed hand. Where once the classics had been the *Gemeingut* – the common property of all cultured Germans – only the elect could now interpret their true meaning. The theatre of the first German democracy was thus arrogantly elitist.[134] That made the public susceptible not only to crude populism but to the siren voices promising a restoration of a German culture open to all. The reactions of an archetypal *Bildungsbürger*, the educationalist Otto Schumann, prove the allure of this. In 1932, Schumann was deeply troubled by the prospect of a Nazi government. He found the party's antisemitism objectionable, and he feared for German culture. Nazi rule would result in a *Primitivierung* – a stripping away of intellect and sophistication. Yet, he wondered, perhaps that very process might prove a boon in the end. It could allow people, once more, 'to *enjoy* Art or Literature [*Dichtung*]', and not be forced to approach them as 'ideological case studies'.[135] That had been Johannes R. Becher's point after the war. The left-wing avant-garde had helped to open the door to the far right.

The people ready to enter were the Weimar group we encountered earlier: Schlösser, Ziegler, Schirach, etc. And it is no accident that they all came from literary backgrounds. They stood for the nexus between nation and language, audience and classical verse that had marked German theatre and national identity before the republic.[136] They could credibly claim to be the heirs of German tradition and the guardians of the nation's identity. It was no accident either that the Nazis spoke of *Werktreue*. Being true to the spirit of a drama and faithful to its text: that would be the guiding principle of their own theatre.[137] The term was well chosen. It appealed to conservative sensibilities.[138] Above all, it suggested incorruptibility: for at bottom, the Nazis hinted, this was a moral issue.[139] The republic's theatre they regarded as fundamentally dishonest. It had bent and twisted the classics for its political ends.[140] Hans Severus Ziegler had not merely inveighed against the 'barren and cold tone' but against *Geschichtsklitterungen* – the 'rewriting of history'.

When the swastika flags appeared on Germany's theatre buildings, the people who had fretted about the intrusion of politics into culture uttered hardly a word of protest: they had become radicalised. The intention of the republic's directors to reveal the ideological relevance of theatre had succeeded: but not in the way the supporters of the republic had intended. The *Bildungsbürgertum* still believed in a separation between culture and politics. Yet they were now willing

34

to make a temporary exception to that rule. Fire, after all, could sometimes only be fought with fire.[141]

The violent expulsion of the avant-garde in the spring of 1933
was experienced by many German conservatives as a liberation. That
owed much to deft Nazi stage management. Yet the left, too, had
played its part. In more ways than one, the theatre of the republic
itself had set the stage for the Third Reich.

2 Visions of a national rebirth: *völkisch* theatre reform

On 20 April 1933, Germany's new leadership assembled for an evening in the theatre. It was the first time the country had celebrated Hitler's birthday as a national holiday. The day was to end with a theatrical treat for the Führer: the première of Hanns Johst's drama *Schlageter*. Johst had dedicated the play to Hitler. It had then been broadcast by the newly nazified German radio in the run-up to the March 1933 elections.[1] Now it was to be staged for the first time. The production was as much a political as a cultural event. The chosen location reflected this: the Prussian State Theatre in Berlin had been the Kaiser's theatre. Then Leopold Jeßner had made it the showcase of republican culture. And just as Jeßner had used his inaugural production there to celebrate the collapse of Imperial Germany, so now the Nazis were celebrating the fall of the republic.[2]

Schlageter was, in its own terms, a signal success. The production was polished, the play itself an effective piece of stagecraft. Rainer Schlösser pronounced it a fitting response to those who 'for so long' had 'made fun ... of our cultural ambitions'.[3] At a personal level, it confirmed Johst's position as the bard of Nazism and advanced the fortunes of many in the cast.[4] Lothar Müthel, playing the title role, was forgiven his earlier closeness to 'the Jew' Max Reinhardt: less than two weeks after the first night of *Schlageter*, he was accepted into the Nazi party, and was subsequently allowed to direct widely. After the *Anschluß*, he took over the reins at Vienna's Burgtheater, perhaps the most august theatrical establishment in Central Europe. Veit Harlan, playing Schlageter's friend, was to make his mark in Nazi cinema as one of Goebbels' most trusted lieutenants. The actress

Emmy Sonnemann, finally, had caught the eye of the man who hosted the production: in due course, she would become Mrs Hermann Göring.

Johst himself was admitted into the Prussian Academy by ministerial decree a fortnight after the première of *Schlageter*, and was immediately elected its president.[5] He was appointed Prussian state councillor and was the recipient of numerous Nazi prizes. He was admitted to the SS in November 1935, where he rose to the eventual rank of *Gruppenführer*, the SS-equivalent of a general. He became a close confidant and personal friend of Himmler. In 1935, Johst also reached the apex of the cultural bureaucracy, when Goebbels appointed him president of the Reich Chamber of Literature.[6] The author of *Schlageter* had thus achieved the rare feat of being equally showered with honours by Göring, Goebbels, Himmler and Rosenberg. Given the notorious factionalism of the Nazi party, such unanimity was striking.[7] *Schlageter* itself went on to be the most widely performed new play in the Reich. Most German theatres produced it in the 1933–4 season. In addition, Johst's play was carried to remote corners of Germany by itinerant Nazi players, members of the *NS-Kampfbühnen*, the party's so-called 'combat troupes'; the play was likewise put on by theatre enthusiasts on open-air stages during the summer months.[8] In all, productions of *Schlageter* appeared in more than a thousand venues in the 1933–4 season; the play entered the school curriculum, and German radio broadcast it no fewer than fifteen times in 1933 alone.[9] If any one drama can be said to have marked the beginning of the Third Reich, it was *Schlageter*.

Johst's play related the life of the *Freikorps* leader Albert Leo Schlageter, who had organised the resistance in the Ruhr against the French a decade earlier. The play ended with a re-enactment of Schlageter's death by firing squad.[10] The actor playing Schlageter stood downstage with his back to the audience. Facing him was a platoon of French soldiers who trained their rifles on him – and thus also on the viewers. The stage was darkened. Then a strong beam of light shone from backstage towards Schlageter *and* the audience. A French soldier approached Schlageter and hit him with the butt of his gun to force him to kneel. This had the effect of allowing the spectators a clear view of the rifles pointing their way. Schlageter then cried

2 *Schlageter*, final scene, in a pencil sketch by Hitler's favourite stage designer, Benno von Arendt.

out, 'Germany – awake! Turn into a flame, into fire! Burn – beyond imagining!' And, as if in response to that cry, the French fired off their guns. A volley of shots rang out in the direction of Schlageter *and* the audience: all light was extinguished. It was perhaps the most effective moment in all of Nazi theatre.

That *Schlageter* was as much an exercise in propaganda as in the dramatic arts has always been obvious. Jeßner's right-hand man, Eckart von Naso, famously described it as 'drumbeat turned drama'. The reviews at the time reflected that too. They called the play 'a national event', beyond the measure of traditional criticism.[11] It is worth pausing, however, to consider how insidiously Johst had manipulated his audiences.

The French invasion of the Ruhr in 1923, over the issue of reparations, had caused a profound national trauma. Germany had been forced to watch impotently while foreign soldiers took the inhabitants of the Ruhr hostage. The responses to that humiliation were partly shaped by traditional gender roles. The First World War – still very present in people's minds a mere five years after the armistice – had reinforced these roles. Males had been cast as the nation's shield and the defenders of her women and children, a view also popularised by German theatre itself with its wartime diet of patriotic plays, shows and musical entertainments.[12] That view of heroic masculinity was now directly challenged by the French invasion. For many German men there was a feeling of having personally failed the Ruhr. It is not too fanciful to suggest that they felt as a father would who had been forced to watch an intruder break into his house and rape his child.

Johst was too fine a writer – and too shrewd a propagandist – to make all this overt. Lesser Nazi dramatists were producing at that time graphic plays about the collective trauma of the post-war years. Scenes of foreign soldiery raping their way through German lands recurred in several of them.[13] Johst's interest, however, was in the *domestic* responses to the post-war crisis. He sought to rekindle the sense of guilt his audience had felt in 1923. To achieve this, he implied a contrast between events on stage and the spectators. Schlageter had fought the French. The audience had not. The patriotism of Berlin audiences in that very theatre had not gone further than watching Jeßner's second *Wilhelm Tell*, chanting the 'Rütli Oath' and singing the national anthem afterwards. In the provinces, too, there had been much patriotic bluster, but few had been willing to risk another war. The Weimar government's policy of passive resistance had been endorsed, albeit regretfully, by the majority of Germans.

The charge of cowardice thus hung in the air. But Johst – and this was the propagandist's stroke of genius – partly absolved the audience from that charge. In his play, he deliberately portrayed some representatives of the Weimar republic as well intentioned in their way. The reviewers of 1933 were struck by that, since it contradicted the established Nazi view. In the words of one critic, the play had offered 'the hand of forgiveness and reconciliation'.[14]

That apparent generosity was not without ulterior motive. It was designed to make the audiences more receptive to Johst's characterisation of the play's hero. Albert Leo Schlageter had been an early exponent of *völkisch* nationalism. That Johst should have presented him as 'the first soldier of the Third Reich' may not seem particularly surprising. It is worth remembering, however, that the people watching the play were not necessarily all Nazis.

Most Germans had rejected the far right at the time of the Ruhr crisis or indeed later. Only a few weeks before the first night of *Schlageter* Germany had gone to the polls. And even in that final democratic election – no longer wholly free – the majority of Germans had failed to vote for Hitler. Johst's aim was to win over to the Nazi cause some of those people.[15] To that end, Schlageter was presented as someone with whom even non-Nazis could potentially identify. Johst had his protagonist rehearse on stage the very arguments which he suspected many in the audience to have held during the Ruhr crisis. All the doubts and hesitations of politically moderate Germans between the wars were here. Then Johst deliberately touched at the psychological wound in his audience. He left it to a woman – the character created in Berlin by Göring's later wife – to urge German men to action. The protagonist, in other words, started out from where the audience might have started out. Johst's Schlageter was a reluctant hero: slow to take up arms, and reaching for them in the heavy knowledge of his likely defeat. That final point was significant.

There was always in National Socialism a profoundly pessimistic streak. Defeat in 1918 had seemed to bear out earlier intimations among the far right of national decline. The manic swagger in the leaders of the supposed master race was in part overcompensation; and it continued to alternate with moments of deepest gloom.[16] At times, this took the form of a pronounced death wish. It was not just Hitler who repeatedly luxuriated in the thought of Germany's utter annihilation in battle. For if their destruction as Nazis and as Germans was decreed, then they wanted to embrace it and feel that they and their nation had died like men. 'Life,' as Johst would later write on the eve of Stalingrad, 'was about learning to die.'[17]

Here is the crucial exchange in Johst's play between a still hesitant Schlageter and the army officer advising him. When Schlageter declares that fighting the French was surely madness, since a renewed conflict would not liberate Germany but destroy it utterly, the officer delivers this reply: 'No! Our despair, the unconditional absolute nature of our despair will destroy the servitude [and] corruption.'[18] That outburst may seem extraordinary enough by any standards but there is more. Johst actually has Schlageter warning the officer that in the process Germany would 'turn into a vast graveyard'. The military man agrees, only to add that death was preferable to a life without dignity or honour. Johst's play was about encouraging non-Nazis to enter into that suicide pact.

To put it in modern psychological terms: Johst aimed to induce 'survivor guilt' in his audience. It is a recognised feature of overwhelming disasters that survivors feel undeserving of their own (relative) luck. After the Great War, guilt was widespread in the men of all combatant nations.[19] The best, many felt, had died. It was this feeling that Johst cynically exploited. Across the graves of the Great War and across Schlageter's corpse on Golzheim heath, Johst confronted his audience with the unspoken question that had been haunting them: 'Why are you still living?'

It was this psychological sophistication that made *Schlageter* so effective in its day – and so contemptible.[20] Johst had exploited the traditional mechanism of classical drama – that of catharsis – for his nefarious ends. For out of guilt, Johst whispered to his audience, could grow redemption. All that was required was to do the right thing now and not fail Germany a second time. That was why, in the play's final scene, Johst carefully pointed the French guns at the audience as much as at the hero. The public should relive the year 1923. This time they, too, should join Schlageter in the face of the guns; and like Schlageter, they should cry a defiant 'Germany awake!'

Those words, of course, were a Nazi party slogan familiar to all.[21] Patriotic sentiment and survivor guilt would have been transformed into political allegiance. The question is whether Johst's strategy worked. There is no conclusive answer. One cannot look into the minds of a nameless crowd decades on: but there is an important clue. In 1923 the theatre audience at the end of *Wilhelm Tell* had spontaneously risen to sing the national anthem. The scene was repeated ten years on at the end of *Schlageter*. Only this time, in 1933, 'Deutschland, Deutschland über alles' was followed by a rendition of the 'Horst Wessel-Lied': the Nazi party anthem.

The final act of a drama, Johst had suggested in an essay some years earlier, should 'take place inside the viewer'.[22] The aim was to create or strengthen ideological commitment through the theatre. In the words of an official in the Propaganda Ministry, theatre should 'energise' the audiences.[23] And one of the panjandrums of Nazi culture, the critic Joseph Magnus Wehner, observed about *Schlageter*, 'The catharsis of this drama lies in the fact that at its end the National Idea has been born inside the viewer.'[24]

Dramas such as Johst's thus had a recognised political function: they served the state. 'The call which has gone out to the theatre is that of "national education",' as another contemporary voice put it.[25] Johst had created for his masters a politicised theatre that equalled, and perhaps exceeded, in its radicalism the practice of the Weimar republic's most avant-garde directors. *Schlageter* was, in a sense, the Nazi equivalent of Piscator's *Gewitter über Gottland*.[26] This should not be reduced to a question of artistic influence. Both the left and the far right wished to press theatre into political service. The parallels in their respective techniques grew out of that shared ambition.[27]

The difference lay in the intended effect. The left sought to induce reflection. Political moderates, such as Jeßner, hoped to strengthen democratic values. The radical left wished to spur people to action. Political education delivered on stage would prompt audiences to act in accordance with their supposed class interests.[28] The Nazis, however, appealed to the spectators' emotions. 'The theatre we are aiming for is a theatre of inner experience [*Erlebnistheater*],' as the dramatist and Propaganda Ministry official Eberhard Wolfgang Möller put it.[29] Johst's *Schlageter*, with its guns trained on the audience in the final scene, and its viewers singing the Nazi party anthem afterwards, was perhaps the most spectacular instance of that *Erlebnistheater*.

Anti-intellectualism worked in the Nazis' favour. Their celebration of instinct and feelings was peculiarly suited to the emotional needs of a traumatised public.[30] The politics of reason – democracy – had, after all, twice presided over mass destitution. And the *Kultur* of reason had chilled the heart. The lesson seemed clear: 'The rape of life by the intellect' had to stop, as Hanns Johst put it.[31] Nazi *Erlebnistheater* was thus the right format at the right time. It appealed to an audience considerably wider than the party's core constituency. The success of *Schlageter* in 1933 is testimony of that. Unlike Piscator's work, Johst's was acceptable to German *Bildungsbürger*, moreover, because it observed the traditional proprieties of German culture. Ostensibly at least, it kept party politics out of the playhouse. Piscator had put a red star on the stage. Johst kept the swastika firmly off-stage. Piscator (and John Heartfield) had festooned the auditorium with Communist slogans.[32] Johst was careful to introduce Nazi phraseology only in the guise of patriotic sentiment. Even the play's inflammatory final scene had been finely judged in that regard.[33]

The success of *Schlageter* across the Reich coincided with a flood of theoretical pronouncements about the theatre in the new Germany. To outside observers it must have seemed as if carefully thought-out Nazi plans had come to fruition. The reality was otherwise. Although there had been much right-wing plotting about the future of German theatre, little of it was specifically National Socialist. The Nazis were latecomers to *Theaterpolitik*. That was true, above all, of the dedicatee of Johst's *Schlageter*: the Führer himself.

There are few substantive references to the stage in Hitler's early speeches in Munich; *Mein Kampf*, too, offers little beyond platitudes.[34] Hitler enjoyed, and was publicly knowledgeable about, what the Germans call *Musiktheater*: opera and operetta, in other words. He cultivated contacts with its practitioners before 1933, and behaved like the Reich's chief operatic impresario thereafter. He decided all the major appointments himself, issued directorial advice and on occasion even determined the sets for particular productions.[35] He was much more reticent about *Sprechtheater*: the theatre of the spoken word. This was, no doubt, a question of personal preference. Yet there were probably also tactical reasons involved. At the beginning of his political career, the future Führer had received voice training from an actor, had experimented on his elocution and tried out gestures for his speeches before mirrors. The affinity between his own techniques and those of the stage was not lost on some of his contemporaries.[36] He may have been wary of highlighting the connections still further.

Yet Hitler's silence on the theatre even among his inner circle is odd in one respect.[37] Munich, which Hitler had made his home on the eve of the Great War, had been the centre of German theatrical modernism. The young Hitler had briefly coincided in that city with Wedekind, Mühsam, Halbe, Lautensack and Panizza. These dramatists had been involved in a regular theatre war with the Bavarian authorities. The air was thick with writs, appeals, manifestos and open letters. Hitler's silence about all this even in later life, given his general penchant for reminiscences, is certainly striking.[38]

Again the reason may have been tactical. The modernist controversy was not limited to the theatre and it did not divide neatly along the expected ideological fault lines.[39] Bavarian censorship seemed to many religiously inspired. And here the anti-Catholic animus of German Protestants, or of Catholic apostates like Hitler himself, complicated matters. Munich theatre had divided Hitler's own constituency (and continued to do so after January 1933).[40] Perhaps Hitler also simply felt out of his depth. He had not received a proper education. His congenital laziness had resulted in his expulsion from the *Gymnasium* in Linz. Later, in Vienna, he had tried to make up for this. He sought to acquire through an eager perusal of the press the semblance of a middle-class education. He duly managed to accumulate a large store of often bizarre detail, which allowed him to create an illusion of hidden depths.[41]

Maintaining that illusion in the theatre was difficult. Hitler was unfamiliar with the canonical plays and lacked the funds to go and see them. By the time money ceased to be a problem – once the royalties from *Mein Kampf* began to flow – it was, in a sense, too late. He was now in the public eye. Knowledge of Germany's theatrical heritage was one of the touchstones of a traditional middle-class education. An injudicious remark by Hitler, revealing the extent of his ignorance, might have done his standing serious harm. Rumours were already circulating about his crushing 'lack of culture'.[42]

That left the party in a conundrum. Towards the end of the Weimar republic, the crisis of German theatre had become part of the nation's political discourse. With box office receipts declining, unemployment in the theatre sector was reaching unprecedented levels. At the same time a large army of cultural malcontents – Alfred Kerr's 'monarchists of the arts' – were effectively boycotting republican theatre. There were votes to be won by making the right kind of noises about the stage. Yet Hitler remained silent. His followers therefore had to improvise.[43] Hans Severus Ziegler assured the public in 1932 that there existed in Germany 'no man ... [with] a more fanatical interest in the arts, and especially the theatre, than Adolf Hitler'.[44] Yet in the absence of supporting evidence, Ziegler was forced to hint at coming revelations. His own embarrassment about this vagueness was palpable.

Ziegler had been witnessing Hitler's silence from close quarters. From 1926 onwards, the Nazi party repeatedly held mass meetings in Weimar's former court theatre. The party was staking its claim on German heritage. In the process, the place where Germany had acquired a republican constitution and where its deputies accepted the Versailles treaty was, so to speak, ideologically fumigated. The early Nazi party rallies also took place in Weimar: against the background of the Goethe-and-Schiller monument.[45] In those surroundings Hitler's silence on the theatre seemed thunderous.

Several of the local dignitaries were unimpressed. Adolf Bartels, the presiding spirit of far-right culture in Weimar, initially saw in Hitler a lesser man than Ludendorff (the joint-supreme commander in the Great War and idol of the far right).[46] *Völkisch* theatre was backing the wrong horse. Hitler duly kept his distance. He devoted all his attention instead to Bayreuth, where the clear-sighted Winifred Wagner had not failed to recognise him as Germany's new Siegfried.[47] Nazi theatre policy, in other words, took shape independently of the Führer. National Socialism may have begun in the streets of Munich; the Third Reich's theatre originated elsewhere. Its roots reach back into a time before the Nazi party had even been constituted.

There had existed in German culture, from the 1880s onwards, a strong anti-modernist undercurrent.[48] It derived its energies from the increasing strength of modernism itself. This cultural phenomenon had a social and regional dimension. It was a protest by small-town and rural Germany against metropolitan arrogance, and by the embattled lower middle-class against the *haute bourgeoisie* and its ways.

The emerging *völkisch* counter-culture was a mixture of tradition and innovation. The celebrations of rural idylls by the *Heimatkunst* movement provided the roots of the Third Reich's blood-and-soil

45

dramas.[49] Nazi theatre would also share the interest in the pagan Teutons (which had superseded the earlier fascination with the Christian Middle Ages). Wilhelmine attempts to explore the mystical 'essence' of people, nations or the universe led to the pseudo-religious plays of the Third Reich.[50] The literature of *Lebensreform* sired, as its bastard progeny, the Nazi dramas about heredity and eugenics.[51] Finally, there were lively pieces about the animal kingdom.[52] Once the traits celebrated in those tales had been transferred to the level of the human species, one quickly arrived at the vitalist plays of the Third Reich, with their excruciating celebrations of maternal instincts or of the alpha male's territorial (and procreative) urges. For what united these various strands of the late nineteenth century, and what made them modern, was the pervading cult of the healthy and strong, with its barely disguised Darwinian undertones.

One might expect to see something of this also in Wilhelmine theatre. Yet the repertoire before the Great War revealed little sign of it.[53] The resulting mismatch between what was offered and what was sought by at least a part of the German public led to lobbying for changes in repertoire policy. The Verband zur Förderung deutscher Theaterkultur – the Association for the Propagation of German Theatre Culture – founded in 1914 was the most prominent of these pressure groups. It aimed to fight what it called 'decadence and decay'.[54] The stage was to be a mirror of 'true German nature: [of] our struggle and work, our tears and laughter'. The rightful function of theatre, the association thought, was to 'give strength and joy once more to our people'.

Those words have a familiar ring to them. They carry echoes of well-worn dramatic theories and of various censorship debates, from the Lex Henze of the 1890s to the campaign against 'filth and trash' in the Weimar republic.[55] Above all, they foreshadow what was to follow. A Nazi organisation bearing as its name those very words 'strength' and 'joy' would play, from the mid-thirties onwards, a significant role in German theatre. *Kraft-durch-Freude* would organise theatregoing schemes and even take over the actual running of individual stage companies. Piscator's old theatre, no less, would emerge as Berlin's first Strength-through-Joy institution; and the ethos of that establishment would be very much in keeping with the sentiments of the theatregoers' association.[56]

One of the association's founders, the Catholic Reichstag deputy Maximilian Pfeiffer, defined its aims as protecting audiences from all that might 'lead them into the shadowy spheres of life'.[57] The original phrase *Nacht des Lebens* is suggestive. It combines the notion of dark deeds with echoes of the word *umnachtet* – insane. To see what this aimed at, let us recall the repertoire of the more progressive German theatres before 1914. There was the sombre Baltic naturalism of Sudermann or Keyserling – both long forgotten as dramatists but influential at the time.[58] There was Gerhard Hauptmann, the Nobel laureate, and his stark social dramas. There were the even darker plays of Ibsen and Strindberg: some of them actually written on German soil. There was the sombre universe of Tolstoi and Gorky, performed in Germany earlier than in most countries.[59] There was the 'aggressive realism' of Wedekind or Sternheim.[60] There was Schnitzler's grimly sardonic vision of Viennese gender relations. Finally, in the run-up to the First World War, came the expressionists with their disturbing explorations of sex and crime, deviance and disorder. The Third Reich would later banish most of these dramatists from its stage.[61] It is tempting, therefore, to conclude that those objecting to theatrical modernism before 1914 had been fascists *avant la lettre*. Yet many of those same plays encountered considerable hostility in Britain and America (and, in some cases, remained banned in Britain until the 1960s). If this was fascism, it was not simply a German phenomenon.[62]

In the 1920s the calls for censorship increased. Significantly, the post-war successor of the theatregoers' association, the Bühnenvolksbund – the Popular Theatre League – soon won important backers: Field Marshal Hindenburg himself endorsed its aims in 1925.[63] With more than 400,000 members across Germany, the League represented a mass phenomenon. Its membership was larger than that of most political parties. It used its power to lobby theatres, and the politicians who held the theatres' purse strings. It supported selected institutions of which it approved, and it run a number of itinerant companies itself. These represented a useful financial threat against *Intendanten* unwilling to cooperate.[64] Here, long before 1933, we encounter in the provinces characteristic features of later Nazi *Theaterpolitik*: the regulatory impulse, the positive delight in censorship and the readiness to resort to blackmail behind the scenes.

The League also anticipated a second strand of Nazi policy: that of actively promoting plays. Rosenberg's Kampfbund, the Hitler Youth, the German Labour Front, the Agrarian League or such outfits as the Reich Colonial League or the Reich Air Raid Protection League all found time to endorse promising dramatists. Even that notable body of *beaux-esprits*, the SA, pronounced on the artistic merit of new plays.[65]

The Kampfbund and Schirach's Hitler Youth went one step further. They published actual model repertoires. Likewise, the Reichsdramaturg Schlösser, as the chief censor, did not simply ban plays: he suggested alternatives to the plays he had struck out on the repertoire lists submitted by individual theatres.[66] This practice takes us back to the man from whom Schlösser and Schirach had learnt their craft.

In the first decade of the twentieth century, Adolf Bartels had been engaged in defining a canon of plays. The purpose was to estab- lish an annual national theatre festival. Weimar should become to drama what Bayreuth was to opera. The intention was to strengthen patriotic sentiment among the young through the experience of Germany's cultural greatness.[67] Bartels was part of a network of men developing similar ideas: August Sauer in Prague; Adam Müller- Guttenbrunn in Vienna; Ernst Wachler and Friedrich Lienhard in Central Germany; Georg Fuchs and Peter Behrens in Darmstadt; and, after the Great War, Hans Poelzig in Berlin. What united these men was a belief in the national mission of the German stage.[68] Theatre, to them, was a means of transforming society by moulding the con- sciousness of the individual spectator. The point is perfectly illus- trated by the plot of Georg Fuchs' playlet *Das Zeichen*, performed in 1901 at the Artists' Colony in Darmstadt. In Fuchs' play, a group of people identified as lacking common purpose await the arrival of a herald. He presents them with a *Zeichen* – a sign or a symbol.[69] It is a diamond: hard and beautiful, and shaped out of compressed dust. In a sense, that was what the theatre reformers of the right aimed to achieve through their own work. They sought to turn an atomised society, where each individual was without consequence, into a strong and shining *Volk*.

Such right-wing ambitions were a profound breach with tradition. They threatened the autonomy of *Kultur* which German *Bildungsbürger* had treasured (and would later seek to defend against the Weimar left). Fuchs was unapologetic about it. Theatre, he explained, was 'not primarily a question of aesthetics, but rather of *Weltanschauung*'.[70] In Wilhelmine Germany that was a minority opinion. Three decades on, it would become official policy: Hitler himself would declare the ideological relevance of the artistic imagination to be paramount; Hanns Johst would dismiss 'the aesthetic sphere' as 'a hollow sphere', which he contrasted with the 'ideological strictness' of his own theatre; and a host of Nazi scribblers would dutifully observe that usefulness to the German people was the proof of true artistry.[71] Fuchs' *Zeichen* stood at the beginning of that process. It failed to achieve the hopes vested in it by its author.[72] Yet the underlying mentality did have potential mass appeal. Take an example from outside the world of theatre: Fritz Lang's celebrated film *Metropolis*. Its plot was essentially a reprise of Fuchs' vision, but with an apocalyptic urgency that had eluded Fuchs.[73] Another ten years on from *Metropolis*, the efforts of herald-like figures and the striving for harmony and beauty against an apocalyptic background would be central to Nazi *Erlebnistheater* (and indeed to Hitler's own aestheticised politics).

Views similar to Fuchs' were also held by the influential architect and designer Peter Behrens. He envisaged theatre as a 'temple of beauty' and saw the general 'harmony of the arts as the beautiful symbol of a strong Volk'.[74] This has a harmless art nouveau ring about it. Yet it is worth considering the corollary of such pronouncements. What if theatre ceased to be devoted to beauty? Then it would also cease to reflect a strong *Volk* and presumably symbolise the opposite of harmony and national strength. Such an attitude, inevitably, led to the issue of blame. Who was responsible for the cultural disharmony? Who sought to sow discord? Who had an interest in weakening the German people? The finger of blame had traditionally been pointed at the French.[75] By the end of the nineteenth century, such accusations were being directed with increasing frequency at the Jews.

Right-wing theatre reform was thus an important indication of Germany's descent into moral and political bankruptcy. The route of that descent was foreshadowed in Fuchs' tracts. The beginnings were conservative. 'Culture is order, is legislation.' Then came the tone of *völkisch* reform. For culture, Fuchs added, 'is *rhythmic formation*': it is

> the artistic form that a *race* imposes on ... its existence; its timing, tonality, and tempo are determined by the rhythm of its *blood* ... Culture is predicated upon a Volk; a Volk is predicated upon *war*; because if it wants to remain a Volk, it must differentiate its blood-realm from that of others.[76]

Fuchs' racism is too obvious to require comment. What is worth pointing out, is the extent to which this passage foreshadows the public face of the Nazi regime. Take the reference to rhythmic formation. It puts one in mind of *Ausdruckstanz* ('dance of expression') or of Hans Niedecken-Gebhard's vast staging of Händel oratorios in the 1920s. These, in turn, influenced the choreography of Nazi power.[77] The opening ceremony of the Berlin Olympics, the synchronised routines of German maidens at various festivities and the marching columns in the arenas were all in a sense versions of Fuchs' rhythmic formation.[78] As in Fuchs' vision, they symbolised the national community while simultaneously seeking to create it in the hearts and minds of the spectators. 'The audience are, as it were, acting out the play within themselves', as the author of the Olympic play of 1936 put it.[79] In the process, the barriers between actors and audience would be broken down. Spectators would cease to be 'private men or women', as another Nazi theorist observed; instead, they would 'experience the feeling of being part ... of the national community to which he or she would be publicly contributing'.[80]

That familiar image of a crowd raising their right arms in the Hitler salute was one form of 'publicly contributing'. The *Sprechchor* (the declamatory chorus) was another.[81] The instances of its deployment ranged from the Nuremberg rallies in peacetime to the Sportpalast speech after the extinction of the Sixth Army at Stalingrad. At that notorious occasion the German people supposedly ratified the proclamation of 'total war' with their rhythmic responses to Goebbels' leading questions.[82] 'Politics had become the drama of the people', as Goebbels himself put it.[83] Illusion masqueraded as reality, and democracy had been replaced by a stage parody of itself. The reality of Nazi power, meanwhile, was celebrated on stage in symbolic form.[84] For both *Sprechchor* and *Ausdruckstanz* also occurred in the *Thingspiel*: the theatrical experiment that marked the Third Reich's early years.[85]

Famously described as a 'mixture of theatre, party rally, oratorio and circus performance', the *Thingspiel* created in effect massive *tableaux vivants* of contemporary life and politics, where the audience became part of the *tableaux*. This blurring of theatre and politics was not unique to Germany or the political right.[86] Its roots lay in the *fêtes* of the French revolution (which, in turn, were a secular adaptation of Catholic ritual). In Germany, as in France, cultural reform was linked with an ideological effort. The aim, in both countries, was that of defining the nation and uniting it against its real or supposed enemies. In Germany, that effort gathered momentum in the final years of the nineteenth century, amid a growing malaise of German conservatives: the Wilhelmine Empire had failed to overcome religious and regional divisions. The disunity was compounded by the erosion of the traditional social structures. By 1914, Germany possessed the world's largest working-class movement. The resulting anti-socialist panic, together with the anti-Catholic prejudice of Protestant liberals and conservatives, paralysed the political institutions.

The crisis further radicalised the right. It led, notoriously, to the antics of the Navy League with its agenda of aggressive expansionism, and to a (failed) trial run of political antisemitism. *Völkisch* theatre reform did not merely coincide with that radicalisation, it was its cultural equivalent. As true *Bildungsbürger*, the theatre reformers believed culture to be at the root of the political problems.[87] Healing German *Kultur* and making it accessible to the entire nation would help overcome the internal divisions. The imperial authorities themselves paid indirect tribute to such beliefs. Wilhelmine postage stamps, for instance, bore as a motto the famous appeal to unity from *Wilhelm Tell*: 'Seid einig, einig, einig.'

Such naïve uses of culture illustrate the difference between old-style conservatism and the new *völkisch* right. The conservative elders believed in the efficacy of patriotic appeals. The theatre reformers were rethinking the basis for such appeals. They were convinced that a unified *Volk* was unlikely to emerge within the traditional theatrical structures. For one thing, the price of theatre tickets effectively excluded part of the *Volk*. The left had responded to this by creating the *Volksbühne* movement with chapters all over Germany and, eventually, its own flagship theatre in Berlin.[88] The ideological stakes had thus been raised, yet the Imperial authorities were proving unable to find an adequate response: bureaucratic chicanery had failed to kill off the *Volksbühne*.

The theatre reformers advocated a change in tactics: the right, too, should woo new audiences. Adam Müller-Guttenbrunn in Vienna had long advocated subsidised theatre tickets for the deserving poor. Bartels now made the issue central to his festival proposals. The Third Reich later took up these suggestions: the Hitler Youth and the German Labour Front implemented them on a vast scale.[89] These schemes were complemented by a huge wartime operation, overseen by Goebbels himself, which focused on the nation-in-arms. German troops from all over Europe were brought back to the Reich to experience the (nazified) Salzburg festival or to listen to Wagner at Bayreuth. The purpose in each case was the same: to 'become one *Volk*' through a common experience of the nation's cultural heritage.[90] The words of an SA-bard, read before performances in theatres across the Reich in 1936, made that explicit. Theatre, Standartenführer Schumann suggested, should prompt audiences to realise 'how fair we are, how great, how pure, how strong'.[91] Such thoughts were exactly what the Wilhelmine reformers had wished to induce three decades earlier.

Widening access was one way of creating a *Volkstheater*; rethinking the theatrical experience itself was another. Georg Fuchs, Peter Behrens (and later Hans Poelzig) concentrated on theatre design. Traditional playhouses, they thought, reflected in their tiered structure of galleries and boxes a stratified society. Individuals would only experience theatre collectively – and be moulded into a collective – if the layout of a theatre assisted that process. (Richard Wagner had reached similar conclusions and designed his festival hall at Bayreuth accordingly.) In *Sprechtheater*, the Hellenes provided the inspiration, as so often with German *Bildungsbürger*. Behrens, Fuchs, Poelzig, and later on the proponents of the Nazi *Thingspiel* all adopted the amphi-theatre of the Greeks in their own designs. Fuchs' Künstlertheater in Munich, which opened in 1908, duly introduced for the first time an amphitheatrical form to a modern urban playhouse.[92]

Another Munich venture combined the reformers' artistic *and* social agenda. In 1910, patriotic Munich burghers founded an associ-ation that sought to sponsor model productions of canonical plays. With tickets at fifty pfennigs, it was designed to be open to all (or at least most) sections of the populace. The stated desire of the organisers to transcend party politics underlined that ambition.[93] So, in a sense, did the venue: the *Volksfestspiele* took place in a huge exhibition hall. The inaugural production of Aeschylus' *Oresteia* – the Greeks again – played before a crowd of 3,000. It was the first major experiment with theatre-in-the-round in modern times. At this point the sectarian efforts of the far right had reached the mainstream: for the man who directed the *Volksfestspiele* was none other than Max Reinhardt.

It would be mischievous to describe the humanist Jewish Max Reinhardt as the creator of Nazi theatre.[94] Yet his influence on the Nazis is unmistakable. Not only was the *Oresteia* chosen to accom-pany the Berlin Olympics, the theatre-in-the-round approach which Reinhardt pioneered, his effort to break down the barriers between audience and players and the emotionalism of his productions were all taken up by the Nazis in one form or another. Likewise, the scale of the Große Schauspielhaus in Berlin, which Hans Poelzig built in 1919 to Reinhardt's specifications, foreshadowed Nazi practice.[95] Reinhardt's use of massed ranks of performers (the 'Theatre of the Thousand'), torches and sweeping searchlights was no less influential. It provided, unmistakably, the exemplar for the Third Reich's political spectacles and for the *Thingspiel*. Yet, as an open-air spectacle, the *Thing* also owed a debt to another strand of theatre reform, which takes us back to the provinces, and to the final name on our list of theatre reformers.

Ernst Wachler was the chief exponent and tireless propagandist of something called the *Naturtheater* movement. He advocated open-air performances in rural settings 'on a patriotic basis'.[96] Open-air theatricals on sites with historical significance had been a common feature in nineteenth-century Germany: they had been an important vector of nationalist sentiment.[97] At the turn of the century there were attempts to institutionalise such plays. This led to a number of projects for vast open-air theatres to be built around major national monuments.[98] Wachler's ideas must be seen in that context. Yet he broke new ground by considering the German countryside itself to be the ultimate national monument. Nature and Art should jointly engender patriotic feelings. The titles of Wachler's tracts tell the story: '*Heimat* as the source of culture' would lead via 'the open-air stage' to a 'rebirth of Germany'.[99]

From 1903 onwards, Wachler attempted to bring this about. His Theater im Thale, in the Harz mountains east of Brunswick, became a point of reference for *völkisch* culture throughout Germany.[100] Special trains brought theatrical pilgrims from as far away as Berlin. It is difficult now to gain the measure of this enterprise. The contrast between the eulogies of its supporters and the derision of its opponents is so pronounced that the two sides would seem to be describing different events. Here is a hostile view by the critic Herbert Ihering. It is worth quoting at length.

> Every spring and summer the amateurs discover their love of theatre ... Affluent burghers [and] generous patriots who stayed away from the ... theatre all winter suddenly brandish ... festival schedules ... They know that, come May, audiences begin to tire a little of theatregoing. This they blame on ... the modern stage ... Back to nature instead! Here in guaranteed genuine country ... deep breaths are breath'd and great passions exhal'd ... Behold the theatre of the Greeks! Were ever Religion, Art, and Nature more closely entwined? ... Back to nature! And thus back to National Art! For can there be a rebirth of National Drama ... in the play-houses of unbalanced metropolitan writers ... [or] in the presence of arrogant reviewers? Nay, 'tis only neath the rustling leaf of immemorial German Oak ... that Germans can learn to feel German once again.[101]

Here are summarised all the clichés surrounding the *Naturtheater*; much the same list was put forward by the *Thingspiel* theorists a quarter of a century later.[102] The Nazis, too, placed their arenas in 'genuine country'. The list of locations speaks for itself: near the Loreley rock high above the Rhine, on a hill above the Neckar valley, amid the Baltic sands on the islands of Rügen and Usedom, or perched on the Annaberg in Silesia.[103] Where an urban setting was unavoidable, the motto was a resolute *rus in urbe*. Take the Dietrich-Eckart-Bühne in Berlin. The site chosen was so sylvan that it has since become known as 'The Theatre in the Glade'. To sophisticated observers, the beauty of the locations could not disguise the artistic shortcomings. The critic Siegfried Jacobsohn called *Naturtheater* a 'hopeless and pitiful ... act of self-deception'.[104] Yet it proved popular enough to spread. By 1911 Julius Bab reported 'wild-eyed prophets of the open-air stage' on the very outskirts of the capital. 'Their destructive legions are closing in,' he exclaimed, '[and] Reinhardt's town trembles.'[105] Some twenty years later, Berlin would indeed fall to destructive legions. Bab, Kerr, Reinhardt and many more would be forced to flee. The open-air spectacle, however, which Bab had reviewed, would receive the Nazi authorities' express approval.[106]

Such continuities abounded. It is important to appreciate the scope of the phenomenon. More than 600 venues came into being in the early twentieth century. This is about three times the number of traditional playhouses then in existence in Germany. It struck Bab as 'remarkable evidence of the German people's love of theatre'.[107] All the more so, he added, since *Naturtheater* received no subsidies. It depended on the 'active participation of broad sections of society'. For once, the Nazis agreed with a Jewish critic: *Naturtheater*, explained the president of the Reich Theatre Chamber, was 'beloved of the people because the people themselves had created [it]'.[108] Inevitably, he contrasted it with the half-empty theatres in the towns where 'Bolshevik experiment had held sway'.

Similar claims were also made for amateur dramatics, which rose markedly in public regard in the early twentieth century. It found particular favour among the young: the youth theatre of the *Wandervogel* movement had in fact inspired *Naturtheater* activists.[109] *Laienspiel* (laymen's theatre), as amateur dramatics came to be called, was another element of the 'conservative revolution' in German popular culture – both before 1918 and after. The same naive idealism that had led the amateur players to reject the materialism of the Kaiser's Germany also placed them in opposition to the republic. The head of the Nazi Theatre Chamber described the amateur ventures in retrospect as 'self-help groups of the nationalist constituency'.[110] Open-air theatre and amateur dramatics became known collectively in the 1920s as *Volkstheater*: the theatre of the people, or rather of the *Volk*. Here were the immediate roots of the *Thingspiel* in the Third Reich; here also was anticipated a part of the wider Nazi repertoire.[111]

In a sense, there had existed between 1890 and 1933 not *one* German theatre but *two*. The history of the urban playhouses is familiar enough. It is the story of triumphant modernism: of Otto Brahm, Jeßner and Piscator, of Hauptmann, Wedekind, Toller and Brecht. Yet once one begins to look more closely, the ghostly outline of the other German stage appears amid the very exhibits of modernist theatre. One example may suffice. It is a printed invitation to a Berlin theatre ball in 1902. It comes with its own satirical conceit. The card pretends to invite disgruntled theatre enthusiasts from the provinces to a protest rally in the capital. Archetypal German small-town names are used for cruel comic effect. All those, the invitation reads, who have 'panted as Romeo ... in Dinglingen and Sangerhausen' or who 'have murdered Julius Caesar between Brauneberg and Kälberstadt' should 'join in our battle-cry, *"Los von Berlin!"* [let's break away from Berlin]'.[112]

It is a remarkable document for social historians. It reflects the existence of anger in the provinces, an awareness of that anger and the condescension with which it met in Berlin.[113] Artistically, the exponents of Berlin theatre may have been on firm ground. Yet their condescension is unappealing. And there was a special circumstance about the avant-garde that would prove fateful. The 1902 invitation made it apparent. For it came complete with a list of names responsible for the lampoon: most of those names were Jewish.

Such jibes played into the hands of antisemites.[114] They made it easy to portray the modern theatre as an essentially Jewish affair.

A perfect example of this comes, retrospectively, from Robert Ley's German Labour Front. It alluded to the famous motto of the *Volksbühne* movement, 'Art for the people'. That, the Labour Front said, had been 'the motto of a mendacious age. For, in reality, there was only ever an attempt to force on the people [*Volk*] the art of the "chosen people".'[115]

Nazi antisemitism should not blind us to the fact that there was something else involved here: a social animus. *Völkisch* theatre reform, from its inception, had also been about class. The right consistently used what we would now call the rhetoric of social exclusion. It presented modernist theatre as the preserve of a pampered arrogant minority in the larger cities. The journalist Friedrich Hussong described Berlin audiences as 'saturated bourgeois', as 'dandies in evening dress' or 'intellectuals with their horn-rimmed spectacles aglow'.[116] Hanns Johst inveighed against 'the snobbery of metropolitan bluff-directors' and 'the arrogance of the cultured'.[117] Hans Hinkel, another central figure in the Nazi cultural bureaucracy, declared that there was 'no place' in the Third Reich's theatre 'for the snobbery and hyper-aestheticism ... of so-called "educated spectators"'.[118] The Reichsdramaturg Schlösser even felt the need to apologise publicly for his privileged cultured background.[119]

Crude populism was thus combined with a rhetoric reminiscent at times of Communist slogans. The Nazis even talked of their opposition to a 'class-based' theatre.[120] Against the divisive metropolitan playhouses they set the supposedly inclusive rural stage. In the country actors and audiences were said to form a natural community. The passion play of Oberammergau and the Swiss peasants putting on their 'national drama' *Wilhelm Tell* provided the standard examples.[121] This was in part an expression of the familiar anti-urban animus of the German right. Yet the desire to be socially inclusive – and to unite a community by means of the theatre – was genuine and central to all *Volkstheater* initiatives. It inspired the Catholic educationalists who revived in the 1920s the medieval mystery plays of Southern Germany; and it drove the attempts to stage the classics in surroundings where 'all social barriers had fallen away', as the *Naturtheater* activist Egon Schmid put it in 1930.[122]

The *Thingspiel* movement originated in this milieu. It was launched through a joint effort of *Naturtheater* representatives, like Egon Schmid, and Catholic theatre activists like Wilhelm Karl Gerst in a series of carefully timed initiatives from late 1931 onwards. The organisation they founded – the Reichsbund zur Förderung der Freilichtspiele (Reich League for the Encouragement of Open-air Theatre) – clearly recognised the imminent end of the republic. The news of Hitler's appointment as chancellor thus found the Reichsbund prepared. Its pronouncements were carefully phrased to appeal to Nazi ears: hence the term *Thingspiel* itself, with its allusion to the ancient Germanic assemblies.[123] The Teutonic credentials were in fact wholly spurious. In reality, Gerst sought to steer the *Thing* not into a neo-pagan but a pro-Catholic direction.[124] This would eventually lead to his dismissal by Goebbels in February 1935.

The open-air activists effectively tried to harness the Nazis for their own ambitions.[125] They were initially able to do so because they had cultivated before 1933 a crucial Nazi contact: the ex-actor and first president of the Reich Theatre Chamber, Otto Laubinger. Laubinger's Nazi credentials were not much more substantial than that of the *Thing* itself. He had joined the party as late as 1932: the year, in which Hans Severus Ziegler had bemoaned the Nazis' lack of impact in the theatre. That lack of impact also explains why Goebbels should have allowed a substantially non-Nazi project like the *Thingspiel* to proceed. There was, quite simply, an absence of viable alternatives.[126]

The *Thing*, of course, was also attractive to the Nazis: it had a useful populist pedigree. More importantly, it represented a coalition of political interests.[127] That, too, was useful, for the Hitler government was itself a coalition containing ministers who were not members of Hitler's party. The Nazis were initially dependent on an informal broader alliance to launch their 'national revolution'. The *Thingspiel* – like Johst's *Schlageter* – was designed to drum up support for this alliance. The *Thing*'s value for the regime lay precisely in the fact that it reached beyond the Nazi constituency in political terms, and that, socially, it complemented plays like *Schlageter*.

Johst's drama is where we started from. It had been written, we noted, with urban middle-class audiences in mind. The *Thingspiel* now aimed at those who had never felt at home in traditional play-houses: it captured an additional segment of German society.[128] As far as Goebbels himself was concerned, the *Thing* had two further advantages. It appealed to his quasi-socialist leanings, and it allowed his ministry to project itself at a time when most traditional playhouses were still under the control of Goebbels' rivals. *Schlageter* had been premiered in Göring's theatre. The *Thing* arenas were Goebbels' own from the start.[129]

It was thus political expediency that allowed the *Thingspiel* to develop. Yet this cannot explain why it should have struck a chord with audiences. For the large crowds flocking to the arenas, the stadiums and exhibition halls to see *Thing* plays did so of their own accord. Even the Nazis could not dragoon people into theatregoing.[130] What then was the secret of the *Thingspiel*'s appeal? The answer may lie in a comment by the Nazi dramatist Eberhard Wolfgang Möller, 'We have lived through tragedy ... we now only need to write it down.'[131] The *Thing* plays were a theatrical comment on recent German history from the vantage of the supposed 'national rebirth' of 1933. The *Thing* presented audiences with a vision of their own recent lives. It was topical theatre, offering an immediacy which more conventional plays or productions rarely achieved. It specifically involved the public: actors and audiences were linked through the use of the *Sprechchor* and the entrances and exits of the players through the ranks of the spectators. The mixture of professional and amateur players, symbolising 'leaders' and 'led', further emphasised the common bonds.[132] The huge numbers involved – no fewer than 17,000 players (and 60,000 viewers) in every performance of *Germany on the March* – suggested the nation in numerical terms alone. The use of lighting, jointly illuminating the stage and parts of the arena, completed the effect. Theatre and nation seemed one.[133]

Here, then, was Georg Fuchs' old dream. Where Fuchs had failed the *Thing* (initially) succeeded. It did so because the emotional responses of the German public had changed since Fuchs' day. There was now an overwhelming desire for national unity – and not just among the political right. The near civil war in the early and, again, in the final years of the Weimar republic had left the country yearning for harmony. The choreography of the *Thing* responded to such long-ings. The mass formations in the arena, the solemnly chanted cho-ruses, all suggested 'rhythmic harmony' and a nation at peace with itself.

The *Thing*'s success in 1933–4 thus demonstrates an uncom-fortable truth: political freedom counts for little if people do not feel in control of their own lives. The Weimar republic had given Germans an unprecedented degree of personal and political freedom. It then left them alone to fend for themselves. For soon after the advent of free-dom the economy collapsed and millions were reduced to abject pov-erty: at the beginning of the 1920s and then a second time at the end of that decade. 'The home owner crushed, the upright bent', said Euringer in his *German Passion*. And specifically on the subject of freedom, he offers this bitter observation: 'Those who have made it to the top are free'; 'the masses are ground underfoot'.[134] By 1933, the overwhelming majority of Germans had been led – through personal experience – to equate freedom with want and democracy with despair.

It is against this background that *Thing* plays with titles such as *German Passion*, the *Düsseldorf Passion* or *The Play of Job, the German* begin to make sense. They were not simply cultural but social and psychological phenomena.[135] They allowed their audiences to re-experience recent history, safe in the knowledge that the night-mare was finally over. The author of *Germany on the March* made that point explicitly. The re-enacted past, he suggested, would induce in the spectators 'righteous wrath' and 'immeasurable anger'.[136] The *Thing* plays are in effect a reflection of the German people's psyche in 1933–4.

That impression is confirmed by the plays submitted to the Propaganda Ministry by amateur playwrights. Their titles speak for themselves: 'Let There Be Light', 'Healed', 'The Crusade against Poverty', 'Bread', 'Eternal Work', 'The Oratorio of Work', 'The Victory of Hallowed Work', 'The Scandal of Inflation', 'The Twilight of the Idols', 'Liberation', etc.[137] The content and ideology of those plays were often 'confused and bordering on madness', as one Nazi censor put it.[138] Yet the difference in that regard between the rejected efforts and those that were staged was only one of degree. There was something inherently unbalanced about the *Thing*. The essence of these plays will elude us unless we recognise that they cannot be judged by artistic criteria alone. The *Thing* was 'the expression of a creed in the rhythm of our new age', as Gerst put it.[139]

Creed and rhythm were the operative terms. 'As soon as the unemployed begin to move again, unemployment vanishes,' we read in the stage direction for Goes' *Sacrificial Flame of Work*.[140] In Heynicke's *Neurode* the mine threatened with closure is saved because the miners believe in its future, and the nation keeps faith with the miners: 'Belief is greater than mere figures [on a balance sheet].'[141] This may sound excruciatingly naive, but it reflects Nazi thinking. More than that: it reflects what actually happened after January 1933. The recovery was achieved, in part, simply by restoring confidence. The 'National Rebirth' did not change economic or social structures; but it did change perceptions, and via those altered perceptions it indirectly changed reality. The *Thingspiel* played its part in that process. By involving the viewers in a pageant about their own lives, the *Thing* suggested that they themselves had become agents of history once more. It gave them the illusion of being in control of their own destinies again.

The *Thingspiel*'s ability to respond to the psychological needs of its viewers was apparent also in another of its recurring themes: that of the dead coming alive. Armies of ghosts appeared in Germany between 1933 and 1935. Faces whitened under their steel helmets, the fallen of the Great War marched in battalion strength across the arenas and open-air stages of the new Reich. The appearance of spirits in the *Thing* might seem proof of its anti-modernism. Yet the fallen had haunted all of Europe after the Great War.[142] Large numbers of people even turned to spiritualism.

Allied nations were able to comfort themselves after 1918 with the thought that the loss of life had bought victory. There was no such consolation for Germans. The deaths and the suffering had been in vain. What made it worse was the apparent indifference of the Weimar authorities. The republic sought to distance itself from the war, which it saw as the Kaiser's war. The consequence, whether intentional or

3 The rising of the dead soldiers from the graves of the Great War in Euringer's *German Passion*, staged at Heidelberg 1935.

not, was to deny the German people a chance to grieve, and the survivors any sense of recognition for their sacrifice.[143] That did real harm to the republic's cause: it made democracy seem cynical and unfeeling.

The theatre of the republic played its part in all this. There had been no shortage of dramas in the 1920s about the war; but their focus was almost exclusively on war as the catalyst of revolution. In that perspective of history, German soldiers were effectively divided into potential revolutionaries or into reactionaries who were little better than murderers.[144] The mass protests that had greeted these highly polemical plays were certainly reactionary; but they were also the protests of people whose own memories of the war simply did not match the scenes on stage. As with 'the rape of the classics', here too the theatre of the republic had added insult to conservative injury.[145] In the retrospective vision of Euringer's *German Passion* the republic was an 'evil spirit' squatting on the war graves and crowing, 'The dead are dead – now Germany is mine.'[146]

The appearance of the ghostly armies in the *Thingspiel* was therefore no accident. The dead had risen to seek justice from the living and to give evidence at the bar of history. The *Thing* as tribunal of the *Volk* might strike us as quintessentially Nazi thinking, were it not for one fact that a decade earlier Arnold Zweig – no Nazi he – had described theatre as 'the nation sitting in judgement upon itself'.[147] Weimar theatre had judged Imperial Germany: in 1933, it was the turn of the republic to be arraigned. In lurid tableaux, the *Thingspiel* fused the Catholic genre of the morality play with an anti-republican pageant: fallen women and prostituted daughters, mixed-raced couples gyrating to jungle beats, the post-war racketeer, the greedy stockbroker and the scheming Marxist intellectual, the working man made redundant, the peasant driven from his land and the masses starving; in short, 'the swamp of corruption … the madhouse that was the republic'.[148]

4 Kurt Heynicke's *Thingspiel The Road to the Reich* at the Heidelberg arena in 1935.

For all their exaggeration, the *Thingspiel*'s scenes had a basis in fact.[149] The depression had been real; so had the profiteering; so, too, had been the change in sexual mores; and so the cold-shouldering of the victims of war. In making the case against the republic, the *Thingspiel* appeared to give meaning at last to the German deaths in the Great War. The fallen had died in the attempt to shield Germany from all that had happened after 1918.[150] Defeat no longer mattered because the cause had been worthy. The peace itself had proved the dead right to have waged war.

Thing plays therefore frequently began with a commemoration of the fallen, and monuments to the dead were erected in the vicinity of the arenas. As in the vision of the *völkisch* reformers, nation and theatre had fused.[151] German history had become a morality play. Its theme was how Germans coped with adversity. In Euringer's *German Passion*, the most successful example of the genre, God and the Devil actually wager for the soul of the Germans. Would they lose faith in themselves? Would they succumb to the temptations of the jazz age? Would they bend down to worship the false idols of internationalism and democracy? These scenes achieved their power in 1933–4 because many in the audience knew that they had been tempted and had succumbed. Morality plays are about the conversion of sinners.[152] So, in a sense, was the *Thingspiel*. Catharsis – theatrical and political – occurred in the ranks of the spectators. By their voluntary presence in the auditorium – that crucible of the nation – they had abjured the republic and all its works; and the army of the risen soldiers had given their blessing. Like the viewers watching *Schlageter* in the urban playhouses, the *Thingspiel* audiences had arrived emotionally in the Third Reich.

3   The uses of the past: from the *Thingspiel* to the Nazi history plays

The Berlin Olympics were a busy time for Nazi propagandists. The games provided an ideal opportunity to influence world opinion with carefully controlled glimpses of life in the 'New Germany'. The monumental architecture of the *Reichssportfeld* and the sumptuous ceremonies of that summer were designed to impress and overawe. Theatre, too, formed part of the grand design: right next to the Olympic stadium a vast open-air arena had been carved out of the hillside. The Dietrich-Eckart Stage, named after Hitler's Munich mentor, was a colossal affair. On its sweeping tiers, it seated no fewer than 20,000 spectators. Elaborate lighting and sound systems pioneered at the Nuremberg rallies were combined with the simple stone seats of a traditional amphitheatre. That combination of the ultramodern and the anachronistic was quintessentially Nazi.[1] So was the classical pose of the entire project. Not since the days of Ancient Greece or Rome had sports and theatre been so closely linked.[2] Not since antiquity had a theatrical arena so obviously been designed to glorify the leader who had built it. The Führer, visitors should conclude, had inherited a city of brick and was leaving one of the finest German granite.

Hitler had taken a close interest in the design and construction of the Dietrich-Eckart Stage.[3] It fell to Goebbels to find a suitable repertoire for it. He commissioned Eberhard Wolfgang Möller to write a verse play for the inauguration. Möller was a young dramatist of proven ability. He had been one of the main exponents of anti-republican theatre in the dying days of the Weimar republic.[4] In 1934 he had been invited to join the Propaganda Ministry and had become an official in its theatre section.

65

The new play for the Dietrich-Eckart Stage was, so to speak, an in-house affair. The plot had been selected by Goebbels himself from various suggestions submitted by Möller, and Goebbels remained involved throughout the writing process.[5] If Johst's *Schlageter* had been the first 'official' drama of the Third Reich, then Möller's *Frankenburger Würfelspiel* – *The Frankenburg Dice Game* – was clearly the second.

Möller's play, however, was not graced by the Führer's presence on the opening night. Hitler had been planning to attend. In fact, he had set out on foot from the Olympic stadium. Then, about halfway on the processional route to the theatre, he turned abruptly, followed by an obsequious train of officials, and headed in the direction of his car. That extraordinary incident – acted out before the eyes of the world – was not a case of dictatorial moodiness. Like Möller's play, it had political roots. To understand what had happened, and how the political function of Nazi theatre had changed since 1933, we need to examine more closely Möller's *Dice Game*.

The plot was historical: a notable departure from previous *Thing* practice. Möller took audiences back to the days of the Counter-Reformation, and across the border into Austria. Upper Austria, the setting of the play, had turned largely Lutheran in the Reformation. In the ensuing decades the Protestant peasantry came under pressure from their Catholic rulers to revert to the old religion. Things came to a head when the peasants of several adjoining villages set upon the newly installed Catholic priests and drove them out of their parishes. Retribution was swift and brutal. A military force was despatched to the area. It corralled the insurgents and demanded that they identify the ringleaders of the assaults on the priests. When the captured men refused to do so, they were told that their lives were forfeit but that half their number would be pardoned. They were then ordered to pair off and dice for their lives. In each case, the man throwing the higher number was set free. The loser was hanged on the spot. In all, thirty-six men were executed. This gruesome affair led to a general uprising of the Upper Austrian peasantry. The insurrection, in turn, ended with the annihilation of the peasants' army and the re-establishment of Catholic practice.

This gory topic Möller and Goebbels had deemed a suitable choice for the Berlin Olympics. One can appreciate why Hitler might have wished to dissociate himself from the play. It threatened to undermine the carefully contrived image of a peaceable Reich. Yet Möller's verse was hardly a temporary aberration: it emanated, after all, from the Propaganda Ministry. Hitler, moreover, is unlikely to have been an innocent bystander in its genesis. From what we know about Goebbels' professional habits, it is difficult to believe that he had not sought the Führer's express approval.[6] All the more so, since the play had as its setting Hitler's actual home region. Frankenburg – the site of the slaughter – lies about midway between Hitler's birthplace of Braunau and Linz, the city of his childhood.[7]

Biographical connections apart, there were obvious political ramifications. To use Austrian history in this way at the Berlin Olympics was tantamount to a Nazi claim on Austria.[8] That such a claim existed was an open secret, and it had met with a forceful response in Vienna: the Nazi party was proscribed in Austria and many of its activists were arrested. Abroad, the government of Chancellor Dollfuß sought to bring about an anti-Hitler coalition. This earned Dollfuß the undying hatred of committed Nazis on both sides of the Austro-German border. In 1934, during an abortive coup orchestrated from Berlin, Dollfuß was murdered. International outrage forced Hitler to distance himself from the failed coup. Yet the Reich continued its propaganda war (and its covert operations) against Austria.

Möller's play must be seen in that context. Recent events offstage added an unmistakable edge to individual lines uttered in the arena. 'In the whole of the Reich you'll find no better Germans than in Austria,' was no harmless tribute in 1936.[9] The proof of subversive intent came in the next line: 'Why,' Möller asked, 'are [they] ... being persecuted?' But even then Möller was not done. He concluded with this observation, directed by the chorus at the Austrian peasants: 'Would that you had weapons!' This was publicly being said in Berlin two years after Austrian Nazis in possession of weapons had unleashed a terrorist campaign in Austria, had murdered the country's chancellor, shot policemen, had blown up railway lines and viaducts and had even staged a full armed incursion from the Reich into Austrian territory.

The *Frankenburger Würfelspiel* was thus a highly inflammatory Nazi comment on the political situation in Austria. The seven-
teenth-century plot selected by Goebbels had been a clever choice. It
provided a degree of diplomatic cover – though ultimately not enough,
it seems, for Hitler to feel able to attend. At the same time, it gave
added historical resonance to the play's ill-disguised propaganda message. For Chancellor Dollfuß and his successor Schuschnigg had
sought to stiffen anti-Nazi resolve by invoking Austria's Catholic
and Habsburg past. Goebbels' strategy thus becomes apparent: he
sought to discredit the moral basis of 'Austrianness'.

The animosity was as much a personal as a political one. The
government in Vienna had denounced the Third Reich as criminal and
had pointedly observed that all political leaders were eventually
accountable for their deeds: God would judge. Goebbels responded by
commissioning a play which arraigned the Viennese authorities (of a
previous century) for their crimes against the *Volk*. Möller's play
called to account the Habsburg Emperor Ferdinand II, his confessor
and the Papal nuncio to the Imperial court. Dramatised past and
political present interlocked. Dollfuß had crushed armed working-
class resistance in February 1934 in a brief but brutal civil war. The
slaughtered peasants of Frankenburg thus stood for the dead workers
of February 1934 as much as for the supposed Nazi martyrs hanged in
Vienna after the July coup. The hidden hand of Rome in the *Dice
Game*, moreover, recalled the role of Mussolini's Italy in supporting
Austria against the Third Reich.[10] Möller's drama thus carried for
contemporary audiences a powerful metaphorical charge.[11] In a
sense, it was the Austrian government itself that was put on trial in
the Dietrich-Eckart arena.

Two telling historical inaccuracies gave the game away. Möller
consistently played down the role of the Bavarians in the Frankenburg
affair. This was no minor detail: Upper Austria had been pawned to the
Habsburgs' Bavarian allies during the Thirty Years' War. It had thus
been Bavarians – rather than Austrians – who planned and carried out
the massacre in 1625. That was a fact traditionally given prominence
inside Austria. Yet Möller placed responsibility for the massacre with
the Emperor in Vienna. What is more, the play referred to Ferdinand,

anachronistically, as the 'Emperor of Austria'. Ferdinand had been Holy Roman (i.e. *German*) Emperor. Given the Third Reich's habit of appropriating all things Austrian (while pointedly avoiding the term 'Austria' itself), that inaccuracy can hardly have been an accident.[12] All the more so, since Möller had gone to some lengths to research the Frankenburg affair.

Surviving Propaganda Ministry files reveal that Möller had sought information from Austrian Nazis who had fled to the Reich.[13] The initial impetus for the play may even have come from those quarters; for the events of Frankenburg were not widely known inside Germany.[14] In Austria, the tercentenary of the Peasants' War in 1926 had raised public awareness. At Frankenburg itself a monument had been erected. Present at its inauguration was an SA detachment – a rare enough sight in the Austria of that period.[15] There had also been a play about the Dice Game (by the proverbial local poet). It had been performed on the historic site by members of the Gymnasts' League, a notoriously pan-German organisation.[16] Here was the kind of ideologically charged amateur open-air theatre we encountered earlier: the 'theatre of the people' which the *völkisch* reformers had been advocating as a source of national regeneration. Unsurprisingly, the Austrian authorities banned the Frankenburg play, along with other *völkisch* dramas about the Peasants' War, during their anti-Nazi clampdown.[17] This in turn increased the propaganda value of Frankenburg for the Third Reich. After the *Anschluß*, the amateur play was revived on a grand scale. Leading Austrian Nazis were in attendance; special trains were laid on to convey the party faithful to the site; and the speeches preceding the play described the Führer as the avenger of the executed peasants and the man who had finally delivered Austria from the Church's chains.[18]

Möller's drama for the Berlin Olympics was thus part of a wider propagandistic effort, to which, in turn, it readily lent itself. The mayor of Passau, for instance, a Bavarian city less than a mile away from Austrian territory, decided in 1937 to order an open-air production of Möller's play. 'I have commanded the *Frankenburger Würfelspiel* to be performed ... as a treat for our ethnic kin beyond the border,' he informed the Propaganda Ministry.[19] The definition of a good play as something that served the interests of the Reich had been no empty rhetoric. As Möller's superior, the Reichsdramaturg Schlösser put it, 'The arts are for us a means to an end: the end being that . . . of perfecting the *Volk*.'[20] Goebbels was even blunter: 'We judge the arts', he declared, 'by the degree of their impact on the *Volk* and the age. Otherwise they are of no interest to us.'[21]

Möller's verse was of interest to Goebbels. Compared to the Nazi drumbeat in *Schlageter* three years earlier, the *Dice Game* might have seemed superficially harmless. In reality, it represented the theatre's total subordination to the Nazi regime. Johst had glorified National Socialism but had acted as an independent agent. Möller made himself a creature of his masters and fashioned a political tool for them.[22]

Yet there was more to the *Frankenburger Würfelspiel* than anti-Austrian propaganda. Its author also had cultural ambitions; and, given Möller's position in the Reichsdramaturgie, these had a political dimension themselves.[23] At issue was the genre which Möller's play represented. Except for its historical setting, the *Dice Game* had all the hallmarks of a *Thingspiel*. It made explicit in its plot the notion of a trial which had been implicit in most earlier *Thing* plays. It had the characteristic motif of the dead coming alive to seek justice: in this case it was Upper Austrian peasants rather than the fallen of the Great War. Möller also retained the mass scenes of earlier *Thing* plays. For the première, no fewer than 1,200 extras had been recruited from the ranks of the Reich Labour Service. (At Erfurt, the following year, the extras even numbered 2,000.)[24] The language of the *Dice Game*, with its pseudo-religious cadences, was likewise reminiscent of the *Thing* plays. These similarities were controversial in 1936 for the term 'Thingspiel' itself had been banned by Goebbels nine months previously.[25]

In the supposed new day of German theatre after January 1933, the *Thing* had proved a false dawn. The initial euphoria had been genuine enough: a new form of theatre with mass appeal appeared to be evolving. It seemed a 'revolutionary breakthrough'.[26] Yet problems soon became apparent. Money was one of them. Building the arenas proved considerably more expensive than had been budgeted for. The initial plans of constructing hundreds of *Thing* sites across the length and breadth of Germany were quietly abandoned. Little more than a dozen were built in the end.[27]

The *Thingspiel* had been a product of the depression. The slump both contributed to the psychological appeal of the new genre and to its expected financial viability. In 1933, there had been an army of unemployed men willing to undertake almost any work for minimal pay. By 1935, they were expecting proper wages again.[28] The situation was made worse by maladministration and extravagance.[29] Arenas envisaged for 1,000 spectators frequently ballooned on the drawing board to hold crowds of 10,000 or even 100,000. (At Annaberg, in the depths of rural Silesia, an arena for 50,000 was actually built.) At Halle – the first *Thing* site to be completed – several costly miles of gas mains had been laid so that an eternal flame could be lit in a 'sanctuary' adjoining the stage. In Heidelberg, the arena was to be hewn from solid rock. When the rock proved harder than expected, the project had to be altered in mid-construction.[30] An exhibition trumpeting the marvels of the new *völkisch* theatre helpfully deflected attention from the problems.[31] The German tourist board, however, was caught out. It had used the Heidelberg *Thing* to lure visitors back to the Reich. Those who had been staying away since 1933 should come and see for themselves. They would find proof that the émigrés had been spreading 'malicious lies' about the state of German culture: for 'at no time had the arts ... been cultivated more assiduously and sympathetically than in the Third Reich'.[32] Those who followed that invitation found a scarred hill-top rather than the expected *Thingplatz*.

The embarrassment, although severe, was transient; the underlying problems were not. The chaos at Heidelberg finally forced Berlin to pause and take stock. Control suddenly tightened in July 1934 over what had been a largely decentralised project.[33] Goebbels himself descended for an inspection of the site. He did not like what he saw and cooled noticeably towards the entire *Thing* enterprise.[34] It was impossible, of course, to abandon the *Thingspiel* altogether: too much capital, literal and figurative, had been invested. The *Thing* was allowed to splutter on for another eighteen months or so. Yet a decisive shift in Nazi theatre policy had occurred. Artistic innovation, with its attendant risks, was dropped in favour of polished traditional theatre.

There had been artistic problems all along. The combination of professional actors and amateurs might have seemed ideologically attractive.[35] In practice, it had not made for a harmonious mix on stage. This was initially outweighed by the satisfaction of having provided work for almost 1,000 unemployed actors. Yet cynics soon suggested that it was obvious why some of those actors had failed to find employment.[36] Complaints about these performers recurred. (In the related case of the *Naturtheater*, some of the actors foisted by the authorities on regional enterprises were apparently bribed *not* to perform.)[37]

The most thorny issue, however, was that of the repertoire. A letter to the Reichsdramaturg in May 1935 speaks for itself. 'During my numerous visits to all manner of *Thing* sites – including the ones under construction – it has gradually dawned on me that it will prove vastly difficult to find suitable plays for them all.'[38] The question of the 'existing or rather the non-existent plays' had, it seems, already been 'repeatedly' discussed in the ministry. Attempts to jump-start the creative process had proved unsuccessful. A conference of promising playwrights had been a 'decidedly temperamental' affair; the resulting drama, however, had not, alas, been of the stageable variety.[39] Perhaps the collective writers' block could be overcome with a tour of the *Thing* sites for potential playwrights?

Here was an echo of Ernst Wachler's turn-of-the-century ideas. The continuity in right-wing thought is unmistakable.[40] The results, too, were similar: viable plays continued to prove elusive. By 1936, the Propaganda Ministry finally admitted defeat. It had been 'a mistake to build the arenas' in the absence of a suitable repertoire.[41] '*Thingspiel*' turned into a non-word. Newspaper editors received instructions to excise references to it even from the transcripts of political speeches, including those 'by senior personages'.[42] The object was to 'end a debate [now] considered undesirable' and to keep from the German public the fact that the debate had been curtailed.[43]

What had not been foreseen was that members of the public might actually challenge the Propaganda Ministry themselves to find out what was happening. The first such communication was by a man who had been commissioned to write a piece about the *Thing*, which his publishers then unaccountably refused to print. The letter created ripples of panic inside the ministry.[44] The suppressed manuscript itself did little to relieve the propagandists' discomfiture. For it contained a perceptive analysis of the *Thingspiel*'s weaknesses. 'Too many people', it suggested, 'have been ignoring the fact that politics and culture obey different laws.'[45] 'One cannot create culture by the means of the propagandist: [for] ... culture recognises no orders, no commands and no marching pace.' These were brave sentiments in 1936. What probably saved the author from unpleasant consequences was that his criticism aimed less at the authorities than at *Thing* writers. Existing *Thing* plays, he declared, had 'been shaped by political and not by cultural demands'. The *Thingspiel* was 'nothing other than the naked reflection of political passion'.[46]

That was well put. It had indeed been 'naked political passion' rather than cold calculation by professional propagandists that had produced the *Thing*. Its core repertoire actually predated the Nazi Seizure of Power.[47] Even the later plays – Eggers' *Dance of Death* (1934) or Heynicke's *Road to the Reich* (1935) – were the fruit of individual initiative and not of ministerial prompting. Theatre in the Third Reich was not a command economy: there were no Four Year Plans. More to the point, there were none of the *Führeraufträge* – the 'Führer commissions' – that kept favoured German architects or sculptors busy.[48] There were none of the 'Führer purchases' which created a market for Nazi art either directly or by example; and, with the sole exception of Möller's *Frankenburger Würfelspiel*, there were no ministerial commissions. This is striking since, in the parallel case of German film, state commissions constituted a central element in Goebbels' strategy.[49] The neglect of the theatre, moreover, was no oversight. When one of the more successful *Thing* authors suggested commissioning plays to alleviate the lack of them, the Propaganda Ministry flatly rejected the proposal.[50]

Goebbels' underlying rationale may not be so difficult to guess. Theatre is not a straightforward commodity. Unlike architecture, sculpture, painting, or indeed film, it does not come as a finished product. Directors and performers need to give a play script (temporal) physical shape.[51] The resulting unpredictability remained a constant worry to the Propaganda Ministry. It may also explain the ministry's limited enthusiasm for theatre as a vector of overt propaganda.[52] Yet it was precisely this element of caution towards the traditional stage that had initially made the *Thingspiel* attractive to the propagandists. The appeal lay, above all, in performance practice.[53]

Acting in *Thing* plays was of necessity a highly stylised affair. The sheer size of the arenas meant that the players' facial expressions could not be made out by most spectators. Small gestures, likewise,

5 The actor Alexander Golling, trying out his costume for the *Frankenburg Dice Game*. The stylised costume was designed to be visible across the vast distances of the Dietrich-Eckart-Arena.

74

did not work.[54] The vast space also influenced voice technique. Subtle modulations gave way to a declamatory style. Voice projection (or successful mastery of microphones) was all.[55] The combined effect of all this was to limit the scope for developing individual traits on a *Thing* stage. The president of the Reich Theatre Chamber himself could thus appear in a *Thingspiel* without fear of upstaging the other players.[56] The format ensured that he became a mere voice resonating from a distant static figure on stage. From the perspective of the audience, that process robbed the characters of all individuality: they became types.[57] And it was precisely this aspect of the *Thing* that Otto Laubinger praised. He contrasted it favourably with more conventional new plays: these, he thought, often showed the right spirit, yet their authors 'had been unwilling or as yet unable to dispense with individual psychological characterisation'.[58]

The flat 'wood-cut' quality of *Thing* characters so often remarked upon was evidently not regarded as a weakness by the *Thing*'s most

6 Hans Niedecken-Gebhardt, directing with the help of a megaphone in the Dietrich-Eckart-Arena.

influential champion.[59] To see in 'the Caller', 'the Herald', 'the German', in characters called 'Rebellion' or 'the Peace of Versailles' evidence of artistic limitation is therefore to miss the point. They were *designed* as types. All ambiguity, all scope for individual interpretation had been removed.[60] Audience responses seemed calculable in advance. Here was the promise of a truly totalitarian theatre.

The corollary of this was that the raised voice was – figuratively and literally – the *Thing*'s only mode of expression. It was, in the words of one theatre activist, 'the speech of the National Socialist leadership turned drama'.[61] The president of the Reich Theatre Chamber concurred: the *Thingspiel* was 'a political demonstration turned theatre'; there was thus no need, Laubinger thought, for a large selection of plays or for dramaturgical niceties. What mattered was that eventually a kind of '*völkisch* liturgy' would develop.[62]

He had in mind something midway between drama and political meeting that would 'bind the national comrades emotionally to the [Nazi] movement': *Erlebnistheater*, in other words.[63] This new 'liturgy' would be performed, with subtle variations to fit the respective occasion, on the great days of the Nazi calendar: the anniversaries of the Seizure of Power and of the Hitler putsch, the Führer's birthday, the summer solstice, etc.[64] The core text of that future 'liturgy' should become so familiar to the 'participating national community' that they would be able to chant the 'responses', much as congregations did in church. This suggestion, Laubinger reported, had met with particular favour among the 'propagandists and *Kulturwarte*' – the Nazi party's cultural officials in the regions.

It does not seem to have occurred to these political high priests that their liturgy might prove counterproductive. Yet the endless repetition took its toll. Audience figures declined, and so did the stature of the *Thingspiel* itself. The banality of its language and sentiments began to stand out uncomfortably. Some members of the public even complained to the Propaganda Ministry about it. 'Where is the shaping hand ... turning sentences into thought, words into an idea, reality into art?' Ideological exhortations in *Thing* plays, the same correspondent observed, frequently sounded 'hollow' [*phrasenhaft*] and 'embarrassing'.[65]

7 *Aufbruch*, the first-ever *Werkspiel*, performed in the grounds of the Siemens plant in Berlin in 1933. Highly skilled industrial workers were playing the part of peasants.

The artistic disenchantment was reinforced by a degree of political disillusion. The right-wing opposition to the Weimar republic had been a broad front. After 1933, parts of that coalition were pushed aside by the new rulers. This was the fate of two core constituencies of the *Thingspiel*: the SA, whose influence ended with the murder of their leaders in 1934, and the religious conservatives, who found themselves sidelined by those worshipping only the Führer.[66] The *Thing*'s eclipse thus reflected the gradual foreclosing of artistic and political avenues in the hardening Third Reich.[67] And it reflected, above all, the altered mood of the wider public. By the mid-1930s, the economic recovery was under way. People were ready to get on with their lives again. The *Thingspiel*'s emphasis on the collective now failed to resonate. That was apparent even in the reviews. A major performance of *Neurode* in 1934 was described as 'calculated to induce yawns'.[68] It was no isolated case. By late 1934, the frequency of the yawns had turned into a political problem. The *Thing* activists were now hoist by

SIEMENS
Spiegellinsen-
Bühnenscheinwerfer

Für Kinolampen 1500 Watt
verwendbar als
Vorbühnenscheinwerfer
Spielflächenscheinwerfer
und Bühnenscheinwerfer

Lampe selbsttätig stets senkrecht
hängend beim Gebrauch des Schein-
werfers zwischen waagerechter
und senkrechter Leuchtrichtung

SIEMENS-SCHUCKERTWERKE AG·BERLIN-SIEMENSSTADT

8 Advertisement for lighting equipment produced by the very workers that provided the performers and audiences of the *Werkspiel Aufbruch*.

their own petard. For if the *Thingspiel* was indeed 'the speech of the National Socialist leadership turned drama', then the half-empty auditoria and the yawning spectators were a troubling sight.

The problem was compounded by the practically uncontrolled proliferation of rough and ready variants of the *Thing*: the so-called *Weihespiele* ('plays of solemnity' or 'dedication') and their close cousin the *Werkspiel* ('the factory play').[69] There had been a rash of these crudely propagandistic playlets after the Nazi Seizure of Power. A playwriting competition organised by the German Labour Front in 1933 is said to have produced over 10,000 entries.[70] As with the *Naturtheater* craze two decades earlier, nowhere in Germany seemed safe. Factories, court yards, schools, stadiums, town squares and indeed *Thing* arenas resounded to the rhythmic chants and choreographed footsteps of party formations whose performing talent rarely matched their political zeal.[71]

In this regard, theatre merely formed part of a wider pattern. The Third Reich's early years were marked by ecstatic amateurism. The auxiliaries of the 'national revolution' were demanding – and initially receiving – their due. From his Swiss exile, the writer Kurt Tucholsky contemplated the scene back home with horrified fascination. He reached a two-word verdict: 'zero talent'.[72] Individual members of the regime arrived at similar conclusions. Hitler himself, if post-war testimonies are to be believed, eventually expressed his displeasure to Goebbels.[73] Whatever the precise chain of events, the raft of new regulations emanating from the Propaganda Ministry from late 1935 onwards was no accident. Even the ostensibly stylistic measures, such as the restrictions on the use of the *Sprechchor* in January 1936, and its complete ban four months later, had a political function. They were designed to rein in the exuberant amateurs as tactfully as possible. When these measures proved insufficient, Goebbels became more direct: he demanded an end to all 'amateurish pranks' (*Unfug*) by party formations.[74]

Allied to the embarrassment were solid political concerns. The regime's slogans threatened to become blunted by excessive use. The Reichsdramaturgie's internal reports document that anxiety. Take the case of a play 'for *Thing* arenas' judged to be 'very solidly crafted and ideologically above reproach'.[75] Yet the censor added a rider. What troubled him was 'the frequency' of plays on similar themes, the 'mechanical repetition' of their sentiments, which '... was progressively wearing out a fine tune'.

Such sentiments point to something fundamental about Nazi theatre: its inability to reflect the contemporary world in a manner acceptable both to audiences and the regime. The *Thing* was one aspect of this; the repertoire of the established playhouses with their solid diet of classics, comedies and history plays was another.[76] The censored stage was a third. Theatrical censorship extended beyond the opponents and victims of National Socialism: a substantial number of *pro-Nazi* plays were also suppressed. Only references to them in the files of the Reichsdramaturgie now survive.[77] It would be possible to write a history of the Third Reich simply by recording the topics of those plays and by quoting from the covering letters or the censor's comments.

Take the case of a twenty-year-old unemployed labourer.[78] This young man had only basic schooling yet he had tried to write an allegorical play about Hitler: the man he regarded as the only hope for those otherwise beyond hope. There are plenty of similar cases: an unemployed war invalid, for instance, with three children to feed and no bread on the table; or a fourteen-year-old girl, who had penned a play in the hope of earning enough to buy Christmas presents for her family (for there would otherwise be nothing to unwrap).[79] Each of these cases reflects an aspect of German reality in the 1930s: of the economic devastation, of the hopes vested by so many in Hitler, but also of the extraordinary social prestige which German theatre continued to enjoy. For at the risk of stating the obvious: all these people regarded it as *worthwhile* to devote their energies to playwriting. They did so either in the hope of economic betterment or simply because they saw the theatre as a forum in which to make their voices heard. In scope and intensity, this phenomenon went beyond the usual efforts of would-be dramatists.[80]

Consider an eighty-four-year-old reaching for his pen to produce a cry from the depths about the fate of his nation.[81] Or take the case of two elderly ladies so moved by the return of the Saar after fifteen years of French occupation that they sat down to write a *Weihespiel*: in the words of the censor, a 'symphony of patriotism ... as bizarre as it is affecting'.[82] Or picture the woman from the Sudetenland who had sent in a play to thank the Führer for the 'wondrous' deliverance of her countrymen.[83] Only the day before, she wrote in the accompanying letter, she had actually seen him in the flesh, in her home town, and would he please excuse the *typed* missive; only, greeting him in the surging crowd, she had dislocated her right shoulder.

That scene – seemingly straight out of Chaplin's *Great Dictator* – was curiously apt: for the farcical frequently threatened to overtake these patriotic playwrights. Their blindness to the true nature of the Nazi regime, moreover, hardly recommends them to posterity. Yet what makes these efforts at playwriting significant is that they were neither propaganda nor attempts to curry favour with the Nazi authorities.[84] They were spontaneous outbursts of passion from ordinary Germans: a kind of passion signally absent from the Reich's professional theatres.

A letter to Goebbels after the *Anschluß* of Austria illustrates the point. In it an Austrian Nazi, still new to life in the Reich, vented his frustration. Theatre directors, he found, were wary of overtly political plays. He had been '"quietly" advised on a number of occasions ... that only ... "tempered passions" were desired by the powers that be'.[85] Surely, he asked, there was nothing 'temperate' about National Socialism?

Yet there had been no mistake. As a reaction to the *Thing*'s extravagance, the Propaganda Ministry had been advocating restraint. In a series of pronouncements from January 1934 onwards, the Reichsdramaturg had discouraged 'outward proximity to the present age'.[86] In May 1936, at the end of the *Thingspiel* era, Goebbels himself confirmed the policy: dramatists were to refrain from contemporary topics (since they were supposedly too close to events to be able to cast them definitively).[87] Finally, in the summer of that year, Möller's *Frankenburger Würfelspiel* provided a demonstration of the kind of political theatre acceptable to the Propaganda Ministry: a verse play, with a Greek-style chorus, and a political message in elaborate historical guise. It was a world away from *Schlageter* three years earlier. The early years of the Third Reich, then, were not simply about *Thing* arena vs. proscenium stage (or about the fate of expressionism).[88] The various stylistic debates were ultimately driven by politics. This, in turn, went beyond the familiar wrangling of rival Nazi potentates. It was about the role of the party rank and file (and of non-party members) in shaping future German theatre; and not least, it was about the self-image of National Socialism.[89] Developments in the theatre reflected the broader transition from Nazism's revolutionary phase to that of entrenched power. Schlösser's much quoted aim of a stylised 'mythical' theatre, transcending history, rather than belonging to a particular period was thus much more than an expression of his own aesthetic preferences.[90]

Nazi theatre effectively embarked on a new course. Out went the plays about the 'national resurgence': or to put it differently, out went the proselytising plays. *Schlageter* itself was effectively banned in 1935.[91] Its no less manipulative 'comic' counterpart, Dietrich Loder's *Konjunktur*, vanished likewise from the repertoire. That play had heaped derision on the pillars of Weimar society and invited the audience to laugh at the thought of the Nazis' supposedly corrupt adversaries being consigned to Dachau.[92] The jocular reference to concentration camps was not the only thing about the play that seemed awkward two years on. Its central comic conceit – so effective in 1933 – that the mass conversions to Nazism that year were a sign of rampant opportunism was problematic in the era of the 'national community'. The final problem for *Konjunktur* was its use of Nazi uniforms and of the Hitler salute: both had become taboo on stage, so as to preserve their potency elsewhere.

Also taboo were representations of prominent Nazis.[93] Several dramatists had actually sought to put Hitler himself on stage. Among the more colourful instances was a play about the Great War, which was to have featured the soul of the wounded Hitler briefly entering heaven before returning to 'further struggle' on earth; the play's other attractions included the daughter of the goddess Germania favouring with her charms a lucky Hermann Göring.[94]

Yet it was not just the grotesque, or the inept, that was weeded out. The plays affected included Möller's *Frankenburger Würfelspiel*. The *Dice Game* was originally to have featured Hitler as the supreme judge in the play's trial scene. In a *coup de théâtre* of some potency, the lighting was to have moved from the figures on stage via the dark night sky to the elevated platform where the Führer was expected to be seated. Wordlessly, by his mere presence, Hitler would have answered the question Möller had put in the mouths of his persecuted Austrian peasants, 'Is there no righteous man [who] ... will put an end to this violent charade?'[95]

Möller's lack of shame should not deflect attention from his capacity for theatrical éclat, or from the fact that this had been curtailed.[96] It is only against such glimpses of what Nazi theatre might have been that the desperate dullness and pitiful mediocrity of the actual propaganda plays becomes fully apparent. For Schlösser's mythical theatre never came about.[97] Instead, there was a stampede into the past. For some dramatists, antiquarianism was a refuge from contemporary politics. For others, however, history became an excuse: a cloak under which they hoped to smuggle their eulogies of the Nazi regime past the censors.[98] All those leaden studies in leadership (*Führertum*) that made up so much of the Third Reich's dramatic output should be seen in this context. They were the price paid for the vigorous policing of the party's ideological copyright.

Ultimately, no one was happy about the situation that had thus arisen. Nationalist writers felt thwarted both in their personal and patriotic capacities. Some even protested. The staunchly right-wing dramatist Hermann Burte, for instance, complained to Schlösser about those 'mining history rather than making history'.[99] The Reichsdramaturg privately agreed; but he could not very well ban the past *as well as* the present.[100] So the mills of recycled history ground on, and the censors groaned openly at the sight of yet another manuscript about Frederick the Great or about Oliver Cromwell (the Lord Protector being a favourite choice of those who would have preferred to write openly about Hitler).[101] And behind every artless play about Cromwell, Caesar, Bonaparte or even Richelieu there lurked a hundred uninspired offerings about some long-forgotten figure or incident from Germany's past. 'Historical drama,' as one reviewer noted in a carefully weighed phrase, '... has forced its way to the forefront, to an extent previously unimaginable'.[102] A letter to the Reichsdramaturg complained at about the same time that 'almost every single new play in recent years' had been an historical play; and while it was possible, the correspondent conceded, that such plays appealed to 'literary types', they seemed 'tired stuff' to 'most ordinary folk'.[103]

The problem was the nature of those plays. Since they were, with very few exceptions, merely vehicles to transport Nazi ideology, they tended to be as preachy as the *Thingspiel* had been. One of the principal offenders, the dramatist (and SS-general) Friedrich Bethge eventually acknowledged as much. 'I have come to realise,' he confided to the Reichsdramaturg, 'that the main weakness of the heroes of National Socialist drama is that ... they keep proclaiming and explaining their ... view of the world'.[104] A Frankfurt critic was brave enough to dissect the problem publicly. 'The characters [in the new historical drama],' she observed, 'lack depth. We have seen it again and again. ... They have no human opponent, for their struggle is in the service of an idea.'[105] Compare this to the complaints about the *Thingspiel*: the charge was that *Thing* characters lacked 'inner motivation' for their actions, since Nazi ideology was simply presented as a given.[106] Not since *Schlageter*, in fact, had any drama proceeded from the assumption that audiences might need to be won over to Nazism. No dramatist could afford to do that after the Seizure of Power: for to do so was to question, by implication at least, the regime's propaganda image of a *Volk* united behind the Führer.

There were people who saw the problem. A party member from Hamburg had sought to address on stage what he regarded as widespread reservations about the party: no theatre had dared touch his play.[107] An SA-man from Silesia protested to Schlösser about the one-dimensional characters in new drama: reducing the opponents of National Socialism to 'mere caricatures', he thought, ultimately diminished the Nazis themselves.[108] Yet, as that SA-man added, self-censorship among directors and producers was so pervasive that more adventurous plays never got anywhere near the stage. It may be more than a coincidence that Hanns Johst gave up writing plays after *Schlageter* and turned to prose.

Audiences voted with their feet. Friedrich Bethge admitted privately that before 1933 none of his plays had survived the first night; all Nazi dramatists, he thought, owed their present access to the stage 'solely to the political conditions created by the Führer'.[109] No less revealing was Bethge's enthusiasm about an audience of Hitler Youth: '*they* had not found my play demanding'.[110] Walther Best – another SS-dramatist – complained to Schlösser that directors had actually told him to his face that Nazi plays emptied theatres.[111] A publisher of such plays advocated repertoire theatres devoted solely to Nazi dramatists. Scheduling individual plays by them, he explained, was pointless. 'For audiences have simply got into the habit of not attending today's standard drama.'[112] Friedrich Hymmen – a so-called 'Hitler Youth dramatist' and thus guaranteed audiences for his dismally plodding plays – was undismayed: true National Socialist dramatists should continue to dispense with dramatic development in favour of ideas and simply ignore the unhappiness of audiences and actors. Another Nazi dramatist, Curt Langenbeck, agreed: there was no need 'to pay the slightest regard to audiences'.[113] It was probably in response to such sentiments that the famous (and vastly popular) Munich satirist Karl Valentin offered his own suggestion: there was nothing for it, he declared with mock ingenuity, theatre-attendance would simply have to be made compulsory; that was the only way to fill empty playhouses.[114] This brings us back to Friedrich Bethge. After the première of his grisly *Anke von Skoepen* – attended by massed ranks of (conscripted) party officials – the local Gauleiter observed, 'People should be driven with clubs to go and see this.'[115]

Against this background the public's enthusiasm for well-crafted *apolitical* evocations of the past assumes significance. If these plays sometimes achieved an echo out of all proportion to their modest merit, it should not necessarily be taken as an indictment of public taste.[116] However, the public's taste is at the heart of another point: that of the actual topics of Nazi history plays. Particular themes predominated. The censors themselves noted a recurring line-up in German history: 'the Ancient Teutons, Frederick the Great, Queen Louise, Bismarck, Hindenburg ... all neatly traipsing along'.[117] Most of that list revolved around one theme: Prussia.

Prussia had long been more than just a geographical term. As Werner Deubel's wartime play *The Last Fortress* put it, Prussia was about 'bearing'.[118] After 1918, the so-called 'Spirit of Potsdam' had been conjured in print and on the cinema screen to discredit the republic.[119] The profusion of Prussian plays in the Third Reich – from Paul Ernst's *Spirit of Prussia* in 1933 to Deubel's *Last Fortress* a decade later – was thus no accident. Yet evocations of Prussia cannot automatically be equated with Nazi sentiment. They might stem from Imperial nostalgia, just as the ancient President Hindenburg had preferred to wear Imperial uniform (complete with pickelhaube) even – or perhaps especially – when in the company of Hitler. Nazi theatre censors were certainly on the look-out for hidden monarchist sentiment. A planned pageant in Silesia in 1939, for instance, outraged the Propaganda Ministry: the tableaux provided an extended glorification of Royal Prussia but failed to reflect either 'in content' or 'language' the Nazi present.[120]

Similar intentions perhaps also underpinned the most spectacular attempt at historical drama in the Third Reich: Hans Rehberg's cycle of plays on the heroic age of Prussia.[121] The glittering productions of these plays under Jürgen Fehling's and Gustaf Gründgens' aegis on the Reich's premier stages became part of the public image of Nazi theatre. Yet the plays themselves cannot readily be subsumed under the heading of 'Nazi drama'. In their range of human emotions and sustained historical imagination they went beyond the Third Reich's conventions. Contemporaries called them 'Shakespearean', which was an astute way of praising something that clearly ran counter to the classicism favoured by the authorities.[122] Rehberg's artistic independence was doubly remarkable, since he had been an early and vociferous supporter of the Nazis. 'One might have expected him to become our foremost National Socialist dramatist,' observed the Rosenberg Office, 'yet his oeuvre to date has scarcely even touched on National Socialist ideology.'[123]

We can thus say that of four prominent Nazi dramatists – Johst, Möller, Rehberg and Bethge – one retired from playwriting, the other sought to rescue some of the artistic legacy of the Weimar years (and promptly fell from grace as a result), the third used his party credentials to disregard utterly Nazi theatre policy (by writing in a Shakespearean vein), and only the least talented of the four ploughed a lonely Nazi furrow.[124]

The comparison between these men is instructive in other ways, too. Rehberg exhibited the fire of Johst (or that of the amateur dramatists); but he turned it into a human passion: the kind of passion the Frankfurt critic had longed for. In the *Seven Years' War*, Rehberg's most successful drama, we see Frederick the Great wreathed in glory; but we also glimpse him at the end of the play as an exhausted old man: war had 'clipped' his 'wings'.[125] Doctrinaire Nazis reacted with dismay and disbelief. If there had not been such a dearth of good writing, Rehberg might well have fallen victim to censorship himself.[126] He achieved his 'Shakespearean' effect of a fully rounded protagonist, moreover, by giving his Frederick real opponents (unlike Bethge's cardboard cut-outs). The identity of those opponents, finally, takes us back to the Berlin Olympics and the Dietrich-Eckart Stage, where we started from: for the historical antithesis of Prussia had always been Austria.

Austro-Prussian rivalry might seem an eighteenth- and nineteenth-century affair. Bismarck appeared to have resolved it, and the Weimar republic actively wooed the Austrians. Yet with the Nazis' accession to power and Dollfuß's defence of Austria's

producer (which in a sense it was, if the ban had been demanded from outside the Propaganda Ministry). Schlösser often enlisted the cooperation of the censored by suggesting that the measure was potentially open to discussion. In the case of *Volk ohne Heimat* he went even further. He specifically described the ban as a 'temporary measure'.[9] Since the offensiveness of Kaergel's play was hardly likely to diminish over time, there was only one thing Schlösser can have meant by this: the ban was to apply only for the duration of the existence of Poland. Schlösser's language, more generally, was certainly suggestive. At one point, he wondered whether 'relations with Poland had already become sufficiently hostile' to grant permits to anti-Polish plays.[10] On another occasion, he spoke of the Propaganda Ministry's 'benevolence to the state of Poland': every part of that phrase was dripping with sarcasm, not least the words 'Poland' and 'state', which constituted an oxymoron in most Nazi minds.[11] After that oxymoron had been abolished by force of arms, the propagandists' true colours finally emerged: they authorised for performance in occupied Warsaw a Nazi comedy about Polish history; the audience of occupiers were invited to laugh at 'Poland's inability to form and sustain a state ...'[12]

The other state which the Nazis considered merely a temporary aberration on the map of Europe was Czechoslovakia. Here there was little diplomatic conciliation. That, too, was reflected in the theatre. There were, for instance, no fewer than fifty-two productions between 1933 and 1936 of *Andreas Hollmann*, an inflammatory play about the fate of the Sudeten Germans under Czech rule. This is doubly revealing because of the identity of the play's author. He was none other than H. C. Kaergel, who not only specialised in anti-Polish drama but also had a fine line in anti-Czech plays. *Andreas Hollmann* was as vulgar and objectionable as *Volk ohne Heimat*; both were viciously anti-Slav. Yet the one play was widely performed, the other banned. It was only when Hitler's preparations for expansion reached a critical point in 1936 and the Reich was briefly at its best behaviour that *Andreas Hollmann*, too, vanished from the stage.[13]

The play's subsequent fate is no less revealing. In November 1937, Schlösser received a letter about *Andreas Hollmann* by a senior civil servant in the Ministry of the Interior. In view of the play's 'thrust' [*Tendenz*], the letter suggested, it would be desirable for the Reichsdramaturg to order productions of *Hollmann* 'in a number of theatres in the near future'.[14] The date of that letter is highly suggestive: only three weeks earlier, Hitler had for the first time revealed to selected generals and civil servants his intention to smash Czechoslovakia. The Reichsdramaturg was almost certainly unaware of that; the matter was top secret. Yet Schlösser could hardly have failed to recognise the significance of the letter addressed to him. Senior civil servants do not write out of the blue to another government department. What is more, the letter mentioned a reception hosted by the Minister of the Interior, thus inviting the inference that the request ultimately came from the minister himself. As he pondered his response, Schlösser did not consult *his* own minister, since Goebbels had effectively been circumvented by that letter. Instead, Schlösser turned to the Foreign Office for advice (but was careful not to reveal what had prompted him to do so). The diplomats were no less circumspect. They replied guardedly that anti-Czech plays 'performed in a state theatre would obviously have a greater ... effect' than 'newspaper articles' did. Repertoire decisions should thus be 'determined by the nature of relations ... at *a given moment*'.[15] Since the Foreign Office, however, also pointed out that anti-Czech articles had been appearing in the press of late, Schlösser took this to be a hint and authorised further performances of *Andreas Hollmann*.[16]

Schlösser's caution may have had its roots in an experience two years earlier which had revealed the other side of the nexus between foreign affairs and the stage. In the far east of Germany, open-air theatre had been taking place since the 1920s in Marienburg castle. That imposing stronghold of the Teutonic Knights had long possessed symbolic significance. Versailles had further heightened its potency: for the river which the castle overlooked had become Germany's new border. Poland had actually claimed *both* banks; but in a referendum the ethnically mixed population voted by well over 90 per cent to stay German. The Marienburg theatricals must be seen in that context. Poland had hoped to silence the sound of the German language in the region. That language would now resonate defiantly from the stage: *Kultur*, as ever, would prove the German nation's strongest shield.

One of the plays specifically written for the Marienburg duly centred on earlier (medieval) Polish attempts to capture the castle. That play, from the pen of a patriotic schoolmaster, was too weak artistically to stay in the repertoire.[17] Yet its nationalist fervour later recommended it to the Third Reich. In 1935, the Association for Germandom Abroad tried to revive the play. (That was the same body whose agitprop about 'the Eastern Marches' we encountered earlier.)

When the Foreign Office in Berlin got wind of all that, it immediately contacted Goebbels, who in turn summoned Schlösser. The Reichsdramaturg tried to brazen things out: the play's theme, he insisted, was past German disunity, and Poland would have no grounds to be offended. Besides, he had already cut the line in the play describing the Poles as 'uniquely treacherous and worthless'.[18] Goebbels may have shared those sentiments privately but he sensed danger and demanded a ban. Yet it was too late for that: the performance schedules had already been published; and if there was one thing the Propaganda Ministry was anxious to avoid above all, it was being *seen* to have changed its mind. Goebbels responded by threatening to hold Schlösser 'personally responsible for any fall-out in foreign affairs'.[19] It might have been the end of Schlösser's career, had he not managed to engineer a 'convenient illness' in 'several leading members of the cast'. All that was arranged with cloak and dagger methods, avoiding the usual channels of communication, lest the Poles (or anyone else) get to hear about it.[20] Not only was theatre repertoire in the Third Reich thus at times subject to the diktat of the Foreign Office, producers and theatre officials all the way up to the Reichsdramaturg were forced to behave like conspirators, and were threatened with dire consequences, should the truth get out.

There was, however, a postscript to the Marienburg affair. The replacement chosen by Schlösser for the suppressed play was Goethe's *Egmont*: a clever choice, given *Egmont*'s theme of national resurgence. Yet a substantial part of the Marienburg audience, who had pre-booked their tickets, disagreed. They boycotted Goethe and insisted on full refunds.[21] It is a useful reminder that theatre in the Third Reich cannot simply be reduced to the level of official structures and policies. Authors and audiences remained factors which the propagandists could control only imperfectly: they could interdict but they could not compel. Similarly, they could encourage but could not create. The theatre of the 'ethnic struggle' was indeed only an indirect outcrop of the Third Reich. It was the result of individual initiative and of a nationalist obsession shared by like-minded audiences. Yet neither the playwrights nor the playgoers involved were necessarily representative of the German nation as a whole. H. C. Kaergel, for instance, was the only professional dramatist in Germany to have written anti-Czech plays.[22] And not all German audiences would have preferred the verse of a patriotic schoolmaster to that of Goethe. Indeed, some Germans failed to warm to nationalist theatre altogether. A play about the fate of the Saar, for instance, was rejected by the theatre in Weimar, on the grounds that 'the fight of the Saarland was hardly likely to be of interest' to local audiences.[23]

This points to something fundamental about German politics and theatre in the inter-war years. Nationalism was not an invariable quantity. It waxed and waned in response to events. Take the most obvious case: the French attempt in 1923 to break up Germany and create a puppet state in the Rhineland. That had resulted in a wave of anti-French plays and productions across Germany.[24] Two years on, emotions were still raw enough to ensure vast audiences for Arnold Bronnen's inflammatory *Rheinische Rebellen*. The play was widely staged, except in the occupied Rhineland itself, where Allied censors had banned even the sale of reading copies (thus proving Bronnen's point about a Rhineland in chains). In Berlin, Jeßner himself directed *Rheinische Rebellen*, complete with a vast German flag that filled the stage. The political left as well as the right in the mid-twenties was capable of feeling outrage about French conduct. Indeed Jeßner used language normally associated with the far right; he proclaimed his Prussian State Theatre a *Kampftheater*: a theatre that was part of the nation's struggle.[25]

Some theatregoers also staged their own protests. Members of a Stuttgart audience in 1924 arrived at the theatre armed with toy trumpets. They used these to disrupt the playing of the 'Marseillaise' during a scene of Büchner's *Danton*.[26] That might seem like archetypal petty nationalism. Yet the scenes in Stuttgart cannot be divorced from the situation in the occupied Rhineland. A few months earlier, the French had fired into an unarmed crowd of protesters in Essen, and had deported into unoccupied Germany some 140,000 Rhinelanders who had taken part in a protest strike. What is more, France had banned the playing of Germany's national anthem in the Rhineland and the Ruhr (i.e. on *German* soil).[27] It is tempting to speculate how French, British or American audiences might have responded to the strains of the 'Deutschlandlied' in comparable circumstances. The Stuttgart protests, moreover, were clearly the work of a minority. Most people in the audience refused to join in. In fact, they started applauding, thus drowning out in turn the noise of the protesters, and allowing the performance to resume. The Stuttgart evidence would suggest that the appeal of aggressive nationalism in the theatre was far from universal.[28]

That impression is confirmed by the wider record of the 1920s and early 1930s. After Chancellor Stresemann's first diplomatic successes (and limited French concessions), no anti-French play achieved a significant impact anywhere in the remaining years of the Weimar republic. Bronnen's own attempt to launch another nationalist vehicle in the theatre – *Reparationen* – received only a muted echo.[29] Passions had cooled inside and outside the playhouse. The lack of interest in the fate of the Saar reported by the theatre in Weimar was thus entirely in keeping with the wider evidence. Final proof of the altered mood, in a sense, came at the Berlin Olympics. When the French team marched into the stadium, they were greeted by a noticeably loud and prolonged cheer from the German spectators. The treaty of Versailles, after all, was dead and buried.[30]

The theatre of the 'ethnic struggle' that emerged almost concurrently with such growing generosity therefore cannot simply be explained in terms of traditional German nationalism. All the more so, since the mood of reaching out to Germany's former enemies also extended to the stage itself. Per Schwenzen's *In the Skies of Europe*, a play advocating Franco-German reconciliation, was produced in no fewer than forty-four theatres in the first season of Nazi rule alone.[31] Another (slightly more equivocal) appeal for friendship with France, Heinz Steguweit's *The Neighbour to the Left*, achieved forty-one

productions between 1936 and 1938.[32] The censors probably allowed
such plays to pass in order to help assuage worries abroad about Nazi
rearmament. If there was deception involved, it was on the part of the
propagandists, and not of the dramatists or their audiences.[33]

That impression is confirmed by the surviving files of the
Reichsdramaturgie. These contain details of a number of plays
fervently advocating friendship with Germany's former enemies.
The regime, however, was determined not to let the peacefulness
get out of hand: nearly all of the plays about 'the reconciliation of
nations', 'the possibility of Franco-German reconciliation', etc. were
banned outright.[34]

The plots of those suppressed plays provide an intriguing
glimpse of the might-have-been. Here was a more peaceful Germany,
which was progressively silenced after 1933. One of these plays revis-
ited a real-life incident on the Franco-German border before the First
World War, where German miners had gone to the rescue of French
colleagues trapped underground.[35] Another play focused on German
and French soldiers throwing presents into each other's trenches during the famous 'Christmas truce' of 1914.[36] A third, more unusually,
even tried to reach out to Germany's eastern neighbours: the play
culminated in the spectacle of Germans and Poles jointly repairing a
broken dam.[37]

The significance of these lost plays does not simply lie in their
sentiments but in the political affiliation of their authors. For these
exponents of reconciliation were not liberal or left-leaning Germans
but confirmed nationalists. Indeed, some of them were Nazis. The
author of the play about the Christmas truce was an 'Old Fighter' no
less (i.e. a member of the party elite of Hitler's earliest followers). The
man preaching German-Polish reconciliation was also a member of
the Nazi party, and his message in 1934 was this: 'Each nation needs
the other; each must let the other live.'[38]

While such views may not have been representative of the Nazi
party as a whole, they cannot simply be disregarded either. The
German stage between the wars did not divide neatly into a pacifist
theatre of the Weimar left and an aggressive theatre of the resurgent
right. The theatre of the right was itself riven between those favouring

peaceful means and the advocates of something altogether more radical. The divide had already become apparent in the second half of the Weimar republic with the resurgence of interest in the Great War.

The wave of *Frontstücke* (plays about the frontline) from 1928 onwards has long been viewed as a harbinger of things to come.[39] Certainly, that was a rare instance where the Third Reich continued enthusiastically what had begun in the republic. In the first two years of Nazi rule, the playhouses of Germany seemed to turn into a second Western front, with the guns opening up in *Langemarck*, *Reims*, the *Battle of the Marne*, etc.[40] So frequent did war drama become that, in 1934, the Propaganda Ministry pleaded publicly with German dramatists to turn their attention to other topics.[41] All this might suggest an undiminished taste among the right for battle: a theatrical link, so to speak, from the aggression of the Kaiser's Germany to that of Hitler. The names involved might indeed seem suggestive: of the five dramatists who launched the *Frontstück* craze – Menzel, Möller, Bethge, Graff and Cremers – the first three were early members of the Nazi party; and of the two who were not, Sigmund Graff later ended up joining the Propaganda Ministry itself, as did Möller. Both men became Schlösser's principal assistants in the business of censoring German theatre. The record does seem damning.

Yet in reality things were rather less clear-cut. Graff's *Endless Road*, the most successful of these plays, had actually been written in collaboration with a young journalist who was a supporter of Chancellor Stresemann; and Stresemann was not only a Nobel peace laureate but a *bête noire* of the German right.[42] Möller's *Douaumont*, meanwhile, had been given its first Berlin production at the Volksbühne: the principal *left-wing* theatre of the republic.[43] The production history of *The Endless Road* was even more remarkable: it had first been staged – in English translation – at the Gate Theatre in London.[44] It was only the favourable notices in Britain that led to productions in Germany. The play's description of soldiers going to their deaths in a mood of quiet resignation was certainly no nationalist glorification of war.[45] Much the same was true of Gerhard Menzel's *Toboggan*, which had been lauded for its stark realism across the political divides of 1928. It was effectively banned after January

1933, Menzel's Nazi party membership notwithstanding. Cremer's *Battle of the Marne*, finally, had also received warm praise for its 'objectivity' from the Weimar critics of all stripes; it was banned by the Nazi authorities a year later.[46] Indeed, almost all plays about the Great War written before 1933 were eventually banned in the Third Reich because they lacked, too obviously, enthusiasm for further slaughter.[47] There were really only two bards of the *Fronterlebnis* – Friedrich Bethge and Heinrich Zerkaulen – whose work corresponded to the Nazi ideal of heroism.[48]

Any attempt to see in war drama the antecedent of the theatre of the 'ethnic struggle' must, in any case, founder over a fundamental point. The *Frontstücke* were not an attempt to win in the theatre a war that had been lost on the battlefield. There were no victories in those plays, or rather no military victories. The Allied nations, moreover, were not the real enemy. The plays aimed, in every sense, at the public at home, then and now. Friedrich Bethge spoke of 'the new German drama' as 'the revenge of the frontline for the way they had been betrayed'.[49] He thus summed up from a Nazi perspective a feeling that extended far beyond the nationalist constituency. It was the anger of a generation of men who felt that their sacrifice, and those of their fallen comrades, had never really been appreciated at home. Right-wing war drama was a family quarrel among Germans about the recent past rather than an ideological preparation for future conquest. For all its specifically German flavour, it had distinct affinities in that regard with the disillusion about the Great War prevalent in Britain in the 1920s and 1930s. The huge success in Germany of R. C. Sherriff's *Journey's End* – no fewer than 120 productions in the course of four seasons – was surely no accident.[50]

If war drama thus tells us little about the theatre of the 'ethnic struggle' and its genesis, it does provide an important indirect clue. With the single exception of E. W. Möller, the authors of the *Frontstücke* had all seen action in the Great War themselves. They had written plays about a world they knew well: a world which haunted their memories. War, as Friedrich Bethge put it, was 'the primary experience [*Grunderlebnis*]' that had made him a dramatist.[51] Bethge had been awarded *two* Iron Crosses and was wounded five times. Heinrich Zerkaulen – who had also volunteered in 1914 and had been grievously wounded two years later on the Eastern Front – said much the same about his own career as a playwright.[52]

It is this personal angle, and the sense of being driven as a writer by the experience of recent history, that provides the link with the theatre of the 'ethnic struggle'. Its authors, too, very often wrote about their own lives even when they were writing about other people or past centuries. The author of *Rhineland Tragedy* was Rhenish himself. H. C Kaergel's anti-Polish *Volk ohne Heimat* was about his native Silesia; his anti-Czech plays *Andreas Hollmann* and *Hockewanzel* were set beyond the very Sudeten hills which he could see from the windows of his house. Friedrich Bethge's family originally hailed from the Eastern lands, which he made the subject of his 'Prussian Trilogy'. Hans Kyser, the author of the vicious anti-Polish drama *Fire on the Border*, was born in the town of Graudenz: that was the same town that had featured in the *Sorrow of the Eastern Marches*, which so exercised the Polish embassy in 1935. Kurt Eggers' Free Corps past provided the biographical link with the Upper Silesia of his *Thingspiel Annaberg*. The unsolicited manuscripts reaching the Propaganda Ministry also showed a frequent link between plays about the borderlands and the background of their authors.[53] Finally, there was the figure of Hans Rehberg, who also came from the 'lost East'. Rehberg sublimated his own loss of *Heimat*, as we have seen, in an almost obsessive celebration of Royal Prussia and its past glories.

What was true of the playwrights, moreover, was often also true of the players, directors or audiences. Max Worgitzki's anti-Polish drama *The Oak Tree at Thorn* was performed by an itinerant troupe across the length and breadth of East Prussia, the region geographically nearest to the town of Thorn (from which it had been separated at Versailles).[54] Felix Lützkendorf's play *Border* was first produced almost within hailing distance of the new border, at Schneidemühl. The nearby town of Nackel, which had woken one morning after the war to discover a border on its outskirts, was clearly still unresigned to the fact some fifteen years later. In 1935, the local amateur dramatic society there wanted to stage a play called *Beyond the Border*. (We know about this because the Nazi authorities banned it in the interest of the supposed new German-Polish amity.)[55] Four year later, when the phoney peace was over, an amateur dramatist offered to Goebbels his own anti-Polish play with the remark, 'There can never be friendship with Poland ... I know the Poles well.' He added, 'For the region that was fought over and is being fought over again is my *Heimat*.'[56]

At the other end of Germany, close to the lands that had until recently been occupied by France, a Lutheran pastor reminisced about a play which had been performed locally. Its topic had been the French Foreign Legion; and it contained, he recalled, moving scenes of desperate young men of various nationalities being 'exploited' by the 'contemptible' French.[57] Even a play advocating reconciliation, like Fritz von Unruh's *Heinrich von Achternach*, contained moments of real bitterness. That play, commissioned in 1925 by Konrad Adenauer (the then mayor of Cologne), featured a sadistic French soldier striking passers-by with his riding crop.[58] Such scenes were rooted in real-life incidents in the Rhineland, where French soldiers conducted their own private acts of revenge for the earlier suffering inflicted on *their* country.

Unruh's thoughtful play, with its pointed references to the devastation in Flanders and Northern France, was very much an exception. The majority of dramatists, players and audiences involved in the theatre of the 'ethnic struggle' failed to see the connection between present German misfortune and past German misconduct: they perceived themselves solely in the role of innocent victims. That this blindness was at the heart of Germany's moral and political downfall in the twentieth century hardly needs pointing out; that the theatre of the 'ethnic struggle' contributed to that downfall is no less obvious. Yet if we focus exclusively on that theatre's blinkered vision of history, we run the risk of falling into the same trap. Certainly, German complaints about the French occupation after the war were undermined by their country's record *during* that war (or the earlier Franco-Prussian War). Yet we, in turn, should not forget that the Rhineland, too, had been occupied before. Under Napoleon, the French had actually annexed the entire left bank. The great cathedral cities of Aachen, Cologne, Mainz and Trier – Germany's historic heartland – had become French at gunpoint. The author of the *Rhineland Tragedy* was born in Aachen, and he had not forgotten.

The Millowitsch theatre company – a well-known institution in Cologne – had not forgotten either, as their repertoire proves.[59] The audiences across Germany who flocked to performances of *Wilhelm Tell* in 1923 remembered it, too. And so did all those writers and scribblers who penned Nazi history plays about the wars of 1812–15, known in Germany as the Wars of Liberation.

The centuries telescoped. *Wilhelm Tell* – written in response to a French invasion – was banned by the French a century later on the Rhine and the Ruhr. The theatre historian Carl Niessen, one of the fathers of the *Thingspiel*, reminded his readers in 1938 both of that ban and of the fact that, in Schiller's day, performances of German plays in the Rhineland had been suppressed in favour of French productions.[60] A century on, one of the first things the French army did after seizing the town of Essen in 1923 was to close the theatre there and place armed guards in front of it. In neighbouring Recklinghausen French soldiers burst into the local theatre during a performance of *King Lear* and cleared the theatre at gunpoint.[61] Further to the south, in Saarbrücken, the town's lively theatre scene in the eighteenth century had ended abruptly with the arrival of the French in 1793: they closed all three local theatres. And there were again all manner of restrictions on theatre in that city and the surrounding region during the period of France's quasi-colonial rule of the Saar between 1918 and 1935.[62] It was no accident, therefore, that Hitler ordered the construction of a huge new theatre in Saarbrücken as 'the Führer's gift' to the returning Saar. East of the Rhine, finally, Euringer's *Thingspiel German Passion* had been performed in the ruins of Heidelberg Castle. Among the spectators, there were many, we may be certain, who knew why that fine palace was in ruins: it had been burnt down in the seventeenth century by the invading armies of Louis XIV during a war, known to history as 'the Rape of the Palatinate'.[63] At every level, theatre was part of that sorry tale which we call the history of Europe. And we will not be able to make sense of either, unless we bear in mind that history did not commence in 1870, in 1914, or for that matter in 1918. It was a continuum; and until Hitler's war changed the rules forever, guilt had been fairly evenly matched between Germany and France.

Nach dem Willen des Führers:

„Gautheater Saarpfalz"

begonnen November 1936 — eingeweiht 9. Oktober 1938

9 'The Führer's gift to the Saar': the new Saarbrücken theatre.

In the case of German-Polish relations, the other recurring topic in German theatre between the wars, guilt was less evenly distributed. Prussia had been instrumental in ending Polish freedom in the eighteenth century; and the Prussian-led German Empire, a century later, had embarked on a policy of repression, targeting the Poles both because of their language and their ancient allegiance to the Catholic Church. If Poles had traditionally featured less on the German stage than the French had, that was perhaps because they had posed no threat.

There was even a degree of sympathy for the plight of those Poles living under the *Russian* yoke. A play by a Polish woman dramatist about the Russian outrages in Poland was actually produced in Berlin and Vienna during the First World War.[64] Staging that play may have been a cynical move by the Central Powers, but perhaps no more so than the claim of Britain and France to fight for freedom, while allying themselves with the Tsarist Empire, the darkest tyranny in Europe at the time. Nations (and theatre audiences) have a pronounced ability to compartmentalise facts, which allows them to go on believing in their own conspicuous national virtue.

102

That phenomenon also explains the sudden emergence in Weimar Germany of anti-Polish drama. During the war, Imperial Germany had overseen the re-establishment of a Polish state in the lands conquered – or perhaps liberated – by the German and Austro-Hungarian armies. The Poles were certainly glad to see the end of Russian rule. Yet two years later, their cousins who had been living under *Prussian* rule were no less glad to see the end of Imperial Germany. In a series of risings against the new German republic, they tried to create facts on the ground before the Allied leaders had come to agree upon the new borders. These events of 1918–21 redefined German perceptions of Poland.

Before the uprisings, Poles had been regarded by (Protestant) Germans in much the same way that Protestant Britons had traditionally regarded the Catholic Irish – namely as amusing and sometimes engaging layabouts, who were obviously unable to govern themselves for as long as they remained in thrall to Romish superstition. And just as the perception of the Irish changed in Britain after the Easter Rising, which seemed to British contemporaries like blackest treason, so the Polish risings appeared to Germans as the work of souls steeped in wickedness. The charges of treachery, ingratitude, cowardice, deceitfulness and of every conceivable human baseness that became the staple of anti-Polish plays were rooted in that sudden shock at the end of the war when the previously docile Poles turned dangerous.[65]

What made it worse was that there existed no neat dividing line between German and Polish areas. Both the province of Posen, where Polish irregulars quickly prevailed, and Upper Silesia, where they encountered stiff resistance, were ethnically mixed. For the Poles, the fighting was about winning freedom. For Germans, it was about their right to stay German: Silesia will fight, and Silesia will be right, so to speak. 'The memories of that glorious fight for our Silesian *Heimat*' were the words chosen by H. C. Kaergel to sum up his play *Volk ohne Heimat*.[66] Kurt Eggers, meanwhile, named his *Thingspiel Annaberg* after the site of the decisive victory of the German Free Corps against the Poles. And of course it was at Annaberg itself that the Nazis built their huge *Thing* arena as a permanent national shrine to the defence of Silesia. As at the Marienburg – or in Saarbrücken in the West – the German language would resound from the stage where Germany's enemies had tried to silence it.

Most of Silesia and East Prussia voted to stay German in the referenda of 1920–1. Most of West Prussia and Posen was awarded to Poland *without* a referendum. In those regions, almost a million Germans abandoned house and home rather than living under Polish rule. They had become, in the title of Kaergel's play, 'a people without *Heimat*'. Like other refugees before or since, they never abandoned the hope of returning one day. All parties in the Weimar republic kept that hope alive: and so, in its own way, did the theatre. Indeed some plays about the 'ethnic struggle' almost took on an official quality. Hans Kyser's *Fire on the Border* had actually been funded by the German Foreign Office, as part of the Weimar republic's campaign for a revision of the Eastern border.[67] The close connection between theatre and foreign policy was thus something the Third Reich inherited, and Schlösser's habit of forwarding all relevant plays to the diplomats for inspection was in a sense merely a natural progression from republican practice.

Yet it was precisely that progression which put a stop to the theatre of the 'ethnic struggle' after 1933. Kyser's *Fire on the Border* was banned because foreign policy aims had changed; and when he completed in 1937 a further play about the Polish corridor, *Clouds on the Horizon*, the response of the Foreign Office was frosty. Not only did the diplomats find unpersuasive the play's 'notion of an hereditary enmity between Germans and Poles', they also objected strongly to the play's ending. The spectacle of 'a Pole [being] killed by a German,' the Foreign Office observed, was 'problematic' and the play thus 'unacceptable'.[68]

Two years later such scenes had become a grim reality: responsibility for the Poles in Berlin had passed from the relatively moderate Foreign Office to the SS. In a sense, it was only fitting, therefore, that an SS-playwright should have turned to the topic of Poland. Friedrich Bethge's 'Prussian Trilogy' represented the final radicalisation of the theatre of the 'ethnic struggle'. *Rebellion over Prussia, Anke von Skoepen* and *Kopernikus* stated emphatically a belief in an hereditary enmity between Germans and Slavs, the existence of which had been denied only two years earlier. Bethge's account of the medieval wars between the Teutonic Knights and the Poles was a chilling exercise in Nazi racism. More than that, it was a barely disguised incitement to genocide. Bethge's message was that the Poles would slit German throats unless the Germans reached for *their* knives first. It may be worth quoting an extended passage from *Anke von Skoepen*. It is from the heroine's account of the Polish conquest of her native town of Gilgenburg in East Prussia:

> When the Slanted-Eyes prevailed ... ape-like, they climbed the town walls. What in Gilgenburg there still was of the male sex, be he boy or four-score-and-ten was cut down like grass by the crescent scimitar ... When the terrified cry went up that the wolves, the Tartars, had crept inside Gilgenburg to savage the defenceless human fold, the women sought refuge in the ... church ... But the axe clove the church door. A shrill cry rent the air ... and the very altar cloth became the bridal bed ... for hundreds of women, virgins – and girls as young as ten; for the wolves from out of the distant steppe turned into ardent bride-grooms. The wine flowed freely, crimson streams, among the bodies undergoing coupling and torturing ... And of the fair women and the delicate girls they took many with them ... as their play-things ... while those lucky enough to have been less desired were left, mutilated fearfully, there in the church, which had been set alight, thus becoming their grave ... Such, gentles, were the 'Polish nuptials' at Gilgenburg – in the year of Grace 1410.[69]

The viciousness of Bethge's racism requires no further comment. His gross distortion of reality is equally palpable: Poles are neither 'slanted-eyed' nor are they 'ape-like' 'Tartars' out of Central Asia. They are frequently blond and blue-eyed, like their German neighbours. It is not for nothing that the SS abducted large numbers of Polish children during the war to raise them as Germans. Germany, moreover, had assimilated peacefully large numbers of Slavs over the centuries: the plethora of Polish names in the telephone directories of any German town is testimony to that. The theatre of the 'ethnic struggle' reflected that, too. Love scenes between individual Germans and Poles recur in the anti-Polish plays (including, in one instance, in a drama written by the brother of a Nazi cabinet minister).[70] Even in Nazi terms, then, Bethge's play did not really make sense.

How, then, to account for this eruption of venom on the stage? Part of the answer must lie buried in the unsavoury recesses of Bethge's own subconscious. The motif of rape, however, also recurs in the literature of colonialism. It has long been recognised as part of the colonisers' strategy of justifying to themselves the patent injustice meted out to 'the natives'. And when Bethge wrote the play, in 1941, Nazi Germany had inflicted on Poland 'colonial' rule of a kind that even Nazis felt the need to justify.

Yet there was a further factor involved. Bethge's 'Prussian Trilogy' contained repeated references to two historic sites: the Marienburg and Tannenberg. The former had become the topic of a whole host of plays in the 1920s that sought to show the present mirrored in the past.[71] Tannenberg, too, possessed a twofold symbolic significance: it was associated with a crushing German defeat in the Middle Ages; but it had also been the site of Field Marshal Hindenburg's decisive victory in 1914 over the Russian armies. And here, finally, we come to the root of the matter.

Whereas fighting on the Western front had taken place deep inside the countries which Germany had invaded, the first major battles in the East were fought on *German* soil. The invasion of East Prussia in the summer of 1914 by the Tsarist armies, and the devastation caused by the fighting, left emotional scars as deep as those in Flanders or Northern France. The Belgians and the French were haunted after 1918 by the thought that the Germans might one day invade again. The East Prussians, likewise, feared another Slav incursion.[72] That fear was heightened by the fact that the Allies had cut off East Prussia from the rest of Germany by creating the Polish corridor. The sense of threat was further increased by the Polish claim on parts of East Prussia at Versailles. That claim revived the memory that in previous centuries, too, Poland had tried to end the German presence in the East. We risk misunderstanding the theatre of the 'ethnic struggle' if we do not recognise the role of fear in its genesis: the fear of the Rhinelanders that, once again, France would try and annexe the entire region; and the fear of the Germans in the East of being driven out of house and home in East Prussia and Silesia.

That fear was never far from the surface in the anti-Polish plays throughout the 1920s and 1930s. And it was increased by the way the German minority was treated inside Poland after 1918. For the Poles took pleasure in reversing the historic roles of masters and servants. Petty humiliations and bureaucratic chicanery continued in the region as before: only the targets now were Germans rather than Poles.[73] While the wish to get even with the Germans may have been understandable, it did little to bring about a reconciliation between the two nations. The theatre of the 'ethnic struggle' was thus the result of specific historic circumstances after 1918, where Germans were the victims of often glaring injustice. To an extent, they had brought that injustice upon themselves by their nation's past conduct. Yet retaliation tends to affect the innocent as well as the guilty. The injustices after the Great War were real and they provoked, particularly in the border regions, widespread cries for vengeance. In the West of Germany, these progressively gave way to a mood of reconciliation, once the occupation had ended. In the East, the mood did not change. Germany never attempted in the Weimar years to reach out to Poland. Equally, Poland did nothing to end the discrimination of the German minority now living inside Polish borders. Yet even here there was sometimes at the individual level a readiness in the most unexpected quarters for a fresh start. The Propaganda Ministry was outraged to receive a play in 1941 which had as its hero a Polish officer; more than that, the Polish officer fell in love with a German girl.[74] Here was a play that preached the polar opposite of what the regime had been propagating and practising. And the author of that play, it should be noted, was a man who had fled his native town of Thorn in 1919 when the region became Polish.

That coded call for reconciliation was silenced by the Propaganda Ministry. Friedrich Bethge's incitement to violence, meanwhile, was produced by no fewer than twenty-one theatres between 1941 and 1943.[75] As such, it provided an illustration for audiences at home of the Third Reich's anti-Slav racial ideology that was turning Eastern Europe into a charnel house. Yet there is a final grim twist: Bethge's descriptions of gang rape, mutilation and mass murder of civilians turned out to be a horribly accurate prediction of what did come to pass in Eastern Germany in 1944–5, when the Red Army took its revenge for German conduct in Russia. As such, Bethge's 'Prussian Trilogy' documents a radicalisation both in Nazi racial policy and in the response it provoked. In its own way, the theatre of 'ethnic struggle' had helped bring about what it had hoped to forestall: the end of German life in the East. For while Bethge sought to justify genocide on the stage, other Nazi bards had grown too busy to write plays: Kurt Eggers, the author of *Annaberg*, was fighting in Russia as part of an SS-unit. He died in action in 1943. The author of the play *Totila* had become *Reichskommissar* for Belorussia, where he oversaw the mass murder of Russians and Jews. (He was killed in his bed, but not in his sleep, by a tank mine placed under the mattress by his Belorussian maid.) One of the principal figures in the Reich Theatre Chamber, Gauleiter Frauenfeld (who advised Möller on his *Frankenburg Dice Game*) was despatched to Germanise the Crimea. Hanns Johst, finally, was now producing racial travelogues about Slav 'hill tribes' in occupied Poland or dashed off little pieces for the papers about the avuncular charm of his travel companion: Heinrich Himmler.[76]

5 'The stream of heredity': theatre in the racial state

In the first half of the twentieth century the issue of race loomed large in German society. Even those not in thrall to the more outlandish theories of the day often exhibited views warped by racial categorisation. Take the following observations on the subject of French colonial troops in the occupied Rhineland. The passage comes from the diary of a then aspirant German dramatist. 'In the Rhineland', he wrote,

> the negroes are sucking all the juice from the land. They are
> impregnating women by the dozen. They do so with impunity,
> merely laughing at the protests of the local population. [Yet]
> the conduct of the population in Germany is exemplary ... These
> people, whose womenfolk are being destroyed ... do not resort to
> lynch mob methods. They grind their teeth but lock themselves
> into their privies as they do so, lest anyone should hear them.
> They do not nail negroes on to doors ... they clench their fists but
> do so safely inside the pockets of their trousers.[1]

The author of those pungent sentiments was no budding Nazi: it was Bertolt Brecht. His diary for 1920 is a suitable warning against simplistic assumptions about racism in German theatre and beyond. For as Brecht's own case demonstrates, racial prejudice was neither the exclusive preserve of the right, nor did it inevitably lead to Nazism. Indeed, there was nothing specifically German even about it. Brecht's reference to racial lynchings, after all, clearly aimed at *American* practices. What was German was the specific forms that racism took, and the occasions around which it crystallised. Take Brecht's own outburst: for all its grotesque exaggeration, it reflected something that was real enough. For the first time, 'negroes' were present on German soil in substantial numbers; and as soldiers of an occupying army, they exercised power. That was the crucial aspect: for black men were then habitually denied equal status by white societies every-where. The Rhineland of the 1920s was probably the only place on earth where black men had authority *over whites*. This heightened the sense of humiliation felt by many Germans: their country, it seemed, now occupied an even lower rung on the international ladder than the 'subject races' of the colonial powers. Few subsequent German accounts of the country's fate after Versailles were complete without a reference to Africans (or Moroccans) on the Rhine. The theatre was no exception. Take Kurt Eggers' *Thingspiel Schüsse bei Krupp – Shots Fired at the Krupp Plant*. The stage directions in the opening scene read: 'a group of Frenchmen, including a number of black men, advance. Some of the [German] women begin to cry.'[2] The reason for the crying is spelt out in the next set of directions: 'a black man kicks a ... [German] woman in her belly; she collapses in agony'. The vio-lence here was probably meant to hint at a kind of violation which could not be shown on stage. Euringer's *German Passion* came close to spelling it out: the figure of the mother whispers in recollection, 'a negro said to me, "don't resist" '.[3] A number of plays that were more explicit still went unperformed.[4] The suggestion that black soldiers were guilty of sexual violence owed more to racist obsession than to reality: while there was indeed a spate of rapes (both of women and boys) for which men in French uniforms were responsible, the perpe-trators were for the most part *white*. However, there is evidence of German women *voluntarily* entering into sexual relations with black soldiers, something many German men evidently found hard to accept.[5] One might note then in the so-called 'Ruhr plays' the charac-teristic nationalist tendency to leaven historical fact with deliberate deception, or possibly self-deception. Yet one should note also the contiguity between the crudely propagandistic *Thingspiele* and Brecht's comments about 'destroyed womenfolk'. It is tempting to look on these cases as paradigms and distinguish between a largely private 'background' racism in the Brechtian mould and an inflamma-tory racism characteristic of Nazi activists. In reality, the dividing line was less neatly drawn. There were examples of extreme racism among non-party members, while people wearing Nazi uniforms sometimes proved capable of the most unexpected views. A young Nazi *Kulturwartin* – a woman cultural official – for instance, had written a play called the *Negro Princess*, which was apparently performed successfully in the early years of the Third Reich and even appeared in print. The play was evidently not to the liking of more orthodox Nazis. There ensued in the playwright's home region a vicious campaign against her by the local sections of the (Nazi) League of German Maidens and the National Socialist Women's League. Things got so ugly that the young woman's mother in desperation turned to Goebbels for help.[6] We know of the affair only because that letter survives; there may have been other cases of which we are unaware.

Certainly, sympathy for other races was not automatically incompatible with robust nationalism. Take the case of a play called *The Holy War*, written in 1928, and submitted to the Nazi censors seven years later.[7] The plot revolved around two young Rhinelanders – brother and sister – who try to resist the post-war occupation of their *Heimat*. Both quickly realise the futility of their efforts in a disarmed Germany. Ever resourceful, they head off to Morocco instead, where they join a local rising against the common oppressors of Germans *and* Arabs: the French. This extravagant plot is, in some ways, less phantastical than it might seem. There was a rising against the French in Morocco in the 1920s and a feeling of kinship with the victims of Allied colonialism was not uncommon in Germany at the time: indeed the play about the Foreign Legion which we encountered earlier pointedly contrasted the friendliness of a young Arab boy with dastardly Gallic conduct.[8] Yet, in *The Holy War*, the object of praise was not a sexually immature boy but a grown man; and that man was portrayed in such glowing terms that the (woman) playwright felt the need to explain her enthusiasm to the (male) censors. 'In Abdul Mohammed,' she wrote in the covering letter, 'I created a great leader [*Führergestalt*]', since 'at the time I knew no true personality of such greatness' and 'I longed for greatness and true leadership'.[9] Besides, she added, Abdul Mohammed's 'posture and character' surely betrayed Nordic ancestry.

It is the transparent excuse of that final sentiment which lifts the play, and the correspondence about it, above the level of the anecdotal.[10] For here is reflected a wider shift in German society characterising the mid-1930s: even those Germans previously free from racial prejudice – or relatively free from it – were learning to be racists in the Nazi mould. The resulting wave of Nordic camouflage was so pronounced that it became the target of the satirists: a theatre troupe of the German Labour Front, for instance, poked fun at those who had turned 'Teuton blonde' with the 'help of a little peroxide'.[11] The censors, certainly, were suspicious of dramatists who paraded their 'racial awareness'; yet the Reichsdramaturgie itself presided over repeated instances of 'nordification', particularly once entire countries and peoples had become unmentionable after the outbreak of war. The English setting of a comedy, for instance, was changed in 1940 to that of a more Nordic (and German-occupied) Norway; and for a performance of Calderón's *La Vida es sueño* in Göring's Prussian State Theatre, 'Poland' became 'Gothland' (the Goths having originally settled in Northern Poland).[12]

Both those textual changes were *volunteered*: respectively, by the play's publisher and the theatre producing it. This is more than just a mere detail: no one in German theatre was actually forced to become racist after January 1933; but *Artbewußtsein* – 'racial awareness' – did constitute a precondition for achieving (or maintaining) access to the stage. The individual had a choice: but it was a stark one between professional withdrawal and political complicity. And here, too, many non-Nazis readily conformed while some among the Nazis' own core constituency unexpectedly bridled.

A particularly striking instance comes not from the realm of theatre itself, but has obvious implications for it. It involved what we would now call airport fiction, namely a serial in which a black character went about vanquishing villains in the lawless world of the United States. Since the villains were white, yet their vanquisher was unambiguously black, the censorship process had spluttered into action. The publisher involved pointed out that he was a 'veteran party member' before launching into a forceful protest.[13] It was 'wholly absurd', he wrote, '... to ban the negro, simply because he is a negro and not unintelligent'. There were, he insisted 'many intelligent negroes', and as for evidence of honourable conduct among them – something also queried by the censors – one had merely to recall the *Askaris* (the native East African regiments) who had gallantly fought alongside the Germans in the Great War. Was there not a slogan, he added, that ran 'Unsere Ehre heißt Treue' (Let loyalty be the source of our honour)?

That was the motto of the SS, and it was being used here by a committed Nazi to plead the cause of 'negroes' in the Third Reich. But there was more. If 'negroes were to be banished from literature', he asked, what was to become of Shakespeare's *Othello*? The reference to *Othello* was a clever move, given Germany's love of the Bard and Hitler's own promise in *Mein Kampf* to restore Shakespeare to his rightful place on the German stage.[14] And as his parting shot, the 'veteran party member' added that in any case the very concept of 'superior' races was alien to true Nazi racial science. Nazism did not claim that 'the Aryan race was essentially better, merely that it was *different*', and that only the mixture of races was problematic. (The negative traits of *both* races supposedly accumulated in the process, while the positive ones evaporated.)[15]

This letter points to something fundamental: the Nazi obsession with race proved in practice a distinctly fraught business. 'Racial theory' was riddled with inconsistencies, allowing contradictory interpretations of what was supposedly hard science. The 'veteran party member' was quite right: Nazi racial theorists had indeed sometimes refrained from claiming that 'Aryans' were superior.[16] (They had been anxious before 1933 to preserve at least a measure of intellectual respectability.) The Nazi leadership had never felt bound by such equivocation, yet they were happy to exploit the ambiguities whenever it suited the Reich's foreign policy needs. The public – or in our case the playwrights and *Intendanten* – were left trying to guess the regime's true intentions. Sympathetic portrayals of other races thus continued to be essayed; but with the single wartime exception of Germany's Japanese allies, they invariably resulted in a ban, often expressed in very harsh tones. A sentimental play about 'a negro boy', for instance, was described by the censor as 'practically a case for the Gestapo'.[17] Yet all-out racism often fared no better: an exercise in nostalgia about Germany's colonial past was likewise proscribed; its 'emphasis on the master–servant approach' was judged to be 'counterproductive'.[18] The Japanese, too, proved an awkward topic. While plays about the 'Yellow Peril' may have been close to the Führer's private thoughts, they were obviously unsuitable in the age of the Berlin–Tokyo axis. Supposed paeans to Germany's Far Eastern allies, meanwhile, frequently met with disapproval from the Japanese themselves. The Propaganda Ministry eventually adopted the precaution of passing all plays touching on Japan to the Japanese embassy for prior approval.[19]

Yet it was not just foreign policy considerations that intervened. Often it was simply the idea of two races living side-by-side that offended. An allegorical play about the downfall of the Vikings is a case in point. Described by the censor as the work of an 'undoubtedly talented author', it was rejected because it contained a scene between a Viking 'Leda and her Black Swan'.[20] The propagandists acknowledged that the author had intended his play as a warning against racial decline; yet they still felt uneasy: the sight of a white woman and a 'negro' embracing on stage would only lead to 'confusion and doubt about the central National Socialist thought on heredity'.

This obsession with the bloodline was to lead to a bizarre and sinister theatrical enterprise involving migrants from Germany's colonies. They had been marooned in Germany by the Great War and, after 1918, were prevented from returning home by Britain, France and Australia, which had divided amongst themselves Germany's African and Pacific empire. The stranded 'colonials' survived tolerably well in Germany. After 1933, however, they attracted the attention of various Nazi organisations, which were greatly exercised by the thought that sexually active 'negroes' were on the loose inside the Reich.[21] Wholesale sterilisation was briefly considered: that fate later befell the children born of German mothers and 'coloured' soldiers in the Rhineland. The 'colonials' escaped the surgeons' knives because of fears that news might leak out and compromise German hopes of renewed colonial expansion. Instead, it was decided to confine the migrants to one place: a practice later also adopted against 'Gypsies', and later still against Jews. The difficulties the migrants encountered in finding employment amid escalating racism furnished the excuse for depriving them of their liberty. The Foreign Office, the *Kolonialpolitische* section of the Nazi party and the Propaganda Ministry jointly agreed to set up a theatrical venture, ostensibly to provide the 'colonials' with employment. Thus was born the *Deutsche Afrika-Schau*: a mixture of theatre, colonial exhibition and travelling circus, which toured the Reich from the spring of 1936 till the summer of 1940. Its involuntary cast of 'colonial negroes' (which included Papuans and Samoans) acted out supposedly characteristic scenes of African life. The paying public encountered happy 'natives' performing before potted palms; the cast encountered grim-faced officials, ever mindful of the 'racial peculiarities of the negroes, especially their powerful urges and their tendency towards sexual excess'.[22] The involvement of the Reich Security Main Office of the SS at subsequent discussions demonstrates that the primary purpose of the *Deutsche Afrika-Schau* was indeed the 'avoidance of interracial sexual congress'.[23]

The *Afrika-Schau* was closed down abruptly in 1940. By then, Nazi racism had reached such a pitch that the mere sight of 'negroes' provoked open hostility from sections of the party and the public alike. In the autumn of 1940, therefore, 'coloured' performers were formally banned from the stage.[24] There was a bloody postscript affecting a leading member of the cast of the *Deutsche Afrika-Schau*: a real-life *Askari* no less, who had fought under the German colours in the First World War and had even sought to enlist again in 1939, perhaps to escape from a life in *tableaux vivants*. He was accused by an informer of having had sexual intercourse with a German woman and was sent to Sachsenhausen concentration camp, where he perished.[25]

What the 'veteran party member' who had treasured the memory of the loyal *Askaris* in 1934 might have made of all that, we do not know; but it underscored his wider point about the threat to *Kultur* and thus to traditional German self-definition. What, he had asked, was to become of Shakespeare's *Othello*? The Third Reich never did find a proper answer to that question. Although there were occasional productions of *Othello*, that traditionally popular play slipped to the margins of the repertoire.[26] Like the parallel cases of *Antony and*

Cleopatra ('Aryan' warrior and racially dubious queen) or indeed *The Merchant of Venice* ('Aryan' Lorenzo and 'Semitic' Jessica), it offended too obviously against National Socialist precepts.[27] The *Merchant*, of course, brings us to the central thrust of Nazi racial policy: the regime's vicious antisemitism.

No one before 1933 could have been in any doubt that a Hitler government would seek to institute antisemitic measures in German theatre: displays of Judeophobia in the playhouse had, after all, become alarmingly common by the early thirties. One example may suffice: in Alfred Neumann's play *Haus Danieli* the Jewish protagonist responded to insults from an army officer by striking the man. The scene provoked a nightly uproar in the auditorium when the play was showing in Berlin, Bochum and Stuttgart in 1930.[28] There was an unmistakable air of menace in the dying days of the republic. Yet even so, contemporaries can perhaps be forgiven for underestimating the gravity of what was to follow. Nazi cultural endeavours had seemed too farcical to seem threatening. Take the self-styled National Theatre Community briefly active in Leipzig in 1925. It had offered, in the words of its organiser, a repertoire free from 'Judeo-Communist anal art'.[29] The local Nazis had been 'attending nightly in uniform, singing in the intervals the [party's] ... battle songs'. Yet for all the lusty singing, the effort had foundered amid a lack of audiences and 'scurrilous reviews in the entire Leipzig press'. Similar ventures elsewhere were similarly short and inglorious.[30] The party's attempts to shape repertoire and ensemble policy via its elected representatives and the various funding committees were a more serious matter.[31] Yet even on that front, the Nazis only encountered partial successes. Nazi regional power in Thuringia had then given a first concrete indication of what a Hitler government might entail: Hans Severus Ziegler's notorious 1930 edict 'Against Negro Culture' had driven most exponents of modernism from Thuringia.[32] Yet the rapid collapse of the Thuringian coalition seemed to suggest, once again, that it would be possible to ride out any Nazi storm.

The Thuringian interlude was revealing in another respect, however: Ziegler's readiness to subsume the Jews under the heading of 'negroes' proved that more was involved here than conventional antisemitism. Many among the German right had in effect created a kind of 'other', which was conceived along racial lines, albeit fairly indistinct ones. We get a glimpse of this mental process from the chief censor Rainer Schlösser himself. In July 1935, only weeks before the promulgation of the Nuremberg laws, Schlösser impatiently dismissed rumours of Jewish ancestry in the author of a popular rural drama. 'The author in question', Schlösser observed, 'has consistently written patriotic plays and it seems wayward to suspect him of being Jewish.'[33] This kind of reasoning would eventually get Schlösser into trouble with Goebbels: in 1938 Schlösser lost his (second) job as head of the Reich Theatre Chamber for having proved insufficiently zealous about 'de-Jewification'.

Yet racial foot-dragging was not limited to Schlösser: it was very common in the early stages of Nazi rule. There was also the related phenomenon of individuals failing to see why Jewishness should automatically be considered a problem. A Nazi *Intendant*, for instance, proposed to the Propaganda Ministry in 1934 the continued employment of a Jewish actress.[34] The Head of the Reich Chamber of Literature spoke out publicly, a year later, in favour of (anti-modern) Jewish writers – and was forced to step down as a result.[35] In the (still Czech-ruled) Sudetenland, local Nazis actually supported a Jewish *Intendant* in his efforts to take over the local theatre at Brüx in 1935: the man's solidly pan-German (and anti-Czech) credentials outweighed his Jewishness.[36] In Reichenberg, the capital of the Sudetenland, pan-Germans continued to patronise the local theatre, even though it was run by a prominent Jewish *Intendant* who had fled SA-terror inside Germany four years earlier. (The local German consul professed himself powerless to do anything about it.)[37]

A local party section in Saxony, meanwhile, had somehow chosen a play by a Jewish author for their next amateur dramatic effort: a full three years into Nazi rule.[38] When those 'party comrades' were challenged about their choice, they made it clear that they could not understand what all the fuss was about: the play was surely quite harmless. Another party functionary approached Schlösser with a suggestion about Shakespeare's *Midsummer Night's Dream*, or rather about Mendelssohn's incidental music for that play. Should one not declare publicly that Mendelssohn's Jewishness was hardly the most pressing concern in 1937 and enjoy once again that sublime music? That suggestion came from the editorial office of the SS-newspaper *Das Schwarze Korps*, probably the most doctrinaire Nazi publication in the entire Reich.[39]

The obverse of this phenomenon was a readiness to detect a Jewish aspect in things one considered disagreeable. Again, one might start in the Reichsdramaturg's office. A manuscript of a play which the censors disliked intensely led them to wonder whether the author was entirely Aryan. Was his gawky handwriting not in some way suggestive? These are 'practically Hebrew characters!' someone scribbled on the margin of the file.[40]

Such thinking – if thinking is quite the word – was not limited to the censors. Take an entirely unconnected case: that of a Berlin schoolmaster teaching German literature. It dates from 1930: well before the advent of the Third Reich. The man in question was greatly exercised by the fact that many of his pupils seemed to prefer modern plays to his beloved German classics. Since a large number of his charges were Jewish, he began to wonder whether the two things might be connected. Then, one day, a particularly precocious young man had the temerity to make fun of Hebbel's ponderous drama *Die Nibelungen*. That boy happened to be Jewish, and now the matter seemed conclusive: 'older German literature', the schoolmaster decided, 'evidently speaks more to people of our blood than to Israelite spirits'.[41]

That schoolmaster was no Nazi: indeed, after he had imprudently published his ruminations in a pedagogical journal, he was troubled by the thought that the Nazis might seek to exploit his contribution. Yet the fact remains that this essentially upright man had been ready to point to race when his treasured German *Kultur* seemed under attack. That put him in uncomfortable proximity to fanatical Nazis like the SS-playwright and *Dramaturg* Walter Best, who spoke of an 'assault on German culture' that had been mounted by the Jews 'with satanic cunning ... ever since the Great War'.[42]

Many Germans – perhaps most Germans even – were less antisemitic than is now often assumed. They were closer to that Berlin schoolmaster than to the SS-dramatist. Yet they lacked the wisdom, the foresight and the moral courage to stand up to their more anti-semitic countrymen while it would still have been possible to do so. For just as the Propaganda Ministry files preserve surprisingly undog-matic views about the Jews, they also contain plenty of cases of hard-ened Judeophobia, of ugly opportunism and simple spite in antisemitic guise. There were people offering plays in the hope, they claimed, of 'enlightening the public' about the Jewish Question.[43] There were anonymous letter writers anxious to alert the authorities that the names they had just seen in a theatre programme were surely Jewish.[44] There were those who saw a chance to turn the tables on their erstwhile social 'betters'. A maidservant, for instance, avenged herself on a man who, she recalled, had been eating 'venison and chocolate cake' while she toiled: that man, she informed her local Gauleiter, was 'not entirely Aryan' yet his works were still being performed; could the 'dear Gauleiter' look into the case?[45] A semi-literate cloakroom attendant at Berlin's Schiller Theatre wrote to Goebbels in a similar vein. Her haughty *Intendant* had cut the pay of all part-time staff. Was the minister aware that the man's wife was actually Jewish? Moreover, 'the Jewess ... had bossed the cloakroom women about and had told them they were too slow'. That sort of thing needed 'sorting out!'[46]

Not all the antisemitic malice was even directed against Jews themselves. There were attempts to harm Aryan competitors by hint-ing at a Jewish background: X 'brazenly shares a household with the family of a Jew who has escaped [abroad],' as someone wrote to their local Gauleiter; *Intendant* Y had systematically favoured Jews in Weimar days, as someone else whispered to the Propaganda Ministry. Nastier still were insinuations about non-Aryan ancestry: did the accent of Z not sometimes sound a little Yiddish?[47] Or consider the letter from a Nazi-appointed *Intendant* to the Propaganda Ministry. He professed himself 'mildly surprised' to have encountered the name of a former colleague who 'had generally been known to be half-Jewish'. 'Without of course wishing to harm ... [him]', the letter continued, 'I thought I should confidentially draw your attention to the matter.' The missive ended on a note of studied disingenuousness: 'I suppose it is possible that he has since managed to prove his Aryan ancestry.'[48] That letter was being written at the height of the deportations to Auschwitz.

Consider, finally, the case of an elderly working-class woman who had submitted a play to Goebbels and was now anxious to hear from the ministry. Could they please confirm receipt of the manuscript? The problem, she explained, was that correspondence kept going missing. If the ministry did not reply, she would be forced to conclude that her play had been 'intercepted by Jewish agents'.[49] Even mental illness can reveal something about the society in which it occurs.

Decades on, it is difficult to form a clear picture of that society and of the theatre in which it operated. The closer one examines the evidence the more contradictory it seems to get: generosity rubs shoulders with spite, selflessness with opportunism, courage with cowardice, hardened Judeophobia with a casual antisemitism that seemed to owe more to tactics than belief. Sometimes the contradictions occurred in the same individual even. Take the actor Heinrich George, who played in several Nazi propaganda films, including the notorious *Jud Süß*. Yet as *Intendant*, he shielded Jewish colleagues at his Berlin theatre all through the Nazi years and in one remarkable case managed to persuade Hitler at the height of the deportations to award full Aryan status to a Jewish actor. Consider also George's great rival Werner Krauß, who actually starred in *Jud Süß* and gave a notoriously nasty interpretation of Shylock when the Third Reich rediscovered *The Merchant of Venice* late in the war. Yet the same man had over several crucial days escorted his (half-Jewish) friend Carl Zuckmayer around Berlin to protect him from misadventure; and when it became obvious that Zuckmayer was indeed in imminent danger of arrest by the Gestapo, Krauß insisted on accompanying him by night train to safety in Prague. (Krauß then returned on the day train to appear in *Hamlet* in Göring's theatre that evening, as though nothing had happened.)[50] It is not easy to make sense of such conduct.

Our knowledge of what came after further complicates matters. *We* know that some of the stage doors and auditorium exits in German theatre ultimately led to Auschwitz. Contemporaries did not have our benefit of hindsight. To say this is not to excuse or trivialise antisemitic sentiment but to remind ourselves that there were different degrees of culpability. The various informers were certainly complicit in the regime's crimes. But what of people like Heinrich George? What of the Berlin schoolmaster with a bee in his bonnet about the classics and Jewish boys? Can we really implicate him in the fate of those boys a decade or so later? And if we do judge him culpable, what about Brecht spouting nonsense about 'negroes' in the Rhineland? Both kinds of prejudice had fearful consequences. Neither Brecht nor the schoolmaster had sought to sponsor violence; neither man supported Nazi policies; yet the fact remains that both men, along with a great many others, had at one point pitched their tent on the slippery slope towards the Nazi racial state.

Germany's descent down that slope after January 1933 may seem to us shamefully swift. To the Nazis, it was agonisingly slow. Goebbels recorded his frustration about delays in 'de-Jewification' in more than a dozen diary entries throughout the second half of the 'thirties.[51] Goebbels' right-hand man in 'de-Jewification' also hinted at Nazi frustration in a speech after Kristallnacht. 'Let us not delude ourselves about the fact,' Hinkel began, 'that the German people were [previously] not nearly as united in their response to the Jewish Question as they are today.'[52] Whether Hinkel actually believed that the Germans had become 'united' in their antisemitism is hard to say. His assertion is contradicted by the Propaganda Ministry's own files. Take the covering letter of an antisemitic play submitted to Goebbels at exactly this time. The letter expressed alarm about public opinion in the aftermath of the Kristallnacht pogrom: the correspondent had been 'taken aback by the extent to which people publicly were expressing sympathy with the Jews, "Those poor Jews" ... "so many innocent Jews"', etc.[53] And Hinkel himself admitted in his speech that even among the antisemites Nazi policies had not met with universal support. He spoke of 'bread-and-butter antisemites' (Brötchenantisemiten), who were solely interested in getting rid of undesired competitors and lacked any real racial awareness; and Hinkel was even more contemptuous of those who exempted baptised Jews from their antisemitism.[54] The antisemitic purges were possible only because they were driven by fully committed sections of the Nazi party prepared to act in advance of public opinion.[55]

In March and April 1933 stormtroopers unleashed a campaign of terror, directed amongst other things on many state theatres. Pressure was also exerted via the newly nazified agencies of state. At Darmstadt, for instance, the police closed down the local theatre, supposedly to maintain law and order in the face of allegedly widespread hostility to the theatre's Jewish *Intendant*.[56] The nazification of town halls and regional diets then added pressure at the level of the theatres' funding bodies. Within a few weeks seventy-five *Intendanten* in publicly funded playhouses across Germany had been removed or had resigned, as against forty-seven who remained in office.[57] Although there were attempts by Göring to establish some degree of control over the process, the SA operated largely unchecked with their trademark brutality. Many of their victims were assaulted and physically ejected from their own theatres. Not all the individuals targeted were Jewish, but no Jewish *Intendant* was unaffected.

These blatantly criminal acts were given an air of pseudo-legality by the state of emergency declared after the Reichstag Fire, which had vested in the SA police powers. The contractual aspects of the purge relied on the so-called Law for the Restoration of the Civil Service of April 1933, which targeted (left-wing) Weimar appointments. A crucial clause also stipulated that any Jews appointed after the First World War were to be sacked, on the grounds that the republic had supposedly given Jews preferential treatment over patriotic Germans.

In the playhouse, the near collapse of the theatre sector at the end of the Weimar era made things especially easy for the Nazis: it allowed them to present their blatantly political purge as an emergency intervention to rescue German theatre from financial, moral and artistic bankruptcy.[58] Antisemitism – an end in itself for large sections of the Nazi party – was firmly presented to the public as a means to an end. Take Wanderschek's influential 1938 history of Nazi theatre. 'The complete elimination of Jewry from the cultural life of the *Volk*,' it reads, 'guaranteed that the stage would once more become "a moral institution", as Schiller had envisaged it.'[59] That such words seemed credible to contemporaries owed much to earlier republican delight in provoking audiences. A huge financial scandal on the eve of the Third Reich involving the Jewish owners of a string of

Berlin theatres provided further ammunition for the Nazis. It allowed Goebbels to declare that Jews had proved themselves 'unfit to be entrusted with German cultural assets'.[60]

The final circumstance that aided the Nazis was the very scale of Jewish success in the theatre. Since Jews had been largely excluded from the old court theatre system in the days of the monarchy, they had created their own venues, which soon eclipsed most court theatres in cultural *cachet*. Max Reinhardt built an entire theatrical empire for himself, combining the roles of director with that of owner and impresario. Similar ventures on a smaller scale existed in many of the larger provincial cities.[61] Commercial theatre catering for more 'lowbrow' tastes was likewise substantially associated with Jewish ventures. The revolution of 1918 then threw open to Jewish talent the former court theatres. Leopold Jeßner had begun his career in his brother's theatre in Königsberg; the republic offered him the Kaiser's theatre. Jeßner's appointment, as was pointed out with only very slight exaggeration, meant that *all* major Berlin theatres were now run by Jews. (Jews, as the antisemites liked to emphasise, made up about 7 per cent of the population). 'Our stage had ceased to belong to us', as the Nazis observed retrospectively.[62] There had been an alien invasion of the German stage, requiring nothing less than its 're-conquest for the nation'.[63]

Hans Severus Ziegler explained that such Jewish dominance had not been an accident. 'The Jewish author', he wrote, 'had been propagated by the Jewish publisher, was recommended to the Jewish *Dramaturg* by a Jewish theatre agency, was then staged by a Jewish director to be praised in the Jewish-owned press'.[64] Such *völkisch* conspiracy theories contained a kernel of truth sufficiently large to win them credibility. It was, for instance, a verifiable fact that almost all leading German and Austrian theatre critics before the Nazi Seizure of Power had been Jewish, and it was true also that many among them had been combative champions of modernism.[65]

While it is problematic to generalise, there is some evidence to suggest that at first hostility was indeed often directed against Jewish *modernists* rather than against Jews *per se*. The abrasive modernist critic Alfred Kerr had to flee within weeks of the Nazi Seizure of

Power; his more traditionally minded and more amiable colleague Julius Bab was able to stay on for several years, albeit in ever more precarious circumstances. Jeßner had to flee at once, while the Nazis are rumoured to have offered Reinhardt 'Aryan' status.[66] Left-wing Jewish dramatists like Ernst Toller or Erich Mühsam were likewise in immediate danger, while the more conservative Carl Zuckmayer was actively courted by parts of the right, his ancestry notwithstanding. As late as October 1935 – *after* the Nuremberg laws – a member of Hitler's inner circle sought to put forward Zuckmayer's name as Germany's contribution for an anthology of contemporary international drama.[67] 'Half-Jewish', noted the Reichsdramaturg in the margin of that memo. And while Goebbels' ministry did indeed seek to remove even 'half-Jews', conservative or otherwise, it is at least open to question whether the public supported that agenda. Certainly, the theatregoers in Saladin Schmitt's thoroughly conservative Bochum playhouse fêted their own half-Jewish leading man. At Horst Caspar's farewell performance in 1939, he received no fewer than 108 curtain calls.[68]

Some 'half-Jews' – Caspar included – were able to continue professionally with Goebbels' express permission. Goebbels considered each case personally, usually in consultation with the Gauleiter of the actor's home region.[69] On at least one occasion, in May 1939, Goebbels deferred judgement to Hitler. War was imminent, yet the head of state found time to peruse the *curricula vitae* of twenty-one actors. Hitler was in generous mood and granted permits even to one half-Jewish actor married to a Jewish wife – normally a hopeless case.[70]

Goebbels, in fact, specifically targeted 'racially mixed' marriages. Actors with Jewish spouses came under intense pressure to seek a divorce; many eventually succumbed to such pressure. The celebrated actor Joachim Gottschalk did not: he opted for suicide, along with his wife, the actress Meta Gottschalk, and their young son. Gottschalk had been harassed for years and was finally banned from the stage in May 1941 in an effort to starve him into submission. The harassment did not even end at death. As Gauleiter of Berlin, Goebbels instructed all the city's cemeteries to deny the Gottschalks burial: he feared a silent protest against the regime at the graveside.

The family were eventually buried in the country outside Berlin; yet a number of Gottschalk's former colleagues did make their way to the funeral, even though Goebbels had threatened reprisals against anyone attending.

The fate of most 'full' Jews in German theatre had been sealed much earlier. The initial purge of the *Intendanten* in the spring of 1933 had deprived German Jews of any realistic chances of employment in publicly owned theatres. The purge had increased the number of antisemites, and those few *Intendanten* who had survived in post were either antisemitic too or had, like the head of the Düsseldorf theatre, been given a Nazi deputy to spy on them. Everybody, moreover, was on probation. The man who supervised the process in Prussia made that plain enough. Of the heads of public playhouses *after the purge* only one-third, Hinkel thought, 'deserve our support' because they had truly 'embraced' Nazism; another third 'can remain *for the time being*, but must be kept under strict observation' until they can be replaced by 'fresh blood of truly National Socialist character'; the final third 'have to be speedily removed' and, if necessary, be encouraged to emigrate.[71]

Hinkel was talking of 'Aryans'. In such conditions the prospects for Jews were all but hopeless. The great actress Agnes Straub used her own fortune to found a private theatre with the sole purpose of giving her Austro-Jewish husband, Leo Reuß, the opportunity to perform. When they arrived in the port of Stettin in 1935 a Nazi mob greeted them with the chant of 'Jews out'.[72]

The Jewish actor Harry Buckwitz was more successful than most in prolonging his career, aided by the fact that no one knew about his ancestry. Whenever the Reich Theatre Chamber sent him a demand to prove his Aryan credentials, he sought employment in a new theatre and he continued the process as soon as officialdom had started to catch up with him again. He eventually decided things were getting too perilous and escaped to Tanganyika, ostensibly on travel.[73] The British authorities had granted him a visa precisely because they thought he was *Aryan* and thus unlikely to stay. Buckwitz had thus arrived in the very land which some in the cast of the *Deutsche Afrika-Schau* had vainly sought to regain.

In November 1935 Goebbels crowed that there was now 'no Jew active in the cultural life of our people'.[74] That was not strictly speaking true: over 300 Jewish performers still clung on precariously at that time.[75] Yet, as far as the ordinary theatregoer was concerned, the Jews had effectively vanished from sight by late 1935. The process was repeated each time the Third Reich expanded, and each time more violently than before: Austro-Jewish theatre practitioners were no longer purged or sacked in 1938: they were often arrested in the playhouses themselves and could escape only with luck and support from abroad.[76] Any Jewish actors or directors overtaken by the advancing German armies thereafter were almost without exception doomed.

The German public received some (highly tendentious) information about what had happened to the vanished Jews. They were told that theatres had been set up in the Reich by the Jewish *Kulturbund* for the sole use of Jewish audiences.[77] Like other racists before or since, the Nazis were at times keen to suggest that their motto was 'separate but equal'. Hans Hinkel, who supervised the *Kulturbund*'s operations, explained that just as German theatres produced no Jewish plays, the new Jewish theatres were not allowed to perform German plays. What could be fairer than that?[78] The public were never told about the desperate circumstances of the *Kulturbund*, of the penury and depression resulting from curtailed careers, sudden isolation in one's native land, or the loneliness of emigration. They were later also told nothing about the final appearances of those Jewish actors who had failed to make it to safety: some of them performed until their strength gave out for their fellow inmates inside the concentration camps.[79]

The persecution of the Jews extended even beyond the Reich's borders. Lavish subsidies channelled through straw-men allowed the Propaganda Ministry to gain influence on the cash-strapped theatres of the ethnic Germans in Czechoslovakia and the Baltic states.[80] Nazi funds came with strings: the theatres involved had to submit to Propaganda Ministry control. To avoid detection, the correspondence between Berlin and the theatres abroad was maintained via couriers. To the same end, the ministry usually permitted a token Jewish actor per theatre (and a token Jewish play or operetta per season), so as to preserve cover. Otherwise, it insisted on rigorous 'de-Jewification'. Similar Nazi attempts in Austria foundered due to the greater vigilance there after the failed Nazi coup.[81] Even Switzerland did not escape Berlin's attention: the Reichsdramaturgie banned all contacts with the Zürich Schauspielhaus at one point because there were 'still too many Jews in that *ensemble*'.[82]

'De-Jewification' also targeted playwrights. If Schlösser had initially been far from zealous on that front, this changed under pressure from the Rosenberg Office, which missed no opportunity to pounce on any oversight by the Propaganda Ministry.[83] It was that very element of competition between rival agencies that led to the rapid radicalisation of Nazi policies in the theatre and elsewhere. The escalation increased the stakes still further: what had been an internal German affair became an international one. Many Jewish playwrights had intially fled to Austria, which acted as a major thorn in the Reich's side in the early years of Nazi rule. Under new *noms de plume* some of these exiled playwrights were able to fool the Propaganda Ministry into granting stage permits for their new plays.[84] Each time Berlin established their true identities, the refugees simply assumed a new name. The Propaganda Ministry eventually decided to reverse the onus of proof: in February 1936 it banned all plays published in Austria from performance in the Reich unless the authors were prepared to submit proof of their Aryan ancestry.[85] With this problem solved, the Propaganda Ministry could turn to plays in translation, where it relied heavily on assistance by foreign antisemites: the ever-helpful Céline, for instance, covertly provided information via the German embassy in Paris.[86] In other cases such help was unavailable: Sheridan's *School for Scandal*, for instance, was held up because 'it had not been possible to prove conclusively [his] Aryan ancestry'.[87]

While considerable energies were thus being expanded off-stage, overt Judeophobia was surprisingly absent from the stage itself. Two references in the Reichsdramaturgie files suggest that this was probably no accident. They date from either side of Kristallnacht in late 1938 and early 1939. Tellingly, both references are in the conditional rather than the indicative: 'If Jewish characters are to be put on stage', reads one; the other reads: 'if there really is to be antisemitic propaganda on stage, which I personally would consider a mistake'.[88] That second reference also speaks of 'the awkwardness of German actors having to imagine their way into Jewish characters'. Since 'imagining one's way into a character' is normally considered to be part of an actor's job, the phrase probably disguised more fundamental worries.

Such worries were spelt out in the actors' journal *Die Bühne* by Elisabeth Frenzel, the wife of one of Schlösser's collaborators in the Reichsdramaturgie. Her article may well reflect official thinking.[89] Playing Jews, she observed, was 'a task requiring ... a high degree of ideological surefootedness'. There were twin dangers for the propagandists. One was that Jewish characters would turn into mere stage villains, thus reducing the propaganda impact. That worry was reflected in the censors' advice to playwrights: 'The Jew and his plotting should only provide the background'.[90] Frenzel in her article made a similar point: 'the actor should not engage in incitement but illustrate and explain our dislike [of the Jews]'.

The second worry for the propagandists was that actors might somehow make Jewish characters appealing. That danger Frenzel could not very well acknowledge; but presumably that is what she meant by 'ideological surefootedness'. The danger was not entirely imaginary. The screen actor and matinée idol Ferdinard Marian would go on to prove the point. In *Jud Süß* he played a Jewish villain who ravished an innocent German maiden. The response to the film was unexpected: Marian received bucketfuls of fan mail from women viewers evidently not averse to sharing the heroine's fate. None of his other screen roles had elicited a comparable echo.

The plays received by the Reichsdramaturgie likewise prove that not every one in the Reich was 'ideologically surefooted'. A play about Bismarck quoted the chancellor as saying, 'I have never been an antisemite.'[91] That was one detail about Bismarck which the Third Reich preferred to forget. A comedy about garrison life contained a scene where the village idiot, asked about his 'religion', replied, 'I'm an antisemite, Sir.'[92] The censors were not amused. They were also grimly disapproving of a comedy which 'poked fun in outrageous fashion' at a schoolmaster and his interest in racial theory.[93] Or take a play entitled *Blood: A Germanic Tragedy*, which contained the line, 'After all, aren't Semites people like you and I?'[94] Such examples of unorthodox thinking – 'courage or chutzpah?', wondered the censors – may not have been very numerous but it is remarkable that they should have occurred at all in material that was being submitted to the Propaganda Ministry no less.

Add to that a substantial number of plays which were antisemitic but nonetheless problematic for the regime. A comedy satirising the readiness of the public to adopt (or drop) antisemitic attitudes depending on who they were talking to may have been designed by its author to expose hypocrisy: yet it threatened to expose much more than that and was banned.[95] Then there were the instances of the wrong kind of antisemitism. A comedy about a 'Jewish smuggler', for instance, ended with the humbled Jew having to consent to the marriage of his son with a German girl: an ending not unlike that of *The Merchant of Venice*, in other words, and banned by irate Nazi officials for the same reasons.[96]

The most frequent problem for the ministry, however, was that plays with Jewish characters were not antisemitic enough. This was most obviously the case of the German and Austrian classics. Lessing's plea for tolerance in *Nathan* vanished from the repertoire early on; Grillparzer's *Jewess of Toledo* – like *The Merchant of Venice* a more ambiguous affair – eventually followed suit. There was, the censor explained, 'altogether too much humanity' in Grillparzer's Jews.[97] Similar objections occurred in modern plays. 'There is still far too much of the positive about the Jew'; 'the figure of the half-Jew is not sufficiently Jewish-negative'; 'increase the antipathy towards the Jew'; etc.[98] Given these various pitfalls, it is scarcely surprising that Jewish stage characters remained conspicuous by their absence. Only the ever-surefooted E. W. Möller created in *Rothschild's Victory at Waterloo* and *The Fall of Carthage* plays that were just right in their antisemitism.[99]

Yet here too, there is an intriguing postscript. It comes in the shape of a letter to Möller by a member of the public urgently seeking help.[100] The problem was that the letter writer was being harassed by an SA-thug ever since he had innocently praised Möller's *Rothschild*.

The dim-witted SA-man had somehow concluded from the title – *Rothschild's Victory* – that a Jewish success was being celebrated in the play and had accused his interlocutor of being in cahoots with the Jews. An attempt to end that misapprehension had only made things worse. The synopsis of Möller's play (a shady 'Jewish' stock market manoeuvre resulting in mass Aryan poverty) had only convinced the SA-man that the play was crypto-Communist into the bargain. If *Rothschild* thus had unexpected consequences for members of the public, *The Fall of Carthage* was to affect the author himself. The play's vivid allusions to the Weimar republic (for Carthage read Weimar) had brought the wrath of the party's Rosenberg section on Möller: the play actually marked the beginning of the end for Möller, the dramatist.

Given the shortage of suitable antisemitic plays in the German canon, Schlösser authorised performances of Marlowe's *Jew of Malta*, even though Germany was at war with Britain at the time.[101] Marlowe's 'pronounced antisemitism' merited a permit, Schlösser explained. He also tried again with *The Merchant of Venice*. As someone who knew his Shakespeare, the Reichsdramaturg remembered the lines by Launcelot that might conceivably be taken to imply that Jessica was not actually Shylock's child.[102] With the help of judicious cuts and one blatant alteration to the text that tentative suggestion was turned into fact; and once Jessica was revealed to have been Aryan after all, there was no obstacle to a Nazi happy end of Aryan lovers united (and the Jew rendered destitute).[103] After successful trial runs 'on several smaller provincial stages', Schlösser felt able to recommend to Goebbels that the ban on the *Merchant* be lifted.[104] Intriguingly, however, the ministry had considerable difficulties in getting a major theatre to stage the Aryanised version. Eventually the ministry managed to twist the arm of Lothar Müthel, whom we first encountered in the original cast of *Schlageter*. More than three years after Schlösser had first began his efforts, *The Merchant* was produced at Müthel's wartime fiefdom, the Vienna Burgtheater. It remained the only truly high-profile *Merchant* in all the years of Nazi rule.[105]

Antisemitism was not the only aspect of Nazi racial policy to prove problematic on stage. In 1941 the Propaganda Ministry sought guidance about 'Gypsies' from the Party Office for Racial Policy. 'Gypsies', the propagandists explained, remained popular with play-wrights and librettists of operettas. The response was forthright: there should be no attempts 'to endow these types yet again on stage with the aura of a harmless and noble race' at a time when 'the party, the state and the police are in action against them'.[106] (The 'Gypsies' were, like the Jews, destined for extermination and had in fact been confined to camps even earlier than the Jews.) Yet here, too, unorthodox thought occurred in the most unlikely quarters. An 'Old Fighter' – a member of the Nazi party since its Munich beginnings, in other words – embarrassed the censors by drawing 'a parallel between the Ancient Teutons and the Gypsies' (since both had been 'nomadic'). That, the censor observed, was a 'Jewish argument'.[107] The propagandists agonised over a suitable turn of phrase to break the news to one of the Führer's oldest and most loyal followers.

There was no such problem with the Nazis' anti-homosexual animus, which was the most widely shared of their murderous obsessions. The complicity here did not end in 1945, and it did not stop at Germany's borders: no detailed research exists in any language on the persecution of gay theatre practitioners, even though the theatrical profession has traditionally contained a disproportionately high percentage of homosexuals. The victims remain largely invisible; yet the most cursory glance at the files reveals instances of actors being arrested, of extensive investigations to root out homosexuality in the theatre, or of plays being banned because of their authors' sexuality.[108]

The Nazi obsession with procreation led to problems of a different kind: of the steady trickle of plays on the topic of heredity, and the need to produce the right kind of offspring in abundant numbers, all but a handful were banned. They threatened to shock the public with their radicalism, or they carried the risk of turning racial policy into the stuff of smutty jokes.[109] The playwrights affected by such bans often enlisted advocates in the party hierarchy to force Goebbels' ministry into granting permits. The number of performances of the most successful play of the genre – *The Stream of Heredity* – may have run into four figures: but the play remained confined to touring companies and small provincial theatres.[110] Such plays conspicuously failed to make it onto the main stages of the Reich.

The same was true of another sub-species of racial drama: in June 1944 the Reichsdramaturg noted 'an alarming rise in the number of plays about the theme of infertile women and a man's right to turn to fertile ones'.[111] Many of these plays were transparent male fantasies about younger women or about polygamy in all but name. Polygamous ambitions in the party may seem a familiar point, since several leading Nazis quietly practised what they preached, but the Reichsdramaturgie files reveal a less well-known phenomenon that shook the censors. In the later stages of the war, when it was becoming clear that almost an entire generation of German men had perished, the ministry received a play advocating *legally sanctioned* polygamy: it was by a *woman* author who had spoken about the issue to women of her acquaintance – some widowed, some unmarried, some who had lost their fiancé. These women evidently despaired of ever having a man to themselves again, and were now ready – or thought they were ready – to share one of the surviving men. Enclosed with the play (which does not survive) came a detailed breakdown of figures.[112] Out of 264 women interviewed by the author, 77 insisted on monogamy (mostly, she added, 'young girls'); 89 said they would be content to ignore a husband's infidelity if that was the price of marriage; 31 said they would devote themselves to a career instead; 54 women advocated polygamy (but insisted on being the 'main wife'); 13 were prepared to settle even for the status of an 'auxiliary wife'.

A few weeks after that play about polygamy had reached the Propaganda Ministry, the theatres were closed and the head of German theatre was reduced to censoring books. Schlösser applied himself to his new task and was soon incensed to discover that someone had tried to smuggle past him an illustrated volume containing a photo of men of six different races. The caption read: 'They may be white, yellow, red, black or brown – apart from the colour of their skin there is less distinguishing them than you might imagine.'[113] A quarter of a century earlier, some German women in the Rhineland had reached the same conclusion and, amid great scandal, had permitted embraces by black men. They were prepared to risk social ostracism in part, one imagines, because there were not enough husbands or even just lovers to go round after the great slaughter in the trenches and on the Russian plain. A generation and another world war later, monogamy itself seemed unsustainable to some despairing women. The very values upon which Western culture had been built and which had been celebrated not least on the German stage – monogamous marriage, the sanctity of laws, and above all respect of human life – had been systematically undermined by Nazi rule. Plays about polygamy proved that as much as the sight of a celebrated actor dead on a kitchen floor beside his family from whom he would not be parted; 'colonial negroes' compelled to turn their lives into a grotesque public spectacle were likewise an indictment of the Nazi regime, as were the emaciated players performing in the very jaws of hell. Theatre, in Schiller's famous phrase, was a 'moral institution': in the Third Reich it reflected all too accurately Germany's moral collapse.

6 The faith of our forefathers: theatre and the Nazi assault on Christianity

The name Heinrich Himmler is not one that readily springs to mind in the context of German theatre. Unlike other leading Nazis, the Reichsführer SS never really fancied himself as a major patron of the arts. Indeed some theatre practitioners who had donned SS-uniforms wondered at times whether they had not backed the wrong horse. 'Attention is constantly being lavished on the Hitler Youth dramatists,' observed a testy Friedrich Bethge in 1941.[1] It was time, he thought, someone also began to champion 'dramatists belonging to the SS'.

Yet Himmler was not completely inactive: he was associated with two vast open-air theatricals in the far north-west of Germany. One, created by the SS itself at Verden near Bremen, re-enacted the historic defeat of the Saxons by Charlemagne. The other venture which Himmler adopted was to achieve an even greater echo. *De Stedinge* had been commissioned in 1934 by the Gauleiter of Oldenburg to commemorate a local anniversary in the region.[2] The play was performed in a Low German patois rooted in fenland soil and as prized by some Nazis as it was impenetrable to the majority of Germans.[3] Written by a competent Low German playwright (who also created one of Nazi theatre's few really successful comedies), *De Stedinge* was at first little more than one of the many *Heimatspiele* glorifying the region of their setting that had long been a feature of rural culture in Germany. It would probably have remained a local affair, had it not been for Goebbels' perennial rival Alfred Rosenberg – and indeed for Himmler. Rosenberg felt outflanked by the Propaganda Ministry in 1934 and was seeking a platform to project his own cultural ambitions: *De Stedinge* offered one.[4] The play, as Rosenberg realised, might be developed as an artistic and ideological alternative to the Propaganda Ministry's *Thingspiel*, with which it shared enough common features to invite comparison.[5] The opening of the 1935 season – the first under Rosenberg's aegis – was duly scheduled to clash with the inauguration of Goebbels' Heidelberg arena.

Like the *Thing*, *De Stedinge* sought to marry landscape and art, to combine amateur players with professional actors, and to inspire in the audience a sense of community. Like the *Thingspiel*, moreover, it was *Erlebnistheater* on a grand scale, with a cast of 650 and audiences ranging between 15,000 and 40,000 spectators per performance. Over the course of a summer the organisers thus hoped to attract a minimum of 150,000–200,000 spectators.[6] *De Stedinge* thus had the same in-built problems from which the *Thingspiel* suffered: the sheer size of the operation was difficult to sustain. By 1936 the organisers were planning to lay on special trains to ensure a steady supply of viewers. Peasants speaking Low German, however, were not an inexhaustible commodity, and one could not bank on the same people attending year after year (a little blood-and-soil drama tended to go a long way). Himmler's interest was thus a life-line for *De Stedinge*: SS-men made up a substantial proportion of the play's audience.

That constituted one difference between *De Stedinge* and the *Thing*, which had been linked to the SA. There were other obvious differences: the *Thingspiel* sought to move audiences by allowing them to re-experience their own lives; *De Stedinge* hoped to move them by conjuring the (supposed) voices of their ancestors. The *Thing* was all national rebirth, *De Stedinge* mystic murmuring and the Voice of Blood. The play, its ideological proponents explained, was not 'a mere interpretation of an historical event but history itself'.[7] That claim was underlined by the staging. Whereas the *Thing* favoured stylised representation, *De Stedinge* plumped for thumping realism: an entire medieval village was constructed to provide an authentic backdrop, so to speak, for the play. And before those thatched cottages there assembled annually a flaxen-haired multitude to be put to death by the men of the cruel Bishop of Bremen. For that was perhaps the most important feature distinguishing *De Stedinge* from the *Thing*: while the *Thingspiel* had sought to fuse nationalism and Christianity, the Northern theatrical was aggressively anti-Christian.

That was precisely what had attracted first Rosenberg's and then Himmler's interest. The SS-play at Verden was likewise evidence of Himmler's anti-Christian animus, extolling as it did the pagan Saxons rather than the Christian Franks. Himmler's name, moreover, also cropped up regularly whenever a piece of crude anti-Christian (and more specifically anti-Catholic) propaganda was staged in a conventional playhouse. Theatre in the early years of the Third Reich thus offered two very different faces to the public: there were evocations of national harmony in the *Thing* arenas and, under the aegis of Rosenberg and Himmler, a snarling attack on the traditional religious beliefs of most Germans.

That contradiction was not wholly surprising: the relationship between the Nazis and the Christian churches had been complicated all along. There was little doubt that Nazism was an irreligious ideology, and that its leaders were atheists (even though the party studiously avoided the use of the term 'atheist', to distinguish themselves from the 'godless' Marxists). Indeed the political left – both Communist and Social Democrat – was even more outspokenly atheist than the Nazis: Christian Germans thus found themselves between a rock and a hard place in the early 1930s.

The Nazis' rabid nationalism, on the other hand, did appeal to some Christians. This was particularly true of Protestants, who had always regarded their Church as a German Church or indeed *the* German Church. It was no accident that the official inauguration of the Third Reich – the highly theatrical 'Day of Potsdam' – should have begun with a Lutheran service, even though almost half of the Reich's population were Catholic. The 'Prussian' version of German history, which was to figure so prominently on the Third Reich's stage, also sounded a distinct anti-Catholic leitmotiv. The endless number of plays about the Saxons vs. Charlemagne, Henry IV vs. Pope Gregory at Canossa, the Protestant reformers vs. Charles V, Prussia vs. Austria, or indeed Möller's Lutheran Austrian peasants vs. their Catholic overlords all contained the same underlying notion: Catholics, being in thrall to Rome, were traitors to German unity and tools of Germany's foreign foes.[8] The Catholic Church, Möller has his Prosecutor say in the *Dice Game*, 'has thrust the sword of civil war into [German] hands'. And Möller lets his two Catholic prelates declare, respectively, 'I am no German ... I served God and my country [i.e. Italy],' and 'I am a stranger to this country [i.e. Germany] and never liked its people.'[9] E. G. Kolbenheyer – another of the Reich's literary heavyweights – seconded such sentiments in his ponderous *Gregory and Henry*. There existed, according to one of Kolbenheyer's prelates, an eternal conflict 'between the Seat of St. Peter and the barb'rous throne north of the Alps' that would only be resolved if one or the other was ground into dust.[10]

That 'Prussian' version of history, eagerly adopted by three prominent Catholic apostates – Hitler, Goebbels and Himmler – served to make Catholics much more suspicious of Nazism than their Protestant compatriots. Almost to the end of the Weimar republic, the Nazis failed to make significant electoral headway in Germany's Catholic regions. And there were good historical reasons for Catholics to be suspicious, not just of the Nazis but of the wider right-wing constituency: Protestant German nationalists under Bismarck had unleashed within living memory ferocious anti-Catholic repression. In scenes not seen since the religious wars of the seventeenth century, vast numbers of Catholic clergy and laity were imprisoned, religious orders proscribed, processions and festivals banned and the faithful harassed by the Prussian authorities.[11] That so-called *Kulturkampf* of the 1880s had deeply scarred German Catholicism. In concluding a Concordat with the Hitler government in 1933, the Vatican was guided, at least in part, by those recent memories: the Concordat was as much appeasement of Protestantism as of Nazism.

Yet there were also areas of potential agreement between both sides. Antisemitism, notoriously, was one such area, even if the more sensationalist claims about Catholic complicity in Nazi crimes are not supported by the evidence. Catholics and Nazis were united, however, in regarding Jews as the ultimate symbol of all they considered most suspect about the modern age, ranging from atonal music via psychoanalysis and feminism to stock market capitalism. The

important aspect here is that all these phenomena were initially dominant after the Great War. The far right and Catholicism both felt that
they were swimming against the tide. In that regard, art mirrored life
most faithfully: surveying the Third Reich's drama in 1943, a literary
critic was moved to remark that the various protagonists were ultimately not battling human opponents but the 'opposing age' itself.[12]
The concepts of the doomed hero and of the 'tragic', and the aim of the
Reichsdramaturg to foster a new type of drama transcending history,
all betrayed a deep unease about the present day. Likewise, the efforts
of Catholic theatre activists to revive the medieval mystery plays after
the Great War and Max Reinhardt's Austro-Catholic *Everyman* at
Salzburg were in their own way attempts to transcend history, or at
least to escape from it temporarily.

History seemed sombre after 1918: the nationalists had seen
their beloved Empire destroyed; the Church had been faced by a wave
of aggressive and often violent secularism in its own heartlands of
France, Mexico and later Spain. (News about events in those countries,
incidentally, reached the German public also via the stage: Catholic
amateur groups performed plays about the plight of their Latin
co-religionists.)[13]

Above all, there was the spectre of Bolshevism: Pope Pius XI had
been papal nuncio in Warsaw when the invading Red Army threatened
that city after the Great War; his successor, Pius XII, had experienced
as nuncio in Munich the short-lived Bavarian Soviet Republic: these
experiences marked both men for life. What was true of the pontiffs
was also true of many papal foot soldiers. Take the case of a priest from
Franconia, whose own plans to produce an amateur play had been
banned by local Nazi officials in 1937: he duly reminded the Nazis
that he had joined the Free Corps in 1919 to fight the 'Spartacists in
Munich', and he had successfully thwarted all attempts by 'Marxist
trade unions to infiltrate [his] village'.[14] The Catholic playwright Leo
Weismantel even included a reference to 'Bolshevism, that pestilence'
in his *Oberammergauer Gelübdespiel*, which was performed in tandem with the Passion Play at Oberammergau in 1934.[15] Pius XI, the
Franconian priest and Leo Weismantel attracted the ire of the Nazi
regime for their defence of Catholicism: yet all three men had initially

sought to come to an arrangement with the Nazis.[16] For on the Eastern horizon there always loomed Soviet Russia, demonstrating just what Communism would mean in practice: monasteries had been closed, their lands seized, churches were being used as grain silos, cathedrals were being dynamited to make way for swimming baths; arbitrary arrest, torture, slave labour and mass murder were the order of the day. Compared to Stalin, Hitler thus seemed in the 1930s very much the lesser of two evils.

Nothing illustrates more perfectly the wider resonance of the Nazis' anti-Bolshevik rhetoric than a parcel received by the Propaganda Ministry in 1937. It had been posted by a French Catholic amateur playwright who felt moved to reach out across the historic divide between his country and Germany. He was sending a play to 'Monsieur le Ministre de l'instruction publique' for use in Nazi propaganda.[17] In his covering letter he wished Nazi Germany well in fighting the good fight against Communism, which, he observed, had brought to the world nothing but 'misery'.

The propagandists, in turn, noted affinities: their French well-wisher lived in the Vendée region, the epitome of a rural France unsullied by republicanism or modern manners. And here the particular opens out into the general again: for both Catholics and Nazis saw in country life a source of moral regeneration for society. In the theatre that showed in a shared enthusiasm for rural drama: the leading Catholic exponents of *Volkstheater* in the Weimar republic, such as Alois Lippl, Julius Maria Becker or Leo Weismantel, had also met with approval among the far right.[18] Similarly, after the *Anschluß*, much of Austrian rural drama received a ready welcome on the Nazi stage.[19] The consensus only broke down where rural drama became overtly ideological: dogmatically Catholic or Nazi 'blood-and-soil'.

Catholics and Nazis also agreed to an extent in their diagnosis of what was wrong with contemporary society. The political left, they thought, reduced people to a mere crowd; democracy and consumer capitalism, on the other hand, had led to an atomised society, bereft of purpose or ideals. In Goes' *Thingspiel Germany on the March* we read that the German *Volk* had neglected its 'soul' and had turned into *Masse Mensch*, the title of Ernst Toller's provocative republican play.[20] Goebbels' collaborator Hans Hinkel spoke of *seelische Verzweiflung* – 'despair gripping the soul' – which had sapped German strength even more terribly than want.[21] The hero in Werner Deubel's play about the Napoleonic wars considered Germany's surest defence to lie in its *Herzenskräfte*, an untranslatable term meaning 'strong hearts' or 'the power of emotions'.[22] It is a similar thought that leads a villainous Communist character in Gerhard Schumann's *The Decision* to speak of his party's aim 'to rip the useless heart' out of German breasts and turn the nation into 'automata'.[23] In Heynicke's *Neurode* the assault comes from capitalist quarters but its effect is similar: in auctioning off the coal mine central to *Neurode*'s plot, much more is being lost, 'What is being auctioned off is the heart of the *Heimat* . . . Our faith is being auctioned off, our hope is being auctioned off, [as is] our confidence, our sacrifice is being auctioned off.'[24] Kolbenheyer's *The Bridge* contrasts the older generation who had spent their lives in 'service to financial interests' with the younger generation who felt stirring within them a 'new faith'.[25] Consider also the engineer in the play *Concrete* by the 'Hitler Youth dramatist' Friedrich Hymmen: 'You are in thrall to the material world,' observes Hymmen's protagonist, 'I wish to transcend it.'[26] Consider further the influential critic Joseph Magnus Wehner, who perceived all around him on stage and in real life, 'lust rather than love . . . hedonism rather than sacrifice, "a job" rather than a calling'.[27] That, Wehner said, had been the fatal gift bequeathed by the Western democracies. And, as if to drive home the point, the wartime critic we quoted earlier spoke of 'the enemy seeking to destroy our highest spiritual values, our very idealism, so as to make way for [their] materialism [and] nihilism'.[28]

Nazi talk of nihilism might seem a particularly glaring case of 'mote and beam' but we should not dismiss it as empty rhetoric. To ignore the role of a perverted idealism in Nazi ideology and culture is to ignore one of the mainsprings of the alarming energies the Third Reich was able to generate. When Nazis talked of 'belief' or 'faith', which they did incessantly on- and off-stage, they clearly did not mean what their Christian compatriots meant by those terms; but, like Christians, Nazis thought that an emotional experience – *Erlebnis* – would lead to a spiritual rebirth, and a new sense of community.[29] In *Neurode* it is the miners' decision to resist the closure of their mine that transforms their community, and significantly it leads the chorus to intone, '*Volk*, you yourself are Faith.'[30] In *Langemarck*, Zerkaulen's drama about trench warfare, it is comradeship that transforms the hearts of the young soldiers and makes possible the following exchange: 'Do you actually believe in God?'; to which – 'after a brief pause' – comes this reply: 'As I [believe] in Germany'.[31] And when the patriotic outburst of Deubel's Gneisenau is dismissed as revolutionary rhetoric by an elder, tone-deaf to the voice of the heart, Gneisenau rejoins that his thoughts about Germany constituted 'religion'.[32]

It was no accident that references to a new 'cultic theatre' should have been so common in the Third Reich. The more observant contemporaries noted that sections of the party were in effect trying to create a new religion and were hoping to use the theatre for their aims.[33] That was explicitly the case in the *Thingspiel* and Otto Laubinger's 'new völkisch liturgy'. It was no less obvious in Rosenberg's rival project. (The concluding line of *De Stedinge* was 'The blood that had been shed here has experienced resurrection.')[34] Yet it was implicit also, as will have become clear, in much of 'conventional' Nazi drama. And it led the SS-dramatist Friedrich Bethge to warn against a closure of the theatres in the final stages of the war. Closing the playhouses would drive 'the middle classes into another kind of religious site [*Kultstätten*] where we would prefer not to see them: namely the churches'.[35]

Clearly, more was involved here than just the traditional veneration of *Kultur* by the German middle classes. To speak of a new religion is perhaps to overstate the case; but those who had lost the Christian faith of their fathers often found in Nazism something that filled the void. They succumbed all the more readily to Nazism's aping of Christian cadences. There were plays submitted to the Propaganda Ministry that combined 'the Führer principle' with 'death and resurrection' or that featured both Horst Wessel (the SA 'martyr') and an evangelist.[36] There was a play about a mining community in the Harz mountains that alternated scenes of SA operations with witches, wood sprites and goblins living underground before it reached a pseudo-Christian conclusion.[37] The Berlin district of Charlottenburg was planning an open-air theatrical in the Olympic Stadium for the Führer's birthday in 1939, which was to have culminated in torch-bearers arranging themselves into a vast cross, which was then to have 'passed on the flame' to another group in the shape of the swastika. The German word for the swastika – *Hakenkreuz* – translates literally as the 'Cross with Angles'.[38]

There was also Richard Euringer's *Dance of Death* (which, unlike the three previous efforts, was performed): it had SA-men 'fallen in combat' painting the 'sign' (i.e. the swastika) on the thresholds of righteous households to assure their inhabitants of 'eternal life'.[39] E. W. Möller strayed temporarily from drama to write a *Christmas Book for German Youth* in 1938: it provoked the wrath of Rosenberg, who thought Möller had 'made the Führer and the National Socialist movement almost look like … Franciscan friars'.[40] Consider, finally, the case of a working-class man from Saxony: an unemployed twenty-year-old cable layer, who was moved to write a play about Hitler and 'the new faith' created by the Führer.[41] The text was riddled with spelling mistakes, and the language was a gauche reworking of Christian phrases; yet that offering proved perfectly the point made by the Nazi theatre activist H. C. Kaergel in 1939, 'Just as the populace moved by religious sentiment in the age of the [medieval] mystery plays re-enacted the symbols of the Church, so now the *Volk* feels the need to express its love of the Führer not just in words but on stage.'[42]

Kaergel's pronouncements may have been a little sweeping; but in a sense he had put his finger on it: the uneasy alliance between Christians and Nazis began to break apart at the precise moment when it became clear to many Christians that a new kind of worship was afoot, where 'love of the Führer' was seeking to replace 'love of God'. On the Nazi side of the equation, the temporary truce ended when it began to dawn on the party that Christianity would not simply whither on the vine.

Since Catholicism retained a greater active following in Germany than Lutheranism, it became the principal target of the Nazi *Kirchenkampf*, the so-called 'struggle against the Church'. In the theatre the first spectacular collision occurred in January 1935 in

Hagen in Westphalia: deep in Catholic territory. The *casus belli* was a pseudo-historical drama about that very defeat of the Saxons under their leader Wittekind which the SS had started to commemorate the year before at Verden. The story was regarded by *völkisch* ideologues as a key moment in German history, and was familiar to generations of schoolchildren from their history primers. It had proved the inspiration, for want of a better word, for a steady stream of plays about Wittekind even before the Nazis came to power. Ten more such efforts were printed or produced in the Third Reich, of which no fewer than four were staged in the 1934–5 season alone.[43] The Propaganda Ministry received Wittekind plays so frequently that the files vividly convey the censors' exasperation.[44] The topic, then, formed part of that wider obsession with the Ancient Teutons to which German adolescents of all ages were prone in the nineteenth and early twentieth centuries. The editor of the Catholic newspaper *Germania* mischievously recalled in 1935 that many of his schoolmates – now respectable members of society – had once tried writing plays about Wittekind themselves.[45] Such enthusiasm for the ancient Germans was only acceptable in adults if it came in decorous academic guise or if it was transmuted into high art, as it had been in Wagner's case. Above all, there was to be no attempt to play off the pagan past against the Christian present. For every *Siegfried* wreathed in Nordic mists, the *Bildungsbürger* expected a *Parzifal*, bathed in the kindly light of Good Friday.

These unwritten conventions were rudely breached by the *völkisch* constituency from the late nineteenth century onwards, and the price its members paid for that transgression was for a long time marginalisation, or even ostracism.[46] Such had been the fate of *Wittekind* by one Edmund Kiß, which the Nazis staged at Hagen in 1935: it had been completely ignored when it first appeared in 1928. Kiß's dramatic effort was little more than an extended anti-Catholic rant. Charlemagne was portrayed as a tool of murderous papal machinations, and the battle at Verden as attempted genocide plotted by the Church. For good measure, Kiß had his Papal nuncio reveal Rome's secret plan, which was supposedly only thwarted at the last moment: blonde German maidens and matrons were to have been taken to a concentration camp on the Rhine, there to be violated by 'scum in human shape' from 'Arabia's plague-ridden harbour towns, [by] Jews, Greeks, Italians and Moors'. The object, Kiß's nuncio explained, was to destroy the Germans through miscegenation: for 'as long as German blood remain[ed] unmixed' the Church would not triumph, not even 'in a thousand years'.[47]

As a glimpse into the unsavoury recesses of the *völkisch* mind, Kiß's desperate farrago could hardly be bettered. Here were all the familiar obsessions of the far right: the inter-racial unions in the occupied Rhineland; the old Protestant notion that Catholics were unreliable citizens; and, not least, the belief growing in far-right circles after the Great War that Christianity itself was part of the problem. The name Kiß gave to his Papal nuncio was 'Isidorus', a name that sounded Jewish to German ears.[48]

The notion that Christianity was irredeemably tainted by Jewishness was widespread in *völkisch* circles. The files of the Reichsdramaturgie bulge with correspondence about plays seeking to expose 'Judo-Catholic desires for subjugating' Germany. Goebbels' collaborator Hinkel told theatre practitioners that 'assimilated Jews' had been working hand in glove with 'those "Christians" using their religion for . . . treason' (i.e. Catholics).[49] Georg Deiniger's play about the Peasants' War – *Peasants under the Yoke* – 'unmasked the Jew and the [Catholic] priest'.[50] Hanns Johst's *Prophets*, written fully a decade before the Third Reich, had contained a scene of Jewish 'usurers' and Romish prelates jointly plotting against Luther – for both Jews and Catholics, Johst intimated, lacked a fatherland.[51] Other *völkisch* authors soon went further. The Kleist Prize laureate Hermann Burte was now attempting to get 'to the heart of things', as he put it: namely the Jewish roots of Christianity. These he had exposed in his play *Christ on Trial*, which had premiered in Switzerland in 1930 (because no one in Germany had been willing to touch it). Five years on, and two years into Nazi rule, it was still being ignored. An exasperated Burte sought to enlist the help of the Propaganda Ministry. His play, he explained, was about belief in the 'Chosen One' – and Burte was *not* referring to Christ. '[T]he Jewish hero,' he observed, 'has to make way for a German one.'[52]

What was happening, then, in 1934–5 was that those on the neo-pagan fringes of German society were demanding to be heard (or staged) in the new Reich. Like the exuberant amateurs in the *Thingspiel* movement, they claimed their reward for years of unrelenting opposition to the republic. That demand met with sympathy by many Nazis at all levels of the party. What seemed to contemporaries like a coordinated effort orchestrated by Goebbels was in reality no such thing.[53] The Propaganda Ministry checked all play texts but did not usually initiate productions. Like *De Stedinge*, most anti-Catholic plays had come about because of decisions taken in the regions: at the level of the Gauleiter, through pressure groups inside town halls or theatre advisory boards.[54] Where such local pressure did not exist, anti-Catholic plays often failed to make it on to the stage, as the SS-playwright Walther Best complained to Schlösser.[55] He had been trying everywhere to get his own anti-Roman effort *Das Reich* staged; yet even the fact that the Reichsführer SS (i.e. Himmler) 'possessed a personal copy of the manuscript' had failed to impress the *Intendanten*.[56]

Anti-Catholic authors often tried to get their plays staged in *Catholic* areas of Germany: there was little point, after all, in preaching to the converted. What precisely they hoped to achieve with their plays is difficult to say. If the object was to provoke, they certainly succeeded. At Hagen, Kiß's grotesque *Wittekind* caused uproar in the auditorium. There were shouts of 'history shall not be falsified'; there was whistling in the galleries; in the stalls people rose from their seats and refused to sit down again when called upon to do so. The theatre eventually had to be cleared by police and SA-men: it was a regular *Theaterskandal*. Catholic theatregoers were adopting methods which the Nazis themselves had practised before 1933. That echo of the Weimar years proved acutely embarrassing to the Nazis.[57] They had, after all, pointed to audience protests as a sign that the 'November State' lacked legitimacy: now there were rebelling audiences in the Third Reich. In this battle of wills between Catholic audiences and the local Nazi authorities, the Nazis blinked first. *Wittekind* was taken off after a mere two performances. As a sop to party feeling two further performances were scheduled (behind closed doors) for party members only. But there was no denying that the protesters had won the day. To complete the humiliation of the local Nazi party, the Westphalian clergy pointedly proceeded to conduct services of expiation, asking Divine forgiveness on behalf of a city that had grievously offended against God.

The repercussions of the affair extended far and wide. The German press was not yet wholly under Nazi control in 1935. The events in Hagen were discussed extensively by independent papers like the liberal *Frankfurter Zeitung* or the Catholic *Germania*.[58] The story was also picked up by the international press: *The Times*, for instance, reported at length about it.[59] Inside Germany, protest telegrams were sent to Hitler, to Goebbels and other members of the regime. The director of the Hagen *Wittekind* had sought to cow audiences by invoking on stage the Propaganda Minister's name.[60] In reality, Goebbels had nothing to do with the production. When news of the rumpus reached him, he sent for the play script, read it – or at least glanced at it – and pronounced it 'utter tripe'.[61]

The Reichsdramaturg, who had been badly shaken by events, sought to insulate his own office against further trouble. In a memo to Goebbels, Schlösser asked for guidance about plays 'touching on religious problems'.[62] He was moved to write, he explained, by a new play about Canossa in the vein of Kolbenheyer's *Gregory and Henry*. Should the production proceed? Goebbels replied with a curt 'yes' but added a significant rider: 'only, no falsification of history'.[63] There duly were no further plays on Wittekind, on Charlemagne or the pagan Saxons.

The Catholics had won a battle, but the *Kirchenkampf* was by no means over. The Propaganda Ministry had merely staged a tactical retreat; in fact, Goebbels' order did not even constitute a proper retreat, since the ministry had never 'pushed' for anti-Catholic plays. If anything, it had sought to restrain the enthusiasm of the neo-pagans. A production of Burte's inflammatory *Christ on Trial*, planned for Berlin in late 1934, was actually stopped by Goebbels at Schlösser's prompting.[64] Schlösser even sought to extend the unofficial ban beyond the Reich's borders. When Burte's publisher informed Schlösser that the State Theatre in the Free City of Danzig was interested in the play, Schlösser ordered them to dissuade Danzig discreetly but firmly.[65] Neither Schlösser nor Goebbels harboured secret sympathies for Rome: they merely possessed greater tactical skill than most regional officials. In Schlösser's case there were also aesthetic objections to the crudity of many *Kirchenkampf* vehicles. 'Even the weapons with which National Socialism fights from the stage must be noble and irreproachable ones', he observed, while trying to stop one particularly crude anti-Catholic effort.[66]

The 'noble' ideological swordsmanship did not, however, preclude passing swipes: Werner Deubel's *Last Fortress*, for instance, may have been about the Napoleonic wars; but it also found time to describe the Pope as 'commanding the immature', before observing that 'there are issues which make us all Protestants if we are not to cease being Germans'.[67] Such needling could always be passed off as artistic freedom, which the Reichsdramaturg was shameless enough to invoke whenever it suited his purposes.

Similarly, Schlösser was prepared to endorse highly tendentious plays about the reformation or pre-reformation days, such as Bethge's *Kopernikus*, Heinz Ortner's much produced *Queen Isabella of Spain* or Felix Dhünen's *Uta von Naumburg* and Heinrich Zerkaulen's *The Horseman* (both about witch trials, 'perverse' Catholic celibacy and healthy 'pagan' sexuality – and both, needless to say, endorsed by Himmler). The palpable ideological intent of such plays could always be passed off as historical fact. The facts, however, tended to be distinctly partisan: a play about the Thirty Years' War was banned by Schlösser because it contained a Jesuit character who struck him as 'all in all, too likeable' to be historically authentic.[68] On the other hand, Schlösser authorised a play about Luther, which achieved the rare feat of uniting Catholics and Protestants in outrage. The public response to the production at Stuttgart in the autumn of 1935 was sufficiently vehement for Goebbels to become involved: coincidentally or not, none of the author's other plays were performed thereafter.[69]

The final type of anti-Catholic agitation on stage focused on the issue of priestly celibacy. From the Nazi perspective, men of the cloth were being prevented from doing their procreative duty for the *Volk*.

This obsession frequently combined with the party's rural enthusiasms: the Propaganda Ministry was inundated with plays about healthy sons of the peasantry throwing off their cassocks as blonde maidens beckoned and instinct won out over Romish superstition. Here, too, Schlösser weeded out the very crudest efforts, including plays by prominent Nazi pens. Friedrich Bethge, for instance, was informed that a staging of his *Blood Sample* 'would I think hardly be in your own interest, my dear Bethge'.[70] When Bethge persisted with a second play about unmarried Catholic clergy, Schlösser authorised it for performance in a deeply *Protestant* suburb of Hamburg, where it duly stirred up apathy.[71]

Artistic merit (or absence thereof) was thus a factor in Schlösser's repertoire policy but not a decisive one: ideological usefulness was. When the prominent actress Käthe Dorsch expressed an interest, via her friend Göring, in reviving Lautensack's *Parsonage Comedy* – a famous Wilhelmine *succès-de-scandale* – Schlösser quickly quashed the proposal.[72] The play, he explained, was 'decidedly inopportune in political terms'. 'Since its plot [revolved around] members of the clergy perpetually getting their house-keepers pregnant, [it] would only result in the clergy appearing human and healthy.' Yet the whole thrust of recent propaganda, Schlösser explained, had been to expose the clergy's 'unnatural practices': so much for National Socialism's 'noble and irreproachable' methods.

Two further anti-Catholic efforts invite scrutiny because they reveal something of the dynamics in the *Kirchenkampf*. The first of these two plays – Otto Erler's *Thor's Guest* – was a neo-pagan drama with literary ambitions. It sought to contrast Catholic self-denial and pagan *joie-de-vivre*. The monk Thysker (the name means 'German' in most Scandinavian languages) is shipwrecked on a Nordic island, where a comely maiden engages him in conversation. When he speaks of his desire 'to bring God' to Northern shores, she asks innocently, 'Why, have you grown tired of him in your own country?'[73] When he calls himself a 'servant of God', she observes that *her* countrymen were free men: for Thor did not wish to be worshipped by 'servants'. And when he lets slip that Christian priests were celibate, she observes that it was a good thing that not all men in his country were priests 'or there would soon be no one left to worship your God'. There are other subtle Nazi touches such as a huge cross practically crushing Thysker, a 'Roman' invasion, the death in battle of the tribal leader, etc. The play concludes with Thysker embracing the pagan faith of his ancestors *and* the comely maiden. Goebbels, who saw a performance of *Thor's Guest* during a visit to Weimar, was scathing about the play: 'it's a dramatised version of Rosenberg's agenda. Unpoetic and artless ... Enough to send anyone to sleep. What would become of German culture were this kind of people to be given free rein?'[74]

What Catholic theatregoers made of Erler's play we do not know. There is no record of public protests to any of the sixty-three productions of *Thor's Guest* in the years 1937–43. Perhaps Catholic audiences were alerted to the likely content of the play by its very title and simply decided to stay away. Catholics appear to have been wary of unfamiliar plays: in the staunchly Catholic city of Mainz, for instance, the mayor reported a decline in attendance at the local theatre in 1935, which, he thought, amounted to a silent boycott by Catholic playgoers.[75] In Baden an official reported that in the Catholic regions of that state 'people run a mile at the very mention of [the words] "Nazi culture"'.[76] Some *Intendanten* may have begun to anticipate such audience responses, tailoring the repertoire accordingly. Evidence of this exists in the case of Linz, in staunchly Catholic Austria. When a theatre exchange with the National Theatre at Weimar threatened to bring to Linz the very production of *Thor's Guest* that had exasperated Goebbels, the Linz *Intendant* requested a change of play: in line, he said, with local audience preferences.[77] It is worth noting, moreover, that the second play of Erler's neo-pagan trilogy – *God's Predicament* – received its première as a *private* performance for the SS-Main Office, and the final instalment – *Blood Friends* – was only staged after further intense pressure by the SS.[78]

The other anti-Catholic play worth considering in greater detail – *The Last Peasant* – was produced in Berlin in January 1936 by a travelling Bavarian company. Here there had been no prior clue to the play's ideological agenda. Audiences presumably expected to see wholesome Bavarian fare, with a little earthy language perhaps to reflect the Carnival mood of January. Instead, they got a tale of a middle-aged priest and his mistress, trying to assuage their guilty consciences by forcing their son into the priesthood too. The lad, however, is rescued in the nick of time by a buxom beauty. This 'comedy' amused the Nazis and the Protestants in the auditorium; the Catholics responded by walking out. The walk-outs were repeated nightly for over a week: either because people kept arriving unawares, or conceivably they had heard and came with the intention of making a stand. The protests took place in the very heart of the Reich's capital: the theatre was a stone's throw away from the Brandenburg Gate and literally round the corner from Hitler's Chancellery and most of the ministries. Schlösser himself hastened down the road from his office to attend a performance and reported back to Goebbels. (E.W. Möller was despatched to observe audiences on another night.)

Schlösser was struck by the outspokenness of the protesters. 'It is remarkable,' he told Goebbels, 'that they combine their protest unabashedly with criticism of National Socialism. One group openly remarked that this sort of thing was only possible for as long as Nazism was *still* in power.'[79] It was the word 'still' that shocked Schlösser most.

The affair of *The Last Peasant* thus demonstrates a number of points. For one thing, all the usual suspects were involved: the production had been organised by Rosenberg's playgoers' association, the NSKG; and Himmler had booked the entire theatre on two nights for the SS.[80] The Propaganda Ministry had misjudged the public reaction in authorising the production, but it was in no hurry to correct its mistake. It clearly intended to sit out the protests, and the affair only ended because Hitler himself intervened. After more than a week of protests practically outside his residence, and with the Olympic Games only months away, the Führer decided that enough was enough. Schlösser was informed of the decision by a senior civil servant and immediately arranged for sudden illness in a leading member of the cast (while threatening all concerned with dire consequences if they should reveal the truth).[81]

There had been an ecclesiastical angle to the affair also: the Bishop of Berlin had protested about the production in a telegram to Goebbels, to which the ministry failed to respond. Count Preising decided to despatch a second telegram a week later, to which

Goebbels again failed to reply.[82] The propagandists had given no quarter to the Church: they had even dispensed with the barest minimum of civility.

A memo by E. W. Möller, dated some eighteen months after the Berlin protests, spelt out the underlying strategy, 'On the orders of Dr Schlösser all complaints from Catholic quarters are to be dealt with in dilatory fashion.'[83] In each case decisions should be determined by the extent of public feeling. The views of the Catholic hierarchy were immaterial to the ministry's decision-making. Take the protest by the Bishop of Speyer in November 1936 about H. C. Kaergel's *Hockewanzel*. That 'comedy' included, among other gems of Nazi subtlety, a scene where a clergyman in his pulpit is overcome by diarrhoea. Nazi and Protestant audiences found it all killingly funny: the play performed to full houses in no fewer than seventy-one productions. As a result, the Bishop's protest was rejected by Schlösser in a letter of studied rudeness.[84]

The Catholic Church is often accused of not having done enough to save the various groups of Nazi victims. The record of the theatre would suggest that the leverage of the Catholic hierarchy was very limited. Senior clerics had intervened forcefully in areas where the Concordat specifically entitled them to do so; and in each case, they failed to extract even the most minor concessions from the regime. In the light of the *Kulturkampf* in the theatre, the later passivity of the Church in the Holocaust might seem motivated at least in part by a painful awareness of its own impotence.

The fate of traditional religious plays fits into this pattern. That may perhaps seem surprising, since the passion play at Oberammergau has often been cited as part of the case against Catholicism in the Third Reich.[85] Hitler's visit to both the 1930 and the 1934 passion and his fond recollections of the play's antisemitism do indeed seem damning.[86] But it is worth noting that there was no passion play at Oberammergau in the next scheduled year of 1940. Ostensibly, that was because of the exigencies of war. Yet all manner of secular openair plays went ahead in 1940, apparently unaffected by that same war. The fate of the other passion plays in Southern Germany and Austria, moreover, strongly suggest that the war was only a convenient excuse for moving against the most famous passion play in the Reich. For of the dozens of other traditional plays, all but one or two had been banned *before* the war.[87]

In Austria, for instance, a number of extremely ancient plays had been stopped immediately after the *Anschluß*. The plays concerned had been performed without any eighteenth- or nineteenth-century accretions and were of an immediacy which we now only associate with theatre in the Third World.[88] Here was true *Volkskultur*, which the Nazis claimed to cherish: yet they closed it down remorselessly. Even passion plays sanctified, so to speak, by nationalist tradition were not safe: at Höritz, in Southern Bohemia, passion plays had begun in the nineteenth century.[89] The local population had used the play to assert the region's (Austro-)German identity against Czech claims in the Habsburg Empire. After 1918, the Höritz play remained a focus of ethnic-German pride inside the new Czechoslovak state. Yet the Nazis closed down the play and forced a blood-and-soil alternative on the villagers (thus blowing their own cover of supposed wartime needs).[90] The local population responded by voting with their feet. In the struggle between Catholic villagers and the Nazi authorities, each side had thus derailed the other side's theatrical ambitions. The final recorded use of the imposing theatre building at Höritz was as a depot for the remaining equipment of Rommel's desert army after the defeat in North Africa.

Bavaria provides a final vignette of the Nazi *Kirchenkampf*. The small town of Rosenheim had been the base of a private touring company that specialised in (Catholic) religious plays. Throughout the early years of the Third Reich, it had toured Southern Germany with its own passion play, to the intense annoyance of local Nazi officials.[91] All attempts to close down the operation had failed because of the director's refusal to be intimidated. For two and half years, his company survived Nazi plotting, scheming and barely disguised threats on an almost daily basis. Then, one night in January 1939, all his costumes, sets and play texts were destroyed in an explosion which ripped through Rosenheim's Catholic Apprentices' Hall. The local police established that a device had been detonated but proved unable to identify the culprits.

7   The manacled muse: theatre and political domination

The Third Reich regarded itself as a strictly hierarchical society organised in accordance with the so-called Führer principle. All individuals within each chain of command theoretically enjoyed untrammelled powers over their subordinates, while owing total obedience to their superiors. At the top of the pyramid stood Hitler. Since the Führer took only an intermittent interest in the non-musical stage, control over German theatre essentially devolved to Joseph Goebbels. Goebbels was, however, overruled by Hitler on a number of occasions. These ranged from the appointment of prominent *Intendanten* to the issue of salaries for the Reich's theatrical stars.[1] Once or twice, Hitler even intervened in repertoire policy: the initial ban on Shakespeare as an enemy dramatist after the outbreak of war, for instance, was lifted on the Führer's personal orders. Yet Goebbels was left to implement the Führer's wishes, and thus enjoyed some leeway in interpreting Hitler's commands. In the case of Shakespeare, Goebbels instructed his own subordinates to limit all theatres to one play by the Bard per season, even though Hitler had not suggested any limitations; and Goebbels saw to it that his own order was enforced. When one of the most prominent theatre practitioners in the Reich tried to ignore the restriction, Goebbels demanded a change in the repertoire plans: Heinrich George, Goebbels observed, was turning Berlin's Schillertheater into a 'Shakespeare Theater'.[2]

While Goebbels was thus capable of intervening in even minor aspects of *Theaterpolitik*, he devolved most day-to-day decisions to his subordinates in two offices set up in 1933: the Theatre Section of the Propaganda Ministry and the Reich Theatre Chamber.[3] Both were based in Berlin at separate addresses but, jointly, kept local offices in

153

the regions: the so-called Reich Propaganda Offices. Known as RPAs by their German acronym, these enforced regulations locally and collated information for the authorities in Berlin.

The appearance of neat organisation was also maintained within these various bodies. The Reich Theatre Chamber was the professional body of all theatre practitioners, who were legally required to be members of it. Anyone denied membership was in effect banned from pursuing a career in the theatre. The Chamber consisted of several subsections, concentrating on legal aspects, opera, dance, cabaret, 'straight theatre', etc. These sections looked after the interests of the members, while simultaneously policing them. The Theatre Section of the Propaganda Ministry itself dealt in similarly ambivalent fashion with the theatres, the publishers and the playwrights. The Section, in turn, was subdivided: the department for publications looked after theatre publishers, the Reichsdramaturgie after the repertoire of individual theatres. All these structures, which had evolved from 1933 to 1937, can be represented in diagrams and flow charts of impressive elegance.

In practice, the whole thing was a messy nightmare for all involved. For a start, the Propaganda Ministry had to fend off persistent attacks by other Nazi organisations: the Rosenberg Office, for instance, thought that theatre should come under its own remit as the chief guardians of ideological purity. It tried, and nearly succeeded, to break the Propaganda Ministry in 1935. In the summer of that year, one of the ministry's spies reported that the Rosenberg men 'were in carnival mood'; 'the cups were being raised till the early hours of the morning' in expectation of imminent victory over the propagandists.[4] The exultation proved premature, yet the Rosenberg Office continued to try and thwart the Propaganda Ministry at every turn, right to the end of the Third Reich.

Then there was Robert Ley's Labour Front, which sought to subsume the theatre sector into its own Office for Leisure Activities. Ley was eventually rebuffed but his subordinates subsequently launched insurrections against the Propaganda Ministry in the regions: itinerant Strength-through-Joy theatre outfits conspicuously ignored ministerial guidelines throughout the later 1930s.[5] The Propaganda

Ministry also had to contend with the substantial figure of Hermann Göring. Although Göring's attempt to establish sole control over theatres in his own Prussian fiefdom ultimately failed, the Propaganda Ministry in turn only ever exercised limited influence on 'the Reich Marshall's theatres'.[6]

The task of bringing about a degree of coherence to Nazi *Theaterpolitik* fell to Goebbels' subordinates: chief among them to Rainer Schlösser as Reichsdramaturg (and President of the Reich Theatre Chamber from 1935 to 1938) and to Otto Laubinger and Ludwig Körner, who were, respectively, Schlösser's predecessor and successor at the Theatre Chamber.[7] A weekly briefing by Schlösser was normally the extent of Goebbels' engagement. It was testimony to Schlösser's administrative and personal skills that there was so little need for Goebbels to become active.

Yet below Schlösser, so to speak, and at times all around him, chaos bubbled merrily. For a glimpse of that chaos, let us consider the route a new play had to take in the Reich to make its way from the author's desk on to the stage. There were *two* bodies of the same ministry which had to scrutinise the play: the publications department to authorise the printing, the Reichsdramaturgie to decide whether or not the play could be performed.[8] Since playwrights had to be members of their own professional body, the Reich Chamber of Literature, there was even a third office that regularly put its oar in. Total confusion was avoided because the heads of these three offices got on reasonably well with each other. Even so, there were awkward moments. In May 1939, for instance, the Reichsdramaturgie was on the verge of authorising a batch of plays when it discovered by chance that the publications department had just banned those very same plays. One of Schlösser's assistants rushed to retrieve from the out tray the letter containing the signed permits. As the official wryly noted, the publisher would have ended up receiving two letters from the same ministry, both invoking Goebbels' name: one letter permitting the plays, the other banning them. In another case, five weeks later, that very thing happened.[9]

Plays that had been cleared were then theoretically available for production. Here the next stage of the process began: *Intendanten* had to submit to the Reichsdramaturgie their proposed repertoire list for each season. Officially, that procedure was described as a service by the Propaganda Ministry to the *Intendanten*: the Reichsdramaturg had been 'authorised to provide advice and information about the uncontroversial nature of individual plays'.[10] Yet it was by no means obvious that a play which had been deemed uncontroversial by the censors the first time round would also be approved the second time. That was less a case of capriciousness than of altered circumstance. To take the most famous example: *Schlageter* was fêted in 1933 but had become politically inopportune a year later. Plays that touched in some way on foreign policy were particularly prone to encounter problems after the original censors' permit had been granted. The Reichsdramaturgie itself might develop doubts and revoke permits; in other cases, it might seek the advice of the Foreign Office (whose officials thus carried out a *third* round of censorship). Similar procedures were also adopted in the case of the Armed Forces, after Göring's Air Ministry had objected strongly to a play about aviators, deemed by them to be insufficiently heroic.[11] More than once, the Foreign Office and the military also changed their minds at an even later stage. The most spectacular case was that of Karl Bunje's comedy about life behind the trenches in the Great War: *The Hare behind the Lines*. It was one of the Third Reich's most successful plays and a particular favourite with servicemen; yet after the outbreak of the Second World War, the High Command suddenly took against the play and forced Schlösser to ban it.[12]

Other ministries or Nazi offices also regularly tried to interfere: the Ministry of Education was exercised about a less than favourable portrayal of teachers, which led it to issue a secret edict banning all plays about schoolmasters; it required a year-long effort by the Propaganda Ministry to get that 'silly' measure revoked.[13] The Health Ministry objected to the stage portrayal of doctors; the Ministry of Justice felt that the majesty of the law was not being adequately conveyed in some other dramatic effort; the police – or rather the Gestapo – objected to a comedy featuring a drunken prison guard.[14] Such scenes surely 'undermined public regard of the prison service and the police'.[15] That particular intervention prompted one of

had neither seen nor read the play ... The basis for his ban was a protest by the chancellor of Jena university – a racial scientist thoroughly devoid of culture – and some tortured phrases by, respectively, a professor of literature, Classics and ... philosophy.[33]

Yet Schlösser felt unable to challenge the bans: all he could do was to try and smooth things over in the Sudetenland, where the playwright Hymmen had lunged out in frustration at the official who had communicated the ban to him. (Hymmen was now awaiting trial for affray.)

All that may seem no more than a string of colourful anecdotes, but news of such incidents spread, and one should not underestimate the cumulative effect on the morale of theatre practitioners. Friedrich Hymmen, who landed that punch, was not a violent man: he was at the end of his tether. An earlier play of his had already been banned, when its Russian setting had become problematic because of the way the war was going.[34] Hymmen thus found himself deprived of income and public standing. What made that particularly hard to bear was the fact that he was a war invalid: he had been blinded by a grenade in Hitler's war, had learnt to cope with his disability and had started writing again only to find himself persecuted by parts of the very regime he had loyally served. The spectacle of a blind playwright lunging out at his tormentors may have been an unusual one even in the Third Reich; yet as a metaphor for Nazi theatre, it does not seem altogether inappropriate.

There is indeed evidence to suggest that the chaotic nature of Nazi rule impacted on the *overall* course of German theatre in the Third Reich. The *Thingspiel*, for instance, failed at least in part because of conflicting messages about it. Otto Laubinger, its great champion, strayed at one point into Schlösser's territory of repertoire policy. *Thing* activists promptly received in speech and print sharply divergent advice from both men about the future direction of the new genre.[35] And Laubinger, in turn, found himself at odds with a man working inside his own Reichsbund but wearing also the hat of a 'Plenipotentiary of the Reich Propaganda Office for the Development of the *Thingspiel*'.[36] The man, noted Laubinger, is thus simultaneously 'my subordinate, my equal, and conceivably even my superior'. Add to that the attempts of Robert Ley's Labour Front and Schirach's Hitler Youth to muscle in on the *Thingspiel* (to say nothing of the constant sniping from Rosenberg in his journal *Bausteine*), and it is not so very difficult to guess why the more gifted Nazi authors should have steered clear of the *Thing*. They evidently had no intention of walking into such an obvious minefield.[37]

Yet even in conventional drama, the ground was treacherous. It is remarkable how many leading Nazi dramatists chose to withdraw from the theatre or were actively forced to do so. Right at the beginning, Hanns Johst was sacked by Göring at the Prussian State Theatre in December 1933. Admittedly that need only have affected Johst's career as *Dramaturg*; but Johst was probably shrewd enough to recognise the writing on the wall. He gave up theatre in favour of becoming a senior official himself (and incidents such as Sauckel's ban three years later must have convinced him that he had made the right choice).

Consider further the case of Walter Erich Schäfer, whose military plays *The Eighteenth of October* and *Lieutenant Váry* were much performed in the Third Reich. He shared Johst's fate and was sacked as *Dramaturg*. The local Nazi potentate in Württemberg actually expelled Schäfer from the state as a 'politically undesirable individual'.[38] Schäfer was able to resume his career in another part of the Reich after Schlösser had taken pity on him; but the plotting continued and took its toll: in 1937, Schäfer suffered a nervous breakdown.[39] He only fully recovered his health *after* the fall of the Third Reich.

The two closest collaborators of Rainer Schlösser, meanwhile, were actually brought down by their party enemies. Sigmund Graff may not have been a particularly serious loss but Möller was. Rosenberg and Himmler had jointly sought to undermine Möller ever since the *Frankenburg Dice Game*, which was too Christian for their tastes.[40] Both Schlösser and Schirach sought to protect Möller; after the ban at Karlsruhe, however, Möller's position became precarious. He eventually sought refuge in the Army, as had Sigmund Graff (and, in another field, the poet Gottfried Benn). Someone who had helped shape Nazi drama had thus turned into a peripheral figure. It

162

is telling that Möller's final play, *The Sacrifice*, received its first-ever performance in 1941 not inside the Reich but at the small theatre of the ethnic German minority at Hermannstadt in Transylvania.

Mention must also be made of Curt Langenbeck, whose neo-classicist verse play *The Traitor* had come closest to Schlösser's ideal future German drama. Langenbeck, too, was brought down by an alliance between Rosenberg and the SS, who both detected in Langenbeck's work coded criticism of the Nazi leadership. For almost three years the Rosenberg Office exercised sustained pressure on all who came into professional contact with Langenbeck. At times, representatives of the Reich Security Main Office of the SS joined in those efforts at intimidation. The Propaganda Ministry was anxious to deny Rosenberg another prominent 'scalp'; yet the pressure was so intense that Langenbeck himself cracked: he resigned as *Dramaturg* at Munich in 1941. Like Möller and Graff, he 'fled to the frontline', as the contemporary phrase had it. In Langenbeck's case, too, there is a telling postscript. Having enlisted with the Navy, he attracted the attention of Admiral Dönitz: and at the admiral's suggestion, Langenbeck proceeded to write a play about submariners. This time it was the Propaganda Ministry itself that issued a ban. Langenbeck, whom Schlösser had considered the brightest hope of Nazi theatre, had effectively become a 'non-person'.[41]

How much of all that was noticed by the public is a matter of conjecture. As consumers of culture, people were confronted with the results of such hidden machinations: a play had vanished; a playwright was suddenly no longer mentioned in the press; but the precise mechanics involved are likely to have remained unknown to most. Certainly, some individuals were conspicuously unaware of what was going on. Amateur playwrights, for instance, often enclosed alongside their manuscripts recommendations from the Rosenberg Office in the touching belief that that would aid their cause with the Propaganda Ministry.

Some Germans probably first began to appreciate the full extent of Nazi cultural repression (and internal party rivalry) in an area where they were actively involved: that of amateur dramatics. The topic has been almost totally neglected by historians and theatre specialists alike: it may have seemed too recondite. Yet amateur dramatics was a mass phenomenon involving, directly or indirectly, tens of millions of Germans. It encompassed village plays and pageants, school or garrison plays, or that peculiarly German phenomenon, the *Burgspiele*: plays performed inside picturesque medieval castles. Above all, amateur dramatics involved the whole gamut of the very societies and organisations historians turn to when they examine civic mentalities in the nineteenth and early twentieth centuries: the bee-keepers, cyclists and gymnasts, the leisure club of the employees of the Reich Railways on the Frankfurt–Basel line, or the *Sparverein* in the local pub, where people turned feeding a piggy bank into an excuse for a little conviviality.[42] All of these outfits were likely to produce periodically an amateur play. The motivation was as much economic as social. The admission charged to non-members helped fill the kitty.[43]

To these groups must be added the dramatic societies proper, which for many of the Reich's citizens, especially in rural areas, probably represented German Theatre. 'The nearest town is three hours away,' wrote one such group of players, 'and people rarely have the chance to go [there].'[44] Financial constraints, moreover, meant that even many urban Germans were unable to attend professional theatre, particularly at the end of the Great Depression. Even the subsidised tickets introduced by the Nazis did not automatically alter that: for a visit to a playhouse meant dressing up, and there were plenty of Germans in the 1930s who simply did not possess an appropriate dress or a good suit. Amateur productions were more relaxed occasions and thus more socially inclusive. The steady rise of the *Laienspiel* in the Weimar republic was probably no accident.

Social inclusiveness also marked the numerous religious plays traditional to the Catholic regions of Germany and the old Habsburg lands. There were nativity plays performed by schoolchildren; there were religious *Lehrstücke* put on by entire villages, by suburban matrons and virgins in the Legion of Mary, or the young apprentices in the urban Kolping hostels.[45] Together, these groups represented a very large section indeed of German (and Austrian) society in the 1930s and 1940s; and all of them became the target of Nazi officialdom.

Otto Laubinger, the first President of the Reich Theatre Chamber, began the harassment of the amateur players. He did so partly in the hope of helping the beleaguered professional theatre sector (by reducing the competition, so to speak). Laubinger was also hoping to 'elevate' the better amateur players by inducting them into the *Thingspiel*. He introduced a system of permits for all open-air productions, which were, after all, in direct competition with his *Thing* ambitions.[46] There followed restrictions on the number of performances allotted to each group, and then all amateur societies not devoted *exclusively* to amateur dramatics were prevented from staging plays.[47]

With Laubinger's death and the end of the *Thingspiel*, the situation eased a little. Yet the Propaganda Ministry itself introduced in 1935 two important new restrictions: all amateur groups were required to seek a licence; they also had to nominate a leader, who required a separate permit. Groups who appointed a Nazi as their leader were usually left in peace thereafter.[48] Those unwilling or unable to so, however, found life very difficult indeed. Catholic drama groups, for instance, had often been led by their priests. The clergy involved now had to prove their 'active support for the National Socialist state'; 'experience has shown that they are normally unable to do that', as one of Goebbels' assistants smugly noted.[49] Göring had already introduced another draconian anti-Catholic measure a year earlier: performances of religious drama were now restricted to religious environments.[50] They could no longer be performed in a field or in a village hall. A narrow interpretation of that edict would have meant the end of most passion plays in Germany, as one priest noted in correspondence with the Propaganda Ministry.[51]

The results of that policy were spelt out inside the Reichsdramaturgie in an exasperated memo some three years later: 'In one Gau they [i.e. passion plays] are banned, in another permitted. In one Gau a sweeping Gestapo ordinance is interpreted in one way, in another Gau another way.' The result had been an avalanche of complaints. There was only one remedy the official suggested: 'I need to be put in a position to launch an all-out attack on the Gestapo ... whose political stupidity quite turns my stomach.'[52]

Characteristically for the Third Reich, it is not even clear which 'sweeping' Gestapo ordinance provoked the official's ire. Since it applied to passion plays, it presumably cannot have been the Gestapo's ban on all 'purely secular' theatricals by 'religious' drama groups, which complemented Göring's ban of *religious* plays on secular occasions. (The Propaganda Ministry, incidentally, appears only to have learnt about the Gestapo ban three years after it had first been imposed.)[53] In a sense it hardly mattered: the official hoping to challenge the Gestapo did not know that his own superior was about to add to the plethora of anti-Catholic measures. In December 1937 the Reichsdramaturg sought Goebbels' approval to ban all plays 'propagating Catholic political aims'. These plays, Schlösser said, did not 'readily furnish an excuse for a ban because they had been very carefully written' but politically they seemed 'highly undesirable'.[54]

It is worth pausing at this point to consider what was happening here. The most senior theatre official in the Reich was proposing to break the Nazis' own law. For there was no *legal* way to ban those plays, as Schlösser clearly realised. He was, after all, sufficiently uneasy about the whole thing to seek formal authorisation; yet Goebbels was no more entitled than Schlösser to alter secretly censorship practice without changing censorship laws. Given the enormities of what the Nazis were planning or had already perpetrated, Schlösser's initiative may seem very small beer indeed. Yet in a society noted for its belief in the sanctity of rules and regulations, such conduct was deeply shocking. It often appears to have shaken contemporaries much more than the open street violence of the years 1933–4, which they regarded essentially as repaying the left in kind for the violence of 1918–19. Consider the reaction of a typical *Bildungsbürger* – the 'father' of the *Thingspiel*, Professor Niessen of Cologne – when he discovered that the permit for his translation of the medieval *Everyman* had been revoked without anyone in the Propaganda Ministry bothering to tell him. (Schlösser decided to ban the play for being too Catholic.) Niessen responded by writing a stinging letter to Schlösser himself. It 'surely constitutes normal practice in a state based on the rule of law to communicate decisions to those affected by them,' he wrote, 'and to explain how those decisions have been arrived at'. And he added, 'I expect both these things from you.'[55] He got neither: instead, an enraged Schlösser sought to get the local Gauleiter to make life difficult for Niessen in Cologne.

At the other end of Germany, in a Silesian village, the local branch of the Association of Catholic Virgins was suddenly denied permission in 1937 to stage its annual play. Since its head could not discover any legal justification for the ban, she wrote to the Führer to complain.[56] The Gestapo in Breslau 'questioned her' a few days later. Consider also the villagers of Nesslwang in Swabia – Catholic, too – who found that their play permits kept being revoked by local officials who had no legal powers to do so. Each time that happened, they protested to Berlin. After several such protests the local party threatened them with arrest.[57] That takes us back to the Reichsdramaturg, who in some ways proved a *Bildungsbürger*, too: he, likewise, was appalled to discover that Nazi officials at local level were systematically breaking the law – and in this case defying his own authority.

For just as Schlösser was seeking to close down Catholic amateur drama, local officials were often trying to stamp out amateur playing altogether; and again, like Schlösser, they refused to be constrained by the law. Anything and everything was liable to be banned, for whatever reason seemed convenient. A play about poachers was stopped 'because there had recently been several cases of poaching in the Gau'.[58] A group of war veterans in Westphalia were astonished to discover that the play they were rehearsing apparently defamed the Armed Forces.[59] A district official in Lower Saxony had banned productions on the advice of a local Nazi schoolmaster, who had objected to the plays' 'constant appeals to God and the Saints' (and the nativity play, he added, was 'simply an insult to Nordic cultural values').[60] Himmler's secret agents in the SD, meanwhile, were agonising over aesthetics. The SD informed Goebbels that it had closed down several drama societies because of their 'appalling artistic ineptitude'.[61] Elsewhere, performances were banned because they had been scheduled too closely to a party event.[62] In Franconia, Strength-through-Joy banned amateurs from performing anything longer than a single-act play; dramatic societies in the region were also told that they had to submit any play to prior censorship by Strength-through-Joy.[63] Neither measure was even legal. In a letter to all regional authorities, and carbon copied to Rudolf Hess at Nazi Party HQ, Goebbels drew attention to such practices. 'All those bans lack all legal basis; they are nonetheless . . . effective, since those wanting to put on a play . . . do not dare to proceed with their planned productions.'[64]

Goebbels' intervention failed to have any perceptible impact. The regime had undermined the rule of law to such an extent that by the late 1930s sudden appeals to respect regulations were simply shrugged off by local Nazi potentates. In desperation, drama societies in many cases responded by seeking shelter under the Strength-through-Joy umbrella. (After the war, such players would be suspected by the Allied occupation authorities of being Nazi sympathisers.)

Drama groups that sought to preserve their independence were watched by party offices with the greatest vigilance: they might contain a suspiciously large number of young men who had formerly been active in a Catholic organisation.[65] In Swabia – a veritable hotbed of Romish amateur dramatics – a group of Catholics had invited into their midst a number of Nazi party members, something that clearly pointed to 'subversive intent' and very likely to a dastardly plot to 'break into our ranks'.[66] Not only had those Swabian players been able to recruit forty-four local villagers for their latest play – including Hitler Youth – they had even ensnared the wife of a Nazi councillor. The lady in question was not to blame: after all, 'how should a simple woman recognise the true significance of things?'

The True Significance of Things, however, was also lost on a group of amateur players in Saxony, who were nearly all Nazi party members and could not understand why they were suddenly not allowed to put on a play as they had been doing for years.[67] Civilians from the Saarland who had been evacuated from the border region at the outbreak of war could not understand either why the Propaganda Ministry explicitly encouraged their plans to mount plays during their temporary exile while their (similarly exiled) regional officials banned their efforts.[68] The officials challenging the ministry in that instance, it should be noted, were not from a rival institution; they were the Saarland RPA: technically Goebbels' own subordinates.

The erosion of the Propaganda Ministry's authority over its own regional offices was not limited to the Saar. When challenged by Berlin about their flouting of Goebbels' edict on amateur dramatics, the RPA for South-eastern Bavaria observed that 'certainly there is the edict;

but ... since then things have moved on'.[69] In Baden, the RPA were even more explicit: 'the notion that something must be permitted because it had not been banned might be true in a purely legalistic sense. The party, however, cannot accept that; and it certainly is entitled to expect from a [drama] society acceptance of a local official's decision, irrespective of the actual legal position.'[70]

Those who now berate Germans for their passivity in the Third Reich might wish to ponder those glimpses of contemporary reality. For here is evidence of Germans challenging the authorities, and conspicuously failing to achieve anything thereby, except to make life more difficult for themselves.

The suppression of amateur dramatics in the Third Reich also demonstrates something else: the paradoxical ability of the Nazi system to neutralise some of the popular anger it had engendered. For the largely unsuccessful efforts of the Propaganda Ministry to intervene on behalf of beleaguered local players appear to have earned it genuine gratitude. A particularly telling case was that of a supplier of theatrical props from Central Germany. The decline of amateur dramatics had put him out of business (along with several of his competitors, with wig makers and a number publishers specialising in plays for amateurs).[71] One might have expected the man to be angry and bitter; yet in a letter to the Propaganda Ministry after he had been forced to sell up, he thanked them volubly for their efforts on his behalf. 'I shall ... challenge anyone who goes around saying, "We're powerless, nobody listens to us." '[72]

The misery induced by the Nazi readiness to ignore rules and regulations of course could also be alleviated on occasion by that same contempt for the rule of law. A publisher from Göttingen had long been in the Propaganda Ministry's sights for purveying too many plays judged *kitschig* (sentimental or trashy). The ministry had therefore decided to deny him – quite illegally – all further permits so as to drive him into bankruptcy. Yet after the man had sought an interview with Schlösser, the Reichsdramaturg noted in a memo, 'The whole thing does indeed now seem quite poignant, particularly since P. has a son in uniform, who has just been badly wounded.' Schlösser therefore proposed to disregard his own previous rulings. After all, he added, 'we are a *Volksministerium* [a ministry for the *Volk*]'.[73] The fiction of a 'listening government' was thus maintained, and the party sometimes ended up winning the gratitude of the very people it had put in chains. That was literally true in the case of an ex-Communist amateur playwright, who was shielded by Schlösser from further persecution after the man had been released from a concentration camp in 1935.[74]

Similar dynamics also occurred at the other end of the social pyramid: at the level of the *Intendanten*, the star actors and directors. They were operating against the same background of unaccountability which the amateurs had encountered. The theatrical elite enjoyed a greater degree of artistic and personal leeway, yet they too were vulnerable to arbitrary decisions. Heinz Hilpert at the Deutsche Theater, for instance, was prevented at one point from staging Gerhart Hauptmann's *The Rats*, for which the sets had already been made. The ministry then demanded that the programmes printed for the replacement of *The Rats* be pulped because Hilpert had praised Hauptmann too effusively for Nazi tastes. (There had been a complaint from Martin Bormann at the party chancellery.) Hilpert also had to endure persistent interference from Goebbels himself, who as Gauleiter of Berlin exercised tight control over 'his' theatres in the capital.[75]

The sense of being at the mercy of the leadership's whims, moreover, extended beyond matters of repertoire. Jürgen Fehling practically fled to Hamburg for a while in 1935 because of party opposition to his Berlin production of Lessing's *Minna*, which had enraged doctrinaire Nazis with a 'negro statue' in the set.[76] A year later, Gustaf Gründgens actually sought refuge abroad. His *Hamlet* had been greeted with a ferociously hostile article in the party daily *Der Völkische Beobachter*. The piece was ostensibly about the play's 'nordic essence' and never mentioned Gründgens by name but the insinuations were unmistakable. Playing Hamlet, it observed, required a heroic outlook on life. 'Only actors who act out their true [heroic] selves are fit for the part.'[77] It was unacceptable, the paper suggested, to play Hamlet 'in the tradition of Oscar Wilde's ... Dorian Gray'. Since Gründgens was gay, he regarded that article not merely as a threat to his career but potentially to his life.

What followed was a perfect illustration of the wholly arbitrary nature of Nazi rule and the dependence it engendered in its subjects. To protect his parents from reprisals, Gründgens had sent a letter to Göring explaining the reasons for his flight. Thereupon, Göring personally rang Gründgens in Switzerland, urging him to return to Berlin for negotiations.[78] Göring gave his word of honour that Gründgens would receive safe conduct back to Switzerland should he wish, but he did dwell on the repercussions Gründgens' emigration might have on his family. As for Gründgens' artistic standing, Göring told Gründgens not to worry: he had already ordered the arrest of the two journalists who had been responsible for the article in the *Völkische Beobachter*. Even where the regime sought to reassure, it revealed its essential lawlessness.

Back in Berlin, Gründgens was met by Göring at the Air Ministry, where they were joined by two frightened Nazi journalists who had just emerged from the Gestapo dungeons in Himmler's HQ, across the road. Gründgens begged for the two men to be released and asked to be given twenty-four hours to consider his position. Göring assented but actually forced Gründgens' hand with an announcement broadcast by Berlin radio that afternoon. Gründgens, who had gone to his doctor, heard of it when two SS-men burst into the surgery, handing him the text of the proclamation: Göring had appointed Gründgens 'Prussian State Councillor', a title that traditionally conferred parliamentary immunity on its bearer. While the concept of such immunity had clearly become a fiction in the Third Reich, the broadcast had nonetheless put everyone on notice that Gründgens enjoyed Göring's personal protection.

Göring proved as good as his word. When Goebbels' assistant Hinkel began to investigate the sexuality of Gründgens' friends and colleagues a year later, possibly at Goebbels' instigation, Göring rapped Hinkel firmly over the knuckles. Hinkel then turned to snooping around at the Berlin Volksbühne, which did not possess Göring's protection.[79]

Those enjoying protection by a senior Nazi paladin were thus constantly aware that their own fates hung by the thinnest of threads. Take the Austrian director Walter Felsenstein, who had been invited back to the Reich from Switzerland in 1939, his Jewish wife notwith-standing. The family were granted exemptions from all anti-Jewish legislation; yet when the mass deportations to Auschwitz began, Felsenstein was sufficiently worried to try and move his family back to Switzerland. He then discovered that they were denied travel per-mits. Nothing happened to the Felsensteins, but the awareness of their vulnerability inevitably dictated their behaviour.[80]

The threat was often far from latent. Otto Falckenberg was arrested in 1933 for having lent a colleague his car to escape from the Reich. He was set free on Heydrich's orders, but only after three days in a Gestapo cell.[81] The actor Fritz Odemar was horse-whipped by an SA unit after he had protested about their taunts at the expense of exiled Jewish actors. Both Falckenberg and Odemar continued to keep their distance from the Nazis; but neither man risked open defiance again.[82] The Austrian stage and screen star Paul Hörbiger stopped going to the swanky Berlin Artists' Club set up by the regime after he had noticed an informer creeping about among the inebriated rev-ellers late at night. At the Vienna Burgtheater actors eventually refused to act alongside a man they (rightly) suspected of being an informer, forcing the *Intendant* to sack the man.[83]

As the regime's paranoia increased after Stalingrad, even the most prominent theatre practitioners were targeted. When Heinrich George was sent on tour to occupied Norway that year, the Reichsdramaturg contacted several people in Oslo. He would be grateful, he wrote, for any 'interesting' details they could provide about George's conduct.[84]

George's colleague Heinz Hilpert fell victim to an informer a year later. He had made philosemitic remarks on a train journey, while sharing a compartment with an old acquaintance. Yet when the train pulled into a station, someone standing on the platform next to the half-open window of the compartment caught a snatch of the conversation, recognised Hilpert and informed the authorities.[85] Since the theatres had by then been closed as part of the Reich's final mobilisation drive, Hilpert was never sacked; but he was punished: he was the only prominent theatre practitioner to be drafted into factory work, even though he was fifty-four years old and had been in poor health.[86] When Goebbels set up the Volkssturm – the 'home army' of old men and young boys that were meant to engage Allied forces in street combat – Hilpert was even called up for active service. He was spared actual combat only because a friendly doctor decided to diagnose a mild heart attack. 'We will stick by you if you will stick by us,' Goebbels had told theatre practitioners in 1933.[87] That promise had always contained an implicit threat.

8 'The final redoubt': theatre and propaganda

Two observations made towards the end of Nazi rule by two very different people illuminate the relationship between theatre and propaganda in the Third Reich. The first comment was by the *Intendant* of Berlin's Deutsches Theater: it was part of that train conversation betrayed by an informer. Heinz Hilpert had expressed his frustration that the theatres in the Reich should answer not to a ministry of culture but to the Propaganda Ministry. That comment was pregnant with meaning. The second observation occurred in a surprisingly frank memorandum by Hans Hinkel. 'In the initial years after the transformation [of January 1933],' wrote Hinkel, 'the party was faced with a predicament ... It lacked the practical experience in ... cultural life to enable it to take charge securely and immediately ...'[1] That fact, Hinkel went on, had not escaped the 'cultured classes'. It led them to 'hope that the revolutionary *élan* of the [Nazi] movement would peter out precisely in the cultural sphere ... *Kultur* would then remain as the final redoubt against the party and the only door still opening on to [politically] neutral ground'.

Hilpert's exasperation with political interference and Hinkel's remarks about the limitations of Nazi power both point to the same fact: theatre in the Third Reich was an uneasy compromise between the Nazi authorities and the cultural elites. The origins of that compromise were recalled by Friedrich Bethge in a wartime letter to Hinkel,

> immediately after the seizure of power, radical party comrades would have preferred to close down all German theatres because there were no Nazis available as *Intendanten*; and [then] you, as Göring's ... adviser, hit upon the ingenious solution of

174

appointing Nazi dramatists as 'chief dramaturgs', thereby creating a new title and ensuring the theatres' survival.[2]

Non-Nazi *Intendanten* judged 'at least halfway acceptable ideologically' were allowed to continue to work because the theatres would have collapsed without them; but the 'technically skilled' were given Nazi 'spine pads'.[3] Bethge pointed out that he was the only such appointee still in office a decade on: a few of his erstwhile peers, like Johst or Möller, had moved on to greater things; the vast majority had been swallowed up again by obscurity.

A similar fate had befallen the handful of genuinely Nazi *Intendanten*. Take Karl-Ludwig Achaz, who had seized control of Max Reinhardt's Deutsches Theater.[4] The main qualification of that passionate if only moderately gifted actor was that he was the son of an industrial magnate who had been an early benefactor of the Nazis. Achaz's tenure lasted just over a year: Goebbels then sacked him and saw to it that Achaz was denied subsequent employment in the theatre, since Achaz had proved himself 'unable to meet . . . artistic requirements'.[5] The other notorious case was that of Count Solms, who had taken over Berlin's Volksbühne. After witnessing a Solms production in the summer of 1936, Goebbels noted in his diary: 'Awful! I shall soon have to move against Solms. Things can't go on like this. Longstanding party member or not, the man's incompetent.'[6] To save face, Solms was offered another large but markedly less prestigious theatre in Berlin. 'He'll prove inadequate there, too,' noted Goebbels grimly.[7] Two years later, Solms was sacked a second time, this time without any prospect of further employment, whereupon he shot himself.

The appointment to prominent positions from 1934 onwards of experienced and decidedly *non*-Nazi theatre practitioners was thus final proof of artistic failure within party ranks. Yet it was also a victory of the party pragmatists over the ideological zealots. For Göring to declare publicly that it was 'easier to turn a great artist over time into a decent National Socialist than to turn a humble party comrade into a great artist' may have been stating the obvious; but it also proved that Göring was quite unembarrassed by the thought of employing people who were, in his own estimation, not remotely Nazi.[8]

This takes us back to Hinkel's memorandum. The party's predicament, Hinkel observed, had been compounded by the fact that there existed within its ranks 'noticeably divergent notions about culture'.[9] The plurality of styles after 1933 was thus no accident. Much more survived of pre-Nazi theatre than might have been expected. At the top of the artistic pyramid, Falckenberg, Fehling, George, Gründgens and Hilpert all enraged sections of the Nazi party with productions which were judged variously to be reminiscent of the 'spirit of the *fin-de-siècle*', to be 'infected by liberalism' or even downright cases of 'art bolshevism'.[10] The 'styles of the period of decadence', noted the Rosenberg Office in 1938, were all still to be found in the Reich.[11] That, it bears repeating, was not simply because the party was bereft of talent: it was the result of internal Nazi disagreement about what should or should not be preserved.

Almost every aspect of German theatre tradition was attacked at one stage or another. The most familiar case may be the debate about expressionism, not least because it seriously embarrassed Goebbels; but the controversies extended far beyond Emil Nolde's canvases, Gottfried Benn's verse or the 'unseemly predominance of the expressionist scream' in individual *Thing* plays.[12] The artistic scene before 1914 divided the Nazis almost as much as the efforts to rescue parts of the Weimar legacy. The *Thingspiel* itself was not just a target in the cultural wars: it had itself been conceived as a battering ram against tradition. The more extreme *Thing* proponents initially aimed at a kind of *völkisch* cultural revolution, which was to sweep away everything connected with the proscenium stage: German theatre was to have undergone compulsory reruralisation.

Even after the defeat of the *Thing* movement much of traditional theatre was under attack. Goethe was widely frowned upon because of his 'individualism'. It required an unlikely alliance between Goebbels and Rosenberg (and their respective subordinates) to rescue Goethe.[13] Schiller may have been the object of Nazi adulation; yet *Don Carlos* and later *Tell* – two core pieces of the German repertoire – became taboo because of their denunciation of tyranny. Lessing was acknowledged as the father of modern German drama but there was the awkwardness of his philosemitic *Nathan*. Hebbel was a

Nazi favourite, yet he had written no fewer than two 'Jewish' plays, and there were other problems, too: his most Teutonic drama, *Die Nibelungen*, invoked Christ in its final line. At the Hebbel festival in Bochum, scandalised party dignitaries summoned the director to their box to protest against such outrageous 'Christian propaganda', which constituted 'an insult to every National Socialist'. The offending verse had to be cut to rescue the production.[14]

The ambivalence extended to another Nazi favourite: Dietrich Grabbe, whose brooding and rarely performed plays were systematically championed by the Reichsdramaturg. Yet the first-ever staging of Grabbe's *Duke Theodor of Gothland* provoked party protests because the play contained a 'negro' character.[15] Kleist fared no better: he may have constituted in Schlösser's words, 'the corner stone' of a Nazi theatre repertoire, yet that did not stop party sniping at *Amphytrion*, which was considered unsuitable for an heroic age.[16]

Shakespeare, too, polarised the party. On the one hand, he had been pronounced a central pillar of German theatre in *Mein Kampf*; various encomia lauded the Bard's supposed 'Nordic', 'Germanic' or even 'German' spirit; Alfred Rosenberg came close to self-parody by praising as inspirational characters Macbeth and Iago; a leading Nazi racial scientist collated Shakespearean quotations for a racial primer to guide the young in their quest for a suitable mate; Shakespeare was even used in a wartime newspaper cartoon to underline the Reich's cultural credentials.[17] Such Nazi appropriation was not just empty talk. The Hitler Youth sponsored a festival where all the history plays were performed on successive nights; nothing like that had been attempted before anywhere in the world, as the organisers proudly pointed out. In the major playhouses, too, some of the Third Reich's most memorable productions were Shakespearean: Werner Krauß's Richard III; the rival interpretations by Rudolf Forster and Gründgens as Richard II; Gründgens, again, as Hamlet; Heinrich George as Falstaff; or Krauß's infamous Shylock. Yet at the same time there were also furious denunciations of Shakespeare, declaring his plays to be 'profoundly un-German' and incompatible with Nazi notions of the heroic.[18]

Consider also the case of the Nobel laureate Gerhard Hauptmann. When Hauptmann turned eighty in 1942, various party outfits were energetically pulling in different directions as to how to mark the occasion.[19] For, although Hauptmann was clearly a national institution, he was synonymous with the 'drama of misery', as doctrinaire Nazis called naturalist theatre, which they blamed for sapping the nation's strength. The ideologically supple Schirach in Vienna and Gauleiter Hanke in Hauptmann's home region of Silesia advocated major festivities (but clashed over the location); Martin Bormann at the Party Chancellery and the Rosenberg Office wanted strictly 'no fuss' about Hauptmann; the Propaganda Ministry favoured modest celebrations; Gauleiter Sauckel of Thuringia marked the occasion by issuing a ban of a Hauptmann play. Hitler himself had remained unaware of the feuding and innocently suggested a lavish birthday edition of Hauptmann's collected works.

Such grotesque Nazi disunity was neither limited to Hauptmann nor to the year 1942.[20] Ibsen's *Ghosts* had been banned a year earlier, after sustained sniping. Yet by then the play had actually been produced more often in the Third Reich than in the Weimar republic; what is more, *Ghosts* was staged twice *after* the ban had been imposed by theatres which somehow managed to get exemptions.[21] The list of Nazi inconsistencies could be extended almost indefinitely. A final example may suffice: Georg Büchner's *Woyzeck*, the ultimate 'misery play' in the German canon, was produced in Frankfurt by the SS-man Bethge.[22]

If there was little agreement about the past, there was still less about the present: various sections of the party favoured their own adopted dramatists and eyed suspiciously those championed by their political rivals. There were 'Hitler Youth dramatists', SS-playwrights, Rosenberg men and those close to the Propaganda Ministry; and only the failure of organisations such as the German Labour Front to attract even minor talents prevented the list from getting longer still.

The dramatic output itself defied definition: 'Nazi theatre' encompassed the expressionist echoes in Johst or Möller, the *agitprop* of the *Thingspiel*, the neo-classicism of Curt Langenbeck or Ernst Bacmeister, Hans Rehberg's 'Shakespearean' plays, dramatised versions of Rosenberg's neo-paganism, blood-and-soil dramas continuing the tradition of the *Volksstück* and E. G. Kolbenheyer's attempts to turn supposed biological destiny into verse drama. No wonder Hinkel found himself confronted by the question as to 'what exactly constituted Nazi culture'.[23]

Publicly, everyone echoed the same slogans. There was to be no more Wilhelmine *l'art pour l'art*; culture now had a definite purpose: it was to serve the interests of the *Volk*. An avalanche of tracts repeated these axioms with wearying regularity. Yet Hinkel himself spoke of the regime discharging its 'duty towards the classics'.[24] Who was serving whom here?

At bottom, there existed two rival conceptions of theatre inside the party. One saw the stage as a platform for propaganda; the other followed a more traditional approach, looking on theatre as a pleasurable civic duty (and a source of national pride). The advocates of open propaganda were initially in ascendance both in the *Thing* arenas and on the proscenium stage. Crude propaganda theatricals were soon marginalised by Goebbels but never vanished completely. A Nazi peasant leader, for instance, was able to dragoon hapless rustics by their hundreds into helping him stage a play he had written about the peasantry's past plight.[25] The German Labour Front encouraged its amateur players to act out scenes about Strength-through-Joy holidays.[26] Coal miners in the Eiffel region were treated to a dramatic offering by an SS-playwright which had failed to make it onto the professional stage.[27] Eugenic enthusiasts trod the boards in village halls and suburban venues to spread the gospel of 'racial health': by September 1935 there had been more than 1,300 performances by such outfits as the 'German Theatre Company for Ethnic Hygiene'.[28] In newly nazified Austria, actors from the Linz theatre created *tableaux vivants* on a carnival float, lampooning 'Yesterday's Men': namely the overthrown Austrian government, Jews and Catholic prelates.[29] Members of the Hitler Youth in a Berlin suburb satirised Chamberlain, Churchill and the House of Commons in sketches accompanying street-collections for Nazi winter-relief late in 1938.[30]

Such propaganda was artless in every sense of the word, yet there were also attempts to combine propagandistic intent with at least a minimum of artistic standard. Otto Laubinger had tried to

Konservative
Partei

10 Members of the Hitler-Youth, in a sketch lampooning the British
Conservative party during street collections for Winter Relief in a Berlin suburb,
November 1938.

steer the *Thing* in that direction: 'what they [i.e. the public] are
taught through the intellect in political meetings, via the papers
and the radio ... [should be] planted into them [on stage] ... through
art, as experience [*Erlebnis*]'.[31] Locally, the link between party propaganda and *Erlebnistheater* was maintained even after Laubinger's
death in 1935: most obviously with *De Stedinge*, but also with the
various performances of Möller's *Frankenburger Würfelspiel*. The
Dice Game, for instance, featured at a party rally in Saxony in
1937.[32] A year later, the play was performed in the hills of the
Erzgebirge, the location having been dictated by propagandistic
intent. The new arena was only a stone's throw away from the
Nazis' next target for expansion: the Sudetenland.

Territorial expansion even brought a final addition to the
Thingspiel canon that year: Karl Springenschmid's *Lamprechtshausner
Weihespiel*, which glorified six Nazi 'martyrs' from a village near
Salzburg, who had been killed in the aftermath of the abortive coup of
1934. The emotional release of Nazi triumph after years on the fringes of

society allowed such crude theatricals to work in newly nazified Austria, as it had done in Germany five years earlier.

Many of the plays which best served the Nazi cause, however, had been written when the Third Reich seemed for its adherents still the stuff of distant dreams, and didacticism had not yet deadened the imagination. Hanns Johst had been active before the Nazis had even formulated their aims. He had started out with the figure of the isolated artist-genius in *The Loner* (1917). In its protagonist, the classical dramatist Grabbe, *The Loner* had anticipated the Reichsdramaturg's tastes. Johst's thematic progression from the artist figure to the leader of men – *The King* (1920), Luther in *Prophets* (1922), *Thomas Paine* (1927) and finally *Schlageter* (1932–3) – was in itself significant. It mirrored, or perhaps anticipated, the lives of Hitler and Goebbels, who both thought of themselves as having sacrificed to the needs of their nation their artistic callings. Hitler told Johst he had seen *The King* ten times: a suspect claim but suggestive nonetheless.[33] Goebbels pronounced himself 'deeply moved' by *Thomas Paine*: much in the play, he noted in his diary, 'reminded me of my own life'.[34]

The other road to Nazism was via the theme of the 'common man betrayed'. That was the route taken by the authors of the *Fronterlebnis*, notably Bethge in *Reims* (1930) and *The Veterans' March* (1932–5) or Zerkaulen in *Langemarck* (1933). These plays succeeded on the cusp between the imploding republic and the emerging Reich because they reflected a wider unease with recent history, rather than a narrowly Nazi interpretation of it. *The Veterans' March* was the least overtly propagandistic of Bethge's dramas, and it promptly became his only reasonably successful play.[35] It had been inspired by a march of American war veterans, protesting against reductions to their meagre pensions. The play was *Erlebnistheater*, where emotional manipulation prepared the ground for the poisonous political seed: namely the contrast between an 'honourable *Volk*' and 'a government without honour'.[36] Bethge had changed the setting from America to Tsarist Russia to prevent audiences from reading an anti-American message into the play. His target, after all, was the *German* republic.

Möller's early plays had likewise reflected public concerns rather than party dogma. Möller had come to the Nazis via Bakhunin and Brecht. Such a route is less surprising than it might seem: a substantial number of Communists embraced Nazism in the 1930s. The phenomenon was sufficiently widespread to receive stage treatment itself: a whole range of Nazi 'conversion' plays in 1933–4 had as their theme working-class youths seeing the light, as Hitler 'sow[ed] peace in German hearts'.[37]

Möller's *Panamaskandal* (1930) was in a sense both a left-wing and a Nazi play: both constituencies regarded democracy, the play's target, as a corrupt affair which habitually ignored the needs of the impoverished masses. The antisemitic overtones of *Panamaskandal* now give the play a strong Nazi flavour; but the original audiences may well have been less forcefully struck by that. *Panamaskandal* was first performed in Frankfurt's Neues Theater, which was *Jewish*-owned and had a substantial Jewish audience: an unlikely setting for genuine Nazi propaganda. Similarly, Möller's *Rothschild's Victory at Waterloo* (1934), with its more overt Judeophobia, was not just an exercise in antisemitism: in its emphasis on the multitude rendered penniless by a stock market manoeuvre enriching the few, it too carried left-wing echoes. The dim-witted SA-man who considered the plot of *Rothschild* crypto-Communist did have a point. The files of the Propaganda Ministry contain a number of examples where the Reich authorities were uncertain whether a play was Nazi propaganda or constituted 'covert Communist agitation'.[38]

Theatre, as the Nazis discovered, is multivalent: different audiences often take away different messages from the same play or even the same production. The Jewish patrons of the Frankfurt Neues Theater probably saw something different in *Panamaskandal* from the Berlin audiences five years later in the Third Reich: the play allowed multiple readings. A member of the 1935 audience noted that very fact: 'good dialogue but no clear overall message [*Linie*], no clear ideological thrust [*Tendenz*], no certainty ... [but] fantastically well acted'.[39] Those words were the considered opinion of Goebbels himself.

The lack of 'certainty' was not limited to *Panamaskandal*. Take Möller's *Rothschild*, which Otto Falckenberg was famously forced to produce in 1936. After the war, Falckenberg's assistant claimed that, together with the leading actor, they had sought to sabotage the Propaganda Ministry's order by presenting the play's Jewish protagonist as a man of initiative rather than as a callous schemer.[40] That may sound like a post-war excuse, yet it is not wholly improbable: for Falckenberg possessed substantial *philo*semitic credentials. It is worth recalling Möller's exasperated correspondent, moreover, whose SA-acquaintance had concluded from a synopsis of *Rothschild* that the play was *pro*-Jewish. The truth of the matter is that we simply do not know what effect Nazi propaganda in the theatre actually had on most German or Austrian audiences.

That goes even for productions where things might seem straightforward, such as the notorious 1943 Vienna *Merchant of Venice*. Detailed descriptions of the production survive, which document that every positive trait in Shylock's character had been excised. Yet those same descriptions suggest that Werner Krauß's lolloping and wildly gesticulating Shylock was not so much a fiend in human form as a pantomime villain.[41] Audiences repeatedly greeted his 'turns' with laughter. That laughter may well have been antisemitic but it was hardly in line with the image of the Jew as a threat to humanity, which was peddled by the Propaganda Ministry outside the playhouse. Krauß's readiness to prostitute his talent in a doctored version of Shakespeare was certainly disgraceful, yet the question is, how useful was his Shylock to the Nazis? The menacing images of the film *The Eternal Jew* were used to prepare the ground for mass murder; but was Krauß's pantomime villain likely to legitimise genocide in the eyes of Viennese audiences?[42]

It may be helpful to recall Marlowe's *Jew of Malta* here, with which the Third Reich also experimented: that play is palpably antisemitic, yet Barrabas' villainy is surely too histrionic to carry conviction with modern audiences. It is hard to believe that Marlowe's tale of poisoned porridge ever *made* anyone antisemitic in the twentieth century. Certainly, the Nazis quickly gave up on Marlowe.[43] Might not something similar have occurred with the Vienna *Merchant*? Committed antisemites, like the party members for whom several special performances were laid on, will have found nothing in the production to challenge their prejudice: Krauß had turned even

Shylock's plea 'if you prick us . . .' into a romp of the Jew performing an act. Yet was that enough to turn less ideologically committed theatre-goers into antisemites? Moreover, if the nazified *Merchant* really had proved effective, why was it never staged again after its Vienna run? Why was Krauß not asked to reprise the role elsewhere? While there can be no definitive answers to these questions, such questions by themselves help to clarify a little the role of theatre in the Third Reich.

There is substantial evidence that neither Goebbels nor Schlösser considered the stage a particularly effective platform for overt propaganda. In November 1939, for instance, Goebbels convened an urgent meeting to commission anti-British propaganda material for 'film, press and radio'.[44] Drama came as an afterthought and only in the form of radio plays: yet Goebbels had approached Hans Rehberg, one of the best Nazi *stage* authors. Was the choice of medium dictated solely by the radio's larger audience or was there also the thought that in its non-visual and pre-recorded format it removed the ambiguities of a live performance on stage? The Propaganda Ministry was noticeably lukewarm in its response to anti-British *stage* plays when these started to be submitted.[45] Rehberg's own offering, *Suezkanal* (1940), was premiered in Danzig, which was hardly the most prestigious of locations.

It was not just that propaganda plays had often been crude or inept (and frequently both). Many had blurted out unwelcome truths. The bards of the ethnic struggle had threatened to give away prematurely the Reich's expansionist aims. Other plays provided disconcerting glimpses of coming savagery at home. Friedrich Griese's blood-and-soil drama *Man of Clay*, for instance, featured a bull of a man who dispensed with every human decency in order to fulfil his biological destiny with a farm-maid of child-bearing age. The play had appalled even *völkisch* critics.[46] The SS-playwright Walter Best presented audiences with the spectacle of a general's wife killing her maid after the girl had seduced her employers' young son. With a corpse at her feet, Best's heroine then calmly announced, 'baseness must be stamped out'. The play provoked 'alarm among petty-bourgeois souls', as a Nazi critic observed.[47] Johst's *Prophets* contained a scene of a medieval pogrom, which might have passed as period colour when the play was written in 1922. After the Nazi seizure of power, however, that scene created a different effect, and it was staged with such relish at the State Theatre in Berlin in 1934 that Göring himself descended on a rehearsal with knotted brows; he duly demanded radical cuts and subsequently sacked the men responsible: Johst as *Dramaturg* and Franz Ulbrich as *Intendant*.[48]

Other plays revealed the irrational nature of Nazism with uncomfortable starkness. When the 'Hitler Youth dramatist' Friedrich Hymmen approached Schlösser with a proposal for a play about workers on a building site, the Reichsdramaturg was initially intrigued. It struck Schlösser as 'thematically exactly the sort of direction in which daring [dramatists] ought finally to venture'.[49] The finished play turned out to be about an engineer who brushed aside all warnings that the structure of the bridge he was building could not withstand a storm. It was not a matter of calculations, he declared, but of will-power. In the final scene the protagonist was shown saving his bridge by personally tightening screws in a gale. That play really did reveal something about National Socialism; and Schlösser was intelligent enough to realise that Hymmen's *Concrete* would do neither Nazi propaganda nor German theatre any favours.[50]

Propaganda plays often seem to have been put on more for the benefit of the party than of the wider public. The various anti-Christian efforts, for instance, which surfaced locally from the mid-1930s onwards, were authorised but not promoted by the Propaganda Ministry. That was in contrast to Schlösser's well-documented efforts to launch other kinds of plays. Older playwrights who had lost their audiences after 1918 were often given discreet assistance.[51] Similarly, Schlösser championed young party dramatists if he detected at least a hint of talent. He would call in favours or flatter selected *Intendanten* by ostensibly turning to them for help.[52] In the case of prominent Nazi playwrights, such as Hitler's deceased mentor Dietrich Eckart, he tended to apply more substantial pressure.[53] The Reichsdramaturg thus influenced theatre repertoire substantially; yet his methods were more modulated than might have been expected. Not only was Schlösser elaborately courteous, he was at times genuinely prepared to listen to counter-arguments.[54] The theatre in Potsdam, for instance, escaped the duty of performing Dietrich Eckart after pleading poverty. The fact that the Nazi bard would empty the playhouse remained unspoken in the correspondence: the *Intendant* tactfully referred to the price of costumes, but Schlösser evidently took the point.[55]

The occasions when Schlösser imposed plays therefore stand out all the more. In July 1939 he asked an assistant to draw up an 'emphatic letter' to twenty-three theatres to get them to stage Felix Dhünen's *Uta von Naumburg*.[56] (Himmler had complained to the Propaganda Ministry that Dhünen's anti-Catholic play had not been staged often enough.) There was an exact parallel five years later when Schlösser came under pressure to endorse an anti-British play by the SS-playwright Walter Best.[57] In both cases, Schlösser clearly did not act out of personal conviction.

Similarly, the Munich *Rothschild* was probably not prompted by a sudden hope that it might spread antisemitism in the Bavarian capital. There was a more immediate need: that of finding a credibly National Socialist play for the 1936 Reich Theatre Festival in that city. Möller was the most talented of the Nazi playwrights; yet as Goebbels himself had noted, Möller's earlier plays were insufficiently Nazi. *Rothschild*, quite simply, was the only option. (The previous year in Hamburg, Dietrich Eckart had been imposed, and in the planning for the 1937 festival, Schlösser advised Goebbels that they had now run out of suitable Nazi plays.)[58] The other famous occasion when Schlösser ordered a theatre to produce a particular play occurred in the summer of 1940, when Gustaf Gründgens was told at very short notice to produce Mussolini's drama *Cavour*. Here the real function of the production was even more apparent than with Möller's *Rothschild*. No one surely can have imagined in 1940 that a weakish play written by the Duce (with a little help from the playwright Forzano) would enthuse Berliners about Hitler's Italian allies. The real purpose was to flatter Mussolini during his state visit. Gründgens had warned Schlösser that the play trailed off badly after its first act; but that did not matter in the slightest, since the visiting author was unlikely to find fault with the structure of his own play. All that was required was a polished production to permit the hosts a suspension of disbelief, and by all accounts Gründgens delivered.

Schlösser actually sent the 'State Councillor' Gründgens a personal thank-you letter. He called the performance 'a singular achievement' and concluded by saying, 'let me thrice raise my hat to [you]'.[59] Schlösser's admiration was genuine; he had just seen supreme proof of theatrical talent: a great director and a stellar cast had turned a real stinker of a play into a tolerable evening in the theatre.

Theatre, in other words, could serve a propaganda function without even containing an explicit propaganda message: the polished production itself was sometimes the message. It is revealing in that regard to contrast Nazi state occasions at the beginning and towards the end of the Third Reich. For the tenth anniversary of the Hitler putsch in November 1933, considerable efforts had been made to find suitably propagandistic fare: a total of nine theatres, for instance, staged Zerkaulen's *Langemarck*, thus equating the 'Nazi martyrs' with wartime sacrifice in the trenches. A further six theatres had selected Friedrich Forster-Burggraf's *Alle gegen einen*, which praised Hitler in the historical guise of a Swedish hero. Yet other theatres staged *Schlageter*. A decade later the picture had changed. In the planning for the tenth anniversary of the Nazi takeover, propaganda plays were in the minority: classics predominated.[60] Provincial theatres, combining *Sprechtheater* and *Musiktheater*, often chose operas or even operettas. On that day of solemn Nazi celebration, selected German and Austrian audiences were thus treated to *The Taming of the Shrew*, *Don Giovanni*, *The Abduction from the Seraglio*, *The Marriage of Figaro* or *The Merry Widow*.[61] The decorous had supplanted the didactic.

Propaganda plays of course continued to surface from time to time. The list for 30 January 1943 actually contained two prime examples of the later years: Paul Appel's paean to Japan, *The Golden Dagger*, and Herbert Reinecker's rallying cry to the Eastern Front, *The Village near Odessa*. Indeed *The Village* was staged by one theatre in three across the Reich over the course of just twelve months.[62] Yet the relatively varied fare in 1943 was a long way from the solid phalanx of propaganda plays ten years earlier.

It is tempting to see in that change evidence of what Hinkel had called the faltering 'revolutionary *élan*' of the Nazis. Certainly, the

doctrinaire Alfred Rosenberg had not just been outmanoeuvred by
Goebbels, he was torpedoed by the German public. Goebbels merely
had to sit back and watch his rival's playgoers' association, the NSKG,
go under. That was also true at individual level: many Nazi appointees
of 1933 did themselves out of their jobs by driving away audiences; and
theatregoers had still not warmed to Nazi fare six years later:
Himmler's security services noted in 1939 that new plays 'have frequently met with [audience] rejection', a fact posing 'serious challenges' for those seeking to create 'a modern National Socialist
repertoire'.[63]

Related initiatives suffered a similar fate: the practice of having
actors give the 'Nazi salute' at curtain calls vanished almost as soon as
it had appeared, since it had tended to turn audience visages to stone.[64]
Success had also eluded the scheme of the Rosenberg men to give
ideological 'pep talks' as curtain raisers. 'Dr Stang spoke introductory
words', reported a Berlin paper in 1933. 'It is to be hoped that this sort
of thing will not become a regular feature.'[65]

The 'bourgeois' newspapers, as the Nazis called the non-Nazi
press, played a prominent part in thwarting Nazi ambitions in the
playhouse. It is not for nothing that Goebbels eventually felt it necessary to ban critical reviews. There had been calls from the start to
move against 'forces seeking to kill off young [Nazi] talent through
irresponsible belittling criticism'.[66] Herbert Ihering was banned by
Count Solms from attending performances at the Volksbühne; Alfred
Mühr was threatened with a 'spell in a concentration camp' for being
too outspoken about Göring's State Theatre.[67] Other critics were more
circumspect, but not necessarily less hostile. The *Frankfurter Zeitung* –
the main paper for liberal *Bildungsbürger* until the Nazis banned it
in 1943 – warned its readers about propaganda plays through coded
language. The paper, noted Schlösser, practically 'winked' at its readers, 'as if to say, "Nazi Culture!"'.[68] A Berlin theatre critic recalled
after the war that his paper developed 'a particular phraseology of
praise', indicating Nazi fare; people, he added, became proficient at
reading between the lines.[69] A paper from Catholic Silesia informed
its readers with touching earnestness about Burte's *Katte*, a desperate
Prussian affair beloved of the Nazis: the première was 'regrettably,

the extinction of the Sixth Army at Stalingard, which the regime had sought to turn into a rallying cry to the home front. Kleist's 'drama of duty' seemed a perfect accompaniment to such propaganda. Hilpert, however, had drained *Homburg* of all heroism in favour of its dreamily romantic qualities. The 'inner distance' in Hilpert's theatre 'to all things Prussian', Schlösser noted, was filling him 'with mounting rage'.[94] For Hilpert had permitted himself a further provocation: in that most Prussian of plays he had cast an *Austrian* actor, Ewald Balser, whose 'bonhomie' suggested Vienna rather than Potsdam. Schlösser considered it a 'typical example of Hilpertian cheek'.

The cleverness of such tactics may be difficult to convey to those unfamiliar with Austro-German culture. A final example may be more obvious: Schiller's *Robbers* is not an antisemitic play but the character of Spiegelberg can be interpreted as being Jewish. In Weimar days, Erich Ziegel had famously exploited that by giving Spiegelberg the features of Trotsky. Gründgens chose to ignore that angle when he directed the play in 1944. He promptly received a letter from a Member of the Reichstag, expressing amid effusive praise a 'sense of regret': why, the Member asked, had Gründgens cut all the 'hints that Spiegelberg might be Jewish'? Surely Spiegelberg's machinations were suggestive to 'anyone who had lived through the last thirty to forty years'?[95] Someone in Gründgens' office highlighted these comments by scribbling a word in the margin: that word read 'danger'.

Making sense of theatre in the Third Reich, we said at the outset, was a matter of perspective. The conduct of Gründgens and Hilpert from the late 1930s onwards, and of Falckenberg and Fehling from the outset, came close at times to open defiance of the regime. Seen from that perspective, the 'saboteurs' on stage, to use Goebbels' term, would almost merit inclusion in the history of the anti-Nazi resistance. Yet those same men had also been repeatedly fêted by the regime, and had all been forced to kowtow. Against the full record of the Nazi years, the star directors' defiance might seem more like remorse at their conspicuous success after 1933.

Yet there is a third perspective, one opening out backwards in time. In its internal report, the Propaganda Ministry had charged Hilpert with organising a 'deliberate flight from the present' (and audiences, noted the officials, were 'regrettably' following Hilpert's lead).[96] By this the officials meant a 'repertoire policy that is useless for our cultural struggle ... [which is] apt to cause depression and to ignore the real problems of today'. That sentence carried distinct echoes of Weimar and Wilhelmine theatre controversies. Hilpert had indeed staged the very naturalist plays to which the Kaiser *and* the Nazis objected; and both Hilpert and Gründgens had produced the 'apolitical' classics which the Nazis *and* the Weimar directors equally regarded as unsuitable to their respective modern ages. For the Nazi Member of the Reichstag who wanted to see Spiegelberg's Jewishness underlined surely had more in common with Erich Ziegel's Weimar approach than with Gründgens' resolute refusal to proffer a ready contemporary reading; and the Hitler Youth from Bremen or the SD spies who berated middle-class audiences for their 'reactionary' attitudes were using rhetoric remarkably like that of the Weimar cultural elites.

Rather than dividing German theatre of the years 1890–1945 into three separate periods, one might note the underlying continuities. Throughout, there was a clash between those advocating a theatre in the service of political aims and those doggedly asserting the stage's independence of politics. In Imperial Germany the advocates of political theatre favoured glorifications of the House of Hohenzollern and of the Prussian-led Empire. The champions of an independent theatre responded with naturalist drama revealing the ugly social reality outside the playhouse, while deflating Wilhelmine pretensions with a Greek chorus or a Shakespearean forest conjured up by Reinhardt's magical hand. After November 1918, the servants of the Crown were replaced by the champions of republicanism, but what remained was the essential divide between those keen to shape the stage in the image of contemporary politics and those believing culture to be *überzeitlich* (transcending time). The Nazi Seizure of Power then brought yet another political dispensation, but in the theatre the old divide remained: the only difference being that the Nazi prophets of the here-and-now were so glaringly untalented that political theatre in the Third Reich had largely collapsed after a single season. The Nazis' artistic bankruptcy then enabled Gründgens, Hilpert *et al.* to recapture the principal playhouses for the *Bildungsbürger* and their favoured eternal verities.

flowering ... All that had seemed dead lived again and grew and was blessed ... by his creative force. Thus Adolf Hitler strode through the wasteland left by the transitory republic.'[13]

The blessing and flowering happened in a few hectic years before territorial expansion placed additional demands on the Führer's 'creative force'. The takeover of Austria and the Sudetenland added some ten million 'national comrades', with essentially penniless theatres. Goebbels noted in his diary at the time, 'I've managed to get another two million [Reichsmark], which I shall distribute among the impecunious theatres.'[14] Only a few months later the annexation of the rump-Czech state widened the field still further. There existed, even after Munich, substantial German minorities in many Czech towns and cities. All these places duly received lavishly renovated German playhouses. Theatre had long been a weapon in the nationality struggle in the old Habsburg lands. Czech students, for instance, had stormed the theatre in Brünn/Brno in 1920 to eject the Germans.[15] The German Brünners, who at the time made up the majority of the town's population, were thereafter limited by their new Czech rulers to two nights per week in the theatre. In other towns, the Bohemian Germans had to make do after 1918 with occasional performances in their native language or were forced to conduct their plays on improvised stages, while the theatres whose construction they had helped to fund were now reserved solely for Czech plays.[16] In a sense, the Nazis ended an injustice only to create a worse one: for performances in Czech were now banned completely in all disputed theatres. The bare statistics – an additional thirteen theatres in the former Czechoslovakia – thus disguise another twist in the spiral of competing German and Czech chauvinisms.

The situation was even starker in Poland, where a further nine playhouses fell under Nazi control in 1939: for whereas Czech theatre life continued throughout the war in those theatres built under Austrian rule specifically for Czech audiences, the Poles were forbidden to set foot in their own playhouses.[17] (The Poles after all had defied the Reich, while most Czechs had chosen collaboration.)

The fall of France then won the Reich the theatres of Alsace-Lorraine and Luxembourg, which were also extensively refurbished:

'before and after' photographs were used, as in the East, to trumpet the Reich's achievement and to denigrate the defeated nations. A picture of rising damp in the Metz theatre, for instance, illustrated what could befall a playhouse in just twenty-odd years of French rule.[18] The invasion of Yugoslavia finally added a further three former Austrian playhouses to the tally, yet even that was not quite the end of it. Theatres were soon also created for the use of German occupiers further afield: Oslo and The Hague got German opera houses, Brussels and Lille German theatres with resident companies; the latter was housed in the 'historic' German theatre that had existed there during the First World War.[19] In the East, too, there were additional stages. The German theatres in the Latvian and Estonian capitals really did deserve to be called historic: they had been founded in the days of the Tsar to cater for the substantial German minority in the region. These theatres had been closed after the Soviet invasion of the Baltic states in 1940 and were reopened after the German invasion a year later. Seemingly oblivious to the slaughter on their doorstep, Riga and Reval performed until April 1944.

It was almost as though the Nazis were waging war solely to be able to reopen theatres. The brutal reality obtruded at first only at the furthest frontiers of that new stage empire: the president of the Reich Theatre Chamber, for instance, referred to the pioneer spirit of the new German theatre in Lodz, which was sited in a street 'crawling with Jews'.[20] Further east, in Minsk, the amateur playwright and mass murderer Wilhelm Kube had created a theatre in a city flattened by the German invaders: the agents of destruction thus masqueraded nightly as bearers of culture. In Warsaw the theatre itself was caught up in the hostilities when the head of the Deutsches Theater in Warschau was shot by the Polish resistance in 1941. (The Wehrmacht retaliated by murdering eighteen Polish hostages.)[21] The 'flowering and growing' had come at a price; and it is not altogether fanciful to say that the price was Germany's soul. What was offered in exchange was not just insubstantial pageants and gilded boxes in which to view them, but often very palpable benefits. Theatre was a living for some Germans: and for them, life had been especially precarious during the Great Depression. Almost half of all German actors are estimated to have been unemployed in the 1932–3 season. For actresses the rate was nearer 60 per cent. In Austria unemployment for men *and* women was still not much short of 60 per cent three years later. What is more, two-thirds of the employed actors were on fixed-term contracts. Given the shortened seasons, that meant that many of those deemed to be working were actually without income for anything up to six months a year.[22] The expansion of the theatre sector meant secure employment for all within a relatively short period. Income began to improve too. At the top end of the profession, actors benefited from a partial exemption from income tax, which had been granted at Hitler's personal suggestion. By the late 1930s, income for the theatrical stars was well in advance of what cabinet ministers earned; and even those at the bottom of the profession were comfortably off.[23] The Nazis also introduced a comprehensive pension scheme, plus fringe benefits ranging from injury pay, homes for injured actors (the 'Goebbels Foundation'), retirement homes for actors (the 'Emmy Göring Foundation') to various recreational facilities.

There was an inflation of honours, with 'State Actors', *Generalintendanten* or even 'State Councillors' now treading the boards. There were prizes, medals and gifts, ranging from framed portraits of the Führer to a country estate for Hitler's favourite stage designer. Even amid the severe shortages in the final phase of the war, the Propaganda Ministry found wine or spirits for favoured actors.[24] And while the bombs were falling on Berlin in 1944, and civil life broke down irretrievably, Goebbels fretted about the provision of flowers for the leading actresses at curtain calls.[25] 'We have elevated actors socially ... in unprecedented fashion, showered them with honours and lavished money upon them,' noted Hans Hinkel, 'without however succeeding in creating for ourselves a reliable corps of National Socialist cultural agents'.[26] The question arises why the Nazis should have lavished so much attention on the stage.

One view current even at the time was that it was all bread-and-circuses.[27] There were supposedly 30 million spectators for the various Strength-through-Joy stage spectacles in 1940; a year later the figure stood at 90 million, and there were no less than 189 million in 1942. Such figures hardly suggest high artistic standards, as some

Nazis themselves observed. Hans Hinkel in fact warned that 'we seriously need to recognise that cultural efforts should not be measured in numbers, mass or statistics'.[28]

One can also point to revealing official pronouncements about the theatre as a break from daily cares and woes; or indeed to Goebbels' advice that a Berlin *Intendant* might increase attendance by casting more attractive actresses.[29] There is also the suggestive tide of comedies flooding the Third Reich's theatres: the most popular plays during Nazi rule included such gems as *Wrangling over Jolanthe* (about a pig being secretly kept in an urban tenement) or *Hilda and the Four Horse-Powers*.[30] Finally, there is the evidence of an SD-report in 1940 which noted that people were not concerned about what plays they might see but 'simply wished to go to the theatre'.[31]

Yet the very same SD-report mentioned the great success of a touring production of *Faust* in rural Mecklenburg. In Berlin there had been Goethe's *Götz* in the Großes Schauspielhaus before an audience of workers; and while Strength-through-Joy emphasised that their theatres were offering 'light, optimistic, life-embracing' fare, the list of plays performed under their aegis included Schiller's *Robbers* and *Wallenstein*, three Shakespeare comedies, and at least in one city even Hebbel and Kleist's *Penthesilea*.[32] The provincial theatres, too, combined comedies and operettas with some of the most heavy-going classics in the German repertoire.[33] Consider also the creation of a special theatre company for the construction workers of the Führer's new highways. The repertoire of the 'Reichsautobahn Stage' was indeed limited to comedies, but those comedies were by Kleist, Lessing or Molière.[34] The performances were introduced by brief lectures on the respective play and its author. Pictures beamed on a white screen by projectors were used as an alternative to programme notes, since some in the audience were likely to be only semi-literate. The artistic standards of the *Reichsautobahnbühne* may have been modest; but the underlying ambition was not. To see how remarkable it was as political and social measure, try and imagine President Roosevelt inviting the construction workers of the Tennessee Valley to the Forest of Arden; or try and picture Churchill treating the dockers of the East End to *Bartholomew Fair* perhaps.

11 Propaganda coverage of the *Reichsautobahnbühne*, the itinerant theatre troupe for motorway construction workers.

The *Reichsautobahnbühne* was an echo of the Wilhelmine reformers: theatre as a sacred cause, uniting the *Volk*.[35] The Nazis had, however, learnt from the failure of the *Thingspiel*: the hopes of assembling all classes in the same audience had died. While lip-service continued to be paid to the idea, in practice each section of the public was now offered its own theatre: the liberal playhouses catered for the *Bildungsbürger*; 'middle-brow' fare was offered to the lower middle classes; and Strength-through-Joy catered for the cultural proletariat.

There is no doubt that the leading Nazis were genuinely hoping to win new cultural enthusiasts.[36] Yet if the workers should not develop a taste for *Kultur*, that would not constitute total Nazi failure: they would then at least have chosen to stay away, rather than feeling excluded by the cultured.

Nazi support for the theatre was thus based both on idealistic and deeply cynical motives; and the two were closely linked. During a visit to Augsburg in 1936, Hitler inspected that city's theatre, an elaborate neo-rococo affair. The Führer was entranced; after an extended rapture, which sorely tested the patience of his entourage, he turned to them sternly and pointed to the building's lamentable state of repair. 'Theatre,' he intoned, 'is the gauge of the cultural standard of any town or nation.'[37] He then ordered the immediate refurbishment of the Augsburg playhouse.

Here was someone publicly embracing the values of the *Bildungsbürger*, namely that politics should be put aside to devote oneself to the service of beauty; but the politician in Hitler also recognised that conspicuous cultivation of *Kultur* might confer legitimacy on his government in the eyes of those who had traditionally despised politics. And the investment might pay off even with other parts of the *Volk*. They might be awed by the lavishness of the Third Reich's style, by the shining exterior of the renovated playhouses, by the massed violins of a Strength-through-Joy operetta or by the fact that, at the Führer's behest, theatre was provided even for navvies knee-deep in mud.

In the Reichstag speech after the passing of the Enabling Law, which inaugurated the Nazi dictatorship, Hitler had expressed his hope that 'the nation's will to endure might manifest itself with particular magnificence in the realm of culture, especially at a time of circumscribed political might'.[38] Theatre, in other words, functioned initially as an alternative to military parades. Germany was still disarmed when the Nazis came to power; there were, at first, no tanks, planes or battleships to show off. The Reich Theatre Festival, the lavish open-air theatricals at Heidelberg or Frankurt, and a host of smaller versions throughout the Reich helped to compensate for the lack of military spectacle; and the reopened playhouses provided

12 Hitler and Goebbels attending a performance of Goethe's *Götz von Berlichingen* in the rebuilt Schiller Theater in Berlin, 1937, with Heinrich George playing Götz.

substitutes for conquest. The mental link would become quite overt after the outbreak of war, with countless references to 'sword and lyre' or Army and *Kultur* being linked symbols of the nation.[39]

By 1938 there would have been no need to rely on theatre as a substitute for military might; but by then the habit had evidently stuck: theatre had become part of the public face of Nazi rule. The sight of senior party figures in the playhouse was a recognised feature of theatregoing in the Third Reich. The phenomenon was by no means limited to Berlin: at a first night in Austria the local party requisitioned the entire grand circle, leading to an official reprimand. (Himmler's SD, too, reported on more than one occasion public indignation about party officials reserving theatre tickets for themselves.)[40]

For all the talk of the '*Volk* and its stage', theatre had reverted to its older role of glorifying Germany's princes. The most shameless illustration of that point occurred on Göring's fiftieth birthday in 1943. A select audience sat in the Kaiser's old Court Theatre, trying to balance theatre programmes the size of a small coffee table book,

STAATLICHES
SCHAUSPIELHAUS

*

Montag, den 11. Januar 1943

AUS ANLASS DES 50. GEBURTSTAGES
DES REICHSMARSCHALLS DES GROSSDEUTSCHEN REICHES
HERMANN GÖRING

*

13 Theatre programme for Göring's fiftieth birthday in 'his' Prussian State
Theatre, 1941.

printed on the thickest, most luxurious paper, so as to point the
contrast with the critical paper shortage outside the auditorium.
(Other theatres had been forced to abandon programmes in favour of
single-sheet playbills.) The birthday treat for the Reich Marshall
consisted of a scene each from *The Prince of Homburg* and
A Midsummer Night's Dream, complete with musical interludes.
Theseus and all the Court of Athens sat in their boxes, so to speak; on
stage, however, there were no 'rude mechanicals' but the cream of the
Reich's acting profession. After all, Göring had charged Gründgens 'to

turn this institution into the finest theatre in Germany – and hence the finest in the world'.[41]

There are countless instances proving both Göring's concern for artistic standards and his colossal vanity. Where the two clashed, the outcome was pre-ordained. When a fire broke out at a stage depot at the time of the Berlin Olympics, the flames threatened to destroy the sets for the entire season; also threatened were decorations intended for Göring's forthcoming garden party. Göring ordered that the rescuers concentrate on the garden ornaments: one could always improvise on stage; but a spoilt garden party was irreparable, all the more so as he was intending to outdo Goebbels' effort.[42]

Yet Göring did also use his power on behalf of others. In the numerous theatre memoirs published after 1945, he emerges at times almost as a patron saint of the German acting profession. It is a matter of record that he shielded a substantial number of theatre practitioners from party zealots. 'His' Prussian State Theatre was enviously described as 'the Island' by those tossed about in stormy seas.[43] Goebbels supposedly referred to it as 'a concentration camp on leave'; and Heinrich George's Schiller Theater, which also enjoyed a degree of protection by Göring, Goebbels apparently called a 'Jew sty'.[44] Since some of the individuals thus protected were not absolutely necessary to maintaining artistic excellence, the question must be asked why Göring should have done so. That question, in turn, points to an important fact: however much one may try to explain the past in terms of structures, ideologies or economics, there always remains a personal factor; and in a political system that had suspended the rule of law, that personal factor might be the only thing keeping individuals from destruction.

Göring genuinely liked the theatre; some of his oldest friends were actors, like the great Käthe Dorsch, to whom he had once been engaged. Göring's wife was an actress too, and both Miss Dorsch and Emmy Göring regularly interceded on behalf of colleagues. Göring went along with that presumably because it was part of the sweetness of life for him to be able to grant wishes, particularly if those wishes were controversial with his peers. He would remonstrate with Käthe Dorsch, fly into a rage, accuse her of being 'completely Jew-ridden';

but he invariably answered her pleas.[45] In the Third Reich's dying days, an embittered Goebbels observed that Göring was 'no Nazi but a sybarite', who had always 'stood aside' from the Nazi movement; 'he engages as much with the party,' Goebbels added, 'as a cow might engage with nuclear physics'.[46]

Yet Goebbels had not been free from sybaritic tendencies himself. The cast of the Deutsches Theater had been invited to go boating with him at his lakeside house on the outskirts of Berlin. (His mistress was in the cast.) Theatrical stars had regularly added glamour to ministerial house parties. 'Gründgens is so amusing. He's such a wonderful *causeur*. What fun we're having!', reads a diary entry in 1936.[47] Pretty actresses had sweetened the hour with their presence. Goebbels, too, had granted audiences to the personable Käthe Dorsch, and had responded to her detailed pleas on behalf of non-Jewish colleagues. (Jewish cases she wisely tackled only with Göring.) 'She is a charming woman,' Goebbels noted in his diary. 'I shall try and help her if I can.'[48] And while Miss Dorsch was clearly off-limits, so to speak, other actresses were not. Martin Bormann acquired an actress-lover, Robert Ley an actress-wife. Other men helped themselves, too: at one point, Goebbels was even moved to observe, 'It is not the purpose of the theatre to facilitate the abduction of women'; yet his own diaries prove that he himself never left the playhouse without having fully sized up the available talent. Indeed, ministerial enthusiasm became a recognised professional hazard for young actresses. The extraordinary symbiosis between theatre and regime in the Third Reich was never just a question of cold political calculation. There existed a mutual fascination between leadership and theatre practitioners; more than that, there was a sense of affinity. Göring and George would jointly carouse. Goebbels felt a mixture of stage performers and politicians made for 'maximum well-being', and while he never reminded anyone that he had written plays himself, it was obvious to all that he knew his stuff in the theatre.[49] Hitler, too, was never happier than in the company of *Künstler* – that untranslatable term of respect which Germans bestow on those active in the arts.

The affinities were unmistakable: 'history will record with astonishment and admiration,' wrote the Reichsdramaturg in 1936,

14 *Künstlerempfang* – a reception for theatre practitioners – at the new Reich Chancellery: the beaming host is surrounded by actors, singers and dancers.

'that the National Socialist movement has brought to power ... artistically gifted individuals'.[50] Carl Zuckmayer was more to the point: the reason why so many theatre practitioners collaborated so readily, he thought, lay in their professional admiration for the Nazis' theatre skills.[51] Hitler's voice coach – a scion of the famous Devrient acting dynasty – was in no doubt either: having seen his pupil perform, he pronounced a Hitler speech 'great theatre in its most elemental form, presented by an able actor'.[52] Piscator observed after the war that Hitler had been the greatest of all directors.[53] Consider also the tribute of the Nazi playwright Lützkendorf after the momentous summer of

1938. What dramatist, asked Lützenkendorf, could hope to equal the three-act drama of 'Berghof, Godesberg and Munich' which the Führer had just created on the political stage?[54] Amid Lützkendorf's sycophancy there surely lurked an element of truth.

To see in the Nazi courting of Germany's theatrical stars mere 'cultural window-dressing' is to close one's eyes to a significant part of Nazi motivation. Certainly, there was abundant cynicism: when Werner Kraus was asked to become vice-president of the Reich Theatre Chamber (and pleaded administrative inexperience), he was actually told that only his name would be required.[55] Yet consider Goebbels' diary entry after he had seen Heinrich George as Götz. The performance had left him, he wrote, with 'goose pimples'.[56] 'The great, great George,' he gushed. Goebbels strove to create goose pimples himself: admiration for a (fellow) performer, the ecstasy of *Erlebnistheater* and an awareness of its political usefulness all combined. When George's rival Werner Krauß celebrated the twenty-fifth anniversary of his first appearance on stage, the Propaganda Ministry arranged for him to reprise on successive nights the greatest parts of his career.[57] It was a quintessentially Nazi gesture, and the fact that it was unprecedented helpfully reflected on the regime. 'The German people,' Goebbels declared, 'are the most theatre-loving and theatre-obsessed people in the world'.[58] 'Theatre,' Goebbels added, 'had found in German culture its deepest and truest expression.' The president of the Reich Theatre Chamber struck a similiar note: while other nations might be as patriotic as the Germans, no one surely equalled the Germans in their love of *Kultur*; and this war was about the defence of culture against 'Eastern nihilism' and soulless 'Western materialism'.[59]

The fact that the theatres had initially been closed in London and Paris at the outbreak of war was prominently reported and contrasted with the situation in Germany. The glossy *Berliner Illustrirte Zeitung* published a photospread of what was on offer in the Reich's capital.[60] Those pictures appeared on the anniversary of the Hitler putsch: subtly, the link had been made between party and *Kultur*. For the claims in the Western democracies that Nazism was destroying Germany's cultural fabric had hit home. There was a telling defensiveness about Goebbels' responses. 'We have never tried to play the part of an ... artistic dictator,' he declared in 1938.[61] 'I did not give orders ... what I gave was money: millions upon millions'. A year later he declared that the 'self-appointed champions' of civilisation should be judged by their deeds not their words: 'the democracies just talk; our theatres perform'.[62] The journal *Die Bühne* examined the advertisements in the *Daily Telegraph* for West End plays in 1941 and noted that, with the single exception of *Heartbreak House*, there was nothing but 'shallow drawing-room comedies and Ivor Novello'.[63] The weekly paper *Das Reich* printed a cartoon in which the spirit of Shakespeare noted the almost total absence of his plays from the contemporary British stage; whereupon the ghosts of Goethe and Wagner assured him that his verse lived on: *in Germany*.[64] And that claim was supported by grand gestures: the great Austrian actor Rudolf Forster had emigrated to the United States when Austrian freedom was extinguished. Yet he found no employment in America and, in despair, returned to Europe via the Pacific and the Trans-Siberian Railway. Goebbels welcomed him 'home' by casting him as Richard II in Berlin.

Two years earlier, Goebbels had publicly conceded that there were limits to artistic freedom in the Reich; those limits, Goebbels

IM OLYMP

„Na, lieber Meister Shakespeare, sie werden ja in Deutschland recht häufig gespielt! Wie steht es denn mit uns in England?"

„Da ist seit je kein großer Unterschied, liebe Meister — dort werden wir alle drei nicht gespielt.

(Maommen dem Reich vom 2. 3. 41)

15 'Well, dear Master Shakespeare, you seem to be staged quite regularly in Germany. How are we faring in England?' – 'Oh, we've long been treated equitably there: [in England] none of us are staged.' Cartoon from *Das Reich* (2 March 1941).

explained, were set by the 'national interest'.[65] In the democracies, he added, it was capitalist interests that dictated what was staged and what was not. As so often in Nazi propaganda, a recognisable element of truth lent credibility to the most shameless Nazi arguments.

Indeed, only a dictatorship could have sustained wartime theatre on the scale the Nazis did. More than a quarter of the Propaganda Ministry's total budget was spent on the theatre: that constituted more than twice the sum devoted to film, and considerably more than was spent on propaganda itself.[66] Funding from Goebbels' ministry, moreover, was just designed to top up the budgets provided by towns and regions; yet these additional funds alone had grown from just 400,000 Reichsmark in 1932–3 to RM 44,845,000 ten years later (at a time of only modest inflation).[67]

Not a single playhouse closed in the first years of the war: indeed one theatre was even built during the war: the Gleiwitz playhouse in Upper Silesia began its inaugural season in February 1944, less than twelve months before the arrival of the Red Army. The touring companies were likewise maintained, and in their new guise of *Fronttheater* they performed for German soldiers all over Europe. One of these companies, the journal *Die Bühne* trumpeted, had travelled more than 20,000 kilometres in the 1941–2 season alone: the equivalent of half the globe's circumference.[68] There was even a film in the cinemas about the *Fronttheater*. Allied intelligence officers viewing a captured copy could not help being impressed by the range of locations from Norway to Greece where the troupe performed in the film and in real life.[69]

Inside the Reich, the great theatre festivals initially continued. Dozens of open-air stages in picturesque rural locations were still playing in the 1943 season; people were conveyed by train to see performances at a time when rolling stock was in short supply and trains were travelling at reduced speed to conserve fuel.[70] Fifteen such festivals where still performing even in the summer of 1944, at a time when the Red Army was threatening East Prussia and the Western Allies were liberating France.

The number of new productions did decline during the war, but it remained very high by the standards of most countries. To sustain

16 Stereotypical wartime propaganda, highlighting the distances covered by an
itinerant theatre group during one season: in this case the equivalent of Berlin to
Cape Town.

repertoire theatre in the provinces, an average of one new production
per fortnight was required, and that average was broadly sustained
until the closure of the theatres in September 1944. Even at the metropolitan playhouses, which could rely on a larger pool of theatregoers,
the provision remained generous: there were still a dozen new productions, for instance, at the Vienna Burgtheater in the 1943–4 season: a
new production a month, after four years of war.[71] Overall, German
and Austrian theatres provided a total of 13,052 new productions in
the war years alone.[72]

The strains, however, showed: in the winter of 1940 many theatres were closed for several weeks due to coal shortages.[73] Given Central European winters, the lack of heating became an existential problem. The Linz theatre in glacial Austria reported on 5 October 1942 that the temperature in the box office – one of the warmest places in the building – had reached only 12 degrees Celsius at noon: yet one was barely into the autumn.[74] Such temperatures, the *Intendant* pointed out, placed people dependent on their voices at real risk. At least one theatre practitioner in the Reich is known to have died of pneumonia after performing on an unheated stage.[75]

The lack of fuel was only a harbinger for other shortages. Before long cloth, wood, paint, nails, glue, etc. – the mundane materials that are required on and behind the stage – were strictly rationed and were soon all but unavailable. The inevitable collapse was staved off for a while by making doubtful purchases in the defeated nations. A handful of theatres tipped off by contacts, for instance, acquired costumes and entire sets in 1941, when the opera of Russian émigrés in Paris was closed down and its effects were auctioned off.[76]

Most theatres in the Reich, however, got little in wartime, and in November 1943 the *Intendanten* were officially informed that it was 'pointless' to request further supplies of anything.[77] Indeed, the theatres themselves began to be seen as sources of raw materials for the war effort. In July 1942 all *Intendanten* received a circular, demanding the surrender of all metal items: anything from props to door handles, brass candelabra or ash trays was to be included.[78] To avoid embarrassing scenes, the theatres were specifically instructed not to remove busts of the Führer.

The greatest shortage, however, was not of material but of men, and with each successive call-up the situation worsened. Backstage hands were the first to go, to be replaced by a motley crew of prisoners-of-war, ethnic Germans from the East, who were practically treated as serfs by the regime, and by foreign labour recruited among the 'friendly nations', i.e. Italians, Slovaks, etc. Yet even such labour was in desperately short supply. The Linz theatre, for instance, may have been one of the more privileged theatres in the Reich, since it enjoyed

Hitler's personal patronage, yet even Linz had to make do with one-third of their normal backstage staff.[79]

The thinning ranks *on* stage caused even greater problems. Among younger men only the most talented were exempted from military duty.[80] Theatres responded by trying to change their repertoires. A Danish comedy about single-sex accommodation became one of the most widely performed plays of the war years, simply because it required no male actors at all.[81] During an inspection of East Prussia in April 1944, a Propaganda Ministry official reported that there was scarcely anything left 'in trousers', so that regular performances had had to give way to 'evenings of poetry and music'.[82] In Austria, the Linz *Intendant* described his own (relative) predicament in vivid terms: the only recent addition to his pool of actors had been an 'elderly man', who was 'of limited use', given his 'extremely conservative acting style', which was compounded by deafness. As replacements for the traditional category of 'youthful hero', Linz had been offered someone invalided out of the Wehrmacht because of arthritic joints; and as for the other candidate, the *Intendant* observed, 'well, the [enclosed] photo surely speaks for itself'.[83]

The strains on everyone in the theatre steadily grew: it was not unheard of for actors or singers to perform seven days in a row, frequently with more than one performance a day. Even though all advertising for the theatre performances had stopped in 1940, demand continued to rise. By February 1943, people were regularly queueing overnight outside the box offices, relieving each other periodically throughout the night.[84]

The Propaganda Ministry responded by insisting on extra performances, while being unable to offer additional resources. Most German and Austrian theatres performed almost 365 days a week during the war. With additional matinées, they frequently achieved between 500 and 600 performances annually, as well as providing frequent 'morning events' of verse and song. The Linz theatre, for instance, reported eighty-nine events in December 1942: in other words almost three per day, every day; and all of that was provided by performers who were given limited food, limited heating, limited public transport to get back from the theatre after performances, and who had to make do with ever more cramped and basic accommodation, as the housing stock was systematically destroyed by Allied bombing.[85]

The air-raids impacted on German theatre even before the play-houses themselves were hit. The remaining men were made aircraft wardens and would often go on duty after a performance, or go on stage after coming off duty. If they had been up all night, they would be excused until 13.00 hours the next day.[86] (Sleepless nights spent in air-raid shelters to the sound of exploding bombs did not count.)

To minimise the effect of a direct hit, theatres were ordered to divide their sets between several locations.[87] That measure placed additional demands on stage crews, who now had to transport the precious cargo over considerable distances. Hitler's preference for elaborate sets compounded matters. The Führer's taste had been for particularly lavish designs, which became known unofficially as *Reichskanzleistil*: 'in the manner of [Speer's] Reich Chancellery'. Indeed, as late as June 1943 Hitler still personally supervised the production of new sets for his adoptive theatre in Linz.[88] When Linz implored the Führer to reduce the size of the sets, since these were simply too heavy to lift for the bedraggled backstage crews, the First Artist indignantly brushed aside such quibbles.[89]

Behind Hitler's back, the Propaganda Ministry had already discreetly advised theatres at the beginning of the 1942–3 season to 'simplify stage sets as far as possible'.[90] The journal *Die Bühne* soon felt it necessary to explain that the increasingly bare stages were by no means to be confused with former Weimar practice.[91] Internally, it was precisely Weimar practice that was used to deal with complaints about lack of resources: in an unmistakable allusion to Jeßner, Goebbels thundered in February 1944 that performances used to take place 'on steps' in Weimar days, and the people involved had been 'thoroughly impressed with themselves about that'.[92]

Before the war, the Strength-through-Joy leader Ley had opined that 'the Führer's greatest gift to the German people' was this: 'that he took away ... all that was ugly and gave ... the beautiful in its stead'.[93] There was a grim irony in the fact that Hitler's war took away from the theatres the beautiful which the Führer's liberal hand had bestowed so prodigiously: until, in the end, the foyers and stages were equally stripped bare. The final Gründgens production in Göring's State Theatre was Schiller's *Robbers*. It was performed on an empty stage with a dais and simple black cloth confining it. The actors were seated during the performance on a row of chairs behind the dais. They would rise, step on the dais for their entries and would sit down again afterwards in full view of the audience.[94] It was perhaps more radical even than Weimar theatre: but the audiences went along with it, because it reflected their own fortunes. Allied bombing had initially been received in Germany in much the same way that the Luftwaffe's raids were greeted in Britain: with a mixture of panic and studied nonchalance. Theatre programmes contained instructions of what to do in a raid and the assurance that *after* the raid the performance would continue at the precise point where it had been interrupted. A performance of a Strength-through-Joy operetta by the Berlin composer Paul Lincke was *twice* interrupted in 1941, and was resumed after each raid.[95] At the end of the performance the organisers even wheeled on a Strength-through-Joy car (the embryonic Volkswagen Beetle) as a foretaste of the good life after victory. Once Allied bombers began to attack in waves and in ever-larger numbers, however, such practices had to be abandoned. The priority now was not to continue individual performances but theatre life itself. Take the case of Düsseldorf: in January 1943 its opera house was destroyed; five months later the town's theatre and its operetta stage were heavily damaged in the same raid. Yet six weeks later the operetta stage had been repaired and the theatre was playing in a school assembly hall. A further three months on, in November 1943, both the (repaired) operetta stage and the school assembly hall were obliterated in a fresh attack. Both institutions, however, were soon playing again in another assembly hall. All that while, moreover, the opera house destroyed in the original attack was being rebuilt: it reopened as a joint venue for opera, operetta and straight plays in May 1944: almost five years into the war.[96]

Düsseldorf was no isolated case. In Hamburg the bombs had totally destroyed the backstage of the opera house but the iron curtain held, thus allowing the authorities to rip out part of the seating in the stalls and turn the old auditorium into an apron stage for the Thalia

Theater, whose own premises had been completely destroyed.[97] In Barmen the theatre was rebuilt twice and only abandoned after it had been destroyed a third time. In Berlin attempts to repair the Komödienhaus were only abandoned after it had been hit for the *fourth* time in January 1944.[98] From mid-1943 onwards, Goebbels demanded detailed monthly reports about Berlin theatres. They read like despatches from the frontline: this theatre hit, that theatre being repaired, a third theatre being rebuilt; the iron curtain in a fourth had held; the roof in a fifth had been damaged (yet three days later that theatre had reopened).[99] At the Deutsches Theater the theatre crew had climbed onto the roof and had managed 'to put out 15 incendiary bombs' dropped on that theatre in a single raid.[100] The Schiller Theater was beyond repair, but its vast canteen was intact: Goethe's *Faust* was performed there with a stellar cast in 1944.

By the end of 1943, two in three Berlin theatres were *heavily* damaged; six months later seventeen theatres were 'operating normally' and five were being rebuilt.[101] Normal operations in 1944, however, involved scheduling plays according to the phases of the moon. In March 1944 Goebbels suggested additional performances at alternative venues to make the most of the nights closest to the full moon, as it would be easier for audiences then to pick their way home through the rubble in the unlighted streets.[102] For it was not just the playhouses that had been hit. Again the reports compiled for Goebbels provide the detail: an actor at the Schiller Theater was left homeless and widowed by a raid; the death of his wife earned him a brief compassionate leave.[103] At the Theater des Volkes, 16 actors were homeless on 24 November 1943; two days later the figure stood at 42. At the Nollendorfplatz, there where 37 homeless actors; and so the report went on, with the express proviso that it made 'no claims to be complete'.[104] By February 1944 so many actors were homeless that the authorities held out little hope for anything other than improvised accommodation. Several actors of the Deutsches Theater were sleeping in a hostel at the Friedrichstraße railway station; they professed to be happy about that arrangement because the dormitory was heated and close to the theatre. Another actress was not so lucky: she fell seriously ill in the freezing cold of February 1944 because her bedroom lacked one wall. In May 1944 an actress at the Schiffbauerndamm theatre was made homeless the third time in a row, with the bombs destroying on each occasion what meagre possessions she had managed to salvage from her previous flat(s). The *Intendant* of the Volksbühne was sleeping in the cloakroom of his theatre after separate air-raids had destroyed both his Berlin flat and his house in the country.[105]

The destruction was not limited to Berlin: after a raid on the town of Kassel, the dead – mostly women and children – were laid out in the town's main square until a carpet of corpses had formed. An actress from the Kassel theatre tried to arrange the singed scraps of clothing to give the dead some measure of dignity. Nine months later, twenty members of that theatre were dead themselves, having asphyxiated in their shelter during an attack. Yet the performances continued, sometimes even in the air-raid shelters themselves; and as far as one can tell decades on, something of that mythical union between performers and playgoers for which the Nazis had vainly striven was achieved in the inferno of the Allied bombs. Here lay the origin of that bond of loyalty between the public and its actors which would be such an obvious feature in post-war Germany and Austria, and which makes it so difficult to gauge in retrospect the artistic quality of these performances. Those that experienced theatre 'under the bombs' often maintained to their dying days that nothing in a lifetime of theatregoing had ever touched them as deeply as the precarious wartime productions. The returning émigrés after the war decried the 'sentimental tone' which they encountered on stage in Germany. Fritz Kortner found it reminiscent of the acting style of New York's Yiddish Theater and he spoke dismissively of an 'oy veh theatre for Aryans' and of a sentimentalism in the self-chosen Nazi ghetto that was every bit as embarrassing as that of the ghettoes imposed on the Jews.[106]

While one may be uncomfortable about attempted parallels between the suffering of Fritz Kortner's Jewish relations and the wartime experiences of 'Aryan' Germans, Kortner's observation nonetheless goes to the heart of things. There existed after the war a mutual incomprehension between the returning émigrés and those that had stayed on under Hitler: the 'Aryans' were never really able to imagine the full horror of racial persecution, of having, like Fritz Kortner, most of one's family murdered. The émigrés, for their part, found it impossible to picture life during the bombing, of waiting nightly for the sound of the planes and the first explosions. That mutual incomprehension has also bedevilled analysis of theatre in the Third Reich. For where one side has tended to see merely unrepentant Nazis defending Hitler's theatre, the other side saw people judging performances which they had not personally witnessed and which had occurred in circumstances beyond imagining.

The journalist Ursula von Kardorff cannot be suspected of pro-Nazi sentiments: several of her friends were in the resistance and her artist family favoured 'degenerate art'. Yet the first post-war production of Brecht's *Threepenny Opera* left her unimpressed. The sardonic style, she felt, failed to work with people who had seen far greater cynicism and had no illusions left.[107] Kardorff did, however, have faith in the actors who had held out in the disintegrating cities, while Nazi officialdom had sought safety in the country. In April 1944 she recorded in her diary that she had spent half a night playing charades with Berlin actors in a hotel: they all had no homes to go to, and Kardorff felt no inclination to return to her own unheated flat.[108] The *Intendant* Paul Rose observed after the war that theatre had turned into 'an anaesthetic: an opiate for performers and viewers alike'.[109]

The drug was suddenly withdrawn in September 1944 when Goebbels shut down all theatres, ostensibly to maximise the war effort. What was portrayed as a forceful act by the Propaganda Ministry was actually a sign of its weakness: it had been hoping to keep at least a quarter of the remaining theatres running in the 1944–5 season.[110] Yet Fate intervened in the shape of Gauleiter Sauckel, who unilaterally ordered the closure of all theatres in his Thuringian fiefdom.[111] To avoid an avalanche of individual decisions that would bury his authority, Goebbels was forced to issue a blanket ban. The ban's implementation confirmed the limits of the ministry's power: more than four months later, a ministry official discovered two actresses and two entire *Fronttheater* companies still playing – illegally – for troops in Silesia; and in Vienna the Burgtheater permitted itself a final gesture of disdain at the Prussian upstarts by continuing its own performances until its coal supplies ran out on 1 February 1945.[112] Ten weeks later, the Red Army entered the city.

The Reichsdramaturg had argued very strongly against a total shut-down. He warned about the 'politico-psychological consequences'.[113] In fact, he foresaw 'exceedingly dangerous repercussions', since theatre practitioners were 'without exception, people of sharp intellect'. Those remarks lead to an important issue: the moral dimension of acting and directing in the Nazi years.

In a famous open letter to Heinrich George, the exiled Brecht drew attention to the disappearance of the Communist actor Hans Otto.[114] Why did George not go and enquire about Otto's fate? That letter was addressed to a man who came close to being the public face of acting in the Third Reich. He toured abroad, serving in effect as an ambassador of Nazi Germany, and he appeared in some of the most notorious propaganda films. Yet the private George appears to have been a very different man.[115] There were no Nazi sentiments but a whole series of well-documented attempts to rescue friends and strangers from persecution. There were people who survived only because of George's help.[116]

The number of genuine Nazis at the top of the acting profession was surprisingly small. It has been well said that those who possessed talent had little need to be Nazis (and those who were Nazis were compensating for lack of talent). The conduct of most theatrical stars after 1933 thus provided variations on the life of George. All made important concessions to the regime; a substantial number, however, also helped its victims.[117] One may see in those rescue efforts evidence of uneasy consciences or even a strategy to insure against Nazi defeat; yet the risks were real. The Austrian stage and screen actor Ferdinand Marian played the Jewish rapist in *Jew Süß*, albeit not by choice. He also risked his life by sheltering in his house his wife's first husband, who was Jewish.[118] Paul Wegener, too, appeared in propaganda films; yet he also collected money to help a Jewish colleague escape from Prague.[119] The scheme was betrayed but Wegener was saved when his co-conspirators contacted the Gestapo to confess, and did so in such numbers that the authorities preferred to hush things up rather than risk a scandal. One wonders how many of today's stern moral judges would have made their way to the Gestapo to throw their own life in the scales?

The question is doubly apposite because of Brecht's letter to George. For sometime after that letter was written, Brecht's former lover, the actress Carola Neher, vanished in that other great killing apparatus of the period: Stalin's gulag. Brecht, it seems, did not heed his own advice and never enquired about Neher's fate, either during his journey through Russia or after the war, when he went to live in East Berlin as the favoured guest of Neher's murderers.

Such moral limitations were not limited to Nazism and Communism. Soon after the war, Senator McCarthy tested the moral fibre of American actors and directors. It may be argued that McCarthy's America cannot be compared to Hitler's Germany, but that argument cuts both ways: for anyone standing up to the senator would not have risked Gestapo dungeons or concentration camps. Yet few did stand up and fewer still chose exile and honour over career, compromise and California.[120]

Actors depend on language: almost all Austro-German émigrés who made it to safety in Britain or America found that their professional life disintegrated before anglophone audiences. Unsurprisingly, people hesitated to leave. Some of those who fled did so only after their efforts to come to an arrangement with the Nazis had failed. Gründgens observed with a degree of bitterness after the war that Albert Bassermann was being held up as a moral exemplar for having emigrated (Bassermann's wife was Jewish). Yet Bassermann had *volunteered* to appear in *Schlageter* in 1933. The real issue perhaps had not been whether to go or stay but how to minimise the concessions to the regime. Everyone in the profession, for instance, had to take part in collecting for Nazi Winter Relief, but some actors at least managed to look sheepish as they did so. No one could escape contact with party dignitaries. In the provinces that might mean mingling with the Gauleiter; in Berlin with Goebbels or Hitler himself. Turning down such invitations was not an option; keeping an inner distance was: one did not have to fawn over the hosts. Likewise, it was not possible to

17 Heinrich George in the costume of Götz, perhaps his most famous part, seen here receiving a donation for Winter Relief from a fan. Artistic and sporting celebrities were summoned each year to the Reich Chancellery to receive a contribution from Hitler's own hand, while a photographer was on hand to record the occasion.

decline presents from them but, again, one could register distance. When the celebrated actor Paul Wegener was given a bust of Goebbels, he buried it in his garden, ostensibly to protect the precious gift from air-raids.

Few prominent actors escaped duties in propaganda films; but again, there were ways of registering distance. When Gründgens was ordered to play in *Ohm Krüger*, he announced that since it was an order he was declining payment.[121] He also told the film's director Emil Jannings, who had espoused the Nazi cause, to revert from the familiar address of *du* to the formal *Sie*: something which for Gründgens' generation was tantamount to striking the man.[122]

Such gestures did not go unnoticed. After the bomb plot of July 1944, Hanns Johst raged about the 'apolitical' guests at the Führer's peacetime parties: the 'grinning smoothies who had weaselled around

18 A sheepish-looking Gustav Gründgens, collecting in costume for Winter Relief during the interval of a performance in the Prussian State Theatre in Berlin.

his apartments like Jesuits'.[123] Johst and Hinkel decided to force all prominent exponents in German culture to declare their allegiance: they were to express their support for Hitler in their own words, which would then be published as a commemorative book. Some eluded the Nazis even then: Paul Wegener's contribution read: 'My belief in the Führer is as great as my belief in German victory.'[124]

With Göring's power declining after Stalingrad, the measure of independence enjoyed by his protégés dwindled. When Goebbels declared total war in February 1943, Gründgens realised that the game, which had never been a game, was up. He persuaded an astonished Göring to allow him to enlist. An Air Force uniform subsequently protected Gründgens both in the Netherlands, where he was stationed, and during his brief stints in Berlin when he directed 'while on leave'.

Less astute and less talented theatre practitioners found it harder to escape being implicated in the regime's crimes. Soon after the proclamation of 'total war', the Linz theatre was ordered to welcome a 'visiting delegation of Police from the East', presumably on leave from genocide.[125] Worse was to come: after the closure of the playhouses in September 1944 the remaining men in the theatre were called up for military duty. In the case of the Führer's 'adopted theatre' in Linz, the able-bodied actors and singers were drafted into the SS and were despatched to guard duty at the nearby concentration camp of Mauthausen.[126] The reality of Nazi *Kultur* had caught up with its servants.

Conclusion

The theatre of the Third Reich continued various strands of German theatre reaching back into the nineteenth century. Nazi theatre, in the narrow sense of the word, took three principal forms: an open-air *völkisch* theatre in the tradition of the Wilhelmine theatre reformers, which sought to create a sense of common national consciousness through a shared theatrical experience (*Erlebnis*); the expressionist theatre of Johst and Möller, which shared some affinities with outdoor *Erlebnistheater*; and a neo-classical theatre, which sought to inculcate a new sense of heroism in German audiences. All three strands had been perceptible before 1933 and all three failed, for different reasons, thereafter.

The Nazis had benefited from widespread opposition to the Weimar cultural experiment, which had alienated in its radicalism and delight in provoking audiences substantial sections of the German public. The theatre of the Third Reich was thus based on a temporary coalition of disgruntled traditionalists and right-wing ideologues. After the fall of the republic, that coalition began to disintegrate, and the resulting conflict between the supporters of apolitical *Kultur* and the advocates of a theatre in the service of the regime was to remain a central aspect of German theatrical life right up to the end of the Third Reich.

The fissures first became apparent in the *Thingspiel* movement. The *Thing* plays had initially achieved considerable resonance by capturing the millenarian mood at the end of the Great Depression and by appealing in their language and themes to a wider nationalist audience. The gradual imposition of a new Nazi orthodoxy alienated the Catholic supporters of the *Thing* movement. The foreclosing of

226

stylistic and ideological variations, moreover, exposed the *Thing*'s inherent artistic weaknesses and accelerated its decline. The proliferation of crudely propagandistic variants – the so-called *Weihespiele* and *Werkspiele* – led to fears inside the party that inept theatrical propaganda might compromise the effectiveness of the regime's own propaganda. That concern led directly to the ban on the *Thingspiel* and a tightening of censorship in the conventional playhouses.

The success of Johst's *Schlageter*, which utterly dominated the German stage in 1933–4, had led to a rash of plays about the Nazi party's rise to power, yet these plays lacked the technical skill and psychological finesse which had made *Schlageter* so effective. The Propaganda Ministry responded by discouraging the use of the present day as a topic. While the Reichsdramaturg sought to encourage a stylised theatre transcending time, and his collaborator Möller offered an effective illustration with the *Frankenburg Dice Game*, the vast majority of playwrights 'took refuge in the past'. Historical plays thus became, almost by default, the dominant genre of the Third Reich's theatre. The resulting tide of antiquarian efforts or of 'Führer plays' in supposedly discreet historical garb succeeded in emptying the theatres in the mid-1930s. The Nazi history plays thus exposed two central weaknesses of Nazi theatre: its essential lack of drama, resulting from the fact that no credible ideological alternative could be presented on stage, which robbed Nazi protagonists of credible, rounded opponents; and the fact that the authorities, Nazi theatre activists and the public all had different priorities or actually favoured differing interpretations of Nazi ideology.

That fact became apparent in the theatre of the ethnic struggle, which was essentially driven by individual playwrights, usually from the contested border regions. Audiences outside those areas remained largely indifferent to these plays, and in fact often appear to have favoured reconciliation with Germany's neighbours. The Propaganda Ministry occasionally sought to exploit the theatre of the ethnic struggle, notably on the eve of the Sudeten crisis, but was otherwise forced to censor plays of which it secretly approved, so as to maintain in the 1930s the fiction of a peaceful Reich.

The issue of race again revealed the lack of ideological orthodoxy in the early years of the Reich. There was no clear consensus even inside the Nazi party about 'negroes', Jews or 'Gypsies'. The most radical sections of the party, however, asserted themselves, resulting in a systematic, brutal and ultimately murderous purge of 'non-Aryan' theatre practitioners. As a topic for plays, however, racial policy became almost taboo, since the radicalism of the ideological zealots threatened to become counterproductive on stage.

Ideological radicalism did produce a backlash in the case of the Nazi assault on Christianity. The neo-pagan plays of the mid- to late 1930s provoked repeated demonstrations among Catholic theatregoers, forcing the Nazi authorities on a number of occasions to end the run of individual plays. The concurrent assault on Catholic amateur drama groups, however, continued unabated and widened out into a determined attempt by local and regional Nazi activists to close down the entire amateur sector. That process revealed the extent to which the Propaganda Ministry had actually lost control over its agents in the regions.

The gradual breakdown of the rule of law shaped theatre in the Third Reich. Censorship became a wholly unpredictable process as agencies outside the Propaganda Ministry began to issue uncoordinated bans. Some of the leading Nazi playwrights – Johst, Möller, Langenbeck, Hymmen, etc. – were affected by sudden edicts from unexpected quarters. By the late 1930s that process was beginning to paralyse the Reich's dramatic production. Sudden attacks by party zealots were also directed at actors, directors and *Intendanten*. The only option for the individuals was flight – either abroad or to the frontline after the outbreak of war – or the search for a Nazi patron powerful enough to defeat the attackers.

With almost every aspect of German theatrical tradition under attack from some quarters, the theatre in the Third Reich created shifting coalitions between the supporters of apolitical *Kultur* and individual members of the Nazi elite. Audience support often proved crucial in rescuing individual careers and in defeating attempts to bring individual playhouses fully under Nazi control. In the leading playhouses especially, the *Bildungsbürger* forced important concessions on the Propaganda Ministry.

An all-out conflict between theatre-practitioners and the regime, however, failed to materialise because there existed a fundamental coincidence of aims. Both the regime and those working in the theatre wished to see the theatre recover after the depression and wanted it to survive in wartime. Aided by lavish subsidies, massive investment and a pronounced sense of affinity between leadership and *Künstler*, theatre became a central feature of Nazi rule and of the Reich's self-image in peace and war. After the tide of war began to turn, vast efforts were expanded to maintain the theatre sector against all the odds. If theatre had earlier reflected the pomp of the regime it now reflected the disintegration of German national life. In the process, the German public began to perceive the theatre again as an institution distinct from the Third Reich. That important psychological shift marked the beginning of the post-Nazi era in German theatre.

Notes

Chapter 1: Weimar: politics in the playhouse

1. The classic case of a combined takeover was Dresden, 7–8 March 1933.
2. On the administrative and legal aspects, see Henning Rischbieter, 'NS-Theaterpolitik', in Rischbieter (ed.), *Theater im 'Dritten Reich': Theaterpolitik, Spielplanstruktur, NS-Dramatik* (Seelze-Velber 2000), pp. 14–20, and Alan Steinweis, *Art, Ideology, and Economy: The Reich Chambers of Music, Theater, and the Visual Arts* (Chapel Hill 1993).
3. On the prominent role of the theatre in right-wing discourses, see Georg Bollenbeck, *Tradition, Avantgarde, Reaktion: Deutsche Kontroversen um die kulturelle Moderne 1880–1945* (Frankfurt 1999).
4. For a survey of the relevant *Memoirenliteratur*, see Ulrich Liebe, *'Verehrt, verfolgt, vergessen': Schauspieler als Nazi-Opfer* (Berlin 1995); Michael Töteberg, ' "Ich möchte hier den Vorhang des Schweigens her-unterlassen": Über die Darstellung des Dritten Reiches in Schauspieler Memoiren, mit einem Exkurs über den Theater-Kritiker Herbert Ihering', in Helmut Asper (ed.), *Im Rampenlicht der 'dunklen Jahre': Aufsätze zum Theater im 'Dritten Reich', Exil und Nachkrieg* (Berlin 1989); see also Helmar Harald Fischer, 'Die Nazis und die Schauspieler', *Theater Heute* 9 (September 1989), pp. 1–21.
5. No comprehensive figures exist. For individual cases, see Oliver Rathkolb, *Führertreu und gottbegnadet: Künstlereliten im Dritten Reich* (Vienna 1991).
6. Peter Gay's classic account of the Weimar era dismisses the conservative resurgence with half a sentence: 'and the country was inundated by the rising tide of Kitsch, much of it politically inspired' (*Weimar Culture: The Outsider as Insider* (London 1968), p. 120). Gay's brevity may be extreme but it is not untypical of studies about Weimar.
7. On the role of culture in widening support for the Nazi party, see Bollenbeck, *Tradition*, pp. 207–89; Jürgen Gimmel, *Die politische*

Organisation kulturellen Ressentiments: Der 'Kampfbund für deutsche Kultur' und das bildungsbürgerliche Unbehagen an der Moderne (Münster 1999); for a succinct account in English, see Alan Steinweis, 'Weimar Culture and the Rise of National Socialism: The Kampfbund für deutsche Kultur', Central European History 24 (Fall 1992), pp. 402–23 and his 'Conservatism National Socialism, and the Cultural Crisis of the Weimar Republic', in Larry Eugene Jones and James Retallack (eds.), Between Reform, Reaction and Resistance: Studies in the History of German Conservatism from 1789 to 1945 (New York 1992), pp. 329–46.

8. A point made insistently in the Third Reich: e.g. Friedrich Neumann, 'Gibt es ein Provinztheater?' Die Bühne 23 (10 December 1940): 'Wo ... der Begriff der Provinz einen Bereich minderen Wertes bezeichnet, da liegt der Einfluß westlichen Denkens vor'. Note that German critics recently awarded their annual prize for outstanding artistic achievement collectively to Germany's Stadttheater ('Lob der Provinz', Der Tagesspiegel, 2 October 2004).

9. On the strong sense of regional identity that underpinned these institutions, see Celia Applegate, A Nation of Provincials: The German Idea of Heimat (Berkeley 1990).

10. For a character sketch of the Prince, see Carl Zuckmayer, Geheimreport (Göttingen 2002), pp. 115–18.

11. See Volker Kern, 'Die Meininger kommen!' Hoftheater und Hofkapelle zwischen 1874 und 1914 unterwegs in Deutschland und Europa (Meiningen 1999), and Steven Deltart, The Meininger Theater, 1776–1926 (Ann Arbor 1981).

12. For details about funding, see Konrad Dussel, Ein neues, ein heroisches Theater? Nationalsozialistische Theaterpolitik und ihre Auswirkungen in der Provinz (Bonn 1998), and his 'Theater in der Krise: Der Topos und die ökonomische Realität in der Weimarer Republik', in Lothar Ehrlich and Jürgen John (eds.), Weimar 1930: Politik und Kultur im Vorfeld der NS-Diktatur (Cologne 1998), pp. 211–24.

13. E.g. Bochum and Duisburg; see Dörte Schmidt and Brigitte Weber, (eds.), Keine Experimentierkunst: Musikleben an Städtischen Theatern der Weimarer Republik (Stuttgart 1995).

14. See, for instance, R. Massek, 'Auflösung des bürgerlichen Theaters', Die Tat 22:12 (March 1931), pp. 993–7; or 'Stirbt das Drama?', Vossische Zeitung (4 April 1926); for a wider discussion of the issue, see Dussel, 'Theater in der Krise'.

15. Erich Kästner, 'Die Unüberwindlichen (Karl Kraus)', in Kästner, Gemischte Gefühle: Literarische Publizistik 1929–1933, vol. II (Berlin 1989), p. 218. On Austrian cultural initiatives abroad, see for instance

the reports by the Reich's embassy in Prague: Václav Král, *Acta occupationis Bohemiae et Moraviae: Die Deutschen in der Tschechoslowakei 1933–1945* (Prague 1964), pp. 146–7.

16. Contrast this with the strenuous Nazi efforts to influence the cultural scene of neighbouring countries. See 'Theaterverhältnisse im Sudetenland': Bundesarchiv Berlin (hereafter BA) R 55/20550.

17. See Wolfgang Bialas and Burkhard Stenzel (eds.), *Die Weimarer Republik zwischen Metropole und Provinz: Intellektuellendiskurse zur politischen Kultur* (Cologne 1996).

18. See *inter al.* Mme de Staël's *De l'Allemagne* (1810) and Friedrich Lienhard's *Wege nach Weimar* (1905–8).

19. Harry, Graf Kessler, *Tagebücher 1918–1937* (Berlin 1967), entry for 7 August 1932.

20. See Justus H. Ulbricht, ' "Deutsche Renaissance": Weimar und die Hoffnung auf die kulturelle Regeneration Deutschlands zwischen 1900 und 1933', in Jürgen John and Volker Wahl (eds.), *Zwischen Konvention und Avantgarde: Doppelstadt Jena-Weimar* (Weimar 1995), pp. 191–208, and ' "Wege nach Weimar" und "deutsche Wiedergeburt": Visionen kultureller Hegemonie im völkischen Netzwerk Thüringens zwischen Jahrhundertwende und "Drittem Reich" ', in Bialas and Stenzel (eds.), *Die Weimarer Republik*, pp. 23–35.

21. On aspects of this in the Third Reich, see Gerwin Strobl 'The Bard of Eugenics: Shakespeare and Racial Activism', *Journal of Contemporary History* 34:3 (1999), pp. 323–36, and 'Shakespeare and the Nazis', *History Today* 5 (June 1997), pp. 16–21. For the politics of German Shakespeare criticism, see Ruth Freifrau von Ledebur, *Der Mythos vom Deutschen Shakespeare: Die deutsche Shakespeare-Gesellschaft zwischen Politik und Wissenschaft 1918–1945* (Cologne 2002).

22. See Ralf Klausnitzer, ' "Wir rücken die Burgen unseres Glaubens auf die Höhen des Kaukasus": "Reichsdramaturg" Rainer Schlösser zwischen Jena-Weimar und Führerbunker', *Zeitschrift für Germanistik* (Neue Folge) 9 (1999), p. 296. See also Schlösser's own references to this: *Das Volk und seine Bühne: Bemerkungen zum Aufbau des deutschen Theaters* (Berlin 1935), p. 27.

23. On the wider background, see Steven Nyole Fuller, *The Nazis' Literary Grandfather: Adolf Bartels and Cultural Extremism* (New York 1995), Thomas Neumann, *Völkisch-nationale Hebbelrezeption: Adolf Bartels und die Weimarer Nationalfestspiele* (Bielefeld 1997), and Ursula Härtl et al. (eds.), *Hier, hier ist Deutschland . . .: von nationalen Kulturkonzepten zur nationalsozialistischen Kulturpolitik* (Göttingen 1997).

24. On Ziegler's impact, see Burkhard Stenzel, 'Das Deutsche Nationaltheater in Weimar', in Ehrlich and John (eds.), *Weimar*, pp. 225–42, and Michael Brunner, 'Das deutsche Nationaltheater in Weimar in den Jahren 1929–44', MA dissertation (Freie Universität Berlin 1994); cf. Ziegler's own wholly unrepentant memoir: *Adolf Hitler aus dem Erleben dargestellt* (Göttingen 1964).

25. See Johst's programmatic piece: 'Deutsch', *Weimarer Blätter* 3 (1921), pp. 380–1.

26. See Städtische Bühnen Erfurt (ed.), *Hitler-Jugend und Theater* (Erfurt s.a.). On Schirach, see Michael Wortmann, *Baldur von Schirach: Hitlers Jugendführer* (Cologne 1982).

27. Cf. Goebbels' telling sigh, 'Schlösser is too much of an aesthete' (Joseph Goebbels, *Die Tagebücher des Joseph Goebbels*, ed. Elke Fröhlich, 23 vols. (Munich 1998–2005), entry for 10 February 1938). The charge of being 'provincial' is no less problematic: Ziegler had studied in Cambridge; Schirach, whose mother was American, was initially brought up in English and spoke only imperfect German as a boy.

28. Cf. Uwe-Karsten Ketelsen's point that the talk of *Ungeist* in much of the German literature about Nazi cultural policies fails to explain their appeal ('Kulturpolitik des III. Reichs und Ansätze zu ihrer Interpretation', *Text und Kontext* 8:2 (1988), pp. 217–42).

29. See Klausnitzer, 'Wir', pp. 294–300.

30. See Stenzel, 'Nationaltheater', pp. 225–6.

31. See the letter of 25 December 1918 by Ernst Hardt to Gerhart Hauptmann, published in Jochen Meyer (ed.), *Briefe an Ernst Hardt: Eine Auswahl aus den Jahren 1898–1947* (Marbach 1975), p. 190.

32. Schirach was given the *Intendanz* at Wiesbaden, where he saw out the long autumn of his professional life: he finally retired in 1943. Goebbels had already diagnosed advanced artistic sclerosis several years earlier. (*Tagebücher*, entry for 16 December 1938).

33. See Manfred Boetzke and Marion Queck, 'Die Theaterverhältnisse nach der Novemberrevolution', in Kunstamt Kreuzberg and Institut für Theaterwissenschaft der Universität Köln (eds.), *Weimarer Republik* (Berlin 1977), pp. 692–7.

34. Günther Rühle may well be right in saying that stylistically little changed in many instances, and that the *Bühnenräte* failed everywhere; but symbols have a potency of their own (*Theater für die Republik: 1917–1933 im Spiegel der Kritik* (rev. edn Berlin 1988), p. 14). Cf. also Jost Hermand's and Frank Trommler's point that contemporaries actually regarded the revolution in the theatre as especially significant (*Die Kultur der Weimarer Republik* (Munich 1978), p. 193).

35. Gay, *Weimar*, p. 120.
36. Carlo Mierendorff, 'Der Skandal am Theater', *Das Tribunal: Hessische Radikale Blätter*, Extrablatt (20 April 1919), reproduced in Boetzke and Queck, 'Theaterverhältnisse', p. 696. Mierendorff went on to be one of the most humane politicians of the Weimar era. In the Third Reich, he joined the Resistance and was murdered by the Nazis.
37. Memorandum by Börries, Freiherr von Münchhausen to Chancellor von Papen, quoted by Werner Mittenzwei, *Der Untergang einer Akademie oder die Mentalität des ewigen Deutschen: Der Einfluß der nationalkonservativen Dichter an der Preußischen Akademie der Künste 1918–1947* (Berlin 1992), p. 26.
38. See Ruth Freydank, 'Das Hoftheater: ein altgewordenes Kulturinstitut', in Freydank (ed.), *Theater als Geschäft: Berlin und seine Privattheater um die Jahrhundertwende* (Berlin 1995), pp. 104–21, and Ute Daniel, *Hoftheater: Zur Geschichte des Theaters und der Höfe im 18. und 19. Jahrhundert* (Stuttgart 1995).
39. 'Zur Dichtkunst abkommandiert', in Helga Bemmann (ed.), *Ludwig Thoma: Immer nur so durchgeschloffen: Humoresken, Bänkellieder und Satiren* (Berlin 1984), pp. 80–1. See the proposals by Ferdinand Avenarius, *Kunstwart* 11 (1900), and their discussion by Ernst Wachler, 'Das deutsche Theater der Zukunft', *Deutsche Volksbühne: Blätter für deutsche Bühnenspiele* 1 (1900), pp. 17–33, reprinted in Christopher Balme (ed.), *Das Theater von Morgen: Texte zur deutschen Theaterreform* (Würzburg 1988), pp. 151–63.
40. Schirach sought legal redress and was eventually awarded compensation.
41. Quoted by Boetzke and Queck, 'Theaterverhältnisse', pp. 693–4.
42. Quoted by Peter Jelavich, *Munich and Theatrical Modernism: Politics, Playwriting and Performance, 1890–1914* (Cambridge, MA 1985), p. 282.
43. Rainer Schlösser, 'Die Bilanz eines Jahrzehnts: Kulturpolitisches Schreckenskabinett', *Völkischer Beobachter* (11–12 and 14 February 1933); see also his 'Die unmoralische Anstalt', *Völkischer Beobachter* (9 January 1932).
44. Johannes R. Becher, 'The Song of Freedom', quoted by Jelavich, *Munich*, p. 279.
45. Ferdinand Avenarius had insisted that Bartels refrain from antisemitic utterances in Avenarius' journal *Der Kunstwart*. See Neumann, *Hebbelrezeption*, p. 26.
46. Goethe- und Schiller-Archiv Weimar, Nachlaß Deetjen, 132/740: Schirach to Werner Deetjen, 28 August 1925.

47. Cf. Adolf Bartels to Börries von Münchhausen, 1 May 1911, quoted by Mittenzwei, *Der Untergang*, p. 162. On concurrent political activities, see Peter Fritzsche, *Rehearsals for Fascism: Populism and Political Mobilization in Weimar Germany* (Oxford 1990).

48. See the reference to a play or sketch called *Stapellauf* in 'Hans Rothe oder des widerspenstigen Shakespeares Zähmung', *Das Schwarze Korps* (14 November 1935).

49. He also became a leading figure in Rosenberg's Kampfbund.

50. Sigmund Graff, *Von S.M. zu N.S.* (Munich 1963). Graff, who had reached Nazism via the Stahlhelm, was for a while Schlösser's right hand in the Propaganda Ministry.

51. Cf. Zuckmayer, *Geheimreport*, p. 57.

52. Von Hülsen, Jeßner's predecessor, and the director of the Tsar's former German Theatre of Moscow were both involved in 'patriotic' theatre ventures. See 'Die nationalen Bühnenbestrebungen' *Neue Preußische Zeitung* (17 September 1924), reproduced in Fischli, 'Zur Herausbildung', p. 903.

53. It may be more than just a coincidence that Baldur von Schirach championed French impressionists even in wartime. See Goebbels, *Tagebücher*, entry for 15 October 1941.

54. Cf. Hermand and Trommler, 'Jeßner setzte auf Konfrontation', in *Die Kultur*, p. 196.

55. On Jeßner, see Günther Rühle, 'Leopold Jeßner: Revolution im Staatstheater', in *Theater in unserer Zeit* (Frankfurt 1976), pp. 47–81; on the wider background, see Michael Patterson, *The Revolution in German Theatre, 1900–1933* (London 1981). On other directors copying Jeßner's style, see, *inter al.*, Paul Wiegler's review of Engel's *Coriolanus* (*BZ am Mittag*, 28 February 1925) or the comments of O. Mrazek on provincial theatre, quoted in Rudolf Fernau, *Als Lied beganns ...* (Frankfurt 1972), p. 172.

56. Cf. Rainer Noltenius, *Dichterfeiern in Deutschland: Rezeptionsgeschichte und Sozialgeschichte am Beispiel der Schiller- und Freiligrathfeiern* (Munich 1984); Gerhard Schmid, 'Die Gedenkjahre 1859 und 1905 als Brennpunkte der bürgerlichen Schiller-Verehrung in Deutschland', in *Impulse: Aufsätze, Quellen, Berichte zur deutschen Klassik und Romantik* (Berlin 1986), pp. 90–114. On the wider background, see Dieter Langewiesche, 'Kulturelle Nationsbildung im Deutschland des 19. Jahrhunderts', in Manfred Hettling *et al.* (eds.), *Nation und Gesellschaft in Deutschland: Historische Essays* (Munich 1996), pp. 46–64; on Tell specifically,

Barbara Piatty, *Tells Theater: Eine Kulturgeschichte in fünf Akten zu Friedrich Schillers Wilhelm Tell* (Basel 2004).

57. See Fritz Kortner's autobiography, *Aller Tage Abend* (Munich 1959), pp. 350–62.

58. On the history of that equation, see Manfed Pfister, 'Hamlet und der deutsche Geist: Die Geschichte einer politischen Interpretation', *Shakespeare Jahrbuch* (West) (1992), pp. 13–38, and Pfister's earlier article 'Germany is Hamlet', *New Comparisons* 2 (1986), pp. 106–26.

59. For details and the principal reviews, see Rühle, *Theater für die Republik*, pp. 763–73. A brief account in English is contained in Wilhelm Hortmann, *Shakespeare on the German Stage* (Cambridge 1998), p. 56.

60. See the coverage in the *Vossische Zeitung* (14 December 1926). See also the renewed debate of 21 March 1927, discussed in Fischli, 'Zur Herausbildung', p. 897.

61. See, for instance, Karl Künkler, 'Hamlet im Frack', *Bausteine zum deutschen Nationaltheater: Organ der Gruppe Theater im Kampfbund für deutsche Kultur* (December 1935), pp. 43–7.

62. *Berliner Tageblatt* (13 December 1919).

63. See BA R 55/20185, 1: Werner Krause to Schlösser, 9 March 1936.

64. See Neil Blackadder, 'Dr Kasten, the Freie Bühne and Audience Resistance to Naturalism', *New Theatre Quarterly* 14:4 (November 1998), pp. 357–65. Cf. also the suggestive evidence of Wilhelmine cartoons: e.g. in Ruth Freydank, *Theater in Berlin: von den Anfängen bis 1945* (Berlin 1988), p. 330.

65. See Wassily Kandinsky's related observations (*Über das Geistige in der Kunst* (Bern 1963), p. 68, quoted by Peter Ulrich Hein, *Die Brücke ins Geisterreich: Kürstlerische Avantgarde zwischen Kulturkritik und Faschismus* (Reinbek 1992), pp. 153–4).

66. Paul Fechter, *Deutsche Allgemeine Zeitung* (13 December 1919). Cf. the remarks by Emil Faktor about Jeßner's *Othello* and the 'Entwöhnungsprozeß' now demanded of audiences, which had not made them 'happier' (*Berliner Börsen-Courier*, 12 November 1921).

67. The expressionists possessed a manic quality much remarked upon; Jeßner was famous for his 'tempo'; Piscator, finally, may have possessed many qualities, but subtlety has not usually been numbered among them.

68. The insults were often quite overt: e.g. the equation of Reinhardt's audiences with docile asses braying on command, in Klabund's 'Reinhardt et circenses' (Klabund, *Emsig dreht sich meine Spule: Brettlverse, Bänkellieder* (Berlin 1972), p. 67).

69. See Hortmann, *Shakespeare*, p. 56.
70. On Austrian theatre after 1918, see Barbara Lesák (ed.), *Von der Pose zum Ausdruck: Theaterfotografie 1900–1930* (Vienna 2003).
71. Quoted by Rühle, *Theater für die Republik*, p. 22.
72. On the crisis, see Dussel, 'Theater in der Krise', pp. 211–24. The repertoire schedules for the summer of 1923 included *Die Frühlingsfee, Die Tugendprinzessin, Der Liebesstreik, Süße Susi* and *Mädi*. Inflation obviously played a role too; but note the parallel with pre-war Munich, where modernism could only be sustained by combining it with 'low-brow' farces (Cf. Jelavich, *Munich*); or see Blumenthal's balancing act in pre-war Berlin (Bärbel Reißmann, 'Geschäftserfolg eines Bühnenautors: Das Lessing-Theater', in Freydank (ed.), *Theater als Geschäft*, pp. 122–33).
73. The arguments are neatly summarised by Rosenberg's right-hand man in the theatre: Walter Stang, 'Vom Sinn und Wesen des Theaters: Kritischer Rückblick und Versuch einer neuen Sinngebung', *Bausteine* 1:1 (October 1933), pp. 1–14, and in Schlösser's earlier 'Die Bilanz eines Jahrzehnts'.
74. See Michael Steinberg, *Austria as Theater and Ideology: The Salzburg Festival* (New York 2000).
75. Dieter Langewiesche, 'Bildungsbürgertum und Liberalismus im 19. Jahrhundert', in Jürgen Kocka (ed.), *Bildungsbürgertum im 19. Jahrhundert* (Stuttgart 1989), p. 112. See also Bollenbeck, *Tradition*, p. 216.
76. Reviewers often specifically highlighted the *cuts*. See, for instance, Norbert Falk's review of *Wallenstein*: '[Jeßner] brüskiert mit Lust … Er befremdet den, der das Vertraute nicht findet, mehr durch das, was er nicht gibt, als durch das, was er … formt' (*BZ am Mittag*, 12 October 1924). Note the suggestion of deliberate provocation. Or take Emil Faktor's praise of Jeßner: the cuts were 'gerechtfertigt. Auch wenn mancher Verzicht weh tat' ('*Don Carlos*', *Berliner Börsen-Courier*, 14 February 1922); or Paul Fechter: 'er [Jeßner] streicht wie immer alles, was blüht, mit sicherer Hand fort' (*Deutsche Allgemeine Zeitung*, 4 December 1926). See also Fechter's verdict on Piscator's production of *Die Räuber*, '[Es] … wurde zusammengestrichen, daß selbst Herrn Jeßner … geschaudert haben muß' (*Deutsche Allgemeine Zeitung*, 13 September 1926). Even Ihering began his review by detailing the famous lines Piscator had cut (*Berliner Börsen-Courier*, 13 September 1926).
77. Arnolt Bronnen, *Anarchie in Sillian*; Ernst Toller, *Die Maschinenstürmer*.

78. See especially the reaction to Piscator's production of Schiller's *Räuber*: 'Sie wollen Schiller hören und nicht Herrn Piscator. . . . Und dann rebellieren sie' (Paul Fechter, *Deutsche Allgemeine Zeitung*, 13 September 1926).

79. Bollenbeck, *Tradition*, p. 272.

80. Rainer Schlösser, 'Kurt Geucke, ein Wanderer zwischen Scholle und Stern', *Deutsches Schrifttum* 17 (1925), p. 2, quoted in Klausnitzer, 'Wir', p. 301.

81. Dussel is surely right to point to the contrast between Reinhardt's professed aim of 'enchantment' and Jeßner's assertion that such things had no place in a modern theatre ('Theater in der Krise', p. 222).

82. See Fechter's revealing comments about Claudius' withered arm (*Deutsche Allgemeine Zeitung*, 4 December 1926).

83. Quoted by Rühle, *Theater für die Republik*, p. 32.

84. See, *inter al.*, Carl Maria Holzapfel, 'Aufbruch zum Nationaltheater', *Deutsche Bühne* (May–June 1934), pp. 5–6, and Hans-Hugo Erdmann, 'Forderungen zum "nationalen" Drama', *Die Neue Literatur* 35:5 (May 1934), p. 266. Recent studies have highlighted the psychological impact of war and hyperinflation: see Jay Winter, *Sites of Memory, Sites of Mourning* (Cambridge 1995), and Bernd Widdig, *Culture and Inflation in Weimar Germany* (Berkeley 2001).

85. Elias Canetti, *Die Fackel im Ohr: Lebensgeschichte 1921–1931* (Munich 1980).

86. Cf., *inter al.*, Leopold Jeßner, 'Politisches Theater' (1927), in Hugo Fetting (ed.), *Leopold Jeßner: Schriften* (Berlin 1979), p. 98, and Arnold Zweig, 'Epoche und Theater', in Max Krell (ed.), *Das deutsche Theater der Gegenwart* (Munich 1923), pp. 22–3.

87. See, for instance, the conservative contributions to the special edition on *Klassikerbearbeitungen* of the magazine *Die Scene* 19 (October/ November 1929).

88. Cf. the response by Friedrich Meinecke after the *Stunde Null*. Peter Gay sees in this the root of the 'German problem'.

89. Becher to Alfred Andersch, 5 May 1948, quoted by Wolfgang Schivelbusch, *In a Cold Crater: Cultural and Intellectual Life in Berlin, 1945–1948* (Berkeley 1998), p. 78. Becher was perhaps responding to Kremlin orthodoxy; yet there is no doubt that, like most exiled Germans, he genuinely sought to understand what had gone wrong.

90. See Alfred Kerr's criticism of Piscator's *Räuber* (*Berliner Tageblatt*, 13 September 1926). Cf. Rühle's judgement on Jeßner: 'Er zerbrach die Verse . . .' (*Theater in unserer Zeit*, p. 60).

91. Kerr, *Berliner Tageblatt* (13 September 1926).

92. Note the way Kerr's language here overlaps with that of the conservative Fechter, who had said of Jeßner's *Hamlet*, 'Das hat mit ... Dichtung wirklich nicht mehr viel zu tun' (*Deutsche Allgemeine Zeitung*, 4 December 1926).

93. *Deutsche Allegemeine Zeitung* (4 December 1926).

94. Hans Severus Ziegler, *Völkischer Beobachter* (Berliner Ausgabe, 9 February 1932). Cf. Emil Faktor's comment a decade earlier in his otherwise friendly review of Jeßner's *Fiesco*: 'Ich führe auf eine zu zielbewußte Dramaturgie manche Ernüchterung zurück' (*Berliner Börsen-Courier*, 7 May 1921).

95. Paul Fechter, *Deutsche Allgemeine Zeitung* (14 February 1922). Cf. also Fritz Engel's comment on Jeßner's *Othello*: a play turned to stone (zur Idee versteint) (*Berliner Tageblatt*, 12 November 1921). Note the parallel with objections to pictorial examples of *Neue Sachlichkeit*: 'Es ist die völlige Seelenlosigkeit, die Lieblosigkeit, die Unmenschlichkeit dieser Werke, ... [die] wir ablehnen' (Karl Kurt Eberlein, *Was ist deutsch an der deutschen Kunst?* (Leipzig 1933), p. 34.

96. Cf. Gay, *Weimar*.

97. See Rühle, 'Leopold Jeßner', p. 58. On prominent exceptions see below.

98. A point made by some Nazis themselves: see Ernst Keppler, 'Jugend und Theater', *Wille und Macht* 2:13 (July 1934), p. 24: 'Dieses Gefühl, das sich im Rausch der Farben und Fahnen, im Klang unserer Kampflieder zu künstlerischer Wirkung steigerte'. Cf. Gudrun Brockhaus, *Schauder und Idylle: Faschismus als Erlebnisangebot* (Munich 1997). See also Peter Ulrich Hein's provocative argument in *Die Brücke* that modernist discourse itself helped prepare the ground for the Third Reich by raising expectations of a *Gesamtkunstwerk*, which modernism proved unable to fulfil.

99. Eugen Kurt Fischer, *Dramaturgie des Rundfunks* (Heidelberg 1942), p. 165, quoted in Wolfram Wessels, *Hörspiele im Dritten Reich* (Bonn 1985), p. 124.

100. There is a suggestive parallel with Catholic ritual versus Protestant sobriety, and the Nazis' failure to make electoral headway in the Catholic regions of Germany.

101. See Hortmann's pertinent warning that the historiography of Weimar culture is often 'openly partisan', and that 'mythifiers' had deliberately and systematically muddied the waters (*Shakespeare*, p. 51).

102. Schmitt's success was acutely embarrassing to the more doctrinaire exponents of republican theatre. Ihering tied himself into knots in explaining away the awkward truth (*Berliner Börsen-Courier*, 27 November 1928).

103. On the often discordant acting styles in Berlin productions, see Rühle, *Theater für die Republik*, pp. 16–18. A brief but effective discussion of Schmitt's style is contained in Hortmann, *Shakespeare*, pp. 93–100. On his productions after 1933, see Jessica Pesch, *Festspiele für ein neues Deutschland? Saladin Schmitts 'Klassikerwochen' am Schauspielhaus Bochum im Dritten Reich* (Herne 1999).

104. Consider Fehling's insistence that the stage was 'not a place for instruction ... but of magic' (quoted by Hortmann, *Shakespeare*, p. 76). On the wider background, see Gerhard Ahrens (ed.), *Das Theater des deutschen Regisseurs Jürgen Fehling* (Berlin 1985), and Fehling's own collected writings: *Die Magie des Theaters: Äußerungen und Aufzeichnungen* (Velber 1965); Frederike Euler, *Der Regisseur und Schauspielpädagoge Otto Falckenberg: Falckenberg-Inszenierungen an den Münchner Kammerspielen* (Munich 1976).

105. For Nazi criticism of Fehling's productions in the Third Reich, see BA R 55/20183, 284–7 and R 55/20210, 314 (discussed below); hostility to Schmitt is apparent in the review of *Coriolanus* quoted by Rischbieter (ed.), *Theater*, p. 123. Nazi ambivalence about Falckenberg is apparent in Heinz Frank, 'Doppelgesicht des deutschen Theaters', *Wille und Macht* 5:10 (May 1937), pp. 36–7.

106. Cf. Rühle's judicious verdict: *Theater für die Republik*, pp. 23–4. See also Markus Moninger's point that talk of Reinhardt as the 'Demiurg szenischer Attraktivität' ignores his 'Suche nach einem die "Klassiker" aktualisierenden Darstellungs-Verismus' (*Shakespeare inszeniert: Das westdeutsche Regietheater und die Theatertradition des 'dritten deutschen Klassikers'* (Tübingen 1996), p. 54). For contemporary recognition of Reinhardt's continuing inventiveness post-1918, see, *inter al.*, Monty Jacobs, *Vossische Zeitung*, 3 November 1924.

107. For pictorial evidence of the republican style spreading into the provinces, see the reproductions of sets in Helmut Grosse, 'Die szenische Entwicklung in Beispielen', in Kunstamt Kreuzberg and Institut für Theaterwissenschaft der Universität Köln (eds.), *Weimarer Republik*, pp. 717–37. See also the contemporary comment of O. Mrazek (i.e. Rudolf Fernau): provincial theatre was merely copying technical aspects of Jeßner's theatre while lacking his insight. 'Die Sucht nach Modernität', Fernau thought, 'umnebelt die Gehirne' (Fernau, *Als Lied*, p. 172).

108. Kerr, 'Blaue Blusen', quoted by Michaela Böhmig, *Das russische Theater in Berlin* (Munich 1990), p. 215.

109. Julius Bab, 'Die deutsche Bühnenkunst', quoted by Wladimir Koljasin, 'Gastspiele russischer Theater in Berlin in den zwanziger und dreißiger Jahren', in Irina Antonowa and Jörn Merkert (eds.), *Berlin Moskau: Moskau Berlin, 1900–1950* (Munich 1995), p. 174.

110. Alfred Döblin, 'Revolution oder Dekadenz?', *Leipziger Tageblatt* (27 April 1923), quoted by Koljasin, 'Gastspiele', p. 174.

111. Alfred Kerr, 'Ostrowski: "Der Wald"', *Berliner Tageblatt* (10 April 1930), quoted by Koljasin, 'Gastspiele', p. 176.

112. Herbert Ihering, 'Meyerhold in der Stresemannstraße', *Berliner Börsen-Courier* (10 April 1930), quoted by Koljasin, 'Gastspiele', p. 176.

113. Quoted by Böhmig, *Das russische Theater*, p. 241.

114. See Hortmann, *Shakespeare*, p. 48.

115. Franz Jung, *Der Weg nach unten*, quoted by Hein, *Die Brücke*, p. 190.

116. E.g. Julius Kulka's concept of 'Emanzipation vom Publikum' ('Theaterreform', in Balme (ed.), *Das Theater*, pp. 98–104). Cf. also Hein's related observation about Kandinsky and Schönberg: 'Ihre "Bühne der Zukunft" war recht eigentlich für eine Aufführung ohne störende Menschen gedacht' (Hein, *Die Brücke*, p. 140).

117. See Zuckmayer's engaging autobiography *Als wärs ein Stück von mir* (Frankfurt 1966). For the attempts by the non-Nazi nationalists to win Zuckmayer to their cause, see Mittenzwei, *Der Untergang*, p. 173.

118. See, *inter al.*, Kortner, *Aller Tage*, pp. 361–2.

119. Thomas Mann, 'Versuch über das Theater', in Balme (ed.), *Das Theater*, p. 213.

120. Zweig, 'Epoche und Theater', pp. 22–3.

121. Quoted by Manfred Boetzke *et al.*, 'Verarbeitung des kulturellen Erbes: Tendenzen der Klassiker-Inszenierung', in Kunstamt Kreuzberg and Institut für Theaterwissenschaft der Universität Köln (eds.), *Weimarer Republik*, p. 749.

122. See Kortner's comment on Jeßner's Richard III, 'Alles war der Machtbegierde unterstellt ... Was sich im Stück dem widersetzte, wurde gestrichen' (*Aller Tage*, p. 379). Cf. Fechter's comment about Piscator's *Räuber* (*Deutsche Allgemeine Zeitung*, 13 September 1926), and Erich Ziegel, who noted retrospectively that 'alles Menschliche' had been 'politisiert' (quoted in Rischbieter, 'NS-Theaterpolitik', p. 145).

123. The term is Brecht's: see Hortmann, *Shakespeare*, p. 85. See also Herbert Ihering, *Reinhardt, Jeßner, Piscator oder Klassikertod?* (Berlin 1928).

124. 'Furchtbar groß ist hier die Angst, im Strom der Zeit sich als Nichtschwimmer zu blamieren' (Alfred Polgar, 'Oktober in Berlin',

quoted by Böhmig, *Das russische Theater*, p. 214). Cf. Karl Kraus'
scathing 1926 poem 'Berlin Theatre' (*Aphorismen und Gedichte*
(Berlin 1984), pp. 278–80).

125. Paul Fechter, 'Don Carlos', *Deutsche Allgemeine Zeitung*,
(14 February 1922). Cf., in revealing contrast, Siegfried Jacobsohn's
republican rapture that in Jeßner's *Fiesco* 'the wenches' had all but
vanished (*Die Weltbühne*, reprinted in Rühle, *Theater für die
Republik*, p. 312).

126. Cf. Michael Patterson's related point, 'that the strength of this theatre
lay in its bold stylistic experimentation rather than in its writing'
(*Revolution*, p. 5). See also Ihering's telling remark about Fritz von
Unruh's *Bonaparte*: 'No director will know what to do with this
Bonaparte, since the speeches do not translate into stage movements'
(*Berliner Börsen-Courier*, 16 February 1927).

127. See Piscator's own account in *Das politische Theater* (Berlin 1929),
pp. 185–6.

128. Berthold Viertel, 'Theater-Zukunft 1919', *Der Neue Weg* (20 June
1919), pp. 317–18.

129. Ihering's observations are discussed in Patterson, *Revolution*, p. 83.
Since Ihering published these comments *during* the Nazi era, his
readers presumably took them as an indictment of Weimar theatre.

130. Cf., from a Nazi perspective, the retrospective remarks of Hermann
Wanderscheck about an 'entfesselte Regiekunst', which had offered
'more to the eye than to the ear' (*Deutsche Dramatik der Gegenwart*
(Berlin 1938)) or Wolfgang Nufer's comment about the 'Zeit der
überhandnehmenden Bildwirkung des Theaters' ('Die dritte Bühne',
Völkische Kultur: Kampfblatt für Kultur und Politik 3 (1935), p. 17).

131. Kraus, *Aphorismen*, pp. 278–80.

132. For the flavour of the Zeitstück, see the illustrations in Hubertus
Schneider, 'Das "Zeitstück": Probleme der Justiz', in Kunstamt
Kreuzberg and Institut für Theaterwissenschaft der Universität Köln
(eds.), *Weimarer Republik*, pp. 835–44. The phenomenon itself is dis-
cussed in 'Das Zeitstück: Drama und Dramaturgie der Demokratie', in
Rühle, *Theater in unserer Zeit*, pp. 82–118.

133. Even where the *Zeitstück* became overtly political – e.g. Rehfisch's
The Dreyfus Affair – it invited audiences to identify with characters on
stage.

134. A point made explicitly by Nazi activists: e.g. Hanns Johst, *Ich glaube!*
(Munich 1928), p. 90, or Walter Stang, 'Vom Sinn', pp. 11–12. See also,
from a left-wing perspective, the revealing joke about Weimar critics
in a sketch of the Kabarett der Komiker, reprinted in Helga Bemmann,

('Introduction', in John London (ed.), *Theatre under the Nazis* (Manchester 2000), p. 5). The chapter 'A Reckoning' – Hitler's thoughts on culture in *Mein Kampf* – merely contains a passing remark in the tradition of complaints about the 'present immorality of the stage'.

35. On opera, see Fred Prieberg, *Musik im NS-Staat* (Frankfurt 1982); and case studies in Henning Rischbieter, 'Die deutsche Theaterlandschaft 1933–1945', in Rischbieter (ed.), *Theater*, pp. 99–261. On operatic sets, see the correspondence on the *Führerausstattungen* in Oberösterreichisches Landesarchiv (OÖLA), Landestheater.

36. See, for instance, Otto Schumann's verdict: 'Daß man sie [i.e. the Nazis] nicht ernst genug genommen hat, mag auch zusammenhängen mit ihrer Schauspielerei, denn geniale Schauspieler sind sie auch' (Hammerstein, *Deutsche Bildung*, p. 129).

37. Note the absence of theatrical *aperçus* in the *Table Talk*.

38. Although Hitler only arrived in the latter stages of that conflict he can hardly have remained unaware of it. The press reported it at length.

39. The satirical magazine *Simplicissimus* was likewise under attack by the censors, as was Munich's cabaret scene.

40. Note Hitler's own defence of Falckenberg, the champion of Strindberg and Wedekind, against repeated attacks from sections of the Nazi party. Note also that Halbe's dramas were revived in the Third Reich or that Lautensack's *Parsonage Comedy* should have found champions in high places after 1933. See 'Spielplan für alle: Theater des Volkes – draußen', *Der Angriff* (24 July 1937) in BA NS 5/VI/6287, 75, or the exchange between Ministerialrat Naumann and Schlösser of early 1939 in BA R 55/20194, 313–6. For attempts to rescue even Frank Wedekind for the Third Reich as a 'vitalist' writer, see A. Strambowski, 'Der Weg zum Deutschen Nationaltheater', *Westfälischer Kurier* (18 May 1934) (cutting in BA R 56 I/ 114, 156).

41. The best account of Hitler's early years is Brigitte Hamann, *Hitler's Vienna: A Dictator's Apprenticeship* (Oxford, 1999).

42. See BA R 56 I/ 119–7: letter of August 1935, Anders to Hinkel: 'der Führer ist als "kulturlos und amusisch verschrieen"'.

43. Goebbels who might have been able to speak on the subject, remained silent, too. This may owe something to his own failure as a dramatist. See David Barnett, 'Joseph Goebbels, Expressionist Dramatist as Minister of Culture', *New Theatre Quarterly* 17:2 (May 2001), pp. 161–9, and Kai Michel, *Vom Poeten zum Demagogen: die schrift-stellerischen Versuche Joseph Goebbels* (Cologne 1999). See also See Karl Christian Führer, 'German Cultural Life and the Crisis of National

Identity during the Depression, 1929–1933', *German Studies Review* 24:3 (October 2001), pp. 461–86.

44. Hans Severus Ziegler, 'Nur Adolf Hitler sichert der Nation eine künstlerische Neubelebung', *Völkischer Beobachter* (4 April 1932).
45. See Stenzel, 'Nationaltheater', pp. 225–42.
46. See Bartels' remarks about Ludendorff in *Der Nationalsozialismus: Deutschlands Rettung* (Leipzig 1924), p. 34, quoted by Neumann, *Hebbelrezeption*, p. 50.
47. See Brigitte Hamann, *Winifred Wagner oder Hitler's Bayreuth* (Munich 2002).
48. An effective overview is provided in Ketelsen, *Völkisch-nationale*.
49. On contemporary awareness of the links between rural anti-modernism and Nazism, see Joseph Roth, 'Gift aus veilchenblauen Kelchen', *Frankfurter Zeitung* (14 December 1930), reprinted in Klaus Vondung, *Völkisch-nationale und nationalsozialistische Literaturtheorie* (Munich 1973), pp. 94–5. For retrospective Nazi accounts, see Adolf Bartels, *Geschichte der deutschen Literatur* (Brunswick 1937), or Helmut Langenbucher, *Volkhafte Dichtung* (Berlin 1941).
50. The untranslatable term *Wesenhaftigkeit* would go on to be a core word in the Nazi argot, especially among Alfred Rosenberg's followers.
51. See Mathildenhöhe Darmstadt (ed.), *Die Lebensreform: Entwürfe zur Neugestaltung von Leben und Kunst um 1900* (Darmstadt 2003).
52. See in particular the work of Hermann Löns, which achieved a mass readership before and after the Great War.
53. The only possible exceptions are again, significantly, the vitalism of Halbe and Kayserling's early dramas.
54. The text of the appeal is reprinted in Eduard Devrient and Willy Stuhlfeld, *Geschichte der deutschen Schauspielkunst* (Berlin 1929), pp. 507–9.
55. See Robin Lenman, 'Art, Society and the Law in Wilhelmine Germany: The Lex Henze', *Oxford German Studies* 8 (1973–4), pp. 84–113; the *Schmutz und Schund* campaign is discussed extensively in Bollenbeck, *Tradition*.
56. Cf. 'Heiligende Kunst', *Der Angriff* (28 November 1936): 'was da stark, was froh, was mutig macht ...', 'Spielplan für alle: Theater des Volkes – draußen', *Der Angriff* (24 July 1937), and Hans Hinkel's reply to an unnamed interviewer in BA R 56 I/ 107, 112.
57. Devrient, *Geschichte*, p. 509. For a glimpse of Pfeiffer's mindset, see the catalogue of his private library kept in the Pfälzische Landesbibliothek at Speyer.
58. For evidence of Sudermann's huge public resonance, see for instance Otto Reuter's wartime revue 'Muttchen hat's Wort', where

'Sudermann' and 'Parzifal' stand paradigmatically for high culture. See Baumeister, *Kriegstheater*, p. 158. On Keyserling, see Dieter Kafitz, 'Die Dramen Eduard von Keyserlings zwischen Naturalismus, Biologismus und Dekadenz', in Kafitz (ed.), *Dramen und Theater der Jahrhundertwende* (Tübingen 1991), pp. 287–304.

59. See Galina Makarowa, 'Das Moskauer und Berliner Theater zu Beginn des 20. Jahrhunderts', in Irina Antonowa, *Berlin-Moskau, Moskau-Berlin 1900–1950* (Munich 1995), p. 43. Cf. the list of playwrights threatening the 'Hort teutscher Kunst' in Gustav Meyrink's satire 'Das Wildschwein Veronika' originally published in *Simplicissimus* (reprinted in Meyrink, *Des deutschen Spießers Wunderhorn* (Berlin 1973), pp. 44–5).

60. The term is Rühle's (*Theater in unserer Zeit*, p. 49).

61. See Hans Severus Ziegler's attempt to harness relevant memories for Nazi causes: 'Schon vor 1918 war jede deutsche Bühne den frechsten Experimenten geöffnet' (Ziegler, 'Nur Adolf'). For a telling pre-war view, see Ernst von Wolzogen's remarks in 'Das Überbrettl', reprinted in Balme, *Theater*, p. 185.

62. Note Suzanne Marchand's warning that we risk misinterpreting German history and culture, if we fail to consider the wider currency and causes of the term 'degeneracy' in 'Nazi Culture: Banality or Barbarism?', *Journal of Modern History* 70:1 (March 1998), pp. 108–18.

63. Hindenburg's message is reproduced in Boetzke and Queck, 'Die Theaterverhältnisse', p. 706.

64. On the League's efforts, see Boetzke and Queck, 'Die Theaterverhältnisse', p. 705.

65. See BA R 55/20168, 350; R 55/20179, 89; R 55/20196, 44 and 312; R 55/20179, 164.

66. For details see Barbara Panse, 'Censorship in Nazi Germany: The Influence of the Reich Ministry of Propaganda on German Theatre and Drama 1933–1945', in Günther Berghaus (ed.), *Fascism and Theatre: Comparative Studies on the Aesthetics and Politics of Performance in Europe 1925–1945* (Providence 1996), pp. 140–56; see also her 'Zeitgenössische Dramatik', in Rischbieter (ed.), *Theater*, pp. 489–721.

67. See 'Die Weimarer Nationalfestspiele', in Neumann, *Hebbelrezeption*, pp. 99–178.

68. On Fuchs, see Jelavich, *Munich*, pp. 187–211; on Behrens and Wachler, see Balme, *Theater*, pp. 175–81 and pp. 151–64 respectively; see also Uwe Puschner, 'Deutsche Reformbühne und völkische Kultstätte: Ernst Wachler und das Harzer Bergtheater', in Puschner, *Handbuch zur 'völkischen Bewegung' 1871–1918* (Munich 1995), pp. 762–69; for a

brief account of Wachler's aims in English, see George Mosse, *The Crisis of German Ideology* (New York 1964), pp. 80–2; on Müller-Guttenbrunn, see Richard S. Geehr, *Adam Müller-Guttenbrunn and the Aryan Theater of Vienna 1898–1903* (Göppingen 1973); on Poelzig, Aedes: Galerie für Architektur und Raum (ed.), *Hans Poelzig, Ein großes Theater und ein kleines Haus* (Berlin, 1986); Krefelder Kunstmuseen (eds.), *Der dramatische Raum: Hans Poelzig: Malerei Theater Film* (Krefeld 1986); see also the monograph by the later president of the Federal Republic Theodor Heuss, which provides a telling perspective from the vantage of the Nazi years: *Hans Poelzig: Bauten und Entwürfe* (Berlin 1939).

69. The play is discussed in Jelavich, *Modernism*, pp. 190–2. NB: The Darmstadt Artists' Colony was one of the centres of German modernism.

70. Georg Fuchs, *Die Revolution des Theaters* (Munich 1909), p. ix (quoted in Jelavich, *Modernism*, p. 198).

71. See Hitler's assertion that true artistic inspiration aimed at 'achieving ideological unity' in the German people: Reichstagsrede, 23 March 1933, in Max Domarus (ed.), *Hitler: Reden und Proklamationen 1932–1945* (Wiesbaden 1973), vol. I; Johst, *Standpunkt*, p. 30. Cf. Johst, *Ich glaube!*, p. 17 and p. 35; and the comments collected in: Vondung, *Völkisch-nationale*, pp. 37–44. Cf. also Stang, 'Vom Sinn'.

72. For details of audience reactions, see Jelavich, *Modernism*, pp. 190–2.

73. In Thea von Harbou's script an amorphous crowd, spiritually starved and excluded from beauty, achieve harmony and strength through the efforts of a herald-like figure.

74. Peter Behrens, *Feste des Lebens und der Kunst: Eine Betrachtung des Theaters als höchstes Kultursymbol* (Leipzig 1900), quoted in Jelavich, *Modernism*, p. 189.

75. See, paradigmatically, the references to 'welscher Tand' in Wagner's *Meistersinger* or, in jest, to 'welsche Art' in Gustav Meyrink, 'Das Wildschwein', in Meyrink, *Des deutschen Spießers Wunderhorn* (Berlin 1987) p. 44.

76. Georg Fuchs, *Der Kaiser, die Kultur, und die Kunst: Betrachtungen über die Zukunft des deutschen Volkes aus den Papieren eines Unverantwortlichen* (Munich 1904), p. 14 (emphasis in the original).

77. See Horst Koegler, 'Vom Ausdruckstanz zum "Bewegungschor" des deutschen Volkes: Rudolf von Laban', in Karl Corino (ed.), *Intellektuelle im Bann des Nationalsozialismus* (Hamburg 1980), pp. 165–79; Hedwig Müller, '. . . jeder Mensch ist ein Tänzer': *Ausdruckstanz in Deutschland zwischen 1900 und 1945* (Gießen

1993); and Valerie Preston-Dunlop, 'Laban and the Nazis', *Dance Theatre Journal* 6:2 (July 1988), pp. 4–7.

78. Carl Diem, the author of the 1936 Olympic *Festspiel* referred to his creation as being less 'dichterischer als vielmehr bewegungsschöpferischer Art' (Diem, *Olympische Jugend: Festspiel* (Berlin 1936), p. 28). See also Hans Ziegelski, 'Sport und Bühnenspiel', *Bausteine* 4:7 (July 1936), p. 194.

79. 'ein Festspiel ... in dem die Zuschauerschaft gewissermaßen ... innerlich mitspielt' (Diem, *Olympische Jugend*, p. 27).

80. Wilhelm von Schramm, *Neubau des deutschen Theaters: Ergebnisse und Forderungen* (Berlin 1934), p. 40.

81. Contemporary commentators specifically linked this with theatre: 'It [the Volk] indicates through short shouts in disciplined choral speech, "... yes! No! *Heil*! etc." acceptance [or] disagreement' (Josef Bauer, 'Natürlicher Aufbau der volkhaften Feier', *Das deutsche Volksspiel* 3 (1935–6), p. 243).

82. The official commemorative volumes for the party rallies include the transcripts of several Sprechchöre (e.g. *Der Parteitag der Freiheit vom 10.–16. September 1935* (Munich 1935), pp. 72–4 and 180–1).

83. Joseph Goebbels, 'Wir halten der Kunst unsere Hand hin: Grundsätzliche Erklärungen über die Aufgaben des deutschen Theaters', *Völkischer Beobachter* (10 May 1933). See also Wolf Braumüller, 'Kurt Heynicke: "Der Weg ins Reich"', *Deutsche Bühnenkorrespondenz* 4:58 (1935), p. 1.

84. This, in turn, was likened to democratic rites: see Goebbels' description of the *Thing* arenas as the 'diets of our day' (quoted in Stommer, *Die inszenierte*, p. 111). On the equation of drama and politics, see also Rainer Schlösser, 'Politik und Drama', *Wille und Macht* 3:11 (June 1935), p. 12, or Frenzel, 'Das Drama der Entscheidung'.

85. There were also personal continuities: Niedecken-Gebhardt himself directed the 1934 *Deutsche Passion* at Heidelberg.

86. For a comparison between the practices of the left and the right in Germany, see Hannelore Wolff, *Volksabstimmung auf der Bühne: Das Theater als Mittel politischer Agitation* (Frankfurt 1985).

87. See, paradigmatically, Fuchs, *Der Kaiser* and his *Deutsche Form: Betrachtungen über die Berliner Jahrhundertausstellung und die Münchner Retrospektive* (Munich 1907).

88. See Andrew Bonnell, *The People's Stage in Imperial Germany: Social Democracy and Culture* (London 2005); on its history post-1918, see Herbert Scherer, 'Die Volksbühnenbewegung und ihre interne Opposition in der Weimarer Republik', *Archiv für Sozialgeschichte* 14

(1974), pp. 213–51, and Almut Schwerd, *Zwischen Sozialdemokratie und Kommunismus: Zur Geschichte der Volksbühne 1918–1933* (Wiesbaden 1975).

89. As an example of the propaganda surrounding this, see 'Zum ersten Male', *Der Angriff* (28 November 1936). Details about subsidised travel to and from open-air theatres in Stommer, *Die inszenierte*, p. 25.

90. Felix Emmel, *Theater aus deutschem Wesen* (Berlin 1937), p. 33. Cf. *Die Bühne* 16 (25 August 1941).

91. 'Heiligende Kunst': Prologue by SA-Standardtenführer Schumann, reprinted in *Der Angriff* (28 November 1936).

92. See Jelavich, *Modernism*, pp. 205–7. There had been an earlier amphitheatrical experiment: the 'Festspiel- und Weihehaus' at Worms, and there was, of course, Wagner's festival hall at Bayreuth. Both drew high praise in the Third Reich. See Julius Petersen, *Geschichtsdrama und nationaler Mythos: Grenzfragen zur Gegenwartsform des Dramas* (Stuttgart 1940), p. 42.

93. On the *Volksfestspiele*, see Jelavich, *Modernism*, pp. 214–17.

94. One might equally blame Reinhardt for inspiring the theatre of Piscator, or the crowd scenes in Hollywood films. Jürgen Fehling did: he regarded Nazi theatre, Piscator and Hollywood as three related disasters. See 'Dichtung und Wahrheit', in Ahrens, *Das Theater*, p. 47.

95. Nazi activists cast a covetous eye on the Große Schauspielhaus in 1933 (see Stommer, *Die inszenierte*, p. 25).

96. See, paradigmatically, Ernst Wachler, *Sommerspiele auf vaterländischer Grundlage* (Berlin 1910). Some theorists distinguished between *Freilufttheater* and *Naturtheater* (see Arthur Kutscher, *Stilkunde des Theaters* (Düsseldorf 1936), p. 75).

97. See Charlotte Tacke, 'Die 1900 Jahrfeier der Schlacht im Teutoburger Wald 1909: Von der klassenlosen Bürgerschaft zur klassenlosen Volksgemeinschaft?', in Manfred Hettling and Paul Nolte (eds.), *Bürgerliche Feste: Symbolische Formen politischen Handelns im 19. Jahrhundert* (Göttingen 1993), pp. 192–230. For retrospective Nazi recognition of patriotic festivals, see Schlösser, *Das Volk und seine Bühne*, p. 40, or Petersen, *Geschichtsdrama*, pp. 40–1.

98. For details, with architectural sketches, see Stommer, *Die inszenierte*, pp. 171–5.

99. Wachler, *Deutsche Wiedergeburt* (Leipzig 1907); *Die Freilichtbühne* (Leipzig 1909); *Heimat als Quelle der Bildung* (Leipzig 1926).

100. The location had first been recommended by Klopstock for performances of the *Hermannsschlacht*. There was thus a direct link with the eighteenth-century reformers. See Kutscher, *Stilkunde*, p. 71.

101. Ihering, quoted in Frank Dittmer, 'Freilufttheater: Dramatisches ohne Dach im 20. Jahrhundert: Dargestellt an Berliner Beispielen', unpublished thesis (Freie Universität Berlin 1991), p. 63.

102. Stommer, *Die inszenierte* contains an exhaustive bibliography of this endlessly repetitive literature. For evidence of the endurance of the clichés even beyond the demise of the *Thing*, see Franz Moraller, 'Das deutsche Freilichtspiel', *Die Bühne* 8 (August 1938), pp. 248–50.

103. For echoes of Wachler's sentiments in the *Thingspiel* theories, see, *inter al.*, Adolf Gentsch, *Die politische Struktur der Theaterführung* (Leipzig 1942), p. 40; Werner Gerth, 'Thingstatt und Thingspiel', *Deutscher Glaube* (1935), pp. 532–5; Alfred Hensel, 'Thingplätze und andere Freilichträume', *Gartenkunst* 47 (1934), pp. 152–7.

104. Jacobsohn, quoted in: Dittmer, *Freilufttheater*, p. 64. Cf. also the negative verdicts of Julius Bab (*Das Theater der Gegenwart: Geschichte der dramatischen Bühne seit 1870* (Leipzig 1928), p. 167) and Kutscher (*Stilkunde*, p. 75).

105. Julius Bab, 'Die Hussiten vor Bernau', *Die Schaubühne* (8 June 1911). Cf. 'Freilufttheater', in Alfred Kerr, *Trotz alledem – es hat gelohnt! Verse und Lieder* (Berlin 1967), p. 71.

106. BA R 55/20188, 332: censorship report on the *Bernauer Hussitenspiel*. See also *Laienspiele* files BA R 55/20440 to 20448. Nazi theatre activists themselves emphasised the continuities: e.g. the newspaper cutting in R 55/20475, 418–25: Hans-Christoph Kaergel, 'Schafft dichterische Volksbühnenspiele', *Volksbühnenwarte: Blätter und Nachrichten für deutsche Volksbühnenspieler* 11–12 (November–December 1939).

107. Bab, *Das Theater*, p. 167. The figure excludes Switzerland and the old Habsburg lands. See Kutscher, *Stilkunde*, pp. 65 and 75. There are no reliable audience figures. Those for the Third Reich in *Die Bühne* 4 (1938) do not tally with figures published elsewhere (details in Stommer, *Die inszenierte*, p. 147). Cf. also Wolf Braumüller, 'Gestaltungswille der Jugend und Freilichttheater', *Die Bühne* 8 (5 August 1938), p. 250. There is a dearth of research on the subject. The best available study is forty years old and has a narrow geographical focus: Barbara Schöpel, *Naturtheater: Studien zum Theater unter freiem Himmel in Südwestdeutschland* (Tübingen 1965). The only study in English discusses post-war performances in the same region: Alison M. Phipps, *An Investigation into South-West German Naturtheater* (Frankfurt 2000). Brief but useful comments are provided in George Mosse, *The Nationalization of the Masses: Mass*

Movements in Germany from the Napoleonic Wars through the Third Reich (New York 1975), pp. 110–14.

108. Otto Laubinger, 'Deutsche Freilichtbühnen', speech in Cologne, 7 July 1933, quoted in Stommer, *Die inszenierte*, p. 29.

109. See Bab, *Das Theater*, p. 167. For retrospective Nazi identification with the aims of the *Laienspiel*, see Gentsch, *Die politische Struktur*, p. 56. See also Ernst Wachler, *'Das Deutsche Theater der Zukunft': Iduna-Taschenbuch auf das Jahr 1903* (Berlin 1903), p. 173. On the Wandervogel's successors, see Werner Kindt, *Dokumentation des Jugendbundes: Die Deutsche Jugendbewegung 1920–1933* (Düsseldorf 1974). On nationalist cultural efforts in youth organisations, see Bruce Campbell, 'Gerhard Roßbach, the Spielschar Ekkehard and the Cultural Attack on the Weimar Republic', in Ehrlich and John (eds.), *Weimar 1930*, pp. 243–60. On school drama groups, see Ulrich Schwedt, *Martin Luserke: Reformpädagogik im Spannungsfeld von pädagogischer Innovation und kulturkritischer Ideologie* (Frankfurt 1993); on parallel efforts elsewhere in Germany, see Peter Wolferdorf, *Stilreform des Laienspiels: eine historisch-kritische Dramaturgie.* (Brunswick 1962).

110. Laubinger, 'Deutsche Freilichtbühnen'. For a documented link between the Nazi Kampfbühne and a *Naturtheater*, see BA R 55/ 20180, 84.

111. See the retrospective Nazi verdict on this in Bruno Nelissen-Haken, 'Das Volks- und Thingspiel', *Hochschule und Ausland* 13:8 (1935), pp. 55–65. For a detailed account of the *Thingspiel* and its genesis, see Stommer, *Die inszenierte*. For an effective introduction to the *Thing* in English, see William Niven, 'The Birth of Nazi Drama? *Thing* Plays', in London (ed.), *Theatre*, pp. 54–95. For continuities in the repertoire, see the careers of Heinz Steguweit, Alois Lippl or Hans-Christoph Kaergel.

112. Invitation to a soirée in Berlin's New Royal Opera House, 13 March 1902, reprinted in Freydank, *Theater als Geschäft*, pp. 18–19.

113. 'Und den Congreß, der helfen soll, beruft sie, weil sie grollt, zu Kroll!' Note also the reference to '*Schmieren-Heimatkunst!*'

114. Cf. Meyrink's famous satire on rural theatre with its recurring references to dung hills and misshapen rustics (Meyrink, 'Das Wildschwein'). Meyrink, too, was Jewish.

115. Press cutting in BA NS 5/VI/6282, 6: 'Deutsches Volksbildungswerk'. *Arbeitertum* (15 December 1936).

116. Friedrich Hussong, *Kurfüstendamm: Zur Kulturgeschichte des Zwischenreichs,* (Berlin 1934), pp. 60–1.

117. Johst, *Ich glaube!*, pp. 73 and 90 respectively.
118. Newspaper cutting in BA NS 5/VI/6282, 12: Hans Hinkel, 'Kein Platz für Muckertum', *Der Angriff* (3 December 1936). See also Hinkel's extended invective on the subject in a further undated manuscript: BA R 56 I/ 107, 240–3.
119. See Schlösser, *Das Volk und seine Bühne*, p. 27 and, again, 'Das Wirken der Jugend im Kulturleben unserer Zeit', *Wille und Macht* 5:1 (January 1937), p. 13.
120. Rudolf Ramlow, 'Volk und Kunst: ungekünstelt', *Bausteine* 3 (1935), p. 232. Cf. also Stang, 'Vom Sinn', p. 10, and 'Gegen die "Klassenkultur" ', *Frankfurter Zeitung* (newspaper cutting in BA NS 5/VI/6283, 46). Compare the review of 'Die Blaue Blusen, in *Die Rote Fahne* (9 October 1927): 'Die Premierentiger, die Geistreichen, die von der "Kultur des Abendlandes" Übersättigten' (reprinted in Schrader, *Kunstmetropole*, p. 218) with Hussong's comments about the same production quoted above.
121. On Oberammergau, see Stang, 'Vom Sinn', p. 5. On 'community spirit' and amateur players, see also Gentsch, *Die politische Struktur*, p. 56. Note also that Gustav Goes cited Oberammergau as the inspiration for his *Aufbricht Deutschland*. See Klaus Sauer, *Lorbeer und Palme: Patriotismus in deutschen Festspielen*, (Munich 1971), p. 185. On the Swiss *Tell*, see Petersen, *Geschichtsdrama*, p. 39.
122. Egon Schmid, quoted in Dittmer, 'Freilufttheater', p. 215. See also the work of Leo Weismantel in Franconia. The Catholic contribution was specifically emphasised by some Nazi proponents of open-air theatre. See BA R 55/20475, 418.
123. The term was invented up by the Cologne theatre historian Carl Niessen. Note, moreover, the striking contrast between Niessen's pseudo-Nazi rhetoric on the subject of the *Thing* and a (later) internal Nazi party assessment which described him as 'displaying considerable indifference' to the Nazi cause. Cf. Niessen, 'Thingplätze und ihre Aufgaben'. Radio manuscript (18 October 1934), quoted in Niven, 'The Birth', p. 58; and BA R 55/127, 194: 'Politische Beurteilung Prof. Carl Niessen', 6 January 1941. On the Reichsbund's strategy in 1932–3, see Stommer, *Die inszenierte*, pp. 24–5 and Michael Dultz, 'Der Aufbau der nationalsozialistischen Thingspielorganisationen 1933/34', in Henning Eichberg *et al.* (eds.), *Massenspiele: NS-Thingspiel, Arbeiterweihespiel und olympisches Zeremoniell* (Stuttgart 1977), pp. 204–5.
124. See the Propaganda Ministry's file on Gerst: BA R 55/20440, 23–6. On the meeting of the Arbeitsgemeinschaft katholischer Schriftsteller convened by Gerst in August 1933, see Stommer, *Die inszenierte*,

p. 35. Note also that Gerst founded a publishing company for play texts – the Volksschaftsverlag – which followed the same Catholic line; he persisted even after his dismissal in 1935 by creating a new Catholic publishing platform, the St.-Georgs-Verlag.

125. William Niven's contention that the Nazis brought the Reichsbund 'under their control' is only true in a longer perspective. Initially, *both* parties in the affair sought to exploit one another.

126. Cf. Hans Hinkel's retrospective remark about a 'Zwangslage' in which 'die Bewegung' found itself in 1933 because 'ihr fehlten in der Breite des kulturellen Lebens die praktischen Erfahrungen' (BA R 56 I / 89, 273). On the failure of earlier Nazi ventures like the NS Volksbühne in 1930–31, see Freydank, *Theater in Berlin*, pp. 426–7.

127. That coalition was originally even wider than the Nazis would later allow. In February 1933 – *after* the Nazi seizure of power – Gerst's Reichsbund still sought the cooperation of Horváth, Toller or Zuckmayer. See Stommer, *Die inszenierte*, p. 24.

128. Cf. Laubinger's revealing remark about Germany's 'palatial theatres' that stood half empty while 'the public was assembling elsewhere in their tens of thousands' (quoted by Dussel, *Ein neues*, p. 122). Cf. also Laubinger's description of the *Thingspiel* as 'die Vorschule des Theaters' ('Deutsche Festspiele', speech at the meeting of the Reichsbund, 23 January 1934, *Theater-Tageblatt* (1934), pp. 1347–8).

129. The Reichsbund specifically emphasised its commitment to 'the economically disadvantaged sections of society' (quoted by Stommer, *Die inszenierte*, p. 24). On Goebbels' brand of National Socialism, see his diaries, 16 April 1925, and Ralf Georg Reuth, *Goebbels* (London 1993). For the minutiae of the struggle for administrative control of the theatre sector, see Rischbieter (ed.), *Theater*, p. 9–23. There appears to have been a brief power struggle with Robert Ley, whose Labour Front was involved in the construction of the *Thing* sites: the Propaganda Ministry quickly prevailed. See Otto Laubinger, 'Freilichtspiele und Thingplätze', *Der Neue Weg* 63 (1934), pp. 174–7.

130. Details of the various promotional activities are discussed in Stommer, *Die inszenierte* and in Niven, 'The Birth'; on radio broadcasts of *Thing* plays, see Wessels, *Hörspiele*, pp. 245–50.

131. Eberhard Wolfgang Möller, 'Die Geburt des Mythos und der Dichter', quoted in Stommer, *Die inszenierte*, p. 25.

132. See Laubinger, 'Deutsche Freilichtbühnen', *Theater-Tageblatt* (7 July 1933).

133. See Carl Maria Holzapfel's comments on theatre as 'Schauplatz der Nation' ('Aufbruch', p. 116) or 'Das ganze Volk in diesem Ring

(Heinrich Zerkaulen, *Der Arbeit die Ehr!* (Berlin s.a.), p. 8). For details about *Germany on the March*, see Stommer, *Die inszenierte*, p. 47.

134. Richard Euringer, *Deutsche Passion* (Berlin 1936), p. 28. On Euringer, see Jürgen Hillesheim, *'Heil Dir Führer! Führ uns an . . .' Der Augsburger Dichter Richard Euringer* (Würzburg 1995).

135. A point rightly emphasised in Günther Berghaus, *Fascism and Theatre: Comparative Studies on the Aesthetics of Politics and Theatre in Europe* (Providence 1996).

136. Gustav Goes, 'Vom Stadion zum Thingspiel', *Bausteine* 3:5 (May 1935), p. 141.

137. BA R 55/20168, 7: 'Ewige Arbeit'; 333: 'Es werde Licht' and 'Genesen'; 369: 'Und was jetzt Andreas? ein Spiel um den Kreuzzug gegen die Not'. R 55/20177, 154: 'Der Sieg des Lichtes'. R 55/20179, 28: 'Götzendämmerung'. R 55/20180, 357: 'Brot'; 358/1: 'Ein Inflationsskandal'. R 55/20182, 263: 'Oratorium der Arbeit'. R 55/20187, 160: 'Sieg der hehren Arbeit' and 'Die Befreiung'.

138. BA R 55/20177, 271: report on August Ott, 'Neue Liturgie'.

139. Wilhelm Karl Gerst, 'Die Thingstätte', *Der Deutsche* (4 July 1934), p. 3 (quoted in Wolff, *Volksabstimmung*, p. 177). On the *Thing's* pseudo-religious function, see Klaus Vondung, *Magie und Manipulation: ideologischer Kult und politische Religion des Nationalsozialismus* (Göttingen 1971). For a more recent discussion of the issues, see also Michael Burleigh, *The Third Reich: A New History* (London 2000).

140. Gustav Goes, *Opferflamme der Arbeit* (Berlin 1934), p. 30.

141. Kurt Heynicke, *Neurode: Ein Spiel von deutscher Arbeit* (Berlin 1935), p. 41.

142. See Winter, *Sites of Memory*.

143. Note the bitterness on this topic in Johst's *Schlageter*, p. 16, or Euringer's *Deutsche Passion*, p. 25. See also Robert W. Whalen, *Bitter Wounds: German Victims of the Great War, 1914–1939* (Ithaca 1984).

144. Günther Rühle describes this as the effect of a kind of unofficial censorship: exponents of republican theatre, he suggests, had actively denied nationalist authors access to the German stage throughout the 1920s (Rühle, *Zeit und Theater: Diktatur und Exil 1933–1945* (Berlin 1974)). Toller's *Hinkemann*, which did focus on the nation's ingratitude to its former soldiers, was unacceptable to right-wing audiences because of Toller's past record in Munich. The uncompromising description of the hero's genital mutilation did not help. Note the unwonted equanimity of Ihering and Kerr: *Berliner Börsen-Courier* (9 December 1923) and *Berliner Tageblatt* (11 December 1922).

145. Cf. Egon Menz, 'Sprechchor und Aufmarsch: Zur Entstehung des Thingspiels', in Horst Denkler und Karl Prümm (eds.), *Die deutsche Literatur im Dritten Reich: Themen, Traditionen, Wirkungen* (Stuttgart 1976), p. 340. On demands for 'truthful representation' of the Great War in the parallel case of the inter-war novel, see Hans-Harald Müller, *Der Krieg und die Schriftsteller: Der Kriegsroman der Weimarer Republik* (Stuttgart 1986) and Matthias Prangel, 'Das Geschäft mit der Wahrheit: Zu einer zentralen Kategorie der Rezeption von Kriegsromanen in der Weimarer Republik', in Jos Hoogeveen and Hans Würzner (eds.), *Ideologie und Literatur (Wissenschaft)* (Amsterdam 1986), pp. 47–78.
146. Euringer, *Deutsche Passion*, p. 9.
147. Zweig, 'Epoche und Theater', pp. 22–3.
148. Euringer, *Deutsche Passion*, p. 25.
149. A point rightly emphasised by Menz ('Sprechchor', pp. 339–40).
150. See the address by the character 'Deutschland' to the 'Frontheer' in Gustav Goes, *Aufbricht Deutschland* (Berlin 1933), p. 17: 'Mehr als vier Jahre hast du mich beschützt ...'.
151. See especially Hans Poelzig's 1932 plan for a combined war memorial and open-air theatre (Krefelder Kunstmuseen (ed.), *Hans Poelzig: Malerei, Theater, Film* (Krefeld 1986)).
152. Cf. Ketelsen's wider point about Christian echoes in *Heroisches Theater*, p. 31.

Chapter 3: The uses of the past: from the *Thingspiel* to the Nazi history plays

1. Cf. Goebbels' own reference to the *Thing* arenas as 'National Socialism made stone' (quoted by Wolff, *Volksabstimmung*, p. 191).
2. Goebbels made the point by referring to the famous opening line of Schiller's Grecian ballad 'Die Kraniche des Ibykus' ('Kampf der Wagen und Gesänge', *Völkischer Beobachter*, 6 May 1933).
3. There was no indication of a planned arena in the original proposals for the Olympic site by the architect Otto March; these were substantially altered after Hitler had inspected the site in October 1933. Otto Laubinger's description of the arena as the Führer's 'generous gift' to German theatre may thus have contained an element of truth (speech at the Reichsbund meeting of January 1934, quoted by Dultz, 'Der Aufbau', p. 226).
4. See Jay Baird, 'Hitler's Muse: The Political Aesthetics of the Poet and Playwright Eberhard Wolfgang Möller', *German Studies Review* 17:2 (May 1994), pp. 269–85.

5. See Glenn Gadberry, 'Eberhard Wolfgang Möller's Thingspiel Das Frankenburger Würfelspiel', in Henning Eichberg, *Massenspiele, NS-Thingspiel, Arbeiterweihespiel und olympisches Zeremoniell* (Stuttgart 1977), pp. 235–51 (based on Gadberry's interview with Möller in 1970; see also Gadberry's dissertation 'E. W. Möller and the National Drama of Nazi Germany: A Study of the Thingspiel and of Möller's *Das Frankenburger Würfelspiel*', unpublished dissertation (University of Wisconsin, Madison 1972), and for the gist of Gadberry's findings, his 'The Thingspiel and *Das Frankenburger Würfelspiel*', *Drama Review* 24:1 (1980), pp. 103–14.

6. Möller's play replaced a planned production of Wagner's *Rienzi* (see the report in *Völkischer Beobachter*, 6 May 1936). Since *Rienzi* was one of Hitler's favourite operas, it is inconceivable that the change of programme occurred without his explicit approval.

7. For evidence of the Propaganda Ministry's extreme caution in all things touching the Führer's home region, see BA R 55/20212, 231. The file dates from 1943, but there is no reason to assume that the ministry would have been any less careful earlier.

8. All the more so, since the Propaganda Ministry had specifically announced that drama at the Berlin Olympics would allow each nation to display 'its own distinctive spirit' ('Kampf der Wagen und Gesänge', *Völkischer Beobachter*, 6 May 1933).

9. Eberhard Wolfgang Möller, 'Frankenburger Würfelspiel', in Günther Rühle, *Zeit und Theater*, p. 359.

10. Möller has the figure of Lamormaini explicitly say that he is 'no German' and had sought to serve his own people (i.e. the Italians) ('Würfelspiel', p. 344).

11. Möller actually uses the term 'Führer' (in the plural) for the peasant leaders ('Würfelspiel', p. 361). The word was otherwise reserved for senior Nazi ranks. For wider evidence of the (Nazi) equation of the victims of the Counter-Reformation with party activists three centuries later, see the reports about the ceremony at Frankenburg in *Die Tagespost* (16 May 1938).

12. The parallels with German film are instructive: see Sabine Hake, 'The Annexation of an Imaginary City: the Topos "Vienna" and the Wien-Film AG', in Hake, *Popular Cinema of the Third Reich* (Austin 2001), pp. 149–71.

13. The line in the play, 'The best [of the Austrians] are forced to flee' was a none too subtle tribute to them ('Würfelspiel', p. 359). On the play's likely sources, see the correspondence of January and February 1936 between Möller and Gauleiter Frauenfeld in: BA R 55/20180,

313–6. Frauenfeld apparently also essayed a play on the Peasants' War himself.

14. The Führer himself repeatedly had occasion to deplore the extent of German ignorance about all things Austrian. See, *inter al.*, Werner Jochmann (ed.), *Adolf Hitler: Monologe im Führerhauptquartier 1941–1944: Die Aufzeichnungen Heinrich Heims* (Hamburg 1980), entry for 25 January 1942. Limited knowledge of Austrian affairs has also undermined post-war German analyses of the *Frankenburger Würfelspiel*. Both Rühle and Stommer fail to spot its political significance. In the case of Egon Menz, one of the foremost authorities on the *Thingspiel*, this blindness allows him even to deny the *Dice Game* all contemporary relevance ('Sprechchor', p. 342).

15. See the retrospective account in *Die Volksstimme* (6 August 1938).

16. The play text survives: Karl Itzinger, *Das Frankenburger Würfelspiel des deutsch-völkischen Turnerbundes* (Wels 1925).

17. E.g. the ban of Ortner's *Stefan Fadinger*, which was to have been premièred at the Burgtheater.

18. See *Die Volksstimme* (4 August 1938).

19. BA R 55/20442, 48: the mayor of Passau to Schlösser, 19 July 1937.

20. Schlösser's term *Vollendung* is ambiguous: it can also mean 'completion'. BA R 55/20440, 147.

21. 'Das Theater im neuen Deutschland', *Theater-Tageblatt* (2 June 1934).

22. See Schlösser's verdict, '[die] am ausgeprägtesten nationalsozialistische dramatische Dichtung' ('Das unsterbliche Gespräch über das Tragische', *Wille und Macht* 5:11 (June 1937), p. 9).

23. Even before he joined the Propaganda Ministry, Möller had been invited to a meeting with Schlösser and Schirach about the future of the *Thingspiel*. Schlösser publicly identified Möller as 'the most talented of the younger playwrights' in his programmatic piece *Das Volk und seine Bühne* (reprinted in Rühle, *Zeit und Theater*, p. 781).

24. See Rühle, *Zeit und Theater*, p. 39.

25. The word *Thingspiel* had been studiously avoided in all things connected with the Olympics, probably out of deference to the Olympic committee. This spared the Propaganda Ministry unexpected blushes after the *Thing* ban.

26. Alfred Mühr, 'Der Durchbruch der künstlerischen Revolution', *Deutsche Mitte* 4 (1934), p. 55. Mühr could suggest, without apparent fear of ridicule, that National Socialism's cultural credentials had been established 'on the strength of plays on *Thing* arenas alone' (ibid.).

27. Stommer gives a figure of 17 (Die *inszenierte*, p. 102), Niven of 16 ('The Birth', p. 56). The distinction between *Thing* arenas and traditional

open-air stages was often fluid. On the issue of cost, see Boguslaw Drewniak, *Das Theater im NS-Staat: Szenarium deutscher Zeitgeschichte 1933–1945* (Düsseldorf 1987), p. 39, and Stommer, *Die inszenierte*, pp. 56–7 and 106–7.

28. Stray *Thing* files in regional archives discovered by Stommer suggest that new restrictions on the job creation schemes in the spring of 1935 effectively brought the construction of *Thing* arenas to a close. (*Die inszenierte*, p. 101).

29. Gerst's financial recklessness greatly aided doctrinaire Nazis in their attempt to unseat the founder of the Reichsbund. See BA R 55/20440, 30–4 and Stang to Rosenberg, 13 March 1934 (NS 8/ 124, 63–4). Stommer argues convincingly that restrictions on job-creation schemes in early 1935 effectively brought the construction of arenas to a close (*Die inszenierte*, p. 101).

30. See Stommer, *Die inszenierte*, pp. 103–14. Completed arenas were often more modest affairs than originally envisaged. The *Thingplatz* at Halle, for instance, was little more than a large semi-circular hollow in the ground with rows of simple wooden benches.

31. The exhibition in Heidelberg town hall of architectural drawings and models of various *Thing* arenas proved a great popular success. See *Neue Mannheimer Zeitung* (2 August 1934). For details on Heidelberg, see Stommer, *Die inszenierte*, pp. 103–14.

32. *BV Nachrichten* (30 January 1934), quoted by Stommer, *Die inszenierte*, p. 73. The Reich Theatre Festival of 1934 had to be staged instead in Heidelberg castle. Perhaps as a result, the production of Euringer's *Deutsche Passion* turned into an unconvincing affair; see the review in *Die Neue Literatur* 35 (1934), p. 653.

33. The administrative chaos involving local authorities, the Reich Labour Service and Gerst's Reichbund is all but impenetrable. An overview is provided in Stommer, *Die inszenierte*, p. 61.

34. Stommer has argued persuasively, on the basis of circumstantial evidence and close attention to dates, that the *Thing* movement's fall from favour began with Goebbels' visit to Heidelberg in July 1934 (see *Die inszenierte*, pp. 74–5).

35. The ideological resonance of a mixture of amateurs and professionals was used by the *Thing*'s proponents inside the party (see BA R 55/20441: Laubinger to Ley, 12 December 1933). See also the retrospective comments by Laubinger's successor in *Thing* affairs, Franz Moraller, who added in June 1936 that 'it had not worked out' ('Bericht von der Auflösung der Spielgemeinschaft Baden', 2 June 1936, quoted by Stommer, *Die inszenierte*, p. 121).

36. See BA R 55/20441, 60: 'Bericht über die bisherige Arbeit des Reichsbundes'. The seasonal aspect – providing work for actors in the summer months when most traditional theatres were closed – was an important argument in favour of the *Thingspiel*. Yet see the complaint about quality in BA R 55/ 201194, 188. Cf. the comment about a 'frightening artistic proletariat' in Wolf Braumüller, 'Die Landschaftsbühne', *Bausteine* 2:7 (1934–5), p. 209.

37. Their place was then taken by amateurs to everyone's satisfaction (see Schöpel, *Naturtheater*, p. 82).

38. BA R 55/20440, 60: Kirchner (i.e. the 'Thingbeauftragter des Reichsarbeitsdienstes') to Schlösser, 27 May 1935. There had been general agreement early on that canonical plays should not be performed on *Thing* stages. Given the state of crisis in municipal and state theatres, the authorities were anxious to avoid anything that might impact on box office takings of traditional playhouses. See R 55/20441, 24: memo for Laubinger, 16 November 1934.

39. This final observation had resulted in a marginal 'richtig!' in Schlösser's own hand. See also the unintentionally revealing report about that meeting itself in BA R 55/20441, 56–7.

40. Cf. Otto Laubinger's sentiments in 'Freilichtspiele und Thingplätze', or the ruminations of the *Völkische Beobachter* (21 July 1936): 'And more clearly than ever one feels ... how greatly Art will be enriched by this fusion with landscape.'

41. 'Bericht von der Auflösung der Spielgemeinschaft Baden', 2 June 1936, quoted by Stommer, *Die inszenierte*, p. 121. The tone of the report may have been partly influenced by the connection of its author, Moraller, with the Rosenberg faction. If so, there was no one left in the Propaganda Ministry willing to challenge that view.

42. See the instructions by the Propaganda Ministry to the press of 23 October 1935 and 22 November 1935 (*NS-Presseanweisungen der Vorkriegszeit: Edition und Dokumentation* (Munich 1998), vol. 1935, items 783, 1761 and 1863). See also the reiteration of the ban, 2 May 1938, 31 January and 24 April 1939 (vol. 1938, item 1274, and vol. 1939, items 334, 1096).

43. See BA R 55/20180, 285: Moraller to Schlösser, undated (*c.* October 1935). Shrewder observers guessed the truth: see, for instance, the letter from a postgraduate student from Dresden to the Reichsdramaturgie, 13 July 1939. The student was planning to write a thesis on open-air theatre. His supervisor had evidently advised him to clear this with the Propaganda Ministry first (R 55/20198, 114). The Reichsdramaturg promptly foresaw 'problems'.

44. See the correspondence between the Reichsdramaturgie and one Lothar Noack (BA R 55/20181, 165–6) of February 1936. Schlösser drafted a carefully worded reply but took the extra precaution of letting a subordinate sign it 'on behalf of the Reichsdramaturg'. Noack, needless to say, was not told that a ban existed.
45. BA R 55/20181, 170–81.
46. Cf. also the strikingly similar conclusions of another communication about the *Thing* reaching the Propaganda Ministry: R 55/20181, 174.
47. Egger's *Job*, Euringer's *Passion*, Goes' *Germany on the March* and Heynicke's *Neurode* were all written before 1933.
48. The only – telling – exception to this were the Führer commissions for stage sets (discussed below). On the wider background, see Jonathan Petropoulos, *Art as Politics* (Chapel Hill 1996).
49. See Felix Möller, *The Film Minister: Goebbels and the Cinema in the Third Reich* (Stuttgart 2000).
50. See the proposal by Richard Euringer in *Der Autor* 9:6 (1934), p. 5. The lack of good-quality *Thing* plays was thus at least in part due to the absence of financial inducements: there was more money to be made by writing for the traditional stage.
51. Goebbels frequently intervened in the production of selected films and gave detailed artistic instructions. The absence of such interventions in the theatre may owe less to a lack of interest than a simple recognition of the theatre's mechanics.
52. See the cautious tone in: Rainer Schlösser, 'Ansprache des Reichsdramaturgen Oberreg.-Rat Dr. Schlösser an den deutschen Dichterkreis', *Der Neue Weg* 63 (1934), pp. 58–60 (reprinted, *inter al.*, in *Theater-Tageblatt* (28 January 1934) and *Völkischer Beobachter* (26 January 1934)). The lavish funding was mainly a reflection of the cultural standing of the theatre in German national life and on Hitler's stated belief that conspicuous cultivation of the arts alone conferred legitimacy on a regime. See, *inter al.*, his programmatic Reichstag speech of 23 March 1933 in Domarus (ed.), *Hitler*.
53. Tellingly, the references to the *Thing*'s political usefulness had been quite overt in 1933: see, paradigmatically, the praise for the *Thing*'s 'pädagogisch-didaktische Qualitäten' (Kurt Fischer, 'Der Chor im nationalen Festspiel', *Deutsches Volksspiel* 1 (1933–4), p. 260). For an effective overview of the sprawling and endlessly repetitive literature on the *Thingspiel* and 'community', see Ketelsen, *Heroisches Theater*.
54. In that regard, the affinity with the theatre of the Greeks so often claimed by the *Thing* movement, was indeed pronounced.

55. Since architectural elegance took precedence over most other considerations in Nazi Germany, the acoustics of *Thing* arenas were imperfect. Elaborate sound systems were thus a necessary feature. See Wolff, *Volksabstimmung*, p. 188.
56. Laubinger appeared in *Germany on the March*; Goebbels was in the audience. See Werner Pleister, 'Kontrolle der Laienspiele?', *Das Deutsche Volksspiel* 1 (1933–4), p. 11.
57. The commentators were quite open about that: see Ferdinand Junghans, 'Die dramaturgische Situation des "Frankenburger Würfelspiels"', *Die Bühne* 2 (1936), p. 475.
58. *Der Neue Weg* 63 (1934) quoted in Dussel, *Ein neues*, p. 122.
59. *Holzschnittartig* was a favourite term in reviews of *Thing* plays and often palpably euphemistic: see, for instance, the reference to 'holzschnittartiger Wucht' in the review of *Fahne empor!*, in *Völkischer Beobachter* (31 May 1934). The play had been judged weak by the censor. See BA R 55/20477, 190–1.
60. See Lothar Müthel's suggestive comment on characterisation (or lack of it) in *Thing* plays: 'Die Einmündung des Einzelfalles in das Geschick der Gemeinschaft' (Johannes Günther, 'Was erwarten Sie vom Freilichttheater?', *Rheinische Landeszeitung*, 28 June 1935), quoted by Stommer, *Die inszenierte*, p. 113. For sceptical voices, see the review of *Neurode* in *Kölnische Zeitung* (22 July 1935), quoted in Stommer, *Die inszenierte*, p. 113. For criticism of the *Thing*'s lack of dramatic tension, see Konrad Dürre, 'Praktische Erfahrungen im Thingspiel', *Das Deutsche Volksspiel* 1 (1933–4), p. 282 or Wilhelm von Schramm, *Neubau des deutschen Theaters: Ergebnisse und Forderungen* (Berlin 1934), p. 51.
61. 'Die zur Handlung gesteigerte politische Rede des nationalsozialistischen Führertums' (Hans Vogel, 'Nochmals "Thingspiele"', *Propyläen* 31 (1934), p. 397).
62. BA, R 55/20441, 77–9: undated memo by Laubinger. Cf. the related thoughts on the opening of the Heidelberg arena: 'Wir glauben an das ewige Deutschland! Gedanken zur Sonnwendfeier auf dem Heiligen Berg' (*Volksgemeinschaft*, 22 June 1935) and 'Weihe der Heidelberger Thingstätte' (*Heidelberger Neueste Nachrichten*, 24 June 1935), quoted by Stommer, *Die inszenierte*, p. 111.
63. Möller expressed a similar line of thought in: 'Die Wendung des deutschen Theaters. Ein Aufriß zum Spiel auf Thingplätzen', *Das Deutsche Volksspiel* 1 (1933–4), p. 149 (reprinted in Vondung, *Völkisch-nationale*, p. 48).
64. See the comments about the Sonnwendfeier at Heidelberg as 'Wegweiser für das künftige dichterische Schaffen', *Heidelberger Neueste*

Nachrichten (24 June 1935), quoted by Stommer, *Die inszenierte*,
p. 111. Cf. parallel efforts in schools: Franz Türk, *Sprechchöre für die
nationalsozialistische Deutsche Schule* (Frankfurt 1935).

65. See respectively BA R 55/20181, 174 and R 55/20180, 370: both by
    Lothar Noack. For similar, if briefer comments, from another corre-
    spondent, see R 55/20184, 141. Cf. also the *published* criticism in
    Erdmann, 'Forderungen zum "nationalen" Drama' about the 'zusam-
    mengestoppelten Kinderreime' and their deleterious effect on the
    'Erlebnisbereitschaft'. The ministry eventually concurred: see its press
    campaign against political pathos: e.g. NS 5/VI/6276, 64
    ('Jungmannschaft der Deutschen Arbeitsfront', *Der Mitteldeutsche*,
    10 March 1936) and 'jeden hohlen Wortschwall'. See also the remark
    'Pathos ist nicht erwünscht' in NS 5/VI/6277, 15: 'Ihr sollt das Gewissen
    der Betriebe sein', *Der Angriff*, undated cutting (1936?); or the reference,
    in R 55/20178, 115, to 'Pegasus auf Sieg Heil dressiert' (late 1935?).
66. The suspicion that the eclipse of the SA damaged the *Thing* appears
    to have been current even at the time. See the revealing remarks by
    Euringer in *Der Führer* (27 July 1934), quoted by Stommer, *Die
    inszenierte*, p. 76.
67. The attacks on the *Thing*'s expressionist echoes, its religious cadences
    and its left-wing heritage are discussed succinctly in Niven, 'The Birth',
    pp. 81–4.
68. Walter Kühn, 'Thingspiel: Das Spiel der völkischen Gemeinschaft',
    Schlesische Monatshefte 11 (1934), p. 460, quoted by Stommer, *Die
    inszenierte*, p. 73. Even Heynicke's *Weg ins Reich* – generally consid-
    ered a much stronger play – was greeted with the observation that 'the
    exceptional site at Heidelberg gave the play its special quality and not
    the other way round'. (*Kölnische Zeitung*, 22 July 1935), quoted by
    Stommer, *Die inszenierte*, p. 113. See the telling remarks in December
    1935 about 'collectivists' and the 'errors of 1934' in the ministry's
    assessment of Adolf Gentsch and Werner Gerth's manuscript 'Das
    Theater als geistiges Führungsmittel' (BA R 55/20180, 352). On the
    wider flagging of enthusiasm for Nazi communal events, see William
    Sheridan Allen, *The Nazi Seizure of Power* (London 1984), pp. 249–64.
69. On the *Werkspiel* and its antecedents, see Wolff, *Volksabstimmung*,
    and Niven, 'The Birth', pp. 81–3.
70. See Rühle, *Zeit und Theater*, p. 37, and Friedhelm Indefrey, 'Über das
    Ergebnis und die Preiszuteilung im Massenschauspielwettbewerb der
    Deutschen Arbeitsfront', *Der Neue Weg* 63 (1934), pp. 230–2.
71. See the undated memo by Otto Laubinger: BA R 55/20441, 99, and the
    related memo on the misuse of *Thing* arenas: R 55/20441, 77–9.

72. Tucholsky to Walter Hasenclever, 17 May 1933 in Kurt Tucholsky, *Briefe: Auswahl 1913 bis 1935* (Berlin 1985), p. 308.
73. See the post-war recollections of Laubinger's successor Moraller, quoted in Stommer, *Die inszenierte*, p. 130; cf. Hitler's surviving criticism of the 'Werkscharen' (BA NS 10/ 44, 3: 'Aktennotiz für Hauptmann Wiedemann', 16 June 1938). Cf. the reference to 'Spießer spielen für Spießer' in 'Jungmannschaft der Deutschen Arbeitsfront', *Der Mitteldeutsche* (10 March 1936) in BA NS 5/VI/6276, 64.
74. *Spielgemeinde* 9 (1936), p. 34, quoted by Stommer, *Die inszenierte*, p. 130.
75. BA R 55/20180, 358; cf. also R 55/20179, 92 or R 55/20177, 21–2.
76. See Thomas Eicher, 'Spielplanstrukturen 1929–1944', in Rischbieter (ed.), *Theater*, pp. 279–486.
77. Barbara Panse has examined the related phenomenon of temporary bans in 'Censorship', pp. 140–56; see also her 'Zensurmaßnahmen der Reichsdramaturgie im Hinblick auf Themenkomplexe', in Rischbieter (ed.), *Theater*, pp. 511–97.
78. BA R 55/20181, 202.
79. See BA R 55/20177, 178 and R 55/20180, 211.
80. Friedrich Bethge, the *Dramaturg* of the Frankfurt theatre, claimed to have been sent on average about 2,000 unsolicited manuscripts annually in the period of 1933–6 (see BA R 55/20186, 55–7: Bethge to Schlösser, 30 April 1936).
81. BA R 55/20185, 109.
82. BA R 55/20195a, 487.
83. BA R 55/20192, 19.
84. The Propaganda Ministry showed itself quite adept in distinguishing genuine enthusiasm from what it called *Konjunkturstücke*: see, paradigmatically, BA R 55/20176, 241.
85. BA R 55/20192, 12: letter to Goebbels, 1 November 1938.
86. Schlösser, 'Ansprache', pp. 58–60. See also his *Das Volk und seine Bühne*. Cf. Stommer's point about a divergence in policy between Laubinger and Schlösser (*Die inszenierte*, p. 55). Clearly, Schlösser's own classicist tastes were a factor, too.
87. Goebbels, speech to the Reichstheaterkammer, printed in *Völkischer Beobachter* (13 May 1936).
88. The vast body of theoretical literature on drama produced in the Third Reich tends to obscure rather than illuminate actual artistic or political practice.
89. See, for instance, the revealing speech of February 1936 by Friedrich Bethge in the Frankfurt theatre, quoted in Bettina Schültke, *Theater*

*oder Propaganda? Die Städtischen Bühnen Frankfurt am Main
1933–1945* (Frankfurt 1997), p. 395. Cf. the related sentiments inside
the Propaganda Ministry, BA R 55/20176, 241: report by Günther
Gablenz of the Reichschrifttumsstelle, 9 July 1935, 'Es ist an der
Zeit, dass diesen Konjunkturschreibern endgültig der Hals abgedreht
wird'.

90. Schlösser himself suggested a link with developments outside the
theatre: BA R 55/20187, 285–91: article for Theateralmanach Frankfurt
am Main (1936?), 'Die strenge und großartige Einfachheit der
Führerbauten entspricht einer hymnischen und chorischen Dichtung,
welche den Ausgangspunkt nicht mehr in privaten und zufälligen psy-
chologischen Quellen sieht.' On the roots of Nazi theatrical classicism,
see Andreas Woehrmann, *Das Programm der Neuklassik: Die
Konzeption einer modernen Tragödie bei Paul Ernst, Wilhelm von
Scholz und Samuel Lublinski* (Frankfurt 1979); on Schlösser's own
tastes, see Klausnitzer, 'Wir'.

91. On the unofficial ban of *Schlageter*, see Panse, 'Zeitgenössische',
pp. 511–5. Wolf Braumüller's dismissive phrase for the *Thing*
repertoire – 'collective heading: "plays about 1918–1933"' also fitted
rather well the repertoire of the proscenium stage (*Freilicht- und
Thingspiel* (Berlin 1935), p. 33).

92. On the resonance of *Konjunktur* in 1933, see Schültke, *Theater*,
p. 265–7.

93. For the way in which that (unofficial) ban was communicated, see BA R
55/20202.

94. BA R 55/20208, 423: 'Carin'. Cf. the comparable case in R 55/20183,
61–2: 'Woas I heut Nacht von moam Führer träumt hoab! Großes
Schauspiel deutscher Gegenwart in 5 Aufzügen'.

95. Möller, 'Würfelspiel', in Rühle, *Zeit und Theater*, p. 367.

96. Möller was to run into more serious trouble with *Der Untergang
Karthagos* (1938), though it is not fully clear if the play itself – or the
direction – offended his party critics most. See Panse, 'Zeitgenössische',
pp. 665–7.

97. Schlösser himself practically admitted as much in: BA R 55/20187,
285–91: article for Theateralmanach Frankfurt am Main (1936?). The
dramatist who came closest to Schlösser's ideal was Curt Langenbeck;
yet Langenbeck was to fall foul of Rosenberg in the *cause célèbre* of *Das
Schwert*. See Panse, 'Zeitgenössische', pp. 575–82, and Rühle, *Zeit und
Theater*, pp. 794–803.

98. Cf. the revealing comment by Arthur Luther: 'es [sind] vor allem die
selbstherrlichen Tyrannennaturen, für die sich die Dichter begeistern'

('Die dramatische Produktion des Jahres 1941', *Die Neue Literatur*, June 1942, p. 128).

99. BA R 55/201901, 239: Hermann Burte to Schlösser, 13 August 1936. Cf. the mixture of ingratiation and complaint by H. C. Kaergel (R 55/20179, 304).

100. See, *inter al.*, BA R 55/20200, 16: 'der Markt an historischen Stücken ist überfrachtet' or Schlösser's public comments in 'Das unsterbliche Gespräch', p. 10.

101. See the comments about *Cromwellstücke* in BA R 55/20181, 63. On the resonance of Cromwell in the Third Reich, see Gerwin Strobl, *The Germanic Isle: Nazi Perceptions of Britain* (Cambridge 2000). For an attempt to tease some underlying order out of the profusion of the Third Reich's dramatic production, see Glen Gadberry, 'The History Plays of the Third Reich', in London, *Theatre*, pp. 96–135.

102. Therese Fromm, 'Kaiser und König', *National-Zeitung* (31 October 1937), quoted by Schültke, *Theater*, p. 432. Cf., a year later, Hans Christoph Mettin's observation that history 'invariably' furnished the plot in new plays: 'Glossen zur Zeit', *Die Tat* 30:1 (1938). See also Hermann Wanderscheck's revealing reference to the 'Schlagwort von der "Flucht in die Historie" ' in his *Deutsche Dramatik*, p. 14.

103. BA R 55/20195, 133–4: covering letter, 'Der neue Bürgermeister', 28 February 1937. There are no reliable statistics for individual genres; the annual tables published in *Die neue Literatur* suggest a *substantial* rise in the number of new history plays but the categories are not clearly defined and about 15 per cent of new plays are simply classed as 'unknown category'.

104. BA R 55/20226: Bethge to Schlösser 29 July 1940.

105. Fromm, 'Kaiser und König', *National-Zeitung* (31 October 1937), quoted by Schültke, *Theater*, p. 432. Cf. the strikingly similar conclusions about a play by a different author by Max von Brück, 'Rebellion um Preußen', *Frankfurter Zeitung* (22 March 1939), quoted by Schültke, *Theater*, p. 367.

106. BA R 55/20180, 370, letter to Goebbels (c. 1936).

107. BA R 55/20191, 16: Prof. Dr. Kuno Ridderdorf to Goebbels, 1 November 1938. Cf. the parallel case in BA R 55/20198, 280: Ernst Karsten to Schlösser, 31 July 1939.

108. BA R 55/20202, 31: letter to Schlösser, 16 August 1935.

109. BA R 55/20226, 200: Bethge to Laubinger, 6 July 1934.

110. BA R 55/20226: Bethge to Schlösser, 2 December 1940 (italics in original).

111. BA R 55/20180, 250: Walther Best to Schlösser, 30 December 1935. Cf. the complaint of the party publishing house about theatres ignoring its

play lists (R 55/21229: Dramaturgisches Büro im Zentralverlag der NSDAP to Schlösser, 16 March 1943).

112. BA R 55/20196, 281: Paul Baumann to Schlösser, 13 January 1941. Cf. the remark by Wolfgang Nufer, 'Was nützen der Bühne die Dichter, die in gläubiger ... Zuversicht schaffen, wenn es nicht gelingt, die Menschen dem Theater zu gewinnen' ('Zur Lage des deutschen Theaters', *Das Volk: Kampfblatt für völkische Kultur und Politik* 1 (1936–7), p. 176).

113. Curt Langenbeck, 'Bemerkungen zum historischen Drama', *Wille und Macht* 6:12 (June 1938), p. 33. On Hymmen's views, see Friedrich Carl Kobbe, 'Auf dem Wege zum Drama', *Die Literatur: Monatsschrift für Literaturfreunde* 41:35 (1939), p. 264. See also Walter Thomas, *Vom Drama unserer Zeit* (Leipzig 1938), p. 59.

114. Karl Valentin, 'Das Theater muß sich ändern', *Wille und Macht* 6:12 (June 1938), p. 37. Note that Valentin's satire was printed on the pages *immediately* following the uncompromising comments by Langenbeck *et al.*

115. BA R 56 I/ 3, 53: Bethge to Hinkel, 23 January 1941.

116. See, for instance, Toni Impekoven's *Das Hofkonzert*. On Schlösser's own views on such fare, see his letter to Goebbels, 26 March 1940 in BA R 55/20202, 171. See also *Die Neuberin*, whose metatheatrical aspects has recently fascinated Glen Gadberry ('Stages of Reform: *Caroline Neuber/ Die Neuberin* in the Third Reich', in Helmut Hal Rennert (ed.), *Essays on Twentieth-Century German Drama and Theater: An American Reception* (New York 2004), pp. 167–75).

117. BA R 55/20184, 90.

118. BA R 55/20204, 94: review of 'Die letzte Festung', *Frankfurter Zeitung* (19 April 1942).

119. See Axel Marquardt *et al.* (eds.), *Preußen im Film* (Berlin 1981).

120. BA R 55 20198, 169: 'Langenbielauer Heimatfestspiel', 17 July 1939; see also R 55/20182, 146 and 187: 'historisches Festspiel "Deutschlands Erwachen"'.

121. On Rehberg, see Rühle, *Zeit und Theater*, pp. 809–18.

122. For contemporary views of Rehberg's real or supposed affinities with Shakespeare, see Otto Friedrich Gaillard, *Hans Rehberg: Der Dichter der 'Preußendramen'* (Rostock 1941); see also Wolf Braumüller, 'Hans Rehberg's Hohenzollerdramen', *Berliner Börsen-Zeitung* (6 April 1938). On the 'anti-Shakespearean' approach of the classicists, see for instance Curt Langenbeck, 'Die Wiedergeburt des Dramas aus dem Geist der Zeit', *Das Innere Reich* 6 (1939–40), pp. 923–57.

123. BA NS 8/ 242, 219: Stang to Schlösser, 1 July 1943.

124. One might add a fifth – Curt Langenbeck – who displayed an independent mind in *The Sword* (upon which he subsequently fell).
125. Hans Rehberg, *Der Siebenjährige Krieg*, reprinted in Rühle, *Zeit und Theater*, p. 500.
126. Rosenberg allegedly called for Rehberg 'to be muffled', 'since he refuses to submit' (quoted by Rühle, *Zeit und Theater*, p. 817). Schlösser made no attempt to interest theatres in Rehberg's plays, as would have been customary in the case of playwrights who were party members, and Rehberg's final plays were no longer premièred in Berlin, which was certainly significant.
127. See the Propaganda Ministry's own emphasis on this in: BA R 55/20200, 5: censor's report on 'Bruderkampf', 18 July 1939.
128. Significantly, both plays were performed in tandem during the 1937 Hitler Youth Theatre Festival at Bochum.
129. BA R 55/20550, 517: undated newspaper cutting from *Egerland* (*c.* October 1935).
130. See, *inter al.*, BA R 55/20550, 51 and 517 or BA R 55/20442, 214. Schlösser himself described *The Prince of Homburg* as the 'Erziehungsdrama eines Volkes, dessen innere Vielfalt naturgemäß zum Zwiespalt neigt' ('Politik und Drama', p. 12).
131. See Hans Daiber, *Schaufenster der Diktaur: Theater im Machtbereich Hitlers* (Düsseldorf 1995), p. 243.
132. See Johann Mugrauer, *Pfarrgemeinde Höritz im Böhmerwalde und seine Passionsspiele* (Tauberbischofsheim 1990), p. 212.
133. See the transcript of the scenes of the Wiener Werkl in BA R 55/20204, 230–43.
134. See the particularly striking example in: BA R 55/20200, 5: censor's report on 'Bruderkampf', 18 July 1939. See also R 55/20191, 17: 'Erzherzog Johann von Österreich', and R 55/20197, 55: 'Der Rademeister'.
135. BA R 55/21229: Schlösser about 'Leuchtfeuer' note to Schmid (*c.* February 1944).
136. 'Das Theater im neuen Deutschland', *Theater-Tageblatt* (2 June 1934).

Chapter 4: Stages of aggression: theatre and the 'ethnic struggle'

1. *Documents on German Foreign Policy, 1919–1945*, series C, vol. I, no. 165, p. 304.
2. BA R 55/20179, 296: Polish Embassy to German Foreign Office, 5 October 1935.
3. BA R 55/20179, 292: Polish Embassy to German Foreign Office, 13 October 1935: One of the lines highlighted was, 'Das Schweinepack

redet von Gerechtigkeit und schleicht sich nachts an die Häuser und zündet sie an' (R 55/20179, 288).

4. BA R 55/20179, 287: Abteilung IV to Schlösser, 4 December 1935.
5. See, for instance, the example of a dramatist approaching the censors a second time after the Saar referendum, 'since things might conceivably be different now' (BA R 55/20178, 210). The ban was reiterated. The principal plays affected are listed in Panse, 'Zeitgenössische', pp. 511–13.
6. See Panse, 'Zeitgenössische', pp. 536–8 and 516–21 respectively.
7. See the suggestive Schlösser 'Vermerk' of 12 April 1939 in BA R 55/20196, 90. On the wider background, see Boguslaw Drewniak, *Polen und Deutschland 1919–1939: Wege und Irrwege kultureller Zusammenarbeit* (Düsseldorf 1999).
8. See BA R 55/20179, 303: Schlösser to Kaergel, 8 January 1936.
9. BA R 55/20179, 305: Schlösser to Kaergel, 31 January 1936.
10. He thought they had not (BA R 55/20196, 90: Schlösser 'Vermerk', 12 April 1939).
11. See BA R 55/20187, 217: Abteilung VI to Schlösser, 'Bei allem Wohlwollen gegenüber dem Staate Polen'.
12. BA R 55/20201, 108: review of 'Hochzeit in Krakau', *Warschauer Zeitung* (3 July 1940).
13. No evidence survives of an actual ban; but the surviving documentation is not necessarily complete. Note, moreover, the case of *Hochwald*, another play about the Sudeten Germans, where there was a ban (BA R 55/20199, 250: Auswärtiges Amt to Schlösser, 9 February 1937).
14. BA R 55/20225, 108: Oberregierungsrat Krebs to Schlösser, 27 November 1937.
15. BA R 55/20225, 110: Auswärtiges Amt to Schlösser, 13 January 1938 (emphasis in original).
16. Hitler was faster than the theatre directors: Czechoslovakia had vanished from the map before *Hollmann* was produced again.
17. See the reference in BA R 55/20445, 39 to the coverage in the *Vossische Zeitung* in 1928: 'es war Volksgottesdienst'.
18. BA R 55/20445, 48: Schlösser to Goebbels, 18 May 1935.
19. BA R 55/20445, 54: Schlösser Aktenvermerk, 20 May 1935.
20. BA R 55/20445, 55: Schlösser to Landesstelle Königsberg, 20 May 1935.
21. BA R 55/20445, 114: Volksbund für das Deutschtum im Ausland to Propaganda Ministry, 30 May 1935.
22. Even among the unsolicited manuscripts reaching the Propaganda Ministry there were, if the surviving files are anything to go by, few anti-Czech plays.

23. BA R 55/20180, 3. Even if this should just have been a polite excuse, the argument chosen is suggestive.
24. See, for instance, Walter Helm, *Ausgewiesen! Lebensbild aus dem besetzten Gebiet in einem Akt* (Langensalza 1924); Hermann Vogt, *Die Peitsche deines Herrn: Schauspiel in einem Akt* (Langensalza 1924). Even Austrian dramatists turned to the topic: e.g. Josef Wenter's *Aus tiefer Not* (1923) and Franz Theodor Csokor, *Besetztes Gebiet: Historisches Stück aus der Gegenwart* (Berlin 1930); on Arnold Bronnen, who was also Austrian, see below.
25. Quoted in Rühle, *Theater für die Republik*, p. 636.
26. See Matthias Bullinger, *Kunstförderung zwischen Monarchie und Republik: Entwicklungen der Kunstförderung in Württemberg zwischen 1900 und 1933 am Beispiel der Theater in Stuttgart, Ulm und Heilbronn* (Frankfurt 1997), pp. 254–9.
27. A point made insistently in the nationalist press: e.g. *Süddeutsche Zeitung* (24 January 1924). On French actions in the Ruhr and on the Rhine see Gerd Krumeich and Joachin Schröder (eds.), *Der Schatten des Weltkrieges: Die Ruhrbesetzung 1923* (Essen 2004), and Conan Fischer, *The Ruhr Crisis* (Oxford 2003).
28. There were links between the Stuttgart *Theaterskandal* and later Nazi theatre, notably in the figure of Georg Schmückle (see below).
29. *Reparationen*, moreover, was only produced a full three years after it had been written: a notable delay, given that Bronnen was considered a leading playwright.
30. Conspicuous friendliness of ordinary Germans towards French and British visitors after 1933 is well documented. The most spectacular instance was the ecstatic welcome given to Prime Ministers Chamberlain and Daladier in Munich (to Hitler's obvious annoyance).
31. Details in Panse, 'Zeitgenössische', pp. 513–14.
32. See ibid., p. 514.
33. Note the frosty response by the Propaganda Ministry to the suggestion by a member of the public to revive *In the Skies of Europe* for the Berlin Olympics (BA R 55/20182, 239).
34. See, *inter al.*, BA R 55/20187, 56; R 55/20699, 404; R 55/20182, 239; R 55/20191a, 521; R 55/20200, 151; R 55/20183, 162. Note also the play about Franco-German reconciliation, actually written by a member of the Propaganda Ministry (R 55/20211, 179).
35. BA R 55/20199, 136
36. BA R 55/20201, 147.
37. That plot, as the author pointed out, had subsequently been authenticated by an incident where East Prussians had crossed the border to help

put out a fire in a Polish village (BA R 55/20199, 136: letter to Schlösser, 8 May 1934).

38. Ibid.

39. Not least by the Nazis themselves. See Heinz Schlötermann, *Das deutsche Weltkriegsdrama 1919–1937: Eine wertkritische Analyse* (Würzburg 1939).

40. Heinrich Zerkaulen, *Jugend von Langemarck* (first performed simultaneously 9 November 1933 in Beuthen, Bonn, Bremen, Darmstadt, Dresden, Greifswald, Hagen, Halle, Kassel and Lübeck); Friedrich Bethge, *Reims* (first performed 27 February 1930 in Osnabrück); Paul Joseph Cremers, *Marneschlacht* (first performed 14 January 1933 in Mannheim).

41. Sigmund Graff, 'Thema Langemarck', *Bausteine* 2 (1934), pp. 58–9.

42. Relatively little is known about this man, Carl Heinz Hintze (see Panse, 'Zeitgenössische', p. 600).

43. For a subsequent Nazi account of that production, and the response of 'the Red season ticket holders', see Wanderscheck, *Deutsche Dramatik*, p. 105.

44. See William Sonnega, 'Anti War Discourse in War Drama: Sigmund Graff and *Die endlose Straße*', in Rennert (ed.), *Essays*, pp. 147–54, and Sonnega's earlier, 'Theatre of the Front: Sigmund Graff and *Die endlose Straße*', in Glen W. Gadberry (ed.), *Theatre in the Third Reich, the Prewar Years* (Westport 1995), pp. 47–64.

45. Alfred Kerr thought that it was impossible not to become a pacifist after seeing that play (*Berliner Tageblatt*, 24 February 1932). Yet Ihering noted, presciently, that the mood of resignation in the play might suit those who like to portray wars as inevitable (*Berliner Börsen-Courier*, 24 February 1932).

46. Quoted in Bruno Fischli, *Die Deutschen-Dämmerung: Zur Genealogie des völkisch-faschistischen Dramas und Theaters* (Bonn 1976), p. 178.

47. For details, see Panse, 'Zeitgenössische', pp. 556–67.

48. However, Bethge's *Reims* contained, from a Nazi perspective, the fundamental flaw of having a hero who deserted from the frontline. In the revised version of 1934, Bethge provides a Nazi happy end: the deserter is pardoned, returns to the front and redeems himself by dying a hero's death.

49. Speech at the Hitler Youth Theatre Conference, Bochum 1937, reprinted in *Das Innere Reich* (June 1934).

50. For production details, see Eicher, 'Spielplanstrukturen', pp. 445–6. For evidence of the high regard for Sherriff's play among the Nazi leadership, see BA R 55/20106, 50: Schlösser to Goebbels, 11 November 1936.

51. Speech at the Hitler Youth Theatre Conference, Bochum 1937, *Das Innere Reich* (June 1937).
52. See Heinrich Zerkaulen, *Erlebnis und Ergebnis* (Leipzig 1939).
53. See BA R 55/20204, 51: *Posen, Herbst 1939*; R 55/20699, 297: *Auf Vorposten*; or R 55/ 20175, 1: *Deutsch bleibt die Saar* as particularly telling examples.
54. BA R 55/20179, 303.
55. BA R 55/20192, 247: letter to Schlösser, 26 November 1935.
56. BA R 55/20699, 297: letter to Goebbels, 8 May 1939.
57. BA R 55/20182, 202: *Der Fremdenlegionär*.
58. See Sauer, *Lorbeer*, pp. 149–57. See also the use of a riding crop as a significant prop in Beyer's *Düsseldorfer Passion*.
59. See the plans, ultimately vetoed by Schlösser, to stage *Meister Burbaum*: a tale about smuggling during the Napoleonic occupation (BA R 55/20197, 285–6).
60. Carl Niessen, 'Westdeutsches Theater im Grenzkampf', *Die Bühne* 12 (6 November 1938).
61. See Barbara Piatti, 'Ein unzerstörbarer Mythos nicht nur für die Schweiz', *Das Parlament* (4 April 2005) and Stanislas Jeanesson, 'Übergriffe der französischen Besatzungsmacht und deutsche Beschwerden', in Krumeich and Schröder (eds.), *Der Schatten*, p. 218.
62. Julius Geist (ed.), *Theater am Westwall: 20 Jahre Kulturarbeit des Landestheaters Saarpfalz* (Neustadt an der Weinstraße 1940). See also Ernst Leopold Stahl, 'Als die "Rheinische Kulturkonferenz" tagte: Aus der Geschichte eines deutschen Landestheaters', *Die Bühne* 24 (28 December 1940).
63. At the 1936 *Reichsfestspiele* in Heidelberg the Reichsdramaturg pointedly reminded audiences of the 'waves of destruction' that had washed over the town. Speech of 12 August 1936, reprinted in *Das Volk* 1 (1936–7), p. 222.
64. See the reference to Gabriela Zapolska's play *Tamtem*, staged in German as *Die Waschauer Zitadelle* in Panse, 'Zeitgenössische', p. 525.
65. See, for instance, the list contained in the official Polish complaint about Kaergel's *Volk ohne Heimat* (BA R 55/20179, 288).
66. BA R 55/20179, 304.
67. See Drewniak, *Das Theater*, p. 236.
68. BA R 55/20226, 381.
69. Quoted in Ketelsen, *Von heroischem Sein*, pp. 25–6.
70. BA R 55/20200, 181: *Die Mongolenschlacht* by the brother of Minister Kerrl; see also R 55/20204, 48: *Posen, Herbst 1939*, and R 55/20204, 340: *Lohhof*.

71. For details, see Drewniak, *Das Theater*, p. 235. For efforts in the Third Reich to create theatre festivals also at Tannenberg, see the suggestions of Kurt Gerlach-Bernau in his *Drama und Nation* (Breslau 1934), pp. 7–8 (Sauer, *Lorbeer*, p. 222).

72. See the thoughtful analysis of these issues in Andreas Kossert, *Ostpreußen: Geschichte und Mythos* (Berlin 2005).

73. Polish officialdom, for instance, closed down almost all German-language secondary schools: see Richard Blanke, *Orphans of Versailles: The Germans in Western Poland, 1918–1939* (Lexington 1993); see also the reference to 'Polish arrogance' in: BA R 55/20699, 297: letter to Goebbels, 8 May 1939.

74. BA R 55/20204, 48: *Posen, Herbst 1939*.

75. See Panse, 'Zeitgenössische', p. 719.

76. See Hanns Johst, *Ruf des Reiches – Echo des Volkes* (Munich 1940). For a complete list of Johst's wartime journalism, see Düsterberg, *Johst*, pp. 429–36.

Chapter 5: 'The stream of heredity': theatre in the racial state

1. Bertolt Brecht, *Tagebücher 1920–1922* (Frankfurt 1975), entry for 25 September 1920.

2. Kurt Eggers, *Schüsse bei Krupp*, p. 8.

3. Richard Euringer, *Deutsche Passion*, p. 24.

4. See, for instance, BA R 55/20178: *Rheinland, 1923*, which contained dialogue about 'Moroccan rapes'. Cf. in R 55/20177, 249 the reference to *Jakob Johannes* and 'die Marokkaner-Szene'.

5. See Katharina Oguntoye, *Eine afro-deutsche Geschichte: Zur Lebenssituation von Afrikanern und Afro-Deutschen in Deutschland 1884–1950* (Berlin 1997); Fatima El-Tayeb, *Schwarze Deutsche: der Diskurs um 'Rasse' und nationale Identität 1890–1933* (Frankfurt 2001). On the French army's own statistics of rape cases, see Jeanesson, 'Übergriffe'.

6. BA R 55/20178, 167: letter to Goebbels, 16 November 1935.

7. BA R 55/20193, 311–4: *Der Heilige Krieg*.

8. BA R 55/20182, 202: *Der Fremdenlegionär*. For overt identification with Africans, see Viktor Klemperer, *Leben sammeln, nicht fragen wozu und warum: Tagebücher 1918–1932* (Berlin 1996), especially the entries for 4 February 1921 and 21 April 1922.

9. BA R 55/20193, 311–4: letter to Hinkel, 13 September 1935.

10. The Reichsdramaturgie, certainly, was unimpressed by the author's reasoning and banned the play.

11. 'Mecherhulda und die 10 Spießersünden', *Preußische Zeitung* (24 November 1936) (newspaper cutting in BA NS 5/VI/6286, 19).

12. See BA R 55/20200, 296: Bühnenverleger to Frenzel, 30 October 1939, re: *Die Kleider meiner Frau*; and R 55/20210, 91: minute by Schlösser of a telephone conversation with Gustaf Gründgens, 18 December 1943.

13. BA R 56/ 1: Dr. Alfred Christoph to Vereinigung der Verleger für Volksliteratur im Deutschen Verlegerverein, 24 September 1934.

14. Adolf Hitler, *Mein Kampf*, trans. Ralph Mannheim (London 1992), p. 324.

15. BA R 56/ 1 (emphasis in original).

16. See in particular the pre-1933 publications of H. F. K. Günther.

17. BA R 55/20182, 206: Intendant Preußisches Staatstheater (acting as censor) to the Amateur Theatre Section of the Propaganda Ministry, 4 December 1935.

18. BA R 55/20195, 183: censorship report for 'Hände weg von Dr. Peters', 23 February 1937. Cf. the case of 'Simba va Ulava' – also about East Africa – where Schlösser urged extreme caution (R 55/20191a, 530).

19. See, *inter al.*, BA R 55/20200, 11; R 55/20208a, 504; R 55/20210, 176.

20. BA R 55/20445, 60: censorship report for 'Vineta', 30 June 1935.

21. Such racism was not specific to Nazi Germany; for British examples, see Ronald Hyam, *Empire and Sexuality: The British Experience* (Manchester 1990).

22. BA R 1001/6382, 126: Schneider to Landesstelle Berlin des Propagandaministeriums, 11 December 1936. On the wider background, see Elisa Forgey, ' "Die große Neger-Trommel der kolonialen Werbung" – die deutsche Afrika-Schau 1935–1943', *WerkstattGeschichte* 9 (1994), pp. 25–33; Marianne Bechhaus Gerst, 'Afrikaner in Deutschland' 1933–1945', *Zeitschrift für Sozialgeschichte des 20. und 21. Jahrhunderts* 4 (1997), pp. 10–31; Heiko Möhle, 'Die "deutsche Gesellschaft für Eingeborenenkunde" ', in Ulrich van der Heyden and Joachim Zeller (eds.), *Kolonialmetropole Berlin: Eine Spurensuche* (Berlin 2002), pp. 243–51.

23. BA R 1001/6382, 262.

24. See Möhle, 'deutsche Gesellschaft', p. 251. They were allowed to continue working for the cinema where they duly appeared in a number of anti-British propaganda films.

25. Bastian Breiter, 'Der Weg des "treuen Askari" ins Konzentrationslager: Der Lebensweg des Mohamed Husen', in van der Heyden and Zeller (eds.), *Kolonialmetropole*, p. 219.

26. Drewniak speaks of 77 productions in 1932, declining to 31 in 1933 and to a mere 19 in 1934 (*Das Theater*, p. 247).

27. There appears to have been an order by Goebbels to stop productions of the *Merchant* (indirectly attested to in BA R 55/20194, 285: Schlösser to Goebbels, 16 July 1940). The number of productions had declined from twenty in 1933 to three in 1937 (see the respective volumes of the *Deutsches Shakespeare-Jahrbuch*).

28. Daiber, *Schaufenster*, p. 29.

29. BA R 55/20188, 401: Hanns Ludwig Kormann to Göring, 29 December 1937. The original term *Afterkunst* is ambiguous: it can mean 'that which comes after Art' but *After*'s primary meaning is anatomical.

30. See Daiber, *Schaufenster*, pp. 23–4; Freydank, *Theater in Berlin*, pp. 426–7; and Steinweis, *Art*, pp. 25–6.

31. See Stenzel, 'Nationaltheater', pp. 229–35, and Dussel, *Ein neues*.

32. See Hildegard Brenner's classic study *Die Kunstpolitik des Nationalsozialismus* (Reinbek 1963); and Stenzel, 'Nationaltheater', pp. 235–41.

33. BA R 55/20177, 192: Schlösser comment to the inquiry by the Reichsbund der deutschen Freilicht- und Volksschauspiele, 20 July 1935.

34. See the proposal by Intendant Nadolle of Memel, 10 October 1934 (BA R 55/20538, 23). There were admittedly tactical considerations involved, since Memel was Lithuanian at the time; yet Nadolle's reasoning is suggestive.

35. See Jan-Pieter Barbian, *Literaturpolitik im 'Dritten Reich': Institutionen, Kompetenzen, Betätigungsfelder* (Munich 1995), pp. 202–4.

36. BA R 55/20550, 469–501.

37. BA R 55/20550, 702: Consulate Reichenberg to Propaganda Ministry, 16 March 1937.

38. See the correspondence between NSV Ortsgruppe Zschornegosda and the Reichsdramaturgie of March–April 1936 (BA R 55/20185, 330–1).

39. BA R 55/20618, 98: Schriftleitung *Das Schwarze Korps* to Schlösser, 11 February 1937. Cf. the reference to the same paper's championing of Hofmannsthal in Wiliam Grange, 'Rules, Regulations and the Reich: Comedy under the Auspices of the Propaganda Ministry', in Rennert (ed.), *Essays*, p. 199; or the unexpected attitude of Friedrich Bethge to Jewish librettists (see Albert Mohr, *Frankfurter Schauspiel 1929–1944* (Frankfurt 1974), pp. 41–2).

40. BA R 55/20183, 217.

41. Martin Havenstein to Otto Schumann, 31 December 1930; published in: Hammerstein, *Deutsche Bildung*, p. 34.

42. Walter Best, 'Gebildet sein, d.h. innerlich reich sein', *Kurhessische Landeszeitung* (5 October 1937) (newspaper cutting in: BA NS 5/VI/

6283, 66). See also the outburst by Hans Severus Ziegler about 'fremd-blütige Barbaren' quoted in Stenzel, 'Nationaltheater', p. 237.

43. BA R 55/20190, 149; see also R 55/20190a, 467; R 55/20192, 93 and 130; R 55/20201, 3; R 55/20213, 474. The list is far from exhaustive. While it is difficult to quantify antisemitic plays since the existing documentation is not necessarily complete, there are suggestive clusters, particularly in the aftermath of Kristallnacht.

44. See, *inter al.*, BA R 55/20210, 1: letter to Propaganda Ministry, 1 December 1942 and R 55/20205, 25: letter to the Reich Chancellery, 23 May 1941.

45. BA R 55/20699, 6: letter to Gauleiter Hofer, 17 April 1939.

46. Quoted in Werner Maser, *Heinrich George: Mensch aus Erde gemacht* (Berlin 1998), pp. 244–5.

47. See BA R 55/ 20141, 42: memorandum by Intendant Iltz, 6 February 1937; R 55/20186, 145: letter to Gauleiter of Hessen-Nassau, 6 October 1937; R 55/20187, 150: letter to Schlösser, 4 November 1935.

48. BA R 55/20207a, 383: Nufer to Schlösser, 14 May 1942.

49. BA R 55/20177, 169: letter to Goebbels, 29 July 1935.

50. See Zuckmayer, *Als wärs ein Stück von mir*, pp. 67–8.

51. See the entries for 4 September and 5 October 1935; 2 July and 11 December 1936; 5 May, 5 June, 21 September, 9 October, 4 November, 24 November, 15 December, 16 December 1937; 13 January, 9 February, 18 May and 27 July 1938; 26 January 1939.

52. Hans Hinkel, ' "Wohin mit den Juden?" Speech at the Lessing-Hochschule', *Die Bühne* 1 (5 January 1939).

53. BA R 55/20193, 30: 'Jahwe über Rußland': covering letter by the author's wife to Goebbels, 3 December 1938.

54. See also the suggestive remarks in Kurt Axmann, 'Das Recht zur Kritik', *Wille und Macht* 3:6 (March 1935), p. 23.

55. For succinct accounts, see Rischbieter, 'NS-Theaterpolitik', pp. 13–28 and Steinweis, *Art*, pp. 103–120.

56. See Steinweis, *Art*, p. 105.

57. Details in Rischbieter, 'NS-Theaterpolitik', pp. 16–17.

58. See, paradigmatically, Aliquis (i.e. Rainer Schlösser), 'Die unmoralische Anstalt', and, retrospectively, Wanderschek, *Deutsche Dramatik*, p. 1.

59. Ibid., p. 9.

60. BA Berlin R 43 II/ 1241: DNB release, 8 February 1934. Cf. also the similar line of argument in R 56 I/ 91, 96. The flight of the Rotter brothers to Liechtenstein had become a *cause célèbre*.

61. See, *inter al.*, Heinrich Riemenschneider, *Theatergeschichte der Stadt Düsseldorf* (Düsseldorf 1987); Thomas Siedhoff, *Das Neue Theater in Frankfurt am Main 1911–1935* (Frankfurt 1985).

62. 'Rede Friedrich Forster-Burggrafs im Prinzregententheater München, gehalten Am Tage seiner Amtseinführung als Leiter des Staatsschauspiels, dem 19. Oktober 1933', *Bausteine* 1:2 (November 1933), p. 44.
63. Wanderschek, *Deutsche Dramatik*, p. 9.
64. Hans Severus Ziegler, *Wende und Weg* (Weimar 1937), pp. 75–6.
65. Biographical details about Jewish theatre reviewers active before 1933 are included at the back of Rühle, *Theater für die Republik*.
66. For details of the Nazi wooing of Reinhardt see Günther Rühle, *Theater in Deutschland: Seine Ereignisse – seine Menschen* (Frankfurt 2007), p. 737.
67. BA R 55/20185, 16–17: Hanfstaengel to Schlösser, 26 October 1935.
68. See Hortmann, *Shakespeare*, p. 101.
69. BDC Entjudung der Einzelkammern, quoted in Steinweis, *Art*, p. 117. A 1939 list of exemptions granted is published in Rathkolb, *Führertreu*, pp. 33–5.
70. BA R 58/992: Tagesmeldung, 25 May 1939, quoted in Steinweis, *Art*, p. 118. See also the detailed discussion in Rathkolb, *Führertreu*.
71. Hinkel, 'Kurzer Jahresbericht über meine Erfahrungen und das Ergebnis der Arbeit des Amtlichen Preußischen Theaterausschusses im Jahre 1933', 31 December 1933, quoted in Rischbieter, 'NS-Theaterpolitik', p. 16 (Hinkel's italics).
72. See Fernau, *Als Lied*.
73. Buckwitz's incredible story continued: when the British threatened to intern him in Dar-es-Salaam at the outbreak of war, he feared contracting malaria and opted to be repatriated to the Reich instead (where he still counted as an Aryan). He then established his supposed Nazi credentials with a pamphlet about 'British misrule' in German East Africa and was rewarded with a licence to operate a hotel in the town of Lodz, whose Jewish population was being murdered at the time. Near the end of the war he correctly foresaw that Germans would be targets of Polish revenge, and thus enlisted in the Wehrmacht, although he was over the age limit. Buckwitz survived. (See Daiber, *Schaufenster*, p. 250.)
74. Goebbels' speech, 15 November 1935, quoted in Steinweis, *Art*, p. 111.
75. See the Listen über die aus der Reichstheaterkammer ausgeschlossenen Juden, jüdischen Mischlinge und mit Juden Verheirateten, BDC file, quoted by Steinweis, *Art*, p. 111.
76. Goebbels himself boasted about the fact at the 1939 Reich Theatre Festival: *Die Bühne* 12 (20 June 1939): For details about Austria, see Oliver Rathkolb, *Führertreu*.

77. There is substantial literature about the *Kulturbund*: see, *inter al.*, Eike Geisel and Henryk M. Broder (eds.), *Premiere und Pogrom: der Jüdische Kulturbund 1933–1941: Texte und Bilder* (Berlin 1992); Rebecca Rovit, 'Collaboration or Survival: Reassessing the Role of the *Jüdischer Kulturbund*' in Gadberry (ed.), *Theatre in the Third Reich*, pp. 141–56; and Rovit, 'Jewish Theatre: Repertory and Censorship in the Jüdischer Kulturbund Berlin', in London (ed.), *Theatre*, pp. 187–221.

78. Hinkel, ' "Wohin mit den Juden?", Speech at the Lessing-Hochschule', *Die Bühne* 1 (5 January 1939).

79. See Michael Patterson and Louise Stafford-Charles, 'The Final Chapter: Theatre in the Concentration Camps of Nazi Germany', in Gadberry (ed.), *Theatre in the Third Reich*, pp. 157–65.

80. See the copious documentation in BA R 55/20550.

81. BA R 55/20188, 551–2.

82. BA R 55/20250, 2.

83. See, for instance, BA R 55/20182, 87.

84. See BA R 55/20179, 64: Vereinigung der Bühnenverleger to Propaganda Ministry, 23 December 1936; cf. R 55/20184, 224; cf. the case of Rudolf Lotha discussed in William Grange, 'Rules', p. 199.

85. BA R 55/20184, 225–6: memo, February 1936.

86. BA R 55/20191a, 332: 18 November 1938. The diplomats enjoined strict confidentiality on the propagandists, since Céline was 'living under constant threat from the Jews'.

87. See the correspondence between the publishers' association and Schlösser of December 1939 in BA R 55/20201, 284–5.

88. BA R 55/20190a, 467: censor report, 9 September 1938: 'Ehrlos?'; R 55/20201, 135: censor's report for 'Elise', 23 March 1939.

89. Elisabeth Frenzel, 'Die Darstellung von Judenrollen', *Die Bühne* 18 (25 September 1940), p. 276. On Frenzel, see Florian Radvan, ' "Mit der Verjudung des deutschen Theaters ist es nicht so schlimm!" Ein kritischer Rückblick auf die Karriere der Literaturwissenschaftlerin Elisabeth Frenzel', *German Life and Letters* 54:1 (January 2001), pp. 25–44.

90. BA R 55/20196, 208. Indeed another play was commended principally for the 'very restrained treatment of the Jewish Question' (R 55/20211, 103: 'Ordonnanz Meise').

91. BA R 55/20185, 340: censor's report for 'Bismarck's Sturz'.

92. BA R 55/20177, 220.

93. BA R 55/20168, 429: censor's report for 'Alpenglühen', 26 August 1934.

94. BA R 55/20183: censor's report for 'Germanische Tragödie: Das Blut', 29 December 1934.

95. BA R 55/20168, 121: 'Ernst Kohl'.
96. BA R 55/20181, 192: Kreisleitung Löbau to Gauleitung, 20 March 1936.
97. BA R 55/20210, 520: censor's report, 11 November 1943.
98. BA R 55/20203, 205: 'Die Botschaft des Ostens'; R 55/20189, 119: Reichsdramaturgie to Roslin Charlemont, 31 January 1939.
99. Elisabeth Frenzel provided a sycophantic tribute to her husband's colleague in her piece for *Die Bühne*.
100. BA R 55/20189, 53: letter to Möller, 25 April 1938.
101. BA R 55/20208a, 340. On contemporary awareness of the relative lack of antisemitic dramatic literature in Germany, see Kurt Sabatzky, *Der Jude in der dramatischen Gestaltung* (Königsberg 1930), and indeed Elisabeth Frenzel, 'Die Darstellung von Judenrollen', *Die Bühne* 18 (25 September 1940), p. 276.
102. See the reference to extensive deliberations in 1939 between Schlösser and the Intendant of the Erfurt theatre in BA R 55/20194, 283–4.
103. 'But though I am a daughter to his blood' (II, iii) became 'But I am not a daughter to his blood', which makes for a passable scansion in German. The production is discussed in Christl Carmann, 'Shylock am Wiener Burgtheater: Versuch einer Analyse der Wechselwirkungen zwischen den Wiener Juden und der Shylockinterpretation', unpublished thesis (Vienna 1972), pp. 280–307.
104. BA R 55/20194, 285: Schlösser to Goebbels, 16 July 1940. That letter, crucially, contains a reference to an earlier ban of the play. The ban does not appear to have extended to teaching *The Merchant* in schools (see the advert for a new school edition, authorised by ministry in 1939, in *Neuphilologische Monatsschrift* 12 (1941), p. 309).
105. See BA R 55/20194, 286–90; there were a handful of productions in the provinces, for instance in Göttingen, and one in Berlin: in a private theatre in a working-class district where *Bildungsbürger* rarely ventured.
106. BA R 55/20203, 109: Rassenpolitische Amt der NSDAP to Dr Lange, 31 March 1941.
107. BA R 55 20198, 184: 'Hervör: ein Schauspiel aus der Weltwende der Germanen'.
108. Akademie der Kunst (ed.) *Goodbye to Berlin? 100 Jahre Schwulenbewegung* (Berlin 1997), pp. 176–85.
109. See, *inter al.*, BA R 55 20198, 16: censor's report for 'Der Kinderkontrollor', 3 July 1939, where these worries are explicitly acknowledged.
110. See BA R 55/20105, 56–7; R 55/20236, 378; cf. *Die Bühne* (Beiblatt) 12 (25 June 1940), p. 8 and *Die Bühne* 17 (8 September 1941), p. 405.

111. BA R 55/20213, 431: memo, 2 June 1944. For a typical example of the genre, see Erich Bauer, *Die Magd des Peter Rottmann*; an instructive review of the play is reprinted in Joseph Wulf, *Theater und Film im Dritten Reich: Eine Dokumentation* (Gütersloh 1964), p. 151.

112. BA R 55/20214, 228: covering letter, 'Die offene Frage', 23 November 1944.

113. BA R 55/20214, 333: Schlösser to Erckmann, 2 August 1944.

Chapter 6: The faith of our forefathers: theatre and the Nazi assault on Christianity

1. BA R 56 I/ 3-49: Bethge to Hinkel, 21 November 1941.

2. For an account of the play's genesis, see 'Stedingsehre: ein Beispiel völkischer Festgestaltung', *Deutsche Bühnen-Korrespondenz* 13 July 1935.

3. The censors actually advised the author to tone down the 'starker Dialekt' (BA R 55/20167, 188: censor's report 'Die Stedinger', 28 May 1934). Several Low and High German variants of the play's title were current at the time: *De Stedinge, De Stedingers, Die Stedinger, Stedingsehre* or *Stedingerehre*.

4. It is surely no coincidence that Rosenberg's NSKG was also involved in the summer of 1934 in a play about Hutten and Luther which was staged on the Wartburg.

5. For a brief discussion, see Stommer, *Die inszenierte*, pp. 115–18.

6. BA R 55/20442, 1: Landesstelle Weser-Ems to Goebbels, 6 January 1936.

7. Wolf Braumüller, 'August Hinrichs "De Stedinge" ', *Deutsche Bühnen-Korrespondenz* 56:4 (1935), p. 1.

8. For a perfect example, see BA R 55/20181, 155–8: 'Deutsche Tragödie'.

9. Eberhard Wolfgang Möller, *Das Frankenburger Würfelspiel* (Berlin 1936), pp. 343–4.

10. E. G. Kolbenheyer, *Gregor und Heinrich*, in Rühle, *Zeit und Theater*, p. 264. For a discussion of the play, see Leigh Clemons, 'Gewalt, Gott, Natur, Volk: The Performance of Nazi Ideology in Kolbenheyer's *Gregor und Heinrich*', in Rennert (ed.), *Essays*, pp. 176–86.

11. See David Blackbourn, *Marpingen: Apparitions of the Virgin Mary in Bismarckian Germany* (Oxford 1993); and Michael Burleigh, *Earthly Powers: The Conflict between Religion and Politics from the French Revolution to the Great War* (London 2005).

12. H. Günther-Konsalik, 'Der Gegenspieler im Drama', *Deutsche Dramaturgie* 2 (1943).

13. See the reference to a play about the 'Kulturkampf in Mexiko' (BA R 55/ 20478, 250).

14. BA R 55/20478, 243: letter by the sexton of Oberriedenberg, 7 January 1937.
15. Quoted in Saul S. Friedman, *The Oberammergau Passion Play: A Lance against Civilization* (Carbondale 1984), p. 125.
16. BA R 55/20208a, 554.
17. BA R 55/20188, 432: B. Clement to Goebbels, 27 October 1937.
18. BA R 55/20475, 418–25.
19. Ranging from the celebrated Tyrolean Exl company to playwrights like Karl Schönherr or Hermann Ortner.
20. Goes, *Aufbricht Deutschland*, p. 25.
21. Hans Hinkel, manuscript 'Arbeiter, seid Kämpfer für deutsche Kultur!' (BA R 56 I/ 107, 241).
22. Werner Deubbel, *Die letzte Festung* (Berlin 1942), p. 71.
23. Gerhard Schumann, *Die Entscheidung* (Berlin 1938), p. 61.
24. Kurt Heynicke, *Neurode: Ein Spiel von deutscher Arbeit.*
25. Quoted in Panse, 'Zeitgenössische', p. 685.
26. Friedrich Wilhelm Hymmen, 'Beton', quoted in Ketelsen, *Vom heroischen Sein*, p. 126.
27. Wehner, *Vom Glanz*, p. 363.
28. Günther-Konsalik, 'Der Gegenspieler', p. 174.
29. See, paradigmatically, Johst, *Ich glaube!* The sense of parallel ambitions among Catholics and Nazis also emerges in Erich Brendler, 'Die Tragik im deutschen Drama vom Naturalismus bis zur Gegenwart', unpublished thesis (Tübingen 1940), pp. 213–14, quoted in Wulf, *Theater*, p. 140.
30. Heynicke, *Neurode*, p. 55.
31. Heinrch Zerkaulen, *Jugend von Langemarck* (Leipzig 1933), p. 28.
32. Deubel, *Die letzte Festung*, p. 72.
33. BA R 55/20181, 174: manuscript 'Thingspiel als Religionsschöpfung'.
34. Quoted in Stommer, *Die inszenierte*, p. 102.
35. BA R 56 I/ 3-9: Bethge to Hinkel, 22 August 1944.
36. BA R 55/20168, 311: 'Der Kadu'; R 55/20200, 261–2: 'Die deutsche Passion'.
37. BA R 55/20186, 237: 'Hilfe Gottes'.
38. BA R 55/20194, 227: censor's report, 'Deutsche Sehnsucht – deutsches Schicksal'.
39. Richard Euringer, *Totentanz: Ein Tanz der lebendig Toten und der erweckten Muskoten* (Hamburg 1935), p. 34.
40. Wulf, *Theater*, p. 208.
41. BA R 55/20181, 199: letter to Reichskulturkammer, 3 August 1935.

42. BA R 55/20475, 418–25. On a recognition of the debt owed by Nazi *Volksstücke* to the mystery plays, see Joseph Maria Lutz, 'Neue Wege zum Volksstück', *Der Neue Weg* 1 (May 1935).
43. For details, see Glen Gadberry, 'An Ancient German Rediscovered: The Nazi Widukind Plays of Forster and Kiß', in Rennert (ed.), *Essays*, p. 164.
44. See BA R 55/20184, 90 or R 55/20176, 25; see also Glen Gadberry, 'Ancient German'.
45. See Walter Hagemann, 'In Sachen Widukind', *Germania* (6 February 1935).
46. See, for instance, R 55 20198, 228: censor's report on plays by W. A. Köhler: 'ist gescheitert . . . an Juden und wohl auch an Katholiken'.
47. Edmund Kiß, *Wittekind* (Berlin 1935), pp. 58–9 and 66 respectively.
48. Goebbels kept referring to the president of the Berlin police force Bernhard Weiss as 'Isidor Weiss'.
49. See respectively, BA R 55/20189, 323: letter to Goebbels, 30 January 1938, and R 56 I/ 107, 29: 'Rede zur Gründung der Fachschaft Bühne, 6 September 1935'.
50. 'Georg Deininger, "Der Bauer im Joch"', *Deutsche Bühnen-Korrespondenz* (19 October 1935), quoted by Wulf, *Theater*, p. 150.
51. Johst, *Propheten* (Munich 1923), p. 53.
52. BA R 55/20191, 239: Burte to Schlösser, 13 August 1936.
53. See the comments in the (Swiss-based) *Deutsche Woche* (8 February 1935), reprinted in Heinz Hürten (ed.), *Deutsche Briefe 1934–1938: Ein Blatt der deutschen katholischen Emigration* (Mainz 1969), p. 197.
54. See, for instance, BA R 55/20180, 1: Intendant Roennecke to Schlösser, 24 December 1935.
55. See the suggestive letter in: BA R 55/20180, 250: Best to Schlösser, 30 December 1935.
56. The play was eventually staged at Guben, a rural backwater in Eastern Germany.
57. Both the protesters and the authorities sought to bolster their arguments by referring to the Weimar republic. For details in the newspaper coverage, see Wulf, *Theater*, pp. 176–7.
58. See the reviews in *Frankfurter Zeitung* (31 January 1935) and *Germania* (1 February 1935).
59. *The Times* (2 and 4 February 1935). See also the *New York Times* (24 February 1935) and the *Deutsche Woche* (8 February 1935) (reprinted in Hürten, *Deutsche Briefe*, p. 197).
60. *Deutsche Woche* (8 February 1935).
61. Goebbels, *Tagebücher*, entry for 22 February 1935.

62. BA R 55/ 20229, 244–5.
63. Goebbels' phrase 'nur keine Geschichtsklitterungen' is ambiguous. Panse discusses the reply at length; however, her reading that Goebbels was 'defiant' seems unpersuasive, given the lack of 'Wittekind' dramas after Hagen ('Zeitgenössische', p. 546).
64. BA R 55/20170, 136. For subsequent reiterations of the ban, see R 55/ 20191, 241 and 253.
65. BA R 55/20182, 282.
66. See BA R 55/20180, 2: Schlösser to *Intendant* of Landestheater Oldenburg, 16 January 1936.
67. Deubel, *Die letzte Festung*, p. 75.
68. BA R 55/20214, 295.
69. BA R 55/20183, 49: letter to Goebbels, 30 January 1936, re: 'Engel Hiltensberger'; and R 55/20179, 306: Schmückle to Goebbels. The play itself was loosely based on a story by Strindberg.
70. BA R 55/20226, 212. Bethge took the hint and revised his play substantially.
71. See the revealing letter by the *Intendant* of the Stadttheater Altona to Bethge, 4 December 1936 (BA R 56 I/ 3, 96).
72. See the correspondence between Ministerialrat Naumann and Schlösser of January and Febuary 1939 (BA R 55/20194, 313 and 316).
73. Otto Erler, *Thors Gast* (Leipzig 1937), pp. 11–12.
74. Goebbels, *Tagebücher*, entry for 31 October 1937.
75. BA R 56 I/ 119, 172: mayor of Mainz to Hinkel, 1 October 1935.
76. BA R 55/20447, 76: report by the Mittelbadische Bühne.
77. OÖLA Landestheater files.
78. BA R 55/20700, 86.
79. BA R 55/20180, 218–21: Schlösser report for Goebbels, via Hanke: 'Der letzte Bauer' (Schlösser's emphasis).
80. See BA R 55/20180, 226: Schlösser to Hanke, 24 January 1936.
81. BA R 55/20180, 225: Schlösser memo, 24 January 1936.
82. See BA R 55/20180, 227: telegram by Count Preising, Bishop of Berlin, to Goebbels, 25 January 1936. It was only after 'illness' had struck that the ministry curtly informed the Bishop of what by then was already common knowledge. See R 55/20180, 226: Propaganda Ministry to Bishop of Berlin, 28 January 1936.
83. BA R 55/20478, 247: Möller memo, 14 October 1937.
84. BA R 55/20225, 104–5. On the productions of *Hockewanzel*, see Panse, 'Zeitgenössische', pp. 674–6.
85. See, notably, Friedman, *Oberammergau*, and Daniel Krochmalnik, 'Oberammergau – "eine deutsche Passion"', in Michael Henker *et al.*

(eds.), *Hört, sehet, weint und liebt: Passionsspiele im alpenländischen Raum* (Munich 1990), p. 211–15.

86. See the discussion of the passage in Friedman, *Oberammergau*, p. 17.
87. For one of the rare exceptions – Waal – see BA R 55/20478, 19.
88. See Karl Konrad Polheim, 'Passionsspiele in Steiermark und Kärnten', in Henker, *Hört*, pp. 33–41.
89. See Pieter M. Judson, 'The Bohemian Oberammergau: Nationalist Tourism in the Austrian Empire', in Judson and Marsha Rozenblit (eds.), *Constructing Nationalities in East Central Europe* (Oxford 2005), pp. 89–106.
90. See *Völkischer Beobachter* (Vienna edition) (12 October 1943). See also Mugrauer, *Pfarrgemeinde*, p. 212.
91. See the voluminous file on Kettl-Wihelmy in BA R 55/20478.

Chapter 7: The manacled muse: theatre and political domination

1. The most famous instance is Heinrich George's appointment in Berlin.
2. BA R 55/ 20290, 410. On Goebbels' restrictions on Shakespeare, see R 55/ 20218, 177–86.
3. For a contemporary view of theatre and the 'Führer principle', see Hans Geisow, *Bühne und Volk* (Leipzig 1933). On the Nazi institutions exercising control over the theatre, see Drewniak, *Das Theater*, pp. 13–27, Rischbieter (ed.), *Theater*, pp. 20–8, and Steinweis, *Art*.
4. Horst Dreßler-Andreß to Abteilung III, 8 June 1935, quoted in Wulf, *Theater*, p. 65.
5. See the voluminous documentation in BA R 55/20476.
6. See the documentation on the Preußische Theaterausschuß in Wulf, *Theater*, pp. 58–9.
7. After Körner had been forced to resign over financial irregularities in 1942, his successor Paul Hartmann wielded no perceptible power.
8. If the play had been submitted to a publisher, the publisher would often informally seek the advice of the censors if the play seemed problematic.
9. See, respectively, BA R 55/20477, 175: Frenzel to Schlösser, 8 May 1939, and R 55/20476a, 485: memo, 19 June 1938.
10. Goebbels edict, 21 August 1933, quoted in Wulf, *Theater*, p. 39.
11. See BA R 55/ 20175, 22–5.
12. The documentation does not survive: for an early attempt to remove the play quietly, see BA R 55/20443, 136.
13. BA R 55/20208a, 413: secret edict, 23 January 1942 (for the revocation of the measure, see R 55/20208a, 416).

14. See BA R 55/20193, 279; R 55/20476a, 449: marginal comment by Graff, 2 January 1939. Cf. also Karl Blanckmeister, 'Im Namen des Volkes', *Die Bühne* 9/10 (20 May 1944).
15. BA R 55/20475, 255: Gestapo to Goebbels, 8 May 1939: re: 'Ein fideler Arrest', and 256: censor's report, 6 June 1939.
16. Kurt Schramm, 'Der Anspruch des Theaters', *Deutsche Allgemeine Zeitung* (19 June 1943).
17. Georg Schmückle, quoted by Daiber, *Schaufenster*, p. 170.
18. BA R 55/20183, 307.
19. See, for instance, the appeal by the Reichsnährstand to boycott Walter Erich Schäfer's play *Schwarzmann und die Magd* ('Gegen Verzerrung des Bauerntums in der Kunst', *Theater-Tageblatt*, 19 October 1935).
20. See BA R 55/20618, 198. Eugen Hadamowsky, *Propaganda und nationale Macht* (Oldenburg 1933), pp. 144–5.
21. BA R 55/ 20150, 412.
22. See Rischbieter (ed.), *Theater*, pp. 78–9.
23. See the collection of documents relating to the ban in Wulf, *Theater*, pp. 79–83.
24. BA R 55/20161, 135.
25. BA R 55/20161, 138.
26. Düsterberg, *Johst*, pp. 249–50 provides details of the speech (but fails to notice the earlier ban).
27. Goebbels, *Tagebücher*, entry for 25 October 1936.
28. The play – *Mary and Lisa* – was about a man turning from his infertile wife to have children by another woman: a topic that attracted the party, while making it nervous of public reactions.
29. BA R 55/20699, 146: Schlösser memo, 13 November 1936.
30. The documents relating to the case do not survive; but see, Goebbels, *Tagebücher*, entry for 3 November 1938.
31. BA R 55/20250, 7: Schlösser to Köhler, 27 October 1943. See also OÖLA Landestheater: Kulturbeauftragter des Gauleiters to *Intendant*, 10 May 1943.
32. BA R 55/20184, 120–1: Schlösser to Schneider-Franke, 27 March 1936.
33. BA R 55/ R 55/20211, 355: Schlösser memo, 3 July 1944.
34. BA R 55/ 20231, 514: Schlösser memo, 24 December 1942.
35. Stommer, *Die inszenierte*, p. 55.
36. BA R 55/20441, 15: Laubinger to Goebbels, 29 November 1934.
37. BA R 55/20441, 45 and 77–9 contain references to plays Hans Rehberg had agreed to write for new *Thing* arenas at Heidelberg and Rügen respectively; Rehberg's interest evidently cooled.
38. Panse, 'Zeitgenössische', p. 612.

39. Ibid., p. 613.
40. See Rühle, *Zeit und Theater*, p. 790.
41. BA R 55/20230, 235–6.
42. For a list of societies regularly staging amateur theatricals, see BA R 55/20476a, 333.
43. On that aspect, see BA R 55/20475, 27.
44. BA R 55/20475, 11.
45. BA R 55/20478, 303: RPA Tyrol to RPA Vienna, 17 August 1938.
46. BA R 55/20441, 60: Bericht über die bisherige Arbeit des Reichsbundes.
47. For examples of bodies affected, see BA R 55/20476a, 333.
48. See BA R 55/20478, 268; and R 55/20475, 138: report by Landrat Calbe, 5 December 1938.
49. BA R 55/20478, 307: Kleinschmidt to Goebbels, 6 October 1937.
50. For evidence of wider discussion of the implications, see BA R 55/20478, 16: Reichskulturkammer to Reichstheaterkammer, 5 March 1937.
51. BA R 55/20478, 288: parish priest of Warendorf/Westfalen to Propaganda Ministry, 25 March 1938.
52. BA R 55/20478, 75: Kleinschmidt to Möller, 7 August 1937.
53. BA R 55/20478, 52: Gestapo to Goebbels, 13 May 1938: 'Ich darf darauf hinweisen, dass ... bereits am 28.6.35 sämtliche Staatspolizeistellen angewiesen habe, rein weltliche Veranstaltungen konfessioneller Vereine zu verbieten'.
54. BA R 55/20478, 4: Schlösser to Goebbels, 23 December 1937.
55. BA R 55/20478, 215: Niessen to Schlösser, 10 November 1940.
56. BA R 55/20478, 240: Landrat Reichenbach i. Schl. to Propaganda Ministry, via Gestapo Breslau, 25 May 1937.
57. BA R 55/20478, 62: Ortsgruppe Nesselwang to Kreisleitung Markt Oberdorf, 19 March 1937.
58. BA R 55/20475, 184: RPA Schwaben to Goebbels, 22 February 1939.
59. BA R 55/20475, 178: Danner to Propaganda Ministry, 3 January 1939.
60. BA R 55/20476a, 418: Landrat Verden to Regierungspräsident Stade, 24 February 1938.
61. BA R 55/20475, 510: Chef der Sicherheitspolizei und des SD to Goebbels, 10 June 1941.
62. BA R 55/20478, 62.
63. BA R 55/20476, 2: Arbeitsgemeinschaft der Laienspiel-Verleger in der Fachschaft Verlag des Bundes Reichsdeutscher Buchhändler to Schlecht, 3 December 1937.
64. BA R 55/20477, 128–9: Goebbels to Landesregierungen, 4 January 1939.
65. BA R 55/20475, 512: Reichsbund to Reichstheaterkammer, 25 July 1941.

66. BA R 55/20478, 73.

67. BA R 55/20475, 11.

68. BA R 55/20475, 442–4.

69. BA R 55/20476a, 478: RPA Bayerische Ostmark to Propaganda Ministry.

70. BA R 55/20475, 235: RPA Baden to Goebbels, 20 January 1939.

71. BA R 55/20476, 13: Tismar to Kleinschmidt, 18 January 1938. Cf. also 132–82: Anträge von Kostümverleih-Geschäften auf Übernahme ihres Fundus infolge Einschränkung von Laienspielaufführungen.

72. BA R 55/20476, 22.

73. BA R 55/20477, 186.

74. See the correspondence between Gauleitung Bayrische Ostmark and Schlösser, August 1935 (BA R 55/20177, 29).

75. See also the cases of *Florian Geyer* at the Volksbühne or of *Cavour* at the Staatstheater (BA R 55/20292, 28–38) or *Rothschild* in Munich.

76. See Drewniak, *Das Theater*, p. 168.

77. Waldemar Hartmann, 'Hamlets politisches Heldentum: Gedanken zum "Hamlet", als der Tragödie nordischen Verantwortungsgefühls', *Völkischer Beobachter* (Berliner Ausgabe) (3 May 1936).

78. See Gründgens' own account, attested to by Swiss friends, in Dagmar Wallach, *Aber ich habe nicht mein Gesicht: Gustaf Gründgens: Eine deutsche Karriere* (Berlin 1999), pp. 99–100.

79. BA R 58 984, 74: meeting in the Hinkel Office, 30 July 1938, quoted by Fricke, *Spiel*, p. 303; see also Rathkolb, *Führertreu*, pp. 140–1.

80. See Fricke, *Spiel*, pp. 154–6.

81. See Daiber, *Schaufenster*, p. 59.

82. See Fricke, *Spiel*, p. 66, and Daiber, *Schaufenster*, p. 234.

83. Ibid., p. 236.

84. BA R 55/ 20291, 235

85. BA R 55/20817.

86. See BA R 55/ 20817, 1 and 5.

87. 'Rede des Propagandaministers Dr. Joseph Goebbels vor den Theaterleitern am 8. Mai 1933', *Das deutsche Drama* 5 (1933), p. 39.

Chapter 8: 'The final redoubt': theatre and propaganda

1. BA R 56 I/89, 273.

2. BA R 56 I/3, 42: Bethge to Hinkel, 10 April 1942.

3. BA RKK file Bethge, Bethge to Hinkel, 15 May 1944.

4. See Wayne Kwam, 'The Nazification of Max Reinhardt's Deutsches Theater Berlin', *Theatre Journal* 40:3 (October 1983).

5. Quoted by Rischbieter, 'NS-Theaterpolitik', p. 73.

6. Goebbels, *Tagebücher*, entry for 9 May 1936.
7. Goebbels, *Tagebücher*, entry for 22 June 1936.
8. Quoted by Jutta Wardetzky, *Theaterpolitik im faschistischen Deutschland: Studien und Dokumente* (Berlin 1983), p. 71.
9. BA R 56 I/89, 273.
10. BA R 55/20183, 284–7; R 55/20205, 275; R 55/20278, 405 and 105–6.
11. Rosenberg Office memo, 20 July 1938, quoted in Wardetzky, *Theaterpolitik*, p. 78.
12. Thus the Propaganda Ministry itself in the summer of 1935: see BA R 55/20184, 145.
13. See Otto Laubinger's thoughts about the season of 1934–5 (Eicher, 'Spielplanstrukturen', pp. 333–4).
14. Daiber, *Schaufenster*, p. 140; on 'unstageable' Hebbel and Lessing plays, see BA R 55/ 20278, 403–4.
15. BA R 55/20188, 226.
16. See Daiber, *Schaufester*, p. 120; on *Amphytrion*, BA NS 8/ 242, 138.
17. See, *inter al.*, Heinrich Bauer, 'Shakespeare – ein germanischer Dichter', *Nationalsozialistische Monatshefte* 41 (1933), pp. 372–3; Gustav L. Plessow, *Um Shakespeares Nordentum* (Aachen 1937). For attacks on Shakespeare, see Wanderscheck, *Deutsche Dramatik*; notably Curt Langenbeck, *Die Wiedergeburt des Dramas aus dem Geist der Zeit* (Munich 1940).
18. See, notably, Gerlach-Bernau, *Drama und Nation*; and Curt Langenbeck, *Wiedergeburt*.
19. See the documents reprinted in Wardetzky, *Theaterpolitik*, pp. 294–6.
20. See Glen Gadberry, 'Gerhart Hauptmann's *Ratten* (1911) at the Rose (1936)', in Rennert (ed.), *Essays*, pp. 187–95.
21. See Eicher, 'Spielplanstukturen', pp. 368–9.
22. Bethge also championed Barlach, Gogol and Yeats. See Mohr, *Frankfurter Schauspiel*, p. 125.
23. BA R 56 I/89, 273.
24. See the undated manuscript in BA R 56 I/109, 157.
25. See the undated cutting from the *Thüringische Bauernzeitung* in BA R 55/20168, 165.
26. 'Wir spielen Müller kommt vom Urlaub heim', *Der Angriff* (26 April 1937) (cutting in BA NS 5 VI/6287, 76).
27. BA R 55/20225, 13.
28. BA R 55/20236, 289 (see also 315 and 378); R 55/20181, 110.
29. Archiv der Stadt Linz, box 'Theaterangelegenheiten', 'Linz lacht und tanzt wieder, Karneval 1939'.
30. See pictures 00248970-1 in the Ullstein-Bilderdienst collection.

31. Laubinger speech of 14 November 1933 to Genossenschaft der Bühnenangehörigen, *Der Neue Weg* 1 (1934), p. 8.
32. BA R 55/20440, 166: Gauappell der NSDAP Sachsen at Kamenz, 13 June 1937.
33. See Daiber, *Schaufenster*, p. 254.
34. Goebbels, *Tagebücher*, entry for 18 November 1935.
35. See the production statistics in Panse, 'Zeitgenössische', pp. 711–17.
36. BA R 55/20226, 222.
37. See the suggestive censor's report for 'Blut wider Blut': BA R 55/20181, 212. See also Zuckmayer, *Geheimreport*, or the striking contemporary impressions of Patrick Leigh Fermor in *A Time of Gifts* (London 1977), pp. 129–30.
38. See, *inter al.*, BA R 55/20178, 37; R 55/20183, 199.
39. Goebbels, *Tagebücher*, entry for 19 September 1935.
40. See Wolfgang Petzet, *Theater: Die Münchner Kammerspiele 1911–1972* (Munich 1973), pp. 279–80.
41. See Carmann, 'Shylock', pp. 280–307. Some of the reviews referred to the threatening element in the character of Shylock, which the production had supposedly demonstrated (e.g. Karl Lahm, 'Shylock der Ostjude', *Deutsche Allgemeine Zeitung*, 19 May 1943); but theatre critics in the Third Reich generally based their comments on the party line: they would find what they thought it best to find.
42. On *The Eternal Jew*, see the copious material in Wulf, *Theater*.
43. On the attempts to heighten the play's impact, see Anon, 'Otto C. A. zur Nedden, '*Der Jude von Malta*: Schauspiel in 5 Akten nach einer Idee von Christoph Marlow [sic]', *Shakespeare Jahrbuch* (1941), pp. 204–5.
44. Goebbels, *Tagebücher*, entry for 23 January 1940.
45. Panse notes that such plays appear only to have been staged in provincial theatres ('Zeitgenössische', pp. 531–2).
46. Friedrich Griese, *Mensch aus Erde gemacht* (Berlin 1933). For critical responses, see Ketelsen, *Vom heroischen Sein*, pp. 135–6.
47. Unidentified newspaper cutting: 'Walter Best "Der General"' (BA R 55/20225, 8).
48. For a detailed account in English, see Elisabeth Schulz-Hostetter, *The Berlin State Theater under the Nazi Regime: A Study of the Administration, Key Productions, and Critical Responses from 1933–1934* (Lewiston 2004), pp. 111–16.
49. BA R 55/20164, 87: Schlösser to Hymmen, 28 January 1937.
50. The play never got beyond its initial production in a small provincial theatre.

51. See, for instance, BA R 55/20194, 332–45. Cf. the documents on Max Halbe reprinted in Wardezky, *Theaterpolitik*, pp. 384–9.
52. BA R 55/20189, 169; 172; 177; 194; 198; 201.
53. Karl Wüstenhagen was ordered to produce Eckart's *Heinrich der Hohenstaufe* for the 1935 Reich Theatre Festival in Hamburg (see Drewniak, *Das Theater*, p. 45).
54. A point made after the war, among others, by Falckenberg's assistant (see Daiber, *Schaufenster*, p. 135).
55. BA R 55/20188, 221; 223. See also the cases of several theatres successfully side-stepping Schlösser's efforts on behalf of the 'Hitler Youth' author Herbert Reinecker in BA R 55/ 21229.
56. BA R 55/20258, 64: Schlösser memo, 8 July 1939.
57. BA R 55/20225, 34–99.
58. See BA R 55/20106, 50: Schlösser to Goebbels, 11 November 1936.
59. Document reproduced in: Wardetzky, *Theaterpolitik*, pp. 322.
60. BA R 55/20098, 314–451.
61. Dussel's study of five provincial theatres found a similiarly varied pattern: one theatre consistently put on propaganda plays on Nazi 'feast' days, another consistently did not, the others changed at some point in the late 1930s from propaganda to non-propaganda. See Dussel, *Ein neues*.
62. Its success owed much to the fact that Schlösser considered it one of the better Nazi efforts and felt duty bound to assist a playwright who, like Schlösser, was affiliated to the Hitler Youth (see the file BA R 55/ 21229). That Herbert Reinecker did possess a measure of dramatic skill is proved by the fact that, after the war, he became a prolific author of police drama for West German television.
63. 'Vierteljahreslagebericht 1939', in Heinz Boberach (ed.), *Meldungen aus dem Reich: Die geheimen Lageberichte des Sicherheitsdienstes der SS* (Herrsching 1985), p. 117.
64. On the introduction of the 'German greeting', see *Deutsche Bühnen-Korrespondenz* (23 October 1933).
65. BA R 56 I/64, 102: Hinkel to Chefredakteur. *BZ am Mittag*, 15 June 1933.
66. Thus Hinkel in an undated manuscript in BA R 56 I/ 109, 157. See also the survey of voices on that topic in Hermann Kepel, 'Theater und Staat im neuen Deutschland', *National-Zeitung* (22 December 1933) in R 56 I/114, 156.
67. See Daiber, *Schaufenster*, p. 162.
68. BA R 55/20207a, 562: Schlösser to Bade, 18 February 1943.
69. Quoted by Daiber, *Schaufenster*, p. 164.
70. Cutting of the *Annaberger Wochenblatt* (1 October 1934) in BA R 55/ 20164, 8.

71. Quoted by Daiber, *Schaufenster*, pp. 164–5.
72. BA R 55/ 21229, unnumbered page. Note the sarcastic use of Gründgens' Christian name.
73. BA R 55/ 21229: Eher to Reichsdramaturgie, 6 April 1943.
74. Ibid. Cf. 'Jahreslagebericht 1938', in Boberach, *Meldungen*, p. 117.
75. BA R 55/20189, 201: Eher to Schlösser, 4 November 1938.
76. BA R 55/20618, 198: HJ-Bann 75 (Bremen) to Schlösser (1937?).
77. For a particularly telling example, see Ilse Pietsch's early post-war thesis: 'Das Theater als politisch-publizistisches Führungsmittel im Dritten Reich' (Münster 1952).
78. Such applause is attested in BA R 55/20183, 285 and R 55/ 20278: report, 2 October 1944.
79. See Daiber, *Schaufenster*, p. 244.
80. Ibid., p. 243.
81. Ibid., p. 343.
82. BA R 55/20618, 204: Schlösser to HJ-Bann 75 [1937?].
83. BA R 56 I/ 3–9: Bethge to Hinkel, 22 August 1944.
84. See the marginal comment in BA R 55/ 21229: Eher to Schlösser, 6 April 1943.
85. Goebbels *Tagebücher*, entry for December 1936; Michael Dillmann, *Heinz Hilpert: Leben und Werk* (Berlin 1990), p. 175; for details of George's repertoire, which made concessions to the war effort but not to Nazi ideology as such, and George's attempts to distinguish between the two, see Fricke, *Spiel*, pp. 185–96.
86. BA R 55/ 20265, 561.
87. See Rathkolb, *Führertreu*, p. 140, and BA R 55/20226, 305–6.
88. See BA R 55/ 20278, 395–7: Schlösser to Goebbels, 3 June 1943.
89. See BA R 55/20278, 158.
90. BA R 55/20278, 289.
91. BA R 55/20278, 288.
92. BA R 55/20183, 284–7.
93. BA R 55/20210, 314: Schlösser to Bade, 11 October 1943.
94. BA R 55/20205, 275: Schlösser to Bade, 29 March 1943.
95. Fabricius to Gründgens, 30 July 1944, reprinted in Walach, *Aber*, p. 120.
96. BA R 55/ 20265, 561.
97. Piscator diary, 11 November 1954, quoted by Daiber, *Schaufenster*, p. 8.
98. Quoted by Daiber, *Schaufenster*, p. 344.
99. Ursula von Kardorff, *Berliner Aufzeichnungen 1942–1945* (Munich 1992), 29 April 1944.
100. See BA R 55/ 20278, 403–4: Schlösser to Goebbels, 17 June 1943.
101. SD-report, 26 February 1942, in Boberach, *Meldungen*, pp. 3371–2.

Chapter 9: The age of Mephistopheles: theatre and power

1. See the illustration in *Die Bühne* 5 (5 March 1939).
2. The statistics are not wholly consistent; the figures here are based on Daiber, *Schaufenster*, p. 325, Rischbieter, 'NS-Theaterpolitik', pp. 42–61, and Hinkel's figures in BA R 56 I/91, 44. See also Dussel, 'Theater in der Krise', and for Austria, Heidemarie Brückl-Zehetner, 'Theater in der Krise', unpublished thesis (Vienna 1988).
3. See, for instance, the speech to the Reichskulturkammer of 15 November 1935, reprinted in *Die Bühne* 11/12 (10 June 1937).
4. See Rischbieter, 'NS-Theaterpolitik', p. 45.
5. See I. G. Brantner, 'Aufbau und Entwicklung', *Das Theater* (Linz) (May 1941), p. 6; see also Regina Thumser, 'Dem Provinzstatus entkommen? Das Linzer Landestheater in der NS-Zeit', in Michael Kügl (ed.), *Promenade 39: Das Landestheater Linz 1803–2003* (Salzburg 2003), pp. 91–132.
6. OÖLA BH Gmunden, Sammelakten Kur-Theater Gmunden, box 99: Mayor Gmunden to Statthalter, 24 February 1941.
7. See *Die Bühne* 15 (15 August 1942).
8. 'Braunaus Bühne einst und jetzt', *Tagespost* (28 September 1943).
9. East Prussia (total population: 2.3 million), for example, possessed an opera house, an operetta stage and a conventional playhouse in Königsberg; there were further playhouses in Memel, Tilsit and Elbing, plus a touring company based in Allenstein, and the theatre festival in the Marienburg.
10. See Wardetzky, *Theaterpolitik*, p. 86.
11. See Drewniak, *Das Theater*, p. 66.
12. Thus on the title page of *Programm des Landestheaters Linz* 1 (1938–9).
13. *Die Bühne* 12 (20 June 1939) and 8 (20 April 1938) respectively.
14. Goebbels, *Tagebücher*, entry for 19 June 1938; see also Daiber, *Schaufenster*, p. 184.
15. See ibid., p. 285. Cf. the devastation of German cinemas in Prague by a Czech nationalist mob discussed in Nancy M. Wingfield, 'When Cinema Became National: "Talkies" and the Anti-German Demonstrations in Prague in 1930', *Austrian History Yearbook* 29 (1999), pp. 113–18.
16. See, for instance, the cases of Budweis or Mährisch-Ostrau.
17. See *Die Bühne* 18 (25 September 1940).
18. See *Die Bühne* 14 (25 July 1940) and 20 (25 October 1940).
19. See William Abbey and Katherina Havekamp, 'Nazi Performances in the German Occupied Territories: The German Theatre in Lille', in London (ed.), *Theatre*, pp. 262–90.

20. *Die Bühne* 23 (10 December 1940).
21. See Daiber, *Schaufenster*, p. 290.
22. See ibid., pp. 33 and 182.
23. For figures, see ibid., pp. 230–1.
24. BA R 55/20108, 437.
25. BA R 55/20251, 155: Schlösser memo, 20 April 1944.
26. BA R 56 I.89, 279. Cf. Johst's anger in R 56 V, 31–2 or Goebbels' disenchantment in his diary in February 1939.
27. See Kardorff, *Aufzeichnungen*, 5 May 1944, distinguishing between genuine *Kultur* and 'KdF-Betrieb'.
28. Undated memorandum in BA R 56 I/ 89, 273.
29. See Goebbels' speech at the Reichstheaterfestwoche Vienna 1939, reprinted in *Die Bühne* 12 (20 June 1939) and BA R 55/202064, 189.
30. Grange, 'Rules', p. 197.
31. SD-report, 17 October 1940, in Boberach (ed.), *Meldungen*, p. 1681.
32. 'Spielplan für alle'.
33. A point made by Staatssekretär Leopold Gutterer in his Salzburg speech; reprinted in *Die Bühne* 15 (15 August 1942). For evidence that there existed party pressure at least in some theatres to *increase* the number of serious plays, see the letter of the Linz Intendant to the office of Dr Fellner, 19 January 1943 (OÖLA, Landestheater).
34. See Hans Knudsen, 'Mit der Reichsautobahnbühne ins Lager', *Die Bühne* 2/3 (1 February 1936); see also the cuttings from *Arbeitertum* (1 December 1936) and *Der Mitteldeutsche* (29 November 1936) in BA NS 5/VI/6286, 7–8; and of the *Berliner Börsen Zeitung* (26 November 1937) in NS 5/VI/6287, 5.
35. For a restatement of that ideal by a conservative *Bildungsbürger*, see Rudolf Binding, 'Schauplatz der Nation', *Programm des Landestheaters Linz* 4 (1938–9).
36. See, for instance, Hitler's own comment about the need to win youth over to theatregoing (BA NS 10/ 44, 3).
37. Quoted in: Daiber, *Schaufenster*, pp. 255–6.
38. Domarus (ed.), *Hitler*, 23 March 1933.
39. Schlösser, 'Heer und Kunstwerk'. See also 'Erste Spielzeit in Metz' in the same issue.
40. OÖLA Landestheater: undated letter to Stadtrat Prof. Heyde (c. April 1941). SD-reports, 13 July 1942 and 8 February 1943, in Boberach (ed.), *Meldungen*, pp. 3939 and 4767.
41. Quoted by Daiber, *Schaufenster*, p. 84; see also Hitler's reported words to that effect, quoted in Rathkolb, *Führertreu*, p. 139.
42. See Daiber, *Schaufenster*, p. 145.

43. See Günther Rühle (ed.), *Bernhard Minetti: Erinnerungen eines Schauspielers* (Stuttgart 1985), pp. 92–3.
44. Daiber, *Schaufenster*, p. 88, and Maser, *Mensch*, p. 235.
45. See Daiber, *Schaufenster*, p. 238.
46. Goebbels, *Tagebücher*, entry for 28 February 1945.
47. Ibid., entry for 5 September 1936.
48. Goebbels, *Tagebücher*, 21 Jan. 1939 and Feb. 1941.
49. Quoted by Rathkolb, *Führertreu*, pp. 144–5.
50. Rainer Schlösser, 'Die kulturelle Sendung Thüringens', speech in Altenburg, 8 Jan. 1936. In: *Die Bühne* 2 (15 Jan. 1936), 337.
51. See Zuckmayer, *Geheimreport*; and Daiber, *Schaufenster*, p. 234.
52. Quoted by Daiber, *Schaufenster*, p. 16.
53. Quoted by Daiber, *Schaufenster*, p. 16.
54. *Die Bühne* 10 (5 Oct. 1938).
55. Daiber, *Schaufenster*, pp. 227–8.
56. Goebbels, *Tagebücher*, 3 Aug. 1935.
57. See Daiber, *Schaufenster*, p. 228.
58. Quoted on the title page of *Programm des Landestheaters Linz* 1 (1939–40).
59. Ludwig Körner, 'Das deutsche Theater, eine Waffe des Geistes', *Die Bühne* 20 Oct. 1939.
60. 'Die Szene des größten Erfolges', *Berliner Illustrirte Zeitung* 9 Nov. 1939.
61. Goebbels' speech at the Reichstheaterfestwoche Vienna; reprinted in: *Die Bühne* 7 (5 July 1938).
62. Joseph Goebbels, 'Die Kulturpolitik im autoritären und im demokratischen Staat', *Die Bühne* 10 (20 May 1939).
63. Dietmar Schmidt, 'Europäische Theater in Berlin', *Die Bühne* 3/4 (20 February 1944).
64. *Das Reich* (2 March 1941).
65. Goebbels, 'Die Kulturpolitik'. See also ' "Faust" in Amerika', *Die Bühne* 18 (25 September 1942).
66. Figures quoted in Birthe Kundrus, 'Totale Unterhaltung?' in Jörg Echternkamp (ed.), *Das Deutsche Reich und der Zweite Weltkrieg*, vol. IX (Munich 2005), p. 115.
67. Drewniak, *Theater*, p. 39.
68. 'Die Theater berichten', *Die Bühne* 19 (10 October 1942).
69. See the entry for *Fronttheater* in SHAEF Psychological Warfare Division, List of Impounded German Films with Comments. Viewed and Graded by Major F. L. Evans and H. J. Lefebre (photocopy in the British Film Institute).

70. BA R 55/20441, 540–60. See also Heinrich Guthmann, 'Freilichtspiel im Kriege', *Die Bühne* 13 (15 June 1942).
71. See Daiber, *Schaufenster*, p. 342. The figures were roughly similar for the main Berlin stages. See Schulz-Hostetter, *The Berlin State Theater*, pp. 197–8.
72. Figures in Kundrus, 'Totale', p. 115.
73. See Wardetzky, *Theaterpolitik*, p. 128.
74. See OÖLA Landestheater, heating permit, 5 October 1942.
75. See Daiber, *Schaufenster*, pp. 336.
76. See OÖLA Landestheater: Laissez-Passer for Ignatz Brantner, 4 November 1941.
77. OÖLA Landestheater: Landesleiter to Intendant, 30 November 1943.
78. OÖLA Landestheater: circular of 13 July 1942.
79. OÖLA Landestheater: Intendant to office Dr Fellner, 19 January 1943.
80. See BA R 55/20099a, 529: Schlösser memo, 8 March 1944.
81. Axel Breidahl, *Aufruhr im Damenstift*.
82. See BA R 55/20448, 118: report by Dr Köhler, April 1944. For a contemporary view on 'masculine' Nazi theatre, see Elisabeth Frenzel, 'Junge Dichter und ein alter Wunsch: Beobachtungen über die Frauenrolle im neuesten Drama', *Die Bühne* 23 (5 December 1939).
83. OÖLA Landestheater: 'Liste männlicher Mitglieder Spielzeit 1944/45', Intendant to Reichstheaterkammer, 6 and 13 May 1944.
84. SD-report, 8 February 1943, in Boberach (ed.), *Meldungen*, p. 4767.
85. OÖLA Landestheater: Intendant to office Dr Fellner, 19 January 1943.
86. OÖLA Landestheater: Danzer to Intendant, 29 October 1942.
87. OÖLA Landestheater: RPA to Intendant, 20 April 1943.
88. OÖLA Landestheater: Arendt to Intendant, 25 October 1942, and Intendant to Danzer, 4 June 1943.
89. OÖLA Landestheater: Intendant to Gauleiter, 8 September 1941.
90. OÖLA Landestheater: RPA to Intendant, 27 October 1942.
91. See Ludwig Cremer, 'Werktreue oder Zeitgeist im Theater?', *Die Bühne* 8 (20 April 1941); see also Friedrich Billerbeck-Gentz, 'Noch einmal – Experiment heute', *Die Bühne* 3/4 (20 February 1944).
92. BA R 55/20250, 235: Schlösser to Lang and Scherzer, 5 February 1944.
93. Robert Ley, 'Arbeiter und Kultur', *Die Bühne* 14 (5 December 1938).
94. See Daiber, *Schaufenster*, p. 345.
95. See ibid., p. 187.
96. See ibid., pp. 333–4.
97. See ibid., p. 335.
98. BA R 55/20099, 142.
99. BA R 55/20099 and R 55/20099a.

100. See BA R 55/20251, 6.
101. BA R 55/20251, 69: Schlösser to Goebbels, 19 May 1944.
102. BA R 55/20099, 132: Goebbels office to Schlösser, 20 March 1944.
103. BA R 55/20099, 623.
104. BA R 55/20250, 40.
105. BA R 55/20250, 77; 98; 115; 129.
106. Kortner, *Aller Tage*, p. 305.
107. Kardorff, *Aufzeichnungen*, 1 October 1945.
108. Ibid., 11 April 1944.
109. Quoted in Daiber, *Schaufenster*, p. 343.
110. See BA R 55/20251, 234; 258; 296.
111. BA R 55/20251, 328: Schlösser to Goebbels, 7 August 1944.
112. BA R 55/20099a, 723: Scherzer to Kochanowski, 5 January 1945; and Daiber, *Schaufenster*, p. 361.
113. BA R 55/20251, 330: Schlösser to Schmidt-Leonhard, 7 August 1944.
114. The letter is discussed in detail in Fricke, *Spiel*, pp. 62–4.
115. On Nazi manipulation of George's public image, see ibid., p. 171.
116. For details, see ibid., pp. 119–21, 158, 215, 258.
117. See the thoughtful analysis in Rathkolb, *Führertreu*, and Dillmann, *Heinz Hilpert*, pp. 157–9.
118. Fricke, *Spiel*, p. 235.
119. See Daiber, *Schaufenster*, p. 287.
120. McCarthy's activities actually persuaded several of the stage refugees from Hitler's Reich to return home: the scenes in McCarthyite America had made it easier for the émigrés to forgive their countrymen in Germany and Austria.
121. Gründgens to Demandowski, 23 December 1940; reprinted in Wallach, *Aber*, p. 62.
122. Gründgens to Jannings, 23 December 1940; reprinted in ibid., p. 61.
123. BA R 56 V / 31, 2: Johst to Hinkel, 31 July 1944.
124. Daiber, *Schaufenster*, p. 356.
125. OÖLA Landestheater: Gaupropagandaleitung to Intendant, 10 June 1943.
126. OÖLA Landestheater: Intendant to Kreisleiter Gmunden, 4 March 1945.

Bibliography

Archival sources
Archiv der Stadt Linz
Theaterangelegenheiten

British Film Institute
SHEAF Psychological Warfare Division, List of Impounded German Films with Comments. Viewed and Graded by Major F. L. Evans and H. J. Lefebre.

Bundesarchiv Berlin (BA)
NS 5 DAF
NS 8 Amt Rosenberg
NS 10 Adjutantur des Führers
R 43 Reichskanzlei
R 55 RMfVP
R 56 RKK

Deutsches Theatermuseum München
Periodika

Goethe- und Schiller-Archiv Weimar
Nachlaß Deetjen

Oberösterreiches Landesarchiv (OÖLA)
BH Gmunden, Sammelakte Kur-Theater
Landestheater

Österreichisches Theatermuseum Wien
Burgtheatermaterialien

Bibliography

Theaterwissenschaftliche Sammlung der Universität Köln
Nachlaß Niedecken-Gebhardt
Kritikensammlung Dr. Steinfeld

Newspapers
Der Angriff
Berliner Börsen-Courier
Berliner Lokal-Anzeiger
Berliner Tageblatt
BV Nachrichten
BZ am Mittag
Deutsche Allgemeine Zeitung
Deutsche Bühnen-Korrespondenz
Deutsche Tageszeitung
Egerland
Frankfurter Zeitung
Germania
Hamburger Nachrichten
Heidelberger Neueste Nachrichten
Kölnische Zeitung
Kurhessische Landeszeitung
Neu Mannheimer Zeitung
Der Mitteldeutsche
Neue Preußische Zeitung
Der Neue Weg
Preußische Zeitung
Rheinische Landeszeitung
Süddeutsche Zeitung
Der Tagesspiegel
Die Tagespost
Tägliche Rundschau
Theater-Tageblatt
Völkischer Beobachter
Die Volkstimme

Vossische Zeitung

Westfälischer Kurier

Published primary sources

Axmann, Kurt, 'Das Recht zur Kritik'. *Wille und Macht* 3:6 (March 1935), p. 23.

Bab, Julius, *Das Theater der Gegenwart: Geschichte der dramatischen Bühne seit 1870*. Leipzig 1928.

    'Die Hussiten vor Bernau'. *Die Schaubühne* (8 June 1911).

Balme, Christopher (ed.), *Das Theater von Morgen: Texte zur deutschen Theaterreform*. Würzburg 1988.

Bartels, Adolf, *Geschichte der deutschen Literatur*. Brunswick 1937.

    Der Nationalsozialismus: Deutschlands Rettung. Leipzig 1924.

    Das Weimarische Hoftheater als Nationalbühne für die deutsche Jugend: Eine Denkschrift. Weimar 1905.

Bauer, Heinrich, 'Shakespeare – ein germanischer Dichter'. *National-sozialistische Monatshefte* 41 (1933), pp. 372–3.

Bauer, Josef, 'Natürlicher Aufbau der volkhaften Feier'. *Das deutsche Volksspiel* 3 (1935–6), p. 243.

Behrens, Peter, *Feste des Lebens und der Kunst: Eine Betrachtung des Theaters als höchstes Kultursymbol*. Leipzig 1900.

Bemmann, Helga (ed.), *Ludwig Thoma: Immer nur so durchgeschloffen: Humoresken, Bänkellieder und Satiren*. Berlin 1984.

Billerbeck-Gentz, Friedrich, 'Noch einmal – Experiment heute'. *Die Bühne* 3/4 (20 February 1944).

Binding, Rudolf, 'Schauplatz der Nation'. *Programm des Landestheaters Linz* 4 (1938–9).

Blanckmeister, Karl, 'Im Namen des Volkes'. *Die Bühne* 9/10 (20 May 1944).

Boberach, Heinz (ed.), *Meldungen aus dem Reich: Die geheimen Lageberichte des Sicherheitsdienstes der SS*. Herrsching 1985.

Branntner, I. G., 'Aufbau und Entwicklung'. *Das Theater* (Linz) May 1941, p. 6.

Braumüller, Wolf, 'August Hinrichs "De Stedinge"', *Deutsche Bühnen-Korrespondenz* 56:4 (1935), p. 1.

Freilicht- und Thingspiel. Berlin 1935.

'Gestaltungswille der Jugend und Freilichttheater'. Die Bühne 8 (5 August 1938), p. 250.

'Hans Rehbergs Hohenzollerdramen'. Berliner Börsen-Zeitung (6 April 1938).

'Kurt Heynicke: "Der Weg in Reich". Deutsche Bühnen-Korrespondenz 4:58 (1935), p. 1.

'Die Landschaftsbühne'. Bausteine 2:7 (1934–5).

'Spiegelfechtereien um das Thema Theater'. Kunst und Volk (1936), p. 435.

Brecht, Bertolt, Tagebücher 1920–1922. Frankfurt 1975.

Brendler, Erich, 'Die Tragik im deutschen Drama vom Naturalismus bis zur Gegenwart'. Unpublished thesis. Tübingen 1940.

Cremer, Ludwig, 'Werktreue oder Zeitgeist im Theater'. Die Bühne 8 (20 April 1941).

Csokor, Theodor, Besetztes Gebiet: Historisches Stück aus der Gegenwart. Berlin 1930.

Deiniger, 'Der Bauer im Joch'. Deutsche Bühnen-Korrespondenz (19 October 1935).

Deubel, Werner, Die letzte Festung. Berlin 1942.

Devrient, Eduard and Willy Stuhlfeld, Geschichte der deutschen Schauspielkunst. Berlin 1929.

Diem, Carl, Olympische Jugend: Festspiel. Berlin 1936.

Domarus, Max (ed.), Hitler: Reden und Proklamationen 1932–1945. Wiesbaden 1973.

Dürre, Konrad, 'Praktische Erfahrungen im Thingspiel'. Das Deutsche Volksspiel 1 (1933–4), p. 282.

Eberlein, Karl Kurt, Was ist deutsch an der deutschen Kunst? Leipzig 1933.

Eggers, Kurt, Schüsse bei Krupp. Hamburg 1937.

Emmel, Felix, Theater aus deutschem Wesen. Berlin 1937.

Erdmann, Hans-Hugo, 'Forderungen zum "nationalen" Drama'. Die Neue Literatur 35:5 (May 1934), p. 266.

Erler, Otto, Thors Gast. Leipzig 1937.

Euringer, Richard, Deutsche Passion. Berlin 1936.

> *Totentanz: Ein Tanz der lebendig Toten und der erweckten Muskoten.* Hamburg 1935.

Fischer, Eugen Kurt, *Dramaturgie des Rundfunks.* Heidelberg 1942.

Fischer, Kurt, 'Der Chor im nationalen Festspiel'. *Deutsches Volksspiel* 1 (1933–4), p. 260.

Frank, Heinz, 'Doppelgesicht des deutschen Theaters'. *Wille und Macht* 5:10 (May 1937), pp. 36–7.

Frenzel, Elisabeth, 'Die Darstellung von Judenrollen'. *Die Bühne* 18 (25 September 1940), p. 276.

> 'Junge Dichter und ein alter Wunsch: Beobachtungen über die Frauenrolle im neuesten Drama'. *Die Bühne* 23 (5 December 1939).

Frenzel, Herbert, 'Das Drama der Entscheidung'. *Die Bühne* 11 (20 October 1938), p. 375.

Frisch, Max, 'Wunder des Lebens'. In Oliver Lubrich (ed.), *Reisen ins Reich: Ausländische Autoren besichtigen Deutschland.* Frankfurt 2004, p. 89.

Fuchs, Georg, *Deutsche Form: Betrachtungen über die Berliner Jahrhundertausstellung und die Münchner Retrospektive.* Munich 1907.

> *Der Kaiser, die Kultur und die Kunst: Betrachtungen über die Zukunft des deutschen Volkes aus den Papieren eines Unverantwortlichen.* Munich 1904.

> *Die Revolution des Theaters.* Munich 1909.

Gaillard, Friedrich, *Hans Rehberg, der Dichter der 'Preußendramen'.* Rostock 1941.

Geisow, Hans, *Bühne und Volk.* Leipzig 1933.

Geist, Julius (ed.), *Theater am Westwall: 20 Jahre Kulturarbeit des Landestheaters Saarpfalz.* Neustadt an der Weinstraße 1940.

Gentsch, Adolf, *Die politische Struktur der Theaterführung.* Leipzig 1942.

Gerlach-Bernau, Kurt, *Drama und Nation.* Breslau 1934.

Gerst, Wilhelm Karl, 'Die Thingstätte'. *Der Deutsche* (4 July 1934).

Gerth, Werner, 'Thingsstatt und Thingspiel'. *Deutscher Glaube* (1935), pp. 532–5.

Goebbels, Joseph, 'Die Kulturpolitik in autoritären und im demokratischen Staat'. *Die Bühne* 10 (20 May 1939).

Die Tagebücher des Joseph Goebbels. Ed. Elke Fröhlich. 23 vols., Munich 1998–2005.

'Wir halten der Kunst unsere Hand hin: Grundsätzliche Erklärungen über die Aufgaben des deutschen Theaters'. *Völkischer Beobachter* (10 May 1933).

Goes, Gustav, *Aufbricht Deutschland*. Berlin 1933.

'Vom Stadion zum Thingspiel'. *Bausteine* 3:5 (May 1935), p. 141.

Günther, Johannes, 'Was erwarten Sie vom Freilichttheater?' *Rheinische Landeszeitung* (28 June 1935).

Guthmann, Heinrich, 'Freilichtspiel im Kriege'. *Die Bühne* 13 (15 June 1942).

Hadamowsky, Eugen, *Propaganda und nationale Macht*. Oldenburg 1933.

Hagemann, Water, 'In Sachen Widukind'. *Germania* (6 February 1935).

Hammerstein, Notker (ed.), *Deutsche Bildung? Briefwechsel zweier Schulmänner: Otto Schumann – Martin Havenstein 1930–1944*. Frankfurt 1988.

Hartmann, Waldemar, 'Hamlets politisches Heldentum: Gedanken zum "Hamlet" als der Tragödie nordischen Verantwortungsgefühls'. *Völkischer Beobachter* (3 May 1936).

Hedler, Friedrich, 'Wiedergeburt der Schauspielkunst aus dem Geist der Dichtung'. *Bausteine* 2 (1934), pp. 97–103.

Helm, Walter, *Ausgewiesen! Lebensbild aus dem besetzten Gebiet in einem Akt*. Langensalza 1924.

Hensel, Alfred, 'Thingplätze und andere Freilichträume'. *Gartenkunst* 47 (1934), pp. 152–7.

Heuss, Theodor, *Hans Poelzig: Bauten und Entwürfe*. Berlin 1939.

Heynicke, Kurt, *Neurode: Ein Spiel von deutscher Arbeit*. Berlin 1935.

Der Weg ins Reich. Berlin 1935.

Hinkel, Hans, 'Kein Platz für Muckertum'. *Der Angriff* (3 December 1936).

'"Wohin mit den Juden?" Speech at the Lessing-Hochschule'. *Die Bühne* 1 (5 January 1939).

Hitler, Adolf, *Mein Kampf*. Trans. Ralph Mannheim. London 1992.

Holzapfel, Carl Maria, 'Aufbruch zum Nationaltheater'. *Deutsche Bühne* (May–June 1934), pp. 5–6.

Hussong, Friedrich, *Kurfürstendamm: Zur Kulturgeschichte des Zwischenreichs*. Berlin 1934.

Ihering, Herbert, *Reinhardt, Jeßner, Piscator oder Klassikertod?* Berlin 1928.

Indefrey, Wilhelm, 'Über das Ergebnis und die Preiszuteilung im Massenschauspielwettbewerb der Deutschen Arbeitsfront'. *Der Neue Weg* 63 (1934), pp. 230–2.

Itzinger, Karl, *Das Frankenburger Würfelspiel des deutsch-völkischen Turnerbundes*. Wels 1925.

Jäckel, Eberhard and Axel Kuhn (eds.), *Hitler: Sämtliche Aufzeichnungen 1905–1924*. Stuttgart 1980.

Jochmann, Werner (ed.), *Adolf Hitler: Monologe im Führerhauptquartier 1941–1944: Die Aufzeichnungen Heinrich Heims*. Hamburg 1980.

Johst, Hanns, 'Deutsch'. *Weimarer Blätter* 3 (1921), pp. 380–1.

   Ich glaube! Munich 1928.

   Propheten. Munich 1923.

   Ruf des Reiches – Echo des Volkes. Munich 1940.

   Schlageter. Munich 1933.

   Standpunkt und Fortschritt. Oldenburg 1933.

Junghans, Ferdinand, 'Die dramaturgische Situation des "Frankenburger Würfelspiels"'. *Die Bühne* 2 (1936), p. 475.

Kaergel, Hans-Christoph, 'Schafft dichterische Volksbühnenspiele'. *Volksbühnenwarte: Blätter und Nachrichten für deutsche Volksbühnenspieler* 11–12 (November–December 1939).

Kardorff, Ursula von, *Berliner Aufzeichnungen 1942–1945*. Munich 1992.

Keppler, Ernst, 'Jugend und Theater'. *Wille und Macht* 2:13 (July 1934), p. 24.

Kerr, Alfred, *Trotz alledem – es hat gelohnt! Verse und Lieder*. Berlin 1967.

Klabund, *Emsig dreht sich meine Spule: Brettlverse, Bänkellieder*. Berlin 1972.

Klemperer, Victor, *Leben sammeln, nicht fragen wozu und warum: Tagebücher 1918–1932*. Berlin 1996.

Knudsen, Hans, 'Mit der Reichsautobahnbühne ins Lager'. *Die Bühne* 2/3 (1 February 1936).

Kobbe, Friedrich Carl, 'Auf dem Wege zum Drama'. *Die Literatur: Monatsschrift für Literaturfreunde* 41:35 (1939), p. 264.

Körner, Ludwig, 'Das deutsche Theater, eine Waffe des Geistes'. *Die Bühne* (20 October 1939).

'Der Sprecher im Dienste des Dichters'. *Die Bühne* 13 (20 November 1938).

Kraus, Karl, *Aphorismen und Gedichte*. Berlin 1984.

Künkler, Karl, 'Der neue Darstellungsstil des Theaters: "Restlose Hingabe an das Erbe der Klassiker" '. *Deutsche Bühnen-Korrespondenz* 3 (1934), pp. 3–4.

'Hamlet im Frack'. *Bausteine zum deutschen Nationaltheater: Organ der Gruppe Theater im Kampfbund für deutsche Kultur* (December 1935), pp. 43–7.

Kutscher, Arthur, *Stilkunde des Theaters*. Düsseldorf 1936.

Langenbeck, Curt, 'Bemerkungen zum historischen Drama'. *Wille und Macht* 6:12 (June 1938), p. 33.

'Die Wiedergeburt des Dramas aus dem Geist der Zeit'. *Das Innere Reich* 6 (1939–40), pp. 923–57.

Die Wiedergeburt des Dramas aus dem Geist der Zeit. Munich 1940.

Langenbucher, Helmut, *Volkhafte Dichtung*. Berlin 1941.

Laubinger, Otto, 'Deutsche Festspiele'. *Theater-Tageblatt* (1934), pp. 1347–8.

'Freilichtspiele und Thingplätze'. *Der Neue Weg* 63 (1934), pp. 174–7.

Ley, Robert, 'Arbeiter und Kultur'. *Die Bühne* 14 (5 December 1938).

Luther, Arthur, 'Die dramatische Produktion des Jahres 1941'. *Die Neue Literatur* (June 1942), p. 128.

Lutz, Josph Maria, 'Neue Wege zum Volksstück'. *Der Neue Weg* 1 (May 1935).

Massek, R. 'Auflösung des bürgerlichen Theaters'. *Die Tat* 22:12 (March 1931), pp. 993–7.

Mettin, Hermann-Christoph, 'Glossen zur Zeit'. *Die Tat* 30:1 (1938).

Meyrink, Gustav, *Des deutschen Spießers Wunderhorn*. Berlin 1973.

Möller, Eberhard Wolfgang, *Das Frankenburger Würfelspiel*. Berlin 1936.

'Wandlungen des deutschen Theaters'. *Hochschule und Ausland* 13:4 (1935), p. 43.

'Die Wendung des Deutschen Theaters. Ein Aufriß zum Spielen auf Thingplätzen'. *Das deutsche Volkspiel* 1 (1933–4), p. 149.

Möller, Felix, *The Film Minister: Goebbels and the Cinema in the Third Reich.* Stuttgart 2000.

Moraller, Franz, 'Das deutsche Freilichtspiel'. *Die Bühne* 8 (August 1938), pp. 248–50.

Mühr, Alfred, 'Der Durchbruch der künstlerischen Revolution'. *Deutsche Mitte* 4 (1934), p. 55.

Nelissen-Haken, Bruno, 'Das deutsche Volks- und Thingspiel'. *Hochschule und Ausland* 13:8 (1935), pp. 55–65.

Neumann, Friedrich, 'Gibt es ein Provinztheater?' *Die Bühne* 23 (10 December 1940).

Niessen, Carl, 'Westdeutsches Theater im Grenzkampf'. *Die Bühne* 12 (6 November 1938).

NS-Presseanweisungen der Vorkriegszeit: Edition und Dokumente. Munich 1998.

Nufer, Wolfgang, 'Die dritte Bühne'. *Völkische Kultur: Kampfblatt für Kultur und Politik* 3 (1935), pp. 14–19.

    'Zur Lage des deutschen Theaters'. *Das Volk: Kampfblatt für völkische Kultur und Politik* 1 (1936–7), p. 176.

Otto C. A. zur Nedden, '*Der Jude von Malta*: Schauspiel in 5 Akten nach einer Idee von Christoph Marlow'. *Shakespeare Jahrbuch* (1941), pp. 204–5.

Der Parteitag der Freiheit vom 10–16. September 1935. Munich 1935.

Petersen, Julius, *Geschichtsdrama und nationaler Mythos: Grenzfragen zur Gegenwartsform des Dramas.* Stuttgart 1940.

Piscator, Erwin, *Das politische Theater.* Berlin 1929.

Pleister, Werner, 'Kontrolle der Laienspiele?' *Das Deutsche Volksspiel* 1 (1933–4), p. 11.

Plessow, Gustav L., *Um Shakespeares Nordentum.* Aachen 1937.

Ramlow, Rudolf, 'Volk und Kunst: ungekünstelt'. *Bausteine* 3 (1935), p. 232.

'Rede Friedrich Forster-Burggrafs im Prinzregentheater München, gehalten am Tage seiner Amtseinführung als Leiter des Staatschauspiels, dem 19. Oktober 1933'. *Bausteine* 1:2 (November 1933), p. 44.

Sabatzky, Kurt, *Der Jude in der dramatischen Gestaltung.* Königsberg 1930.

Schirach, Baldur von, 'Haltet das Wort heilig!' *Die Bühne* 16 (25 August 1940).

Schlösser, Rainer, 'Die Bilanz eines Jahrzehnts: Kulturpolitisches Schreckenskabinett'. *Völkischer Beobachter* (11–12 and 14 February 1933).

'Heer und Kunstwerk: Zwei Symbole'. *Die Bühne* 16 (25 August 1941).

'Die kulturelle Sendung Thüringens'. *Die Bühne* (15 January 1936), p. 337.

'Kurt Geucke, ein Wanderer zwischen Scholle und Stern'. *Deutsches Schrifttum* 17 (1925).

'Politik und Drama'. *Wille und Macht* 3:11 (June 1935), p. 12.

'Die unmoralische Anstalt'. *Völkischer Beobachter* (9 January 1932).

'Das unsterbliche Gespräch über das Tragische', *Wille and Macht* 5:11 (June 1937), p. 9

Das Volk und seine Bühne: Bemerkungen zum Aufbau des deutschen Theaters. Berlin 1935.

'Das Wirken der Jugend im Kulturleben unserer Zeit'. *Wille und Macht* 5:1 (Jan. 1937), p. 13.

'Das Wunder des gesprochenen Wortes'. *Die Bühne* 23 (20 December 1940).

Schlötermann, Heinz, *Das deutsche Weltkriegsdrama 1919–1937: Eine wertkritische Analyse*. Würzburg 1939.

Schmidt, Dietmar, 'Europäische Theater in Berlin'. *Die Bühne* 3/4 (20 February 1944).

Schramm, Kurt, 'Der Anspruch des Theaters'. *Deutsche Allgemeine Zeitung* (19 June 1943).

Schramm, Wilhelm von, *Neubau des deutschen Theaters: Ergebnisse und Forderungen*. Berlin 1934.

Schumann, Gerhard, *Die Entscheidung*. Berlin 1938.

'Spielplan für alle: Theater des Volkes – draußen'. *Der Angriff* (24 July 1937).

Städtische Bühnen Erfurt (ed.), *Hitler-Jugend und Theater*. Erfurt s.a.

Stahl, Ernst Leopold, 'Als die "Rheinische Kulturkonferenz" tagte: Aus der Geschichte eines deutschen Landestheaters'. *Die Bühne* 24 (28 December 1940).

Stang, Walter, 'Vom Sinn und Wesen des Theaters: Kritischer Rückblick und Versuch einer neuen Sinngebung'. *Bausteine* 1:1 (October 1933), pp. 1–14.

'Stedingsehre: ein Beispiel völkischer Festgestaltung'. *Deutsche Bühnen-Korrespondenz* (13 July 1935).

'Stirbt das Drama?' *Vossische Zeitung* (4 April 1926).

Strambowski, 'Der Weg zum Deutschen Nationaltheater'. *Westfälischer Kurier* (18 May 1934).

'Die Szene des größten Erfolges'. *Berliner Illustrirte Zeitung* (9 November 1939).

Thomas, Walter, *Vom Drama unserer Zeit*. Leipzig 1938.

Trautmann, H., 'Nationalerziehung'. *Volksbildung* 64 (1934), p. 13.

Tucholsky, Kurt, *Briefe: Auswahl 1913 bis 1935*. Berlin 1985.

Türk, Franz, *Sprechchöre für die nationalsozialistische Deutsche Schule*. Frankfurt 1935.

Valentin, Karl, 'Das Theater muß sich ändern'. *Wille und Macht* 6:12 (June 1938), p. 37.

Viertel, Berthold, 'Theater-Zukunft 1919'. *Der Neue Weg* (20 June 1919), pp. 317–18.

Vogel, Hans, 'Nochmals "Thingspiele"'. *Propyläen* 31 (1934), p. 397.

Vogt, Hermann, *Die Peitsche deines Herrn: Schauspiel in einem Akt*. Langensalza 1924.

Wachler, Ernst, 'Das Deutsche Theater der Zukunft'. *Deutsche Volksbühne: Blätter für deutsche Bühnenspiele* 1 (1900), pp. 17–33.
　'Das Deutsche Theater der Zukunft': Iduna-Taschenbuch auf das Jahr 1903. Berlin 1903.
　Deutsche Wiedergeburt. Leipzig 1907.
　Die Freilichtbühne. Leipzig 1909.
　Heimat als Quelle der Bildung. 1926.
　Sommerspiele auf vaterländischer Grundlage. Berlin 1910.

Wanderschek, Hermann, *Deutsche Dramatik der Gegenwart*. Berlin 1938.

Wehner, Joseph Magnus, *Vom Glanz und Leben deutscher Bühne*. Hamburg 1941.

Wulf, Joseph, *Theater und Film im Dritten Reich: Eine Dokumentation*. Gütersloh 1964.

Zabludowski, Nina, 'Ein Reinhardt-Jubiläum'. *Die Scene* 20 (1930), pp. 48–9.

Bibliography

Zerkaulen, Heinrich, *Der Arbeit die Ehr!* Berlin s.a.
  Erlebnis und Ergebnis. Leipzig 1939.
  Jugend von Langemarck. Leipzig 1933.
Ziegelski, Hans, 'Sport und Bühnenspiel'. *Bausteine* 4:7 (July 1936), p. 194.
Ziegler, Hans Severus, 'Nur Adolf Hitler sichert der Nation eine künstlerische Neubelebung'. *Völkischer Beobachter* (4 April 1932).
  Wende und Weg. Weimar 1937.
Zweig, Arnold, 'Epoche und Theater'. In Max Krell (ed.), *Das deutsche Theater der Gegenwart.* Munich 1923, pp. 22–3.

Secondary sources

Abbey, William and Katherina Havekamp, 'Nazi Performances in the German Occupied Teritories: The German Theatre in Lille'. In London (ed.), *Theatre*, pp. 262–90.
Aedes: Galerie für Architektur und Raum (ed.), *Hans Poelzig, Ein großes Theater und ein kleines Haus.* Berlin 1986.
Ahrens, Gerhard, *Das Theater des deutschen Regisseurs Jürgen Fehling.* Berlin 1985.
Akademie der Kunst (ed.), *Goodbye to Berlin? 100 Jahre Schwulenbewegung.* Berlin 1997.
Allen, William Sheridan, *The Nazi Seizure of Power.* London 1984.
Antonowa, Irina, *Berlin-Moskau, Moskau-Berlin 1900–1950.* Munich 1995.
Applegate, Celia, *A Nation of Provincials: The German Idea of Heimat.* Berkeley 1990.
Baird, Jay, 'Hitler's Muse: The Political Aesthetics of the Poet and Playwright Eberhard Wolfgang Möller'. *German Studies Review* 17:2 (May 1994), pp. 269–85.
Barbian, Jan-Pieter, *Literaturpolitik im 'Dritten Reich': Institutionen, Kompetenzen, Betätigungsfelder.* Munich 1995.
Barnett, David, 'Joseph Goebbels, Expressionist Dramatist as Minister of Culture'. *New Theatre Quarterly* 17:2 (May 2001), pp. 161–9.
Bärsch, Claus-Ekkehard, *Die politische Religion des Nationalsozialismus: die religiöse Dimension der NS-Ideologie in den Schriften Dietrich Eckarts, Joseph Goebbels, Alfred Rosenbergs und Adolf Hitlers.* Munich 1998.

Baumeister, Martin, *Kriegstheater: Großstadt, Front und Massenkultur 1914–1918*. Essen 2005.

Bemmann, Helga, *Berliner Musenkinder-Memoiren: Eine heitere Chronik von 1900–1930*. Berlin 1987.

Berghaus, Günther, *Fascism and Theatre: Comparative Studies on the Aesthetics of Politics and Theatre in Europe*. Providence 1996.

Bialas, Wolfgang and Burkhard Stenzel (eds.), *Die Weimarer Republik zwischen Metropole und Provinz: Intellektuellendiskurse zur politischen Kultur*. Cologne 1996.

Blackadder, Neil, 'Dr Karsten, the Freie Bühne and Audience Resistance to Naturalism'. *New Theatre Quarterly* 14:4 (November 1998), pp. 357–65.

Blackbourne, David, *Marpingen: Apparitions of the Virgin Mary in Bismarckian Germany*. Oxford 1993.

Blanke, Richard, *Orphans of Versailles: The Germans in Western Poland, 1918–1939*. Lexington 1993.

Boetzke, Manfred *et al.*, 'Verarbeitung des kulturellen Erbes: Tendenzen der Klassiker-Inszenierung'. In Kunstamt Kreuzberg and Institut für Theaterwissenschaft der Universität Köln (eds.), *Weimarer Republik*, pp. 739–57.

Boetzke, Manfred and Marion Queck, 'Die Theaterverhältnisse nach der Novemberrevolution'. In Kunstamt Kreuzberg and Institut für Theaterwissenschaft der Universität Köln (eds.), *Weimarer Republik*. pp. 692–7.

Böhmig, Michaela, *Das russische Theater in Berlin*. Munich 1990.

Bollenbeck, Georg, *Tradition, Avantgarde, Reaktion: Deutsche Kontroversen um die kulturelle Moderne 1880–1945*. Frankfurt 1999.

Bonnell, Andrew, *The People's Stage in Imperial Germany: Social Democracy and Culture*. London 2005.

Breiter, Bastian, 'Der Weg des "treuen Askari" ins Konzentrationslager: Der Lebensweg des Mohammed Husen'. In van der Heyden and Zeller (eds.), *Kolonialmetropole*, pp. 215–9.

Brenner, Hildegard, *Die Kunstpolitik des Nationalsozialismus*. Reinbek 1963.

Brockhaus, Gudrun, *Schauder und Idylle: Faschismus als Erlebnisangebot*. Munich 1997.

Bibliography

Brückl-Zehetner, Heidemarie, 'Theater in der Krise'. Unpublished thesis. Vienna 1988.

Brunner, Michael, 'Das deutsche Nationaltheater in Weimar in den Jahren 1929–44'. MA dissertation. Freie Universität Berlin 1994.

Bullinger, Matthias, *Kunstförderung zwischen Monarchie und Republik: Entwicklungen der Kunstförderung in Württemberg zwischen 1900 und 1933 am Beispiel der Theater in Stuttgart, Ulm und Heilbronn.* Frankfurt 1997.

Burleigh, Michael, *Earthly Powers: The Conflict between Religion and Politics from the French Revolution to the Great War.* London 2005.

The Third Reich: A New History. London 2000.

Campbell, Bruce, 'Gerhard Roßbach, the Spielschar Ekkehard and the Cultural Attack on the Weimar Republic'. In Ehrlich and John, *Weimar 1930,* pp. 243–60.

Cannetti, Elias, *Die Fackel im Ohr: Lebensgeschichte 1921–1931.* Munich 1980.

Carmann, Christl, 'Shylock am Wiener Burgtheater: Versuch einer Analyse der Wechselwirkungen zwischen den Wiener Juden und der Shylockinterpretation'. Unpublished thesis. Vienna 1972.

Clemmons, Leigh, 'Gewalt, Gott, Natur, Volk: The Performance of Nazi Ideology in Kolbenheyer's *Gregor und Heinrich*'. In Rennert (ed.), *Essays,* pp. 176–86.

Daiber, Hans, *Schaufenster der Diktatur: Theater im Machtbereich Hitlers.* Düsseldorf 1995.

Daniel, Ute, *Hoftheater: Zur Geschichte des Theaters und der Höfe im 18. und 19. Jahrhundert.* Stuttgart 1995.

Deltart, Steven, *The Meininger Theater, 1776–1926.* Ann Arbor 1981.

Dillmann, Michael, *Heinz Hilpert: Leben und Werk.* Berlin 1990.

Dittmer, Frank, 'Freilufttheater: Dramatisches ohne Dach im 20. Jahrhundert: Dargestellt an Berliner Beispielen'. Unpublished thesis. Freie Universität Berlin 1991.

Drewniak, Boguslaw, *Polen und Deutschland 1919–39: Wege und Irrwege kultureller Zusammenarbeit.* Düsseldorf 1999.

Das Theater im NS-Staat: Szenarium deutscher Zeitgeschichte 1933–1945. Düsseldorf 1987.

Dultz, Michael, 'Der Aufbau der nationalsozialistischen Thingspielorgani-
sationen 1933/34'. In Henning Eichberg et al. (eds.), *Massenspiele:
NS-Thingspiel, Arbeiterweihespiel und olympisches Zeremoniell.*
Stuttgart 1977, pp. 202–34.

Dussel, Konrad, *'Ein neues, ein heroisches Theater! Nationalsozialistische Theaterpolitik und ihre Auswirkungen in der Provinz.*
Bonn 1998.

'Theater in der Krise: Der Topos und die ökonomische
Realität in der Weimarer Republik'. In Ehrlich and John (eds.),
Weimar, pp. 211–24.

Düsterberg, Rolf, *Hanns Johst: 'Der Barde der SS': Karrieren eines deutschen Dichters.* Paderborn 2004.

Ehrlich, Lothar and Jürgen John (eds.), *Weimar 1930: Politik und Kultur
im Vorfeld der NS-Diktatur.* Cologne 1998.

Eicher, Thomas, 'Spielplanstrukturen 1929–1944'. In Rischbieter,
Theater, 279–486.

El-Tayeb, Fatima, *Schwarze Deutsche: der Diskurs um 'Rasse' und nationale Identität 1890–1933.* Frankfurt 2001.

Euler, Friedricke, *Der Regisseur und Schauspielpädagoge Otto Falckenberg:
Falckenberg-Inszenierungen an den Münchner Kammerspielen.*
Munich 1976.

Fehling, Jürgen, *Äußerungen und Aufzeichnungen.* Velber 1965.

Fernau, Rudolf, *Als Lied beganns ...* Frankfurt 1972.

Fetting, Hugo (ed.), *Leopold Jeßner: Schriften.* Berlin 1979.

Fischer, Conan, *The Ruhr Crisis.* Oxford 2003.

Fischer, Harald Helmut, 'Die Nazis und die Schauspieler'. *Theater Heute*
9 (September 1989), pp. 1–21.

Fischli, Bruno, Die Deutschen-Dämmerung: Zur Genealogie des völkisch-
faschistischen Dramas und Theaters. Bonn 1976.

'Zur Herausbildung von Formen faschistischer Öffent-
lichkeit in der Weimarer Republik'. In Kunstamt Kreuzberg and
Institut für Theaterwissenschaft der Universität Köln (eds.), *Weimarer Republik*, pp. 891–922.

Forgey, Elisa, '"Die große Neger-Trommel der kolonialen Werbung" – die
deutsche Afrika-Schau 1935–1943'. *WerkstattGeschichte* 9 (1994),
pp. 25–33.

Freydank, Ruth, 'Das Hoftheater: Ein altgewordenes Kulturinstitut'. In Freydank (ed.), *Theater als Geschäft*, pp. 104–21.

    (ed.), *Theater als Geschäft: Berlin und seine Privattheater um die Jahrhundertwende*. Berlin 1995.

    Theater in Berlin: von den Anfängen bis 1945. Berlin 1988.

Fricke, Kurt, *Spiel am Abgrund: Heinrich George: eine politische Biographie*. Halle 2000.

Friedmann, Saul S., *The Oberammergau Passion Play: A Lance against Civilization*. Carbondale 1984.

Fritzsche, Peter, *Rehearsals for Fascism: Populism and Political Mobilization in Weimar Germany*. Oxford 1990.

Führer, Karl Christian, 'German Cultural Life and the Crisis of National Identity during the Depression, 1929–1933'. *German Studies Review* 24:3 (October 2001), pp. 461–86.

Fuller, Steven Nyole, *The Nazis' Literary Grandfather: Adolf Bartels and Cultural Extremism*. New York 1995.

Gadberry, Glenn, 'An Ancient German Rediscovered: The Nazi Widukind Plays of Forster and Kiß'. In Rennert (ed.), *Essays*, pp. 155–66.

    'Eberhard Wolgang Möller's Thingspiel Das Frankenburger Würfelspiel'. In Henning Eichberg, *Massenspiele, NS-Thingspiel, Arbeiterweihespiel und olympische Zeremoniell*. Stuttgart 1977, pp. 235–31.

    'E. W Möller and the National Drama of Nazi Germany: A Study of the Thingspiel and of Möller's *Das Frankenburger Würfelspiel*'. Unpublished dissertation. University of Wisconsin, Madison 1972.

    'Gerhard Hauptmann's *Ratten* (1911) at the Rose (1936)'. In Rennert (ed.), *Essays*, pp. 187–95.

    'The History Plays of the Third Reich'. In London, *Theatre*, pp. 96–135.

    'Stages of Reform: *Caroline Neuber / Die Neuberin* in the Third Reich'. In Rennert (ed.), *Essays*, pp. 167–75.

    (ed.), *Theatre in the Third Reich, the Prewar Years*. Westport 1995.

    'The Thingspiel and *Das Frankenburger Würfelspiel*'. *Drama Review* 24:1 (1980), pp. 103–14.

Bibliography

Gay, Peter, *Weimar Culture: The Outsider as Insider.* London 1968.

Gehr, Richard S., *Adam Müller-Guttenbrunn and the Aryan Theatre of Vienna 1898–1903.* Göppingen 1973.

Geisel, Eike and Henryk M. Broder (eds.), *Premiere und Pogrom: der Jüdische Kulturbund 1933–1941: Texte und Bilder* (Berlin 1992).

Gerst, Marianne Bechhaus, 'Afrikaner in Deutschland 1933–1945'. *Zeitschrift für Sozialgeschichte des 20. und 21. Jahrhunderts* 4 (1997), pp. 10–31.

Gimmel, Jürgen, *Die politische Organisation des Ressentiments: Der 'Kampfbund für deutsche Kultur' und das bildungsbürgerliche Unbehagen an der Moderne.* Münster 1999.

Graff, Sigmund, 'Thema Langemarck'. *Bausteine* 2 (1934), pp. 58–9.

Von S. M. zu N. S. Munich 1963.

Grange, William, 'Rules, Regulations and the Reich: Comedy under the Auspices of the Propaganda Ministry'. In Rennert (ed.), *Essays.*

Grosse, Helmut, 'Die szenische Entwicklung an Beispielen'. In Kunstamt Kreuzberg and Institut für Theaterwissenschaft der Universität Köln (eds.), *Weimarer Republik*, pp. 717–37.

Günther-Konsalik, H., 'Der Gegenspieler im Drama'. *Deutsche Dramaturgie* 2 (1943).

Hake, Sabine, 'The Annexation of an Imaginary City: The Topos "Vienna" and The Wien-Film AG'. In Hake, *Popular Cinema of the Third Reich.* Austin 2001, pp. 149–71.

Hammann, Brigitte, *Hitler's Vienna, A Dictator's Apprenticeship.* Oxford 1999.

Winifred Wagner oder Hitlers Bayreuth. Munich 2002.

Härtl, Ursula *et al.* (eds.), *Hier, hier ist Deutschland ...: von nationalen Kulturkonzepten zur nationalsozialistischen Kulturpolitik.* Göttingen 1997.

Hein, Peter Ulrich, *Die Brücke ins Geisterreich: Künstlerische Avantgarde zwischen Kulturkritik und Faschismus.* Reinbek 1992.

Henker, Michael *et al.* (eds.), *Hört, sehet, weint und liebt: Passionsspiele im alpenländischen Raum.* Munich 1990.

Hermand, Jost and Frank Trommler, *Die Kultur der Weimarer Republik.* Munich 1978.

Hillesheim, Elisabeth, *Die Erschaffung eines Märtyrers: Das Bild Albert Leo Schlageters in der deutschen Literatur von 1923 bis 1945.* Frankfurt 1994.

Hillesheim, Jürgen, *'Heil Dir Führer! Führ uns an ...' Der Augsburger Dichter Richard Euringer.* Würzburg 1995.

Hortmann, Wilhelm, *Shakespeare on the German Stage.* Cambridge 1998.

Hürten, Heinz, *Deutsche Briefe 1934–1938: Ein Blatt der deutschen katholischen Emigration.* Mainz 1969.

Hyam, Ronald, *Empire and Sexuality: The British Experience.* Manchester 1990.

Jeanesson, Stanislas, Übergriffe der französischen Besatzungsmacht und deutsche Beschwerden'. In Krumeich and Schröder (eds.), *Der Schatten.*

Jelavich, Peter, *Munich and Theatrical Modernism: Politics, Playwriting and Performance, 1890–1914.* Cambridge, MA 1985.

Judson, Pieter M., 'The Bohemian Oberammergau: Nationalist Tourism in the Austrian Empire', in Judson and Marsha Rozenblit (eds.), *Constructing Nationalities in East Central Europe.* Oxford 2005, pp. 89–106.

Kafitz, Dieter, 'Die Dramen Eduard von Kayserlings zwischen Naturalismus, Biologismus und Dekadenz'. In Kafitz (ed.), *Dramen und Theater der Jahrhundertwende.* Tübingen 1991, pp. 287–304.

Kern, Volker, *'Die Meininger kommen!' Hoftheater und Hofkapelle zwischen 1874 und 1914 unterwegs in Deutschland und Europa.* Meiningen 1999.

Kessler, Harry Graf, *Tagebücher 1918–1937.* Berlin 1967.

Ketelsen, Uwe-Karsten, *Heroisches Theater: Untersuchungen zur Dramentheorie des Dritten Reichs.* Bonn 1968.

      'Kulturpolitik des III. Reichs und Ansätze zu ihrer Interpretation'. *Text und Kontext* 8:2 (1988), pp. 217–42.

      Völkisch-nationale und nationalsozialistische Literatur in Deutschland 1890–1945. Stuttgart 1976.

      Von heroischem Sein und völkischem Tod: Zur Dramatik des Dritten Reichs. Bonn 1970.

Bibliography

Killy, Walter (ed.), *Literatur Lexikon: Autoren und Werke deutscher Sprache*. Vol. VI. Gütersloh 1990.

Kindt, Werner, *Dokumentation des Jugendbundes: Die Deutsche Jugendbewegung 1920–1933*. Düsseldorf 1974.

Kiß, Edmund, *Wittekind*. Recklinghusen 1935.

Klausnitzer, Ralf, ' "Wir rücken die Burgen unseres Glaubens auf die Höhen des Kaukasus": "Reichsdramaturg" Rainer Schlösser zwischen Jena-Weimar und Führerbunker'. *Zeitschrift für Germanistik* (Neue Folge) 9 (1999).

Koegler, Horst, 'Vom Ausdruckstanz zum "Bewegungschor" des deutschen Volkes: Rudolf von Laban'. In Karl Corino (ed.), *Intellektuelle im Bann des Nationalsozialismus*. Hamburg 1980, p. 165–79.

Koljasin, Wladimir, 'Gastspiele russischer Theater in Berlin in den zwanziger und dreißiger Jahren'. In Irina Antonowa and Jörn Meckert (eds.), *Berlin Moskau, 1900–1950*. Munich 1995, pp. 173–8.

Kortner, Fritz, *Aller Tage Abend*. Munich 1959.

Kossert, Andreas, *Ostpreußen: Geschichte und Mythos*. Berlin 2005.

Král, Václav, *Acta occupationis Bohemiae et Moraviae: Die Deutschen in der Tschechoslowakei 1933–1945*. Prague 1964.

Krefelder Kunstmuseen (eds.), *Der dramatische Raum: Hans Poelzig: Malerei Theater Film*. Krefeld 1986.

Krochmalnik, Daniel, 'Oberammergau – "eine deutsche Passion" '. In Henker *et al.* (eds.), *Hört*, pp. 211–15.

Krumeich, Gerd and Joachin Schröder (eds.), *Der Schatten des Weltkrieges: Die Ruhrbesetzung 1923*. Essen 2004.

Kundrus, Birthe, 'Totale Unterhaltung?'. In Jörg Echternkamp (ed.), *Das Deutsche Reich und der Zweite Weltkrieg*. Vol. IX. Munich 2005.

Kunstamt Kreuzberg and Institut für Theaterwissenschaft der Universität Köln (eds.), *Weimarer Republik*. Berlin 1977.

Kwam, Wayne, 'The Nazification of Max Reinhardt's Deutsches Theater in Berlin'. *Theatre Journal* 40:3 (October 1983).

Langewiesche, Dieter, 'Bildungsbürgertum und Liberalismus im 19. Jahrhundert'. In Jürgen Kocka (ed.), *Bildungsbürgertum im 19. Jahrhundert*. Stuttgart 1989, pp. 95–121.

'Kulturelle Nationsbildung im Deutschland des 19. Jahrhunderts'. In Manfred Hettling *et al.* (eds.), *Nation und Gesellschaft in Deutschland: Historische Essays.* Munich 1996, pp. 46–64.

Ledebur, Ruth Freifrau von, *Der Mythos vom Deutschen Shakespeare: Die deutsche Shakespeare-Gesellschaft zwischen Politik und Wissenschaft 1918–1945.* Cologne 2002.

Leigh Fermor, Patrick, *A Time of Gifts.* London 1977.

Lenman, Robin, 'Art, Society and the Law in Wilhelmine Germany: The Lex Henze'. *Oxford German Studies* 8 (1973–4), pp. 84–113.

Lesák, Barbara (ed.), *Von der Pose zum Ausdruck: Theaterfotografie 1900–1930.* Vienna 2003.

Liebe, Ulrich, *'Verehrt, verfolgt, vergessen': Schauspieler als Nazi-Opfer.* Berlin 1995.

'Lob der Provinz'. *Der Tagesspiegel* (2 October 2004).

London, John (ed.), *Theatre under the Nazis.* Manchester 2004.

Makarowa, Galina, 'Das Moskauer und Berliner Theater zu Beginn des 20. Jahrhunderts'. In Antonowa, *Berlin-Moskau*, pp. 43–6.

Mann, Golo, *Erinnerungen und Gedanken: Eine Jugend in Deutschland.* Frankfurt 1981.

Marchand, Suzanne, 'Nazi Culture: Banality or Barbarism?' *Journal of Modern History* 70:1 (March 1998), pp. 108–18.

Marquardt, Axel *et al.* (eds.), *Preußen im Film.* Berlin 1981.

Maser, Werner, *Heinrich George: Mensch aus Erde gemacht.* Berlin 1998.

Mathildenhöhe Darmstadt (ed.), *Die Lebensreform: Entwürfe zur Neugestaltung von Leben und Kunst um 1900.* Darmstadt 2003.

Mennemeier, Franz Norbert, 'Vom Expressionismus zum Faschismus (Hanns Johst)'. In Mennemaier, *Modernes deutsches Drama: Kritiken und Charakteristiken.* Vol. II. Munich 1975.

Menz, Egon, 'Sprechchor und Aufmarsch: Zur Entstehung des Thingspiels'. In Horst Denkler und Karl Prümm (eds.), *Die Deutsche Literatur im Dritten Reich: Themen, Traditionen, Wirkungen.* Stuttgart 1976, pp. 330–46.

Meyer, Jochen (ed.), *Briefe an Ernst Hardt: Eine Auswahl aus den Jahren 1898–1947.* Marbach 1975.

Meyrink, Gustav, 'Das Wildschwein'. In Meyrink, *Des deutschen Spießers Wunderhorn*. Berlin 1987.

Michel, Kai, *Die schriftstellerischen Versuche Joseph Goebbels*. Cologne 1999.

Mittenzwei, Werner, *Der Untergang einer Akademie oder die Mentalität des ewigen Deutschen: Der Einfluß der nationalkonservativen Dichter an der Preußischen Akademie der Künste 1918–1947*. Berlin 1992.

Möhle, Heiko, 'Die "deutsche Gesellschaft für Eingeborenenkunde"'. In van der Heyden and Zeller (eds.), *Kolonialmetropole*, pp. 243–51.

Mohr, Albert, *Das Frankfurter Schauspiel 1929–1944*. Frankfurt 1974.

Moninger, Markus, *Shakespeare inszeniert: Das westdeutsche Regietheater und die Theatertradition des 'dritten deutschen Klassikers'*. Tübingen 1996.

Mosse, George, *The Crisis of German Ideology*. New York 1964.

    The Nationalization of the Masses: Mass Movements in Germany from the Napoleonic Wars through the Third Reich. New York 1975.

Mugrauer, Johann, *Pfarrgemeinde Höritz im Böhmerwalde und seine Passionsspiele*. Tauberbischofsheim 1990.

Müller, Hans-Harald, *Der Krieg und die Schriftsteller: Der Kriegsroman der Weimarer Republik*. Stuttgart 1986.

Müller, Hedwig, '. . . jeder Mensch ist ein Tänzer': Ausdruckstanz in Deutschland zwischen 1900 und 1945*. Gießen 1993.

Neumann, Thomas, *Völkisch-nationale Hebbelrezeption: Adolf Bartels und die Weimarer Nationalfestspiele*. Bielefeld 1997.

Niven, William, 'The Birth of Nazi Drama? *Thing* Plays'. In London (ed.), *Theatre*, pp. 54–95.

Noltenius, Rainer, *Dichterfeiern in Deutschland: Rezeptionsgeschichte und Sozialgeschichte am Beispiel der Schiller- und Freiligrathfeiern*. Munich 1984.

Oguntoye, Katharina, *Eine afro-deutsche Geschichte: Zur Lebenssituation von Afrikanern und Afro-Deutschen in Deutschland 1884–1950*. Berlin 1997.

Panse, Barbara, 'Censorship in Nazi Germany: The Influence of the Reich Ministry of Propaganda on German Theatre and Drama 1933–1945'.

In Günther Berghaus (ed.), *Fascism and Theatre: Comparative Studies on the Aesthetic and Politics of Performance in Europe 1925–1945*. Providence 1996, pp. 140–56.

'Zeitgenössische Dramatik'. In Rischbieter (ed.), *Theater*, pp. 489–721.

'Zensurmaßnahmen der Reichsdramaturgie im Hinblick auf Themenkomplexe', in Rischbieter (ed.), *Theater*, pp. 511–97.

Patterson, Michael, *The Revolution in German Theatre, 1900–1933*. London 1981.

Patterson, Michael and Louise Stafford-Charles, 'The Final Chapter: Theatre in the Concentration Camps of Nazi Germany'. In Gadberry (ed.), *Theatre in the Third Reich*, pp. 157–65.

Pesch, Jessica, *Festspiele für ein neues Deutschland? Saladin Schmitts 'Klassikerwoche' am Schauspielhaus Bochum im Dritten Reich*. Herne 1999.

Petropoulos, Jonathan, *Art as Politics*. Chapel Hill 1996.

Petzet, Wolfgang, *Theater: Die Münchner Kammerspiele*. Munich 1973.

Pfister, Manfred, 'Germany Is Hamlet'. *New Comparisons* 2 (1986), pp. 106–26.

'Hamlet und der deutsche Geist: Die Geschichte einer politischen Interpretation'. *Shakespeare Jahrbuch* (West) (1992), pp. 13–38.

Phipps, Alison M., *An Investigation into South-West German Naturtheater*. Frankfurt 2000.

Piatty, Barbara, *Tells Theater: Eine Kulturgeschichte in fünf Akten zu Friedrich Schillers Wilhelm Tell*. Basel 2004.

'Ein unzerstörbarer Mythos nicht nur für die Schweiz'. *Das Parlament* (4 April 2005).

Pietsch, Ilse, 'Das Theater als politisch-publizistisches Führungsmittel im Dritten Reich'. Unpublished thesis. Münster 1952.

Polheim, Konrad, 'Passionsspiele in Steiermark und Kärnten'. In Henker *et al.* (eds.), *Hört*, pp. 33–41.

Prangel, Matthias, 'Das Geschäft mit der Wahrheit: Zu einer zentralen Kategorie der Rezeption von Kriegsromanen in der Weimarer Republik'. In Jos Hoogeveen and Hans Würzner (eds.), *Ideologie und Literatur (Wissenschaft)*. Amsterdam 1986, pp. 47–78.

Preston-Dunlop, Valerie, 'Laban and the Nazis'. *Dance Theatre Journal* 6:2 (July 1988), pp. 4–7.

Prieberg, Fred, *Musik im NS-Staat*. Frankfurt 1982.

Puschner, Uwe, 'Deutsche Reformbühne und völkische Kultstätte: Ernst Wachler und das Harzer Bergtheater'. In Puschner, *Handbuch zur 'völkischen Bewegung' 1871–1918*. Munich 1995, pp. 762–9.

Radvan, Florian, ' "Mit der Verjudung des deutschen Theaters ist es nicht so schlimm!" Ein kritischer Rückblick auf die Karriere der Literaturwissenschaftlerin Elisabeth Frenzel'. *German Life and Letters* 54:1 (January 2001), pp. 25–44.

Rathkolb, Oliver, *Führertreu und gottbegnadet: Künstlereliten im Dritten Reich*. Vienna 1991.

Reißmann, Bärbel, 'Geschäftserfolg eines Bühnenautors: Das Lessing-Theater'. In Freydank (ed.), *Theater als Geschäft*, pp. 122–33.

Rennert, Helmut Hal (ed.), *Essays on Twentieth-Century German Drama and Theater: An American Reception*. New York 2004, pp. 167–75.

Reuth, Ralf-Georg, *Goebbels*. London 1993.

Riemenschneider, Heinrich, *Theatergeschichte der Stadt Düsseldorf*. Düsseldorf 1987.

Rischbieter, Henning, 'Die deutsche Theaterlandschaft 1933–1945'. In Rischbieter (ed.), *Theater*, pp. 99–261.

  'NS-Theaterpolitik'. In Rischbieter (ed.), *Theater*, pp. 14–20.

  (ed.), *Theater im 'Dritten Reich': Theaterpolitik, Spielplanstruktur, NS-Dramatik*. Seelze-Velber 2000.

Ritchie, J. M., 'Johst's *Schlageter* and the End of the Weimar Republic'. In A. F. Bance (ed.), *Weimar Germany: Writers and Politics*. Edinburgh 1982, pp. 153–67.

Rovit, Rebecca, 'Collaboration or Survival: Reassessing the Role of the *Jüdischer Kulturbund*'. In Gadberry (ed.), *Theatre in the Third Reich*, pp. 141–56.

  'Jewish Theatre: Repertory and Censorship in the Jüdischer Kulturbund Berlin'. In London (ed.), *Theatre*, pp. 187–221.

Rühle, Günther (ed.), *Bernhard Minetti: Erinnerungen eines Schauspielers*. Stuttgart 1985.

'Leopold Jeßner: Revolution im Staatstheater'. In Rühle, *Theater in unserer Zeit*, pp. 47–81.

Theater für die Republik: 1917–1933 im Spiegel der Kritik. Rev. edn Berlin 1988.

Theater in Deutschland: Seine Ereignisse – seine Menschen. Frankfurt 2007.

Theater in unserer Zeit. Frankfurt 1976.

Zeit und Theater: Diktatur und Exil 1933–1945. Berlin 1974.

'Das Zeitstück: Drama und Dramaturgie der Demokratie'. In Rühle, *Theater in unserer Zeit*, pp. 82–118.

Sauer, Klaus, *Lorbeer und Palme: Patriotismus in deutschen Festspielen.* Munich 1971.

Scherer, Herbert, 'Die Volksbühnenbewegung und ihre interne Opposition in der Weimarer Republik'. *Archiv für Sozialgeschichte* 14 (1974), pp. 213–51.

Schievelbusch, Wolfgang, *In a Cold Crater: Cultural and Intellectual Life in Berlin, 1945–1948.* Berkeley 1998.

Schmid, Gerhard, 'Die Gedenkjahre 1859 und 1905 als Brennpunkte der bürgerlichen Schiller-Verehrung in Deutschland'. In *Impulse: Aufsätze, Quellen, Berichte zur deutschen Klassik und Romantik.* Berlin 1986, pp. 90–114.

Schmidt, Dörte and Brigitte Weber (eds.), *Keine Experimentierkunst: Musikleben an Städtischen Theatern der Weimarer Republik.* Stuttgart 1995.

Schneider, Hubertus, 'Das "Zeitstück": Probleme der Justiz'. In Kunstamt Kreuzberg and Institut für Theaterwissenschaft der Universität Köln (eds.), *Weimarer Republic*, pp. 835–44.

Schöpel, Barbara, *Naturtheater: Studien zum Theater unter freien Himmel in Südwestdeutschland.* Tübingen 1965.

Schrader, Bärbel and Jürgen Schebera, *Kunstmetropole Berlin 1918–1933.* Berlin 1987.

Schültke, Bettina, *Theater oder Propaganda? Die Städtischen Bühnen Frankfurt am Main 1933–1945.* Frankfurt 1997.

Schulz-Hostetter, Elisabeth, *The Berlin State Theater under the Nazi Regime: A Study of the Administration, Key Productions, and Critical Responses from 1933–1934.* Lewiston 2004.

Schwedt, Ulrich, *Martin Luserke: Reformpädagogik im Spannungsfeld von pädagogischer Innovation und kulturkritischer Ideologie.* Frankfurt 1993.

Schwerd, Almut, *Zwischen Sozialdemokratie und Kommunismus: Zur Geschichte der Volksbühne 1918–1933.* Wiesbaden 1975.

Siedhoff, Thomas, *Das Neue Theater in Frankfurt am Main 1911–1935.* Frankfurt 1985.

Sonnega, William, 'Anti War Discourse in War Drama: Sigmund Graff and *Die endlose Straße'.* In Rennert (ed.), *Essays,* pp. 147–54.

'Theatre of the Front: Sigmund Graff and *Die endlose Straße'.* In Gadberry (ed.), *Theatre in the Third Reich,* pp. 47–64.

Steinberg, Michael, *Austria as Theater and Ideology: The Salzburg Festival.* New York 2000.

Steinweis, Alan, *Art, Ideology and Economy: The Reich Chambers of Music, Theater, and the Visual Arts.* Chapel Hill 1993.

'Conservatism, National Socialism, and the Cultural Crisis of the Weimar Republic'. In Larry Eugene Jones and James Retallack (eds.), *Between Reform, Reaction and Resistance: Studies in the History of German Conservatism from 1879 to 1945.* New York 1992, pp. 329–46.

'Weimar Culture and the Rise of National Socialism: The *Kampfbund für deutsche Kultur'. Central European History* 24 (Fall 1992), pp. 402–23.

Stenzel, Burkhard, 'Das Deutsche Nationaltheater in Weimar'. In Ehrlich and John (eds.), *Weimar 1930,* pp. 225–42.

Stern, Fritz, *The Politics of Cultural Despair.* Berkeley 1974.

Stommer, Rainer, *Die inszenierte Volksgemeinschaft: Die Thingspielbewegung im Dritten Reich.* Marburg 1985.

Strobl, Gerwin, 'The Bard of Eugenics: Shakespeare and Racial Activism'. *Journal of Contemporary History* 34:3 (1999), pp. 323–36.

The Germanic Isle: Nazi Perceptions of Britain. Cambridge 2000.

'Shakespeare and the Nazis'. *History Today* 5 (June 1997), pp. 16–21.

Tacke, Charlotte, 'Die 1900 Jahrfeier der Schlacht im Teutoburger Wald 1909: Von der klassenlosen Bürgerschaft zur klassenlosen

Volksgemeinschaft?' In Manfred Hettling and Paul Nolte (eds.), *Bürgerliche Feste: Symbolische Formen politischen Handelns im 19. Jahrhundert*. Göttingen 1993, pp. 192–230.

Theweleit, Klaus, *Male Fantasies*. Cambridge 1987.

Thumser, Regina, 'Dem Provinzstatus entkommen? Das Linzer Landestheater in der NS-Zeit'. In Michael Kügl (ed.), *Promenade 39: Das Landestheater Linz 1803–2003*. Salzburg 2003, pp. 91–132.

Töteberg, Michael, ' "Ich möchte hier den Vorhang des Schweigens herunterlassen": Über die Darstellung des Dritten Reiches in Schauspieler Memoiren, mit einem Exkurs über den Theater-Kritiker Herbert Ihering'. In Helmut Asper (ed.), *Im Rampenlicht der 'dunklen Jahre': Aufsätze zum Theater im 'Dritten Reich', Exil und Nachkrieg*. Berlin 1989.

Ulbricht, Justus H., ' "Deutsche Renaissance": Weimar und die Hoffnung auf die kulturelle Regeneration Deutschlands zwischen 1900 und 1933'. In Jürgen John and Volker Wahl (eds.), *Zwischen Konvention und Avantgarde: Doppelstadt Jena-Weimar*. Weimar 1995.

"Wege nach Weimar" und "deutsche Wiedergeburt": Visionen kultureller Hegemonie im völkischen Netzwerk Thüringens zwischen Jahrhundertwende und "Drittem Reich" '. In Bialas and Stenzel (eds.), *Die Weimarer Republik*, pp. 23–35.

van der Heyden and Joachim Zeller (eds.), *Kolonialmetropole Berlin: Eine Spurensuche*. Berlin 2002.

Vondung, Klaus, *Magie und Manipulation: ideologischer Kult und politische Religion des Nationalsozialismus*. Göttingen 1971.

Völkisch-nationale und nationalsozialistische Literaturtheorie. Munich 1973.

Wallach, Dagmar, *Aber ich habe nicht mein Gesicht: Gustaf Gründgens: Eine deutsche Karriere*. Berlin 1999.

Wardetzky, Jutta, *Theaterpolitik im faschistischen Deutschland: Studien und Dokumente*. Berlin 1983.

Wessels, Wolfram, *Hörspiele im Dritten Reich*. Bonn 1985.

Whalen, Robert W., *Bitter Wounds: German Victims of the Great War, 1914–1939*. Ithaca 1984.

Widdig, Bernd, *Culture and Inflation in Weimar Germany*. Berkeley 2001.

Wingfield, Nancy M., 'When Cinema Became National: "Talkies" and the Anti-German Demonstrations in Prague in 1930'. *Austrian History Yearbook* 29 (1999), pp. 113–18.

Winter, Jay, *Sites of Memory, Sites of Mourning*. Cambridge 1995.

Woehrmann, Andreas, *Das Programm der Neuklassik: Die Konzeption einer modernen Tragödie bei Paul Ernst, Wilhelm von Scholz und Samuel Lublinski*. Frankfurt 1979.

Wolferdorf, Peter, *Stilreform des Laienspiels: eine historisch-kritische Dramaturgie*. Brunswick 1962.

Wolff, Hannelore, *Volksabstimmung auf der Bühne: Das Theater als Mittel politischer Agitation*. Frankfurt 1985.

Wortmann, Michael, *Baldur von Schirach: Hitlers Jugendführer*. Cologne 1982.

Wulf, Joseph, *Theater und Film in Dritten Reich: Eine Dokumentation*. Gütersloh 1964.

Ziegler, Hans Severus, *Adolf Hitler aus dem Erleben dargestellt*. Göttingen 1964.

Zuckmayer, Carl, *Als wärs ein Stück von mir*. Frankfurt 1966.

    Geheimreport. Göttingen 2002.

Index